The Schüssel Era in Austria

Günter Bischof, Fritz Plasser (Eds.)

CONTEMPORARY AUSTRIAN STUDIES Volume 18

UNO PRESS

innsbruck university press

Printed in the United States of America.

Published and distributed in the United States by
University of New Orleans Press:
ISBN 978-1-60801-009-7

UNO PRESS

Published and distributed in Europe by
Innsbruck University Press:
ISBN 978-3-902719-29-4

iup

Library of Congress Control Number: 2009936824

Contemporary Austrian Studies

Sponsored by the University of New Orleans and Universität Innsbruck

Publication of this volume has been made possible through generous grants from the Austrian Ministries of Foreign Affairs through the Austrian Cultural Forum in New York as well as the Ministry of Science and Research. The Austrian Marshall Plan Anniversary Foundation in Vienna has been very generous in supporting CenterAustria at the University of New Orleans and its publications series. The College of Liberal Arts at the University of New Orleans and the *Auslandsamt* of the University of Innsbruck provided additional financial support as did the Cultural Office of the City of Innsbruck.

Table of Contents

II. Policies and Policy Changes

FORUM

BOOK REVIEWS

ANNUAL REVIEW

INTRODUCTION

Fritz Plasser and Günter Bischof

The seven years of Wolfgang Schüssel's chancellorship (2000-2007) represent a departure from traditional policies and governmental style in Austria. They are also characterized by passing a reform agenda that will have lasting impact. As a consequence of his governing style, Schüssel was prepared to accept a greater intensity in domestic political conflict and policy innovations. He cast aside long-standing traditions in the formation of post-World War II national governments when he took office in February 2000. First, the "Schüssel era" ended the reign of grand coalition governments that had dominated Austrian national politics since 1987 (following in the postwar tradition of such grand coalition governments from 1945 to 1966). Second, in spite of massive and unprecedented resistance from Thomas Klestil, Austria's president in 2000 when the Schüssel government was formed, Schüssel launched a coalition government with Jörg Haider's *Freiheitliche Partei Österreichs* (FPÖ), the right-wing populist and *enfante terrible* in the Austrian political arena since the mid-1980s.

A reluctant President Klestil appointed Schüssel chancellor of an ÖVP/FPÖ "small" coalition government. Although the *Österreichische Volkspartei* (ÖVP) had suffered a severe defeat at the polls in the fall 1999 national elections—placing third behind the FPÖ for the first time in postwar political history—the shrewd political negotiator Schüssel managed to finagle himself into the position of chancellor. For the first time since 1970 when the Josef Klaus government was voted out of office, the ÖVP seized the Federal Chancellor's office on the Ballhausplatz again. Managing to become chancellor in 2000 was Schüssel's strategic masterpiece of sorts. It showed his readiness to take political risks and demonstrated his superb tactical skills in the minefield of Austria's quotidian contentious political infighting.

None of Schüssel's predecessors at the helm of Austrian politics entered office under comparably dramatic circumstances. Daily protests and demonstrations by his numerous detractors on the Left overshadowed the first weeks of his government's activities. Critical pundits and commentators described his chancellorship as a definite break with the consensual tradition of Austrian politics. A stubborn Schüssel did not budge, even though he found himself confronted domestically by the stubborn resistance of the *Sozialdemokratische Partei Österreichs* (SPÖ), which emerged as the strongest party on the polls in 1999, but was not successful in finding coalition partners. The SPÖ found itself ill-suited for the oppositional role it undertook for the first time in thirty years. Internationally, the new Schüssel government found itself utterly isolated for a few months by the novel sanctions launched by the governments of the fourteen remaining states of the European Union.

The EU-14 sanctions actually represented an embargo of communications and the end of direct talks and negotiations with the chancellor of the ÖVP/FPÖ-government. Schüssel was treated as a leper and outcast in the European political arena. These sanctions were rescinded in the fall of 2000 when relations between the heads of governments of the fourteen states of the European Union and the Schüssel government were normalized. During this phase, another defining character trait of Wolfgang Schüssel's became visible: his ability to cope with extraordinary stress and his iron will to stand up to political pressure coming from outside the country.

In spite of this turbulent start to his chancellorship, Schüssel remained extremely active in domestic politics. Under the motto "speed kills," he launched a host of political reform projects during his first year in office. He immediately set up special commissions to deal with restitution issues regarding former slave laborers exploited by the Nazis on Austrian terrain during World War II and Jewish victims whose property had been aryanized. Chancellor Schüssel was eager to remove unacceptable old blockages of economic and social policies; he was fighting political gridlock Austrian style. This brought out an additional trait of Schüssel's political leadership style: his determination to forge ahead actively with new policies and bring about political change. Schüssel felt that the chancellor's office offered a much broader range of executive leadership potential than his cautious predecessors had practiced.

The first coalition with the FPÖ was short-lived. Tensions and strategic disagreements quickly escalated in the coalition. Personnel conflicts proliferated within the FPÖ primarily because the FPÖ did not have a sufficient pool of politically experienced people to fill its ministerial assignments in the coalition. This caused Schüssel in the summer of 2002 to end prematurely the coalition government with the FPÖ. During the following parliamentary elections, Schüssel's ÖVP was triumphant in the polls. Voters catapulted the ÖVP from 26.9 percent to 42.3 percent of the vote, while the FPÖ ignominiously sank from 26.9 percent back to 10.0 percent. Coalition negotiations with the Green Party collapsed quickly, not the least due to Schüssel's half-hearted negotiations. Instead, Schüssel formed a new coalition government with the substantially weakened FPÖ in January 2003. No longer the junior partner, he naturally was in a much stronger position now.

As chancellor of a coalition, which political pundits have described as a quasi-single party government, Schüssel in record time succeeded in speeding up his reform agenda. He launched a decisive reform of the Austrian pension system. Some constituencies in his own electorate felt that this pension reform was too radical. In retrospect, this 2003 pension reform marks a turning point in the chancellorship of Wolfgang Schüssel. Critiques of his governing style became shriller, general discontent with his governing activities increased, and losses during regional elections showed that unfavorable attitudes towards the ÖVP were emerging across the country. The controversial pension reform of 2003 showed a further trait of Schüssel's governing style: his tendency for stubbornness and underestimating public moods and attitudes that were critical and leery of his ambitious reform agenda.

In the 2006 parliamentary elections, Schüssel paid the price for his overreaching reform agenda that was considered too ambitious in large parts of the electorate. Losing 8 percent of its 2002 supporters, the ÖVP slipped back into second place behind the SPÖ. Schüssel again conducted the tough coalition negotiations. A new grand coalition government emerged between the SPÖ and the ÖVP, but with a Social Democratic chancellor. Chancellor Alfred Gusenbauer's new government only lasted for two years. While in 2007 Schüssel was forced to relinquish his chancellorship, he did not withdraw from the political arena altogether. In 2007/2008 he led the ÖVP faction in the Austrian Parliament. Once more, he exerted great influence in the SPÖ/ÖVP coalition government, but this time not as an executive leader in the Ballhausplatz but as a legislative whip on the Ring. Schüssel hereby revealed another remarkable character trait: his stoic ability to accept personal defeats and political backlashes unperturbed.

The Schüssel era in Austria represents a remarkable time-span regarding recent Austrian history. The lasting changes and innovations in domestic and foreign policies directed by Schüssel's personal and executive leadership style are under scrutiny in these scholarly essays. It is too early to tell how far Austria changed politically, socially, and culturally under Schüssel's chancellorship. Yet the constraints and contradictions of his government's activities are analyzed in the present volume from different perspectives and disciplines. These essays are designed to be a first draft of recent history and start the debate on Wolfgang Schüssel's place in the post-World War II political arena. These essays' goal is to frame the historiographical agenda of the Schüssel era and to initiate the conversation on Schüssel's place in postwar Austrian politics beyond the chatter of the pundits in the news media. The volume is designed to offer a first assessment of Schüssel as chancellor like earlier volumes of *Contemporary Austrian Studies* (*CAS*) did for Chancellors Bruno Kreisky and Franz Vranitzky.

The editors have divided the fourteen essays into two sections. The contributions in the first section deal with Wolfgang Schüssel's political personality and leadership style. Specific policies and policy changes are the focus of the contributions in the second section. The legacies of the Schüssel years are placed in context in a concluding chapter.

A special Forum on Austrian Studies Today complements the topical essays in this volume. The Forum essays were delivered as papers at the 2008 German Studies Association meeting in St. Paul, Minnesota, in memory of the deceased great Austrian Germanist Wendelin Schmidt-Dengler, who had passed away in Vienna only weeks before the meeting and who was scheduled to sit on the panel to discuss the "disturbing creativity" in recent Austrian literature; this was the hallmark of some of Austria's most famous artists and writers—their inclination to irritate the public and produce scandals. The historian Ernst Hanisch once called this phenomenon a streak of self-hatred among Austrian intellectuals and writers. Other essays assess the state of Austrian-Jewish studies and the need "to reimagine Jewishness as an integral part of Austrianness and to reimagine Austrianness as the partial product and reflection of specifically Jewish contributions," as Leslie Morris writes. The lively state of Austrian literature and cultural studies in the United States, especially as seen through the journal *Modern Austrian Literature*, is the focus of another Forum essay. Yet another contribution assesses the Austrian intellectual tradition by looking at both the relationships of today's little Austria to the larger historical Austria as well as Austria's relationship with German language and culture. As in every *CAS* annual publication, book reviews and a review of Austrian politics in the year 2008 complete the volume.

Finally, we treasure the opportunity to thank the people who have made this volume possible, first and foremost our contributors with the timely submission of their manuscripts and their good cheer in suffering through the extensive copy-editing process with us. Fritz Plasser has commissioned the bulk of the topical essays. In New Orleans and at UNO, Michael Maier from the University of Vienna, the 2008/2009 Austrian Ministry of Science dissertation fellow at CenterAustria, addressed the daily tracking of manuscripts with wonderful efficiency and aplomb. We hope his own dissertation research on the challenges of integrating returning Austrian *Wehrmacht* soldiers after World War II back into Austrian society did not suffer too much from the demands of his job as assistant to the editors. Jennifer Shimek at Loyola University of New Orleans performed the demanding work of copy-editing the essays and stream-lining them to our style-sheet in a timely fashion and with her usual superb skill and good cheer. Gertraud Griessner was pinch-hitting when needed. In Innsbruck, Ellen Palli has produced photo-ready copy of the final manuscripts with her usual professional skill in spite of the numerous tables in the topical essays. Franz Mathis has supported out endeavours when and wherever needed. Franz Mathis is retiring from the University of Innsbruck and his job as Senate Representative of the University of Innsbruck for the UNO partnership treaty. He has been the most professional and helpful of colleagues. He also helped to shepherd the publication of the volume to a new publisher after seventeen years of publishing *CAS* with Transaction Publishers.

Funding for the publication of this volume has come from the Universities of New Orleans and Innsbruck through their partnership agreement, as well as from the Austrian Foreign Ministry through the Austrian Cultural Forum in New York and the Marshall Plan Anniversary Foundation in Vienna as a generous institutional supporter of CenterAustria. Martin Rauchbauer in New York has been kind in being our liaison with the Ministry for European and International Affairs in Vienna and Ambassador Emil Brix.

Innsbruck/Larose, June 2009

I. PERSONALITY AND LEADERSHIP

The Political Personality of Wolfgang Schüssel

Peter Gerlich

If you cannot clothe yourself in lionskin use foxpelt.
– *Gracian*

Introduction

The public image of Wolfgang Schüssel is shrouded in controversy. To some extent, this is not surprising; each and every politician, particularly if still active, has supporters and opponents. But his case seems nevertheless a special one. As federal chancellor, he broke taboos of traditional politics and tried to introduce change to Austrian political culture: for many observers, patterns of far too much consensus were replaced by controversy and even conflict in a quite unprecedented way. Sometimes one had the impression that consociational democracy was not so much replaced by mere political competition—which would have been the generally more accepted mode of democratic rule—but rather, at least as far as public debates were concerned, with something almost approaching civil war. All that was also a consequence of a process of transition which has not only affected the former socialist countries in Eastern Europe, but Western and Central Europe as well.

As Wolfgang Schüssel stepped down from his last position of power, the chair of the parliamentary caucus of the People's Party (*Österreichische Volkspartei*, or ÖVP), and took his seat among the parliamentary backbenchers, Hans Rauscher, the dean of Austrian journalism, attempted in a brief comment to sum up the pros and cons of the previous chancellor's personality. According to Rauscher, Schüssel merited a differentiated appraisal. He could on the one hand be considered a rare politician: very intelligent, determined, even bold. On the other hand a certain intellectual hubris had to be noted. Schüssel had started as a modernizer—rising up to the challenges of transition—at the beginning by rightly privatizing the nationalized industries. He proceeded from a clearly defined vision, namely to create an Austria that was more competitive and effective, less controlled by political officials and big economic interest groups. However, he failed to effectively challenge the costly governmental bureaucracy. To try to carry out reforms with the help of the extreme right proved, according to Rauscher, not only a moral but also a practical impossibility and led to a cynicism on Schüssel's part which strongly contrasted with his more upbeat beginnings.[1]

While it is certainly too early to describe and judge with anything approaching a definitive portrait the political personality of somebody who only recently left his high executive office and who might still provide some political surprises, one could nevertheless contribute towards such a picture. This article focuses on the public image of the former chancellor in terms of the way in which he was perceived by commentators and the general public. Therefore, after a brief summary of Schüssel's career, it seems appropriate to place it into the context of experiences and challenges to which he was exposed and which to some extent influenced his political behavior as well as to introduce some theoretical perspectives, placing his performance into a more general framework. Finally, a provisional scoreboard of achievements and failures and of the contradictory judgments by which his performance has been evaluated will be attempted.

Three main questions about Schüssel's time in politics can be posed. First to what extent did Schüssel succeed as a politician and to what extent did he fail and for which reasons? Second, did he manage during his period in office to introduce major changes in Austria? Third, what does his experience reveal about the characteristics of the Austrian political system in view of possible strategies for constitutional change?

An Overview of Schüssel's Career

With the benefit of hindsight, Wolfgang Schüssel's political career appears almost typical, a slow rising through the ranks. If one looks more closely, some aspects appear rather remarkable, however.[2]

What might be termed his political apprenticeship started in 1968 when, after finishing the study of law, he joined the staff of the People's Party parliamentary party. He was just twenty-three years old and at that time considered a bright and promising young man with considerable intellectual capacities. Those who founded the academic discipline of political science in Austria at that time remember that he and his counterpart Heinz Fischer of the Social Democrats, who worked in a similar parliamentary role, were asked to join this effort as representatives of the two then relevant political parties.[3]

In 1975, Schüssel was recruited by the powerful interest representative Rudolf Sallinger as secretary general of his Business League, the very influential representative of economic interests in the People's Party. This choice was unusual for several reasons. First Schüssel had no business background, second he was at thirty-four which was quite young for such an important position, and third he appeared if anything relatively critical of the corporatist mentality of social partnership of which Sallinger was an essential representative. Sallinger, however, wanted "fresh blood" in his organization, and the two got along very well, Sallinger serving as a kind of benevolent father figure for the somewhat unruly younger man.[4] During this time, Schüssel's political convictions, the belief in a slim if strong state, not quite in line with traditional corporatist concepts, was consolidated and often publicly expressed.[5]

In 1979, Schüssel became a member of the Austrian Parliament, a return to his previous place of work in a now more elevated position. He was a devoted and very active parliamentarian and supposedly mentioned at some later point that the only position he ever coveted was that of a chairman of the People's Party parliamentary group. Party politicians in Austria are culturally not supposed to show signs of ambition; this admission on Schüssel's part sounds a little daring in the local context. At thirty-four, Schüssel was once again quite young to hold a position normally only reached about a dozen or so years later.[6]

The next essential step up the political ladder happened in 1989 when he was at age forty-four elevated to the position of a member of the cabinet. He served first as Federal Minister of Economic Affairs, later as Federal Minister of Foreign Affairs and as Vice-Chancellor. In these capacities, he played a decisive role in first preparing Austria for EU membership and then actually leading it into the Union as well as chairing the Ministerial Council during Austria's first EU presidency in 1998. During this time, his international reputation, which may still be considered remarkable even today, was built up. The only slight irritation which occurred during this time was the so-called "breakfast affair" which consisted of a journalist publishing negative remarks about leading German and Danish officials which Schüssel had confided to him off the record.[7] It is quite possible that his earlier easygoing relationship with the media suffered because of this experience. Schüssel became more careful and maybe even taciturn.

In 1995 during one of the People's Party's recurrent leadership crises, Schüssel was, at age fifty, elected chairman of the party. It was obvious that the party was, as usual, quite divided. Before his election there was, as Franz Fischler recounts, not much of a discussion, "As so often, what was not said was almost more important than what was said,"[8] but afterwards Schüssel managed to consolidate the party with a very emotional and effective speech to the nominating convention. Yet Schüssel even joked, although more in private, that he would also soon be thrown out again as many of his predecessors had been. Ultimately, he would remain chairman for a record eleven years and retreat only after losing the 2006 election and, therefore, also the position of chancellor.

This position he reached in 2000 after actually coming in only as a narrow third in the election of 1999. In spite of the protests of the Social Democrats and of Federal President Thomas Klestil, who would have preferred a continuation of grand coalition government to an uproar among the governments of the European Union, Schüssel formed a center right coalition with the controversial Jörg Haider of the radical right Freedom Party (*Freiheitliche Partei Österreichs*, or FPÖ). Haider himself did not enter the cabinet and remained in his position as governor of the state of Carinthia. The other EU governments imposed so-called "sanctions" on Austria, a policy of socially isolating its representatives, measures which ultimately only strengthened the new government at home, even if its domestic critics continuously demonstrated against the new "black-blue" cabinet. President Klestil remained critical and demonstrated this by a stern demeanor when swearing in the cabinet. As Manfried Welan has correctly noted, something akin to an Austrian cohabitation regime was initiated when a government was instituted on the basis of a parliamentary majority against the explicit wishes of the president.[9]

By forming this controversial coalition, Schüssel certainly hoped to be able to realize his long-standing program of reform which would not have been possible in a traditional grand coalition. The achievement of his strategy, first negotiating with the Social Democrats until they gave up and then concluding an agreement with the Freedomites and forcing a reluctant president to appoint this government, was generally considered Schüssel's tactical masterpiece. The high ranking American diplomat Stuart Eizenstat, who at that time negotiated with Schüssel a resolution to the question of restitution for Jewish victims of Austrian Nazism, expressed understanding for Schüssel's tactics which he saw as a means of reaching reasonable goals, "I had been in politics long enough to know that the thirst for power at the top all too often produces unpalatable relationships."[10]

In 2002, the black-blue coalition broke up, mainly because Jörg Haider, who had not joined the cabinet, became jealous of the relatively popular representatives of his party in the government. In the following election, Schüssel managed to achieve a resounding electoral victory. As clear winner, he had a choice of three options for forming a government by joining with the Social Democrats, the Greens, or the FPÖ. To the surprise of many including the Greens themselves, he started to negotiate with this party. "Black-green" would have been an unprecedented arrangement, at least on the national level. The negotiations were taken relatively seriously, but ultimately foundered, probably because more radical elements of the Greens did not want to compromise themselves. After rather perfunctory talks with the Social Democrats, Schüssel returned to the much weakened FPÖ and formed a "black-blue" coalition again, which allowed him to govern the country until the next regularly scheduled elections in 2006.[11]

In 2004, the FPÖ broke up. Haider founded a party of his own, the Alliance for the Future of Austria (*Bündnis Zukunft Österreich*, or BZÖ), which remained in the government, while the remnant FPÖ went into opposition. During Schüssel's time in office, a number of reform measures mainly of a neoliberal orientation, especially pension reform and the introduction of university tuition fees, were carried out. At the same time, the Chancellor appeared to become more and more reluctant to engage in much publicity and acquired the epithet of the "silent chancellor" (*Schweigekanzler*).[12]

Maybe for these but also for more general reasons, Schüssel lost the election in 2006 and stepped down both as chancellor and party chairman, retreating to the position of chairman of the parliamentary party.[13] After Jörg Haider's death in an automobile accident, the last hope for a possible reunification of the right-wing parties, a return to power, and, thus, keeping his own party together vanished for Schüssel, and he withdrew to a mere backbencher position in the Peoples Party's parliamentary group.

The ups and downs of Schüssel's career can be summed up fairly succinctly: a relatively quick rise to the top, a masterly negotiation achievement from a position of weakness in 2000, an electoral victory in 2002 (the meaning of which he probably overestimated), and an electoral and political defeat in 2007 which ended the political era of Schüssel if, indeed, it may be called an era.

Personal Character and Life Experiences

Some of Schüssel's personality traits stand out and certainly distinguish him from average Austrian politicians. Many observers and commentators have noted his enormous intellectual capacities, the tactician's quick ability to recognize opportunities and display tenacity in pursuing negotiations, which often led opposition negotiators ultimately to capitulate. In this, his tactical finesse appeared remarkable.[14]

But in addition he was also a successful team player, organizing his colleagues and supporters well, keeping a notoriously contentious party together for a relatively long time, and demonstrating, particularly in his earlier phases, a remarkable ability for interpersonal empathy.

At the same time, he always remained true to his convictions. Unlike other politicians for whom it is often difficult to define what they really believe, he always stuck to his political goal of making Austria fit for a more competitive international environment without forgetting in the process some of his basic conservative and Catholic values.

Schüssel could be very articulate if he chose to do so, but increasingly withdrew from the glare of the public limelight. To some extent, this coincided with a very unpretentious, even lighthearted, lifestyle. Some establishment observers noted with disdain how Schüssel would appear without any pretensions at semiofficial occasions and how he preserved the privacy of his family. Non-conservative commentators remarked how Schüssel differed from many of his party colleagues: he did not drink, did not engage in manly activities like deer hunting, and scorned the male bonding quite usual in conservative political circles.[15]

Speculatively, some of these traits could be seen in connection with the milieus and experiences Schüssel went through in his youth. His mother experienced the wages of war very intensely when she, while being pregnant with her son, was buried for two days under the rubble in the basement of a heavily bombed house in Vienna.[16]

Schüssel's firm European convictions as a means to establish a zone and period of peace have to be seen in this context. Schüssel's father, who was divorced from his mother and somewhat distant from his family, was even further estranged from his son after the son found out only at age sixteen that the father had been close to the Nazi party during the war.[17]

This also explains Schüssel's intense involvement with questions of restitution and compensation for Nazi victims which had been rather neglected by earlier governments. The lack of a father figure might also explain his relationship with Sallinger as well as a certain reluctance to play a national father figure himself, a temptation to which some of his predecessors had more easily succumbed. However, Schüssel certainly is, even if this did not become obvious to the general public, a family man, understanding women and children and working extremely well with female collaborators and even authoring children's books.

Education in the famous Schottengymnasium, a Catholic institution with a liberal reputation, certainly provided an opportunity for Schüssel to develop intellectual and organizational capacities and also provided a firm ideological foundation grounded in the Benedictine tradition of this establishment. Schüssel always maintained this connection and even periodically attended religious and spiritual seminars together with his governmental colleagues and collaborators.[18]

Schüssel's training at the University of Vienna Law School did not lead, as in so many other cases, to traditional authoritarian attitudes. Rather, they gave Schüssel an understanding of legal instruments and their limits for politics, which top politicians who have a business school background, for example, often sadly lack.

Of great influence must also have been Catholic youth and student organizations, which in the late 1960s, following the spirit of the time, became quite liberal, allowing Schüssel to playact, perform as a musician, and even work as a radio commentator. These experiences were, of course, also essential for networking on the one hand and for forming firm political convictions on the other.[19]

His political career provided from the very beginning opportunities to study different milieus and become a tactician and power broker. He had the chance to experience, intensely study, and understand parliament, bureaucracy, political parties, and interest groups. His involvement in European affairs opened his political horizon to an extent that other national politicians maybe increasingly lack.

Some of these assumptions about personal experiences remain, of course, speculation. Experiences form a personality only to some extent. Any person's character is, in a sense, a law unto itself. Schüssel's positive personality traits can be seen in this light, just like those which led him to make political mistakes, overestimate his own capacity and, ultimately, face political failure.[20]

Professional Achievements and Failures

As head of government, Schüssel faced a considerable array of problems and challenges. Some of them were the result of specific Austrian traditions; others followed from the fact that the country, like all of Europe, East and West alike, experienced (and still experience) a period of rapid transition.

The new problems were not only the consequences of economic globalization and international competition, but also of technological and demographic change. Questions of regulation in fields of technological innovation as well as problems of financing the increasing costs of the welfare state with an aging population complicated the social agenda. More specifically, Austria had to accommodate itself to the new role of a member state of the European Union. The somewhat ill-advised and also misplaced sanctions of the other EU governments did not make this task easier for a devoted European like Wolfgang Schüssel. The EU sanctions had to be lifted after several months when a committee of wise men concluded that the FPÖ, while not to everybody's liking, was not a neo-Fascist party after all. The other EU governments had to accept that their action, even if well intentioned, had certainly not been well informed. This was underscored the fact that of all postwar Austrian governments, it was precisely the one suspected of neo-Fascist tendencies which concluded a relatively generous program of restitution and compensation for Austrian Nazi victims.[21]

Some say Schüssel had to prove his democratic credentials and that was certainly true, but he nevertheless indeed *did* attempt to rectify old injustices. The Austrian government also performed well during its second European presidency in 2006 and helped to take up the opportunities provided by the Union's eastern enlargement. Likewise, the Schüssel government at last attempted to come to grips with some of the challenges of technological and demographical change. Wherever the chancellor had to negotiate internationally as well as nationally, he was often quite successful, while his appeals to the general public did not always succeed to the same extent, if one disregards the one big electoral success in 2004 which was, perhaps, more a defeat of his opponents than his own victory.

Specific traditions that party and government chairman Schüssel had to face were the conflicts inside his own party between representatives of different interest groups or different bureaucratic departments. Given this, he achieved a remarkably successful record. The record *vis-à-vis* the other parties was much more ambivalent. Schüssel dared to break old traditions and even taboos in attempting a different governmental strategy, antagonizing not only a traditional Austrian hegemonic alliance of social partners (the federal president and the powerful *Kronenzeitung*),[22] but also alienating the general public who would not follow him down these new avenues. To an extent which was surprising to many outside observers, large sections of the public were mobilized by his opponents to protest the legitimacy of his admittedly legal and constitutional actions. For many Austrians, who used to equate democracy with consociationalism, Schüssel's competitive democracy strategy appeared unacceptable. In addition, this criticism implied that the competitive democratic system of Austria's written constitution should be replaced by a kind of *Konkordanzdemokratie*, a consociational pattern of Austria's unwritten "real" constitution in which all relevant political parties should by law be represented in the government.

Schüssel did not have the strength to convince critics to follow him in his attempt to reform the country in view of changed conditions. This became particularly obvious as regards the accusation that the new government advocated policies which supposedly made Austria a "socially chilly" place. Austrians, used to a relatively generous welfare system, did not appreciate losing some of their perks, even if they were difficult to finance. Once again, Schüssel did not successfully manage to convince the public of the long-term reasonableness of his fiscal measures.

An interesting question is whether Schüssel, by taking them into his government, did "domesticate" Haider and the FPÖ. In the short run, he succeeded up to a point; in a longer perspective, however, he did not, and it remained to Haider himself to ultimately take himself—if not his party (or even parties)—out of the game. Strangely enough, in doing so he (probably) also ended the career of his supposed domesticator.

So, again, the record is a mixed one. Schüssel's challenges were many. In some respects, Schüssel succeeded; in others, he failed. In a democratic environment, all politicians will lose the support of the voters sooner or later. But to have tried something new before being replaced or even having introduced a greater change of policy distinguishes the more successful political leader from the less successful one.

Evaluating Schüssel's Achievements and Failures

Political theory has from its very beginnings speculated about the qualities and requirements of the good political leader.[23] Max Weber in his classical lecture of 1919 "Politics as a Vocation"[24] specifically demanded of politicians a sense of vision, a recognition of ethical responsibility, and a sense of tactical proportion, "the slow drilling of heavy logs."[25] It is probable that to a great extent Wolfgang Schüssel fulfilled these requirements.[26]

Recent critics of Weber have, however, pointed out that his analysis was based on the experiences of an era which was not yet characterized by modern mass media and a consumer oriented society. A leader nowadays also has to define political goals, communicate with supporters and opponents, and convince others and inspire passions in order to have a majority accept his leadership and be willing to support him or her.[27] As one political scientist has noted, a precondition for electoral success today is that politicians have to demonstrate charisma, not necessarily to have it, but to act convincingly as if they had.[28] These requirements were only partially fulfilled by Wolfgang Schüssel.

A study of the role of heads of government in Europe after the Second World War showed that leaders who were considered not only mere politicians but also statesmen were both able to organize and negotiate (often behind closed doors) and also to appeal successfully to the public and to convince them to accept the policies thus organized and negotiated.[29] Statesmen who exercise effective leadership[30] in contrast to mere politicians have to play two roles; they have to be both chairmen and chieftains, or to use a very traditional metaphor, foxes as well as lions.[31] To be only one or the other means not to rise to greatness. In all countries, one does find mere chairmen, but also mere chieftains. But in every country, politicians who were considered the most successful leaders were also considered effective in both respects. Schüssel certainly has been a remarkable organizer and an even more remarkable negotiator. His tactical skill in his role of chief executive was surprising, but he lacked or maybe chose to lack the capacity to lead, to convince, to mobilize the passions of his fellow citizens. He did this even less toward the end of his term of office, maybe more at the beginning. He seemed to have been convinced, especially after his electoral success in 2002, that the public would trust him and follow him not matter what. But it did not work out like that.

One should, however, not underestimate the achievement of being a good chairman under present day political conditions in Europe where, according to many observers, government is replaced by governance.[32] Traditional forms of top-down decision making, even inside the government, no longer work. Governmental institutions have to be continuously reformed and made more efficient. Multilevel politics means that politicians have to coordinate different levels of formulating and implementing policies, especially on both the European and the domestic level. The state has to slim down and allow market forces to work—an assumption that more recently has been somewhat called into question. Additionally, modern techniques of political management have to be applied. In all these respects, Wolfgang Schüssel was rather successful. In particular, his capacity to succeed in multilevel governance was considerable and is illustrated by the fact that his international reputation, even today, remains high.

So why did he ultimately fail in the sense of not inspiring the Austrian electorate to further support his successful achievements in organizing and managing the complex governance process? One should not underestimate the strength of the resistance to change in a very traditional society such as Austria. The long-lasting practice of consociational and corporatist politics does not easily allow politicians to mobilize a majority as happens in other Western democracies that have practiced competitive democracy and applied a different electoral system for a longer time. A majority electoral system instead of proportional representation might have provided the kind of clear support and mandate for the chief executive that would have been needed in order to successfully carry out far-reaching plans of reform. Moreover, as has been pointed out above, to be in office means sooner or later creating a negative majority of voters dissatisfied by one measure or the other. There is a political shelf-life to every government. Comprehensive comparative studies of Western democracies have shown that the chances of reelection have, on the average, been reduced over time. Voters have become more critical, more volatile, and expect change almost for change's sake.[33] Finally, close observers of Schüssel have noted that being successful in 2002 had set in motion an overestimation of his own capacities, a certain form of hubris.[34] Power corrupts, even if it's not absolute.[35] Even a modest and intellectually capable person like Wolfgang Schüssel may have fallen prey to that tendency, not having tried hard enough and likewise not having changed his somewhat exhausted team before the 2006 showdown.[36]

To sum up the achievements and the failures of Wolfgang Schüssel, on the positive side one can say that he pursued with tenacity a political program of consequence which seemed reasonable to many observers and stuck to it even against the feelings of vocal sectors of the public and even against the powerful rainbow press[37]—something that cannot be said about some of his successors. He proved a superior tactician and negotiator, especially on the European level. He exhibited an unusual amount of political spontaneity and, at the same time, personal modesty. Stuart Eizenstat came to appreciate him: "Despite his slight build his energy, intelligence and intensity made him a significant presence."[38] About the restitution negotiations, Eizenstat testifies, "He truly wanted a solution and was acting in a political environment that was (very) difficult."[39]

On the other hand, Schüssel broke a political taboo by governing with political outsiders which ultimately did lead to his downfall. But he tried to do something new, to introduce change in a very inflexible political environment. He failed to communicate successfully with the public, or out of a certain sense of hubris choose not to do so. In addition, he could not really overcome the opposition to his policy goals at home.

Has Schüssel succeeded in changing Austria? To some extent, yes. His policies and the forces mobilized by EU membership and increased internationalization have changed structures and attitudes. Privatization has progressed even if presently, under the impression of the economic crises, the clock may, as in other sectors, be turned back. The pension system has been reformed up to a point. But many areas still remain resistant to change. Constitutional reform and the reorganization of federalism and of certain sectors of the state bureaucracy have not succeeded. No effective new start has been possible in the education system or as regards research and development.[40] On the political level,

Austria has returned to a grand coalition government which to an almost absurd extent woos the rainbow press and is supported by it.

In a recent essay, Manfried Welan has in comparative perspective reflected about possible alternative major reforms of the Austrian constitutional system which certainly relate to Schüssel's successes and failures as chief executive.[41] He made clear that Schüssel proved, as had been shown in France twenty years before, that in a semipresidential system, a parliamentary majority can overrule an unwilling president and establish a regime of cohabitation. So semipresidentialism works and need not be changed. However, it is also obvious that the introduction of a majority electoral system such as in the United Kingdom would make it much easier to give a chief executive a clear mandate to introduce reforms (which Schüssel never received), but also allow voters to hold the chief executive fully responsible at the next elections. Finally, if, on the other hand, a *Konkordanzsystem*, a consociational constitution as in Switzerland, would be introduced (because as the strong opposition to Schüssel has demonstrated, this corresponds to a strongly held conviction in Austrian political culture) then, of course, the other aspect of the Swiss system such as the intensive emphasis on referendums would be necessary in order to keep the government democratically responsible. For all this finesse in short-term tactical matters, Schüssel did not take up these reforms which, in a long-term perspective, would have made the political system much more efficient and more democratic at the same time.

The problem is, however, that under the new situation of global economic crisis conditions have not become easier, but more difficult. International competition will not decrease, but increase.[42] Austria will need political leadership and ingenuity even more than before, maybe more than Wolfgang Schüssel could provide, but certainly not less.

Notes

1. Hans Rauscher, "Schüssel," *Der Standard*, 2 Oct. 2008; on Schüssel, see also Peter Pelinka, *Wolfgang Schüssel: Eine politische Biografie* (Vienna: Ueberreuter, 2003).

2. Andreas Khol, et al., "Wolfgang Schüssel—ein politischer Lebenslauf," in *Zukunft denken: Festschrift für Wolfgang Schüssel*, ed. Andreas Kohl et al. (Vienna: Oldenbourg, 2005), 9 ff.

3. Heinz Fischer, *Reflexionen* (Vienna: Kremayer & Scheriau, 1998), 152, 187.

4. Alfred Payrleitner, "Der Cellospieler," in Khol et al., *Zukunft denken*, 393ff.

5. See, for example, Johannes Hawlik and Wolfgang Schüssel, *Staat lass nach* (Vienna: Herold, 1985).

6. See Herbert Dachs et al., eds., *Die Politiker* (Vienna: Manz, 1995), 613ff.

7. See Pelinka, *Wolfgang Schüssel*, 149 and 170f.

8. Franz Fischler, *Erinnerungen* (Vienna: Ueberreuter, 2006), 105.

9. Manfried Welan, *Entwicklungsmöglichkeiten des Regierungssystems* (Vienna: Boku, 2009).

10. Stuart E. Eizenstat, *Imperfect Justice* (New York: Public Affairs, 2003), 291.

11. Ibid, 20ff.

12. Payrleitner, "Der Cellospieler," 401; and Fischler, *Erinnerungen*, 105.

13. Fritz Plasser and Peter A. Ulram, eds., *Wechselwahlen. Analysen zur Nationalratswahl 2006* (Vienna: Facultas, 2007), 33.

14. Pelinka, *Wolfgang Schüssel*, 196.

15. Ibid., 192.

16. Ibid., 175.

17. Ibid., 176.

18. Ibid., 174; and Joachim Riedl, *Der Wendekanzler* (Vienna: Czernin, 2001), 98.

19. Pelinka, *Wolfgang Schüssel*, 186; and Riedl, *Der Wendekanzler*, 58.

20. Robert Isaak, *Individuals in World Politics*, 2nd ed. (Belmont: Duxbury, 1981); and Wolfgang C. Müller, "Persönlichkeit und Politik," in *Die Politiker*, ed. Herbert Dachs et al. (Vienna: Manz, 1995).

21. Peter Berger, *Kurze Geschichte Österreichs im 20. Jahrhundert* (Vienna: Facultas, 2007).

22. Pelinka, *Wolfgang Schüssel*, 172.

23. See Johannes Pollak et al., eds., *Politik und Persönlichkeit* (Vienna: Facultas, 2008).

24. Max Weber, *Politik als Beruf* (Munich: Duncker, 1919); and Dirk Kaesler, ed., *Leidenschaft und Augenmaß* (Ramsen: Tenschert, 2008), 7ff.

25. Riedl, *Der Wendekanzler*, 21.

26. Ibid., 21.

27. Andreas Zielecke, "Helden und Waschlappen," *Süddeutsche Zeitung*, 6 Sept. 2008, p. 13.

28. Helmut Berking et al., eds., *Politikertypen in Europa* (Frankfurt: Fischer, 1994), 280ff.

29. Peter Gerlich and Wolfgang C. Müller, *Images of Chief-Executive Leadership: A Comparative Exploration* (Working Paper/ University Vienna 1988).

30. See Regina M. Jankowitsch, "Political Leadership," in *Politik und Persönlichkeit*, ed. Johannes Pollak et al. (Vienna: Facultas, 2008), 197ff.

31. The initial quote of this article is from Baltasar Gracian's *Art of Worldy Wisdom*, trans. Joseph Jacobs (Whitefish, MT: Kessinger, 2003), reputedly one of Wolfgang Schüssel's favorite books. Some observers have assumed that he was influenced by the traditional *Rule of Saint Benedict*, regulating the behavior of abbot and monks in Benedictine monasteries. While this book certainly reads as a very modern text in many ways, it can be assumed that Schüssel prefered the less stern and sober but more realistic and slightly cynical political manual of Baltasar Gracian. See Baltasar Gracian, *Hand-Orakel* (Frankfurt: Insel, 1986).

32. Peter Gerlich, "Sozialpartnerschaft in Zeiten der Governance," in *Festschrift 60 Jahre Wirtschaftskammer Österreich*, ed. Wirtschaftskammer Österreich (Vienna: WKO, 2006), 49.

33. Kaare Strom et al., eds., *Cabinets and Coalition Bargaining* (Oxford: Oxford UP, 2008), 403ff.

34. Fritz Plasser as quoted in Riedl, *Der Wendekanzler*, 31.

35. See David Owen, *In Sickness and in Power: Illness in Heads of Government during the Last 100 Years* (New York: Prager, 2008) and Sherwin B. Nuland, "Political Disorders," *Foreign Affairs* 87.6 (Nov./Dec. 2008): 148-51.

36. The lightheartedness of Schüssel's support team was expressed by one of its members who recollected in retrospect that they playfully expressed three wishes at the three Christmas parties which took place before important decisions in 1999, 2002 and 2006. In the first year, they wished for a black-blue government, in the second year for a black-green, and in the third for black-red, however under a chancellor Schüssel. The first wish was granted, the second and the third remained unfulfilled. Santa Claus does not intervene in politics. If true, the anecdote demonstrates the political flexibility of Schüssel and his team.

37. Pelinka, *Wolfgang Schüssel*, 172.

38. Eizenstat, *Imperfect Justice*, 91.

39. Ibid., 305.

40. See Payrleitner, "Der Cellospieler," 400; Andreas Unterberger, "Austria semper reformanda," in Khol et al., *Zukunft denken*, 423ff.; Pelinka, 196ff.; Emmerich Tálos, ed., *Schwarz-Blau: Eine Bilanz des "Neu-Regierens"* (Vienna: LitVerlag, 2006).

41. Welan, *Entwicklungsmöglichkeiten*.

42. Markus Beyrer, "Reformen für Österreich," in Khol et al., *Zukunft denken*, 356.

Rollercoaster: Schüssels' Electoral (Mis)fortunes and the Dynamics of Public Approval

Fritz Plasser and Peter A. Ulram

Wolfgang Schüssel's political career and the electoral performance of the Austrian People's Party (*Österreichische Volkspartei*, or ÖVP) between 1995, the year in which Schüssel took over the party chair, and 2006, the year when an electoral defeat ended his chancellorship, compare to a political rollercoaster ride. Under Schüssel's leadership, the ÖVP fell to third place among Austria's major political parties for the first time in 1999, rose in 2002 after a fulminant election victory to become the strongest party by far, and fell again back to the second place behind the Social Democratic Party of Austria (*Sozialdemokratische Partei Österreichs*, or SPÖ) in 2006.[1] Twice Schüssel terminated the government coalition prematurely. In 1995, he canceled the great coalition with the SPÖ on short notice, thereby provoking early elections which, however, did not bring the expected gains for the ÖVP. In 2002, he terminated the coalition partnership again in face of chaotic controversies within the Freedom Party of Austria (*Freiheitliche Partei Österreichs*, or FPÖ) and called for new elections which brought him—in contrast to the year 1995—a triumphal election victory.

After the parliamentary elections of 1999 that ended with an electoral disaster for both the SPÖ and ÖVP, Schüssel decided to form a coalition government with Jörg Haider's FPÖ and took over the chancellorship in 2000. After thirty years, the ÖVP became the chancellor party again due to Schüssel. In May 1995, when Schüssel took over the party chair of the ÖVP, the party had a voting share of 27.7 percent according to the results of the elections in 1994. In 1995, this share rose slightly to 28.3 percent.[2] In 1999, the ÖVP fell back again to 26.9 percent.[3] In 2002, the ÖVP rose again under Chancellor Schüssel to a share of 42.3 percent and became the clearly strongest parliamentary party.[4] In 2006, after a loss of 8.0 percent of the votes, the party fell back again to 34.3 percent and landed slightly behind the SPÖ (35.3 percent), which now placed the chancellorship in the SPÖ's hands.[5]

Between 1995 and 2006, Schüssel had three SPÖ chairs as his competitors: Chancellor Franz Vranitzky (1995-1997), Chancellor Viktor Klima (1997-1999), and chair of the oppositional SPÖ Alfred Gusenbauer (2000-2006). As vice-chancellor and chancellor, Schüssel has been part of three coalition governments. As vice-chancellor, he governed between 1995 and 1999 in a grand coalition government with the SPÖ. As chancellor, he led a coalition with the FPÖ from 2000 to 2002, which he continued until 2006, although he was forced to base this coalition between 2005 and 2006 on the Alliance for the Future of Austria (*Bündnis Zukunft Österreich*, or BZÖ), an offshoot party founded by Haider after the break-up of the FPÖ.

His relationship to the European Union was also characterized by several ups and downs. In 1994, Schüssel belonged to the core of the team negotiating the modalities of Austria's admission to the European Union (EU) and was highly engaged in the accession which occurred in 1995. In 2000, being chancellor of a coalition government between the ÖVP and FPÖ, he had to cope with the sanctions imposed by the EU14 and the break-up of communication with the EU elites. After the termination of the sanctions, Schüssel not only returned as chief of government to the circle of the EU elites, but also engaged himself anew in a deepening of European integration and the enlargement of the European Union. Political, personal, and electoral (mis)fortunes characterize the Schüssel years in Austria. In the center of this essay stands the public perception of Schüssel, the dynamics and the cycles of public approval, and his image with the Austrian voters. How did the approval ratings for Schüssel change over the course of time, how satisfied was the population with his government's activity, which attributes primarily determined Schüssel's public persona, and what did the image of Chancellor Schüssel mean for the election successes and defeats—those are the central questions to be analyzed in the following sections.

Schüssel's Public Approval

Schüssel started his political career as secretary general of the *Österreichische Wirtschaftsbund* (the representation of business in the ÖVP) and was elected a member of parliament in 1979. He became well known in the party and by a wider public for his innovative approach to economic policy, in particular, by asking for economic liberalization and a re-dimensioning of state interventionism. Thus he was considered a politician who challenged traditional concepts albeit doing so while being firmly rooted within the established party structure. At a time of severe problems in the state-owned industries and growing dissatisfaction with the increasing burden of taxation as well as the distribution of taxpayer's money,[6] this image contributed to his enjoying a high degree of public approval. During his time as minister of economics and trade, nearly six out of ten respondents had a good opinion of Schüssel, while only about one-quarter held a bad one. However, the premature elections of 1995 did not result in the lead that the ÖVP desired, and his previous election as party chairman had been accompanied by considerable internal conflicts. His public rating then declined sharply, never again to reach the positive levels of the previous years.

The late 1990s were characterized by the rise of the right-wing populist FPÖ under Haider and of oppositional parties in general which meant a sound electoral defeat of both the SPÖ and the ÖVP in 1999, catapulting the FPÖ to the position of the second largest party. Schüssel responded to this challenge which came as a shock to the great majority of the party leadership – in an active, if controversial, way—by forming a coalition with the FPÖ and taking over the position of federal chancel-

Table 1
Schüssel's Public Rating, 1989-2006, in Percentage and Percentage Point Difference (PPD)*

Year	Good Opinion	No Good Opinion	PPD
1989	49	24	25
1990	50	28	22
1991	57	26	31
1992	58	24	34
1993	59	26	33
1994	60	26	34
1996	50	50	±0
1997	56	40	16
1998	50	40	10
2000	49	42	7
2001	45	41	4
2002	43	46	-3
2003	33	55	-22
2004	42	44	-2
2005	44	47	-3
2006	53	41	12

*Average values per year.

Source: GfK Austria, National Surveys (1989-2006).

lor. As a consequence, neither the electoral misfortune nor the following sanctions of the EU 14 which had to be abandoned after a few months left a lasting impact on his public approval. Actually the latter might have proven helpful for the chancellor who presented himself as a strong and tough national leader keeping at bay overly nationalistic outbreaks (of the FPÖ).

Contrary to a rather agitated media and intellectual discourse in Austria and abroad and a series of protest activities organized mostly by the (now oppositional) SPÖ and smaller left-wing groups, the majority of the electorate responded to the formation of the ÖVP-FPÖ coalition in a moderate way. The predominant wait-and-see attribute[7] was also reflected in a slightly positive evaluation of the new government in its first year: 52 percent declared satisfaction with the performance of the coalition, while 46 percent took a negative view. Conflicts within the government as well as in the FPÖ led to an erosion of consensus, but the opposition parties could not take full advantage of this because these parties, especially the Social Democrats, had great difficulties coming to terms with the new political situation. As a matter of fact, the great bulk of irritated FPÖ voters (who had voted for political change in 1999 but not for continuous strife and often inexperienced and unprepared FPÖ ministers) deserted their former party for the ÖVP rather than the SPÖ in the 2002 elections. Nevertheless, many people had looked for something else and when—after the failure of the negotiations with the Greens—the old coalition was installed again, these expectations remained disappointed.

More important, however, were the effects of a restrictive budgetary politics, cuts in social welfare, and, most of all, the pension reform of 2003. The latter was not only badly communicated, but the initial proposals were also generally seen as causing unacceptable social hardships. Not surprisingly, the public reaction proved to be overly critical, and the country witnessed its first large-scale strike in many years. Subsequent modifications smothered many of the measures, but not the negative impact on the popularity of the government. Satisfaction with the government fell to a (up to then) historical low of 32 percent with 67 percent expressing dissatisfaction.

Even though there was an improvement in the following years—also partly due to the economic recovery—negative votes outweighed positive ones at the eve of the 2006 elections.

These developments also overshadowed Schüssel's personal ratings. In 2003, the share of "good opinion" fell to a mere 33 percent with a slow upward trend thereafter. The year 2006 saw a further increase of good opinions about the chancellor and a concomitant decrease of bad opinions, but the ground for the electoral misfortune of the coming autumn had already been laid. The elections of 2006 were much less a plebiscite about the person of the chancellor than an expression of diffuse discomfort with the main governing party, the ÖVP.

Table 2
Satisfaction with Government Coalition (ÖVP-FPÖ/BZÖ), 2000-2006, in Percentage and Percentage Point Difference (PPD)*

Year	Satisfied	Not Satisfied	PPD
2000	52	46	+6
2001	48	49	-1
2002	46	51	-5
2003	32	67	-45
2004	37	59	-22
2005	36	61	-25
2006/1st quarter	38	58	-18
2006/2nd quarter	42	54	-12

*Annual or quarterly averages

Source: GfK Austria, National Surveys (2000-2006).

Candidate Image: Schüssel's Public Persona

Only a few voters get an opportunity to meet their party's top candidate personally. The great majority of voters gains their picture of the top candidate from information and impressions communicated via the mass media. These perceptions of the chancellor candidates are called candidate images. They are multi-dimensional concepts including evaluative components both on the cognitive and affective level. According to Oscar Gabriel and Katja Neller,[8] candidate images relate to three aspects on which voters judge them: the overall judgment about the candidates, the evaluation of their personality characteristics, and an evaluation of their political competence or politically relevant attributes. Generally, candidate images refer to "issue positions, character traits and are likely to include psychical appearance, style of communication, and nonverbal behavior."[9] For Anthony King, candidate images are a reference to four attributes of party leaders or presidential candidates: "their physical appearance, their native intelligence, their character or temperament, and their political style."[10]

While King reduces the concept of candidate image mostly to personal traits, character, integrity, and personal qualities and style, Frank Brettschneider and Kenneth Hacker also consider perceptions of issue-related competence of a leader as central components of candidate image.[11] In fact, numerous studies point to considerable message-image interactions,[12] just as candidate images and party images affect each other. Brettschneider differentiates between four dimensions of candidate image: the evaluation of political viewpoints and the ability for the solution of concrete problems, the qualities of leadership (leadership strength, decision making, and power to act and persuade), personal integrity (honesty, reliability, trustworthiness) and non-political attributes (looks, charisma, age, and social background).[13] Table 3 is based on this typology and presents the public perception of Wolfgang Schüssel from his time as vice-chancellor in a grand coalition under Chancellor Vranitzky (1996) and Chancellor Klima (1998) as well as Schüssel's image as chancellor in a small coalition with the FPÖ (2000-2004).

In 1996, primarily three attributes defined the public image of Schüssel: his competence in economic questions, his ability to represent Austria's interests in Europe, and the courage to make unpopular decisions which was credited to him. At that time, Schüssel was responsible for the Department of Economy and Trade and had only in 1995 taken over the ÖVP party chair and, succeeding Erhard Busek, also the position of vice-chancellor in the grand coalition. Only few months later, he canceled the cooperation with the SPÖ on account of considerable disagreements in budgetary policies and called for new elections which, however, did not result in the hoped for gains. Schüssel had to accept a meager increase of only 0.5 percent, while the SPÖ and Chancellor Vranitzky gained 3.2 percent. Two years later, the image of Schüssel in the perception of the public had not essentially changed. Competence in matters of economy as well as the representation of Austrian interests in Europe were central image qualities of the ÖVP vice-chancellor, who in the meantime had changed from the Department of Economic Affairs to the Department of Foreign Affairs in 1998. Leadership qualities were less ascribed to him in 1998 than only two years earlier. His public appearance in the dimensions of integrity and trustworthiness as well as personal qualities and style continued to be less pronounced characteristics.

Table 3
Schüssel's Public Image, 1996-2004, in Percentage of Responses

Describes Wolfgang Schüssel according to interviewed persons	Vice-Chancellor 1996	Vice-Chancellor 1998	Chancellor 2000	Chancellor 2004
Dimension: Competence				
Knows a lot about the economy	44	41	30	29
Represents Austria's interests in Europe well	39	35	33	23
Is able to cope with serious problems	18	7	24	21
Takes care that Austria is well governed	NA	NA	24	18
Dimension: Leadership qualities				
Has the courage for unpopular decisions	37	16	41	36
Gives clear directions	25	11	21	22
Has real leadership qualities	17	5	18	14
Has a forceful impact	17	22	21	26
Dimension: Integrity, trustworthiness				
Stands up for what he says	19	13	18	15
Trustworthy	18	12	18	15
Understands people's problems	13	13	17	8
Dimension: Personal attributes				
Makes an appealing impression	18	18	23	18
Looks good on TV	23	23	23	26

NA: not applicable

Source: GfK Austria, National Surveys (1995-2004).

Leadership and his somehow less prominent competence characterized Schüssel's public image in 2004, too. Attributes relating to trustworthiness and understanding of people's problems continued to be less pronounced. Schüssel was perceived as a leading chancellor, but not as a caring leader. In 2002, Schüssel celebrated an overwhelming electoral success and led the ÖVP to first place with a gain of 15.4 percent which led to a further rise of his leadership image. However, the forceful course of reforms and partially drastic changes in pension policies and the social system left its traces on the public's perception of Schüssel.[14] In 2004, only 8 percent of interviewed persons believed that Schüssel was able to understand the needs and problems of the people. His leadership by conviction was opposed by a deficit of caring compassion, which was to contribute to his loss of votes and the end of his chancellorship in the campaign of 2006.

During the campaign of 2006, the ÖVP and SPÖ not only competed with different issues and profiles of competence regarding voter-relevant problems, but also with chancellor candidates whose images were defined by different strengths. These differences in the appearance of the two chancellor candidates become visible in their evaluations. Schüssel was, compared to Gusenbauer, perceived as politically more experienced by far, a person who knows his way in European politics, has the required strength of leadership, and keeps a clear head, even in difficult situations. He was seen as considerably more powerful than Gusenbauer, was believed to make a much better appearance on television, and signaled the courage for decisive actions. While the public image of the acting chancellor focused upon leadership, strength, competence, and resilience in crises, so was the image of Gusenbauer primarily characterized by social competence (strives for social balance, meets the needs of people, and understands their problems). Apart from this social competence and affinity to the citizens, which harmonized with public opinion and appealed to the large-scale expectations of the population, the data also points out pronounced deficits in all dimensions relating to leadership strength and competence of decision making and crisis management. A strong leadership personality—the acting chancellor—was therefore confronted with a challenger who was reflecting social expectations, promising not primarily leadership, but caring understanding. This was the central polarity of the campaign for chancellor and the choice given to primarily personality-oriented voters.

The relevance of the polarity of the two chancellor images is clearer if a closer look is taken at the changes in the appearance of both candidates. In January 2006, 59 percent were under the impression that Gusenbauer cared about the needs of people. Four years earlier, only 41 percent had this impression. On the other hand, only 32 percent still believed that Schüssel met the needs of the people. During the campaign of 2002, this was still the opinion of 48 percent of voters. In the estimation of the electorate, a chancellor in a leading role had apparently distanced himself too much from the emotional needs of the people, while his challenger signaled—despite having less leadership strength, but based on the image of his party—more concern about everyday problems.

Table 4
Images of Chancellor Candidates in 2002 and 2006, in Percentage of Responses

Quality	Schüssel 2002	Schüssel 2006	Gusenbauer 2002	Gusenbauer 2006
Has political experience	85	81	11	14
Has better appearance on TV	70	67	18	24
Keeps a clear head in difficult situations	70	70	19	22
Able to represent Austria's interests in Europe well	68	67	24	23
Has a strong, forceful impact	61	68	28	25
Has courage to decisive action	57	61	31	33
Presents clear goals for Austria	56	58	32	32
Can be trusted	51	43	31	40
Meets the needs of people	48	32	41	59
Understands people's problems	NA	23	NA	67
Takes care of social balance	NA	21	NA	73

NA: not applicable

Source: GfK Austria, National Surveys (2002-2006).

The influence of issue-oriented attitudes and expectations on the images of the candidates makes the quantification of the importance of candidates' personalities upon the voting decision quite difficult because it depends not only on the attractiveness of the preferred candidate but also on the acceptability of his party. If voters decisively refuse to vote for a particular party, they also vote against it if they prefer its candidate.[15] This tendency can be seen in the data regarding a (hypothetical) direct vote for a chancellor. If it had been possible to vote for a chancellor directly, 49 percent would have chosen Schüssel and only 40 percent Gusenbauer. However, taking a closer look, Schüssel's chancellor-bonus has to be differentiated by party defectors and newcomers.

Every second party defector from the ÖVP or from the SPÖ preferred as chancellor not the candidate of the party for which the person actually voted, but the chancellor-candidate of the party he or she voted against. As much as 7 percent of the SPÖ voters would not have elected the chancellor candidate of their own party if they could have voted directly for the chancellor. However, it was not the chancellor candidates but the parties with issue-oriented profiles of achievement and competence that were up for election, and they finally determined the results. The strength in Schüssel's image for the voting decision of ÖVP voters were clearly more relevant than the strength in Gusenbauer's image for SPÖ voters. While 24 percent of the ÖVP voters primarily oriented themselves on the personality of the ÖVP chancellor candidate, the same was only true for 8 percent of the SPÖ voters. SPÖ voters obviously placed more importance on their expectations of issue competence regarding problems of high importance to them, rather than on the personality of the top candidate. Therefore, the highest share of issue-oriented voters can be found among SPÖ voters, while ÖVP voters by comparison have the lowest share of primarily issue-oriented voters.

The Chancellor's lack of sensibility for everyday social problems, support of drastic reform measures, and projection of a leadership style which was interpreted as aloof led to a loss of 8 percent for the ÖVP, a loss of first place, and the end of the six-year chancellorship of Wolfgang Schüssel. This defeat did not come as a surprise. Prior to the campaign, 80 percent of the people interviewed had mentioned Schüssel's lack of concern for the socially underprivileged as a reason for ending his chancellorship, 69 percent referred to his tendency to make decisions alone, and 67 percent to his readiness to make deep cuts in social payments; considerable groups of ÖVP voters agreed with this criticism of the content and style of Schüssel's chancellorship. In 2006, Schüssel's leadership strength could no longer compensate for these weaknesses in his image as had been the case in 2002. Policy-related image traits played a more important role for the evaluation of candidate images than questions of style, personal qualities, and performance on TV. The dynamics and trends of Schüssel's public perception confirm the evidence from several studies which conclude "that issues of performance and issues of policy loom much larger in most voters' minds than do issues of personality."[16]

Candidate Voting: Personalization of the Voting Decision

The concentration of election campaigns on the image and performance of top candidates, increasing personalization of campaign reporting in the mass media, and higher importance of candidate-centered motives for voting decisions are part of the standard diagnoses of a progressive *Americanization* of the political competition in Austria.[17] In fact, campaign strategists tend to stress factors like their candidates' image, credibility, and strength in decision making. These election campaigns concentrate on the personality and image of top candidates not only in the United States, but also in countries with party-list voting systems as in the majority of Western European states. Attentive observers of the campaign practices in Western Europe, where proportional representation is the predominant election formula and the decisive vote is given to the party, speak of a trend of *presidentialization* of European parliamentary campaigns in the sense of moving away from party-centered election campaigns toward media-centered personality campaigns.[18]

Far more differentiation is applied by election research toward the value and importance of candidate-oriented election motives. Controversy exists among election researchers about whether the share of personality voters actually increased during the past years and whether personality attributes of candidates have gained importance in voters' decisions; most researchers warn against an overestimation of candidate-oriented election motives.[19] The cautious restraint of election research toward the actual importance of *candidate voting* also becomes understandable in the light of trends in Austrian election studies. Since the middle of the 1980s, the share of primarily candidate-motivated voters did not rise, but drop. While in 1986, 45 percent of the voters still mostly named the image and personality of the top candidates of the chosen party as the main cause for their voting decision; in 2002, such voters amounted to only 30 percent of the electorate and in 2006 only 16 percent.[20]

Apparently the trend to *candidate voting* depends upon the personalities offered by political parties; the attraction, competence, and credibility of individual top candidates; and the degree of personalization of the strategies of communication and election campaigning. If several parties have politically attractive top candidates and focus their campaign strategies primarily upon the public image of their top candidates, the share of candidate-oriented voters increases, too. If, however, there is a lack of candidates who are convincing via the mass media and if controversial issues and policies are at the center of the campaign with individual parties placing more importance upon the problem solving competence assigned to their parties, then the share of candidate-motivated voters will subsequently be lower. As a consequence, the shares of candidate-motivated voters will *vary* between the party electorates depending upon their current strategic competitive position. In 1986, the SPÖ focused its campaign primarily on the image and alleged competence of Chancellor Vranitzky who had only been in office for four months. At that time, for 61 percent of the SPÖ voters the personality of the SPÖ top candidate was the primary reason for their personal voting decision, while only 28 percent of the ÖVP voters pointed out that the ÖVP top candidate had been the reason for their choice of party. In 1986, 71 percent of those voting for the FPÖ referred to Haider, who had only taken over the party chair a few weeks prior to election day; he was to shape decisively the image and appearance of the newly formed FPÖ regarding strategy and style in the following election campaigns, too.

The growth of *candidate voting* can also be seen as an indicator for *cycles* of the elective attraction of individual candidates. While in 1986 61 percent of the SPÖ voters primarily gave the personality of Vranitzky as the main reason for their choice, in 1995—in spite of additional gains for the SPÖ—only 37 percent of SPÖ voters could be classified as candidate-motivated voters. In 2002, only 23 percent of SPÖ voters stated that the personality of their top candidate, Gusenbauer, had been the decisive reason for their choice.[21] Issue- and party-competence (70 percent), factors guided by traditions and interests (56 percent), and tactical considerations regarding coalitions (38 percent) were more relevant for the SPÖ voters in 2002 than factors referring to the personality of the candidate. In 2006, only 8 percent of the SPÖ voters named the chancellor candidate of the SPÖ, Alfred Gusenbauer, as a central election motive, but 53 percent of the SPÖ voters mentioned current issues as main reason for their voting decision.

The development of candidate-motivated voting took a different course within the ÖVP electorate. In 1990 under Josef Riegler, only 19 percent of the ÖVP voters referred to the personality of the top candidate as reason for their choice, and this share of candidate-motivated ÖVP voters reached an even lower value with Busek as the top candidate in 1994; however, the share of ÖVP *candidate voters* reached the highest value up to that date under Schüssel with 37 percent in 1995. During the election of 1999 when the ÖVP received its worst result to date with a share of only 26.9 percent, only 22 percent of ÖVP voters could still be classified as Schüssel voters. In 2002, 36 percent of the ÖVP voters referred to the personality of the ÖVP chancellor as the reason for their party choice. Although the ÖVP campaign had almost exclusively focused upon the image of the chancellor, issues and party competences (62 percent) and traditional party allegiance and interests (55 percent) still were more widespread reasons for the election decision of ÖVP voters than primarily personality-oriented factors. This does not lower the factual communicative and mobilizing effect of the personality of the chancellor as represented in the mass media, but *relativizes* simple explanations about the voter decision in 2002 as exclusively personality-related. Also in 2006, the ÖVP campaign was focused upon the image and leadership qualities of Schüssel with the candidate standing in the center of the election campaign. Yet the image and personality of Schüssel only turned out to be the central election motive for 24 percent of the ÖVP voters.

The available data trends also relativize the widespread assumption that non-party-affiliated swing-voters orient themselves more strongly on the profiles of candidates and personality attributes than party-affiliated core voters.[22] With 30 percent, the share of candidate-motivated voters among swing-voters is congruent with the share of *candidate voters* among core-voters, whereby ÖVP newcomers oriented themselves tendentially more on the personality of Schüssel than did SPÖ newcomers on the personality of the top candidate Gusenbauer. In 2006, 51 percent of the *candidate voters* elected the ÖVP, only 18 percent the SPÖ, 14 percent the Greens, and only 8 percent the FPÖ. At the parliamentary election in 1999, however, 31 percent of the candidate-motivated voters had chosen the FPÖ, 34 percent the SPÖ, and only 17 percent the ÖVP.

In 2006, the issue-oriented voter was the most represented type of voter by far. At that time, 47 percent could be classified as primarily oriented on issue competence of the chosen party. With a share of 37 percent, traditional voters, for whom the party's affinity to the past and group-specific identities determined the election decision, were the next largest group of voters. The type of the personality-oriented voter followed in third place with a share of 16 percent. Three-quarters of the personality-oriented voters were party-affiliated core voters of a particular party. Among the swing-voters, only 14 percent of candidate-oriented voters primarily felt attracted by the top candidate of their chosen party at the parliamentary elections in 2006, but more than 20 percent mentioned criticism of leading politicians of the parties for which they declined to vote.[23] The personality of both chancellor candidates undoubtedly influenced the voting decision in 2006 and favored more strongly the chances for electing the ÖVP rather than the SPÖ. However, the more issue orientations and expectations of content gained importance for voters' party choice, the weaker the influence of personality and chancellor preference became upon the final voting decision.

Conclusion

The last two decades saw profound changes of the Austrian party system. Structural and affective ties between voters and parties weakened and were accompanied by a considerable confidence gap.[24] Voters began to strengthen new parties like the Greens or old parties which had adapted a populist style (FPÖ, BZÖ). Although both traditional parties suffered from these developments, the ÖVP was more vulnerable since it was hampered by its difficult position as the minor partner in the "grand" (SPÖ-ÖVP) coalition—getting most of the blame but little of the praise—and the dominance of corporatist and regional interests in the party organization.

Table 5
Indications of Political Change in Austria, 1979-2008, in Percent

Group	1979	1986	1990	1994/5	1999	2001/2	2006	2008
Traditional Voters*	56	39	34	31	26	25	24	18
Party Members	23	23	18	13	n.a.	15	12	12
Mobile Voters**	16	18	26	44	46	53	60	n.a.
Party Changers**	7	16	17	19	18	24	25	28
ÖVP Share of Valid Vote****	41.9	41.3	32.1	27.7	26.9	42.3	34.3	26.0
ÖVP and SPÖ Share of Valid Vote****	92.9	84.4	74.9	62.6	60.1	78.7	69.6	55.3
FPÖ and BZÖ Share of Valid Vote****	6.1	9.7	16.6	22.5	26.9	10.0	16.1	28.2
Other Parties' Share of Valid Vote****	1.0	5.8	8.7	15.0	13.1	11.1	15.2	16.5

*voters who always vote for the same party even if they sometimes do not agree with the party's position or actions; **voters who have already shifted from one party to another in national or regional elections; ***national elections 1979, 1986, 1994, 1999, 2002, 2006, 2008; ****voters who changed their vote with respect to the prior national election

Source: GfK Austria, Representative Surveys or Exit Polls (1979-2008).

Schüssel, who had started his political career as an advocate for sectoral reforms and a supporter of the grand coalition evidently became aware of the restrictions inherent in these positions and looked for new options. His first try did not bring the desired results and led to a deterioration of his formerly high sympathy ratings. Four years later, the move to form a coalition with the FPÖ proved more successful. It made him chancellor and brought the ÖVP into a much better strategic position, especially since the FPÖ once in government could not deliver what it had promised when in opposition. Yet what the chancellor lost in popularity, he gained in leadership. His second term in office after the landslide victory of 2002 was characterized by a strong emphasis on reform politics and a pointed pro-European agenda. This focus, however, came with a price: real or imagined losers of cuts in the social welfare and pension system deserted the ÖVP, first in the polls and later in the polling booths. Furthermore, Schüssel's personal leadership style led to friction with some of the "big players" in the party, and his relationship with the media was anything but a close one. Schüssel was considered a strong and determined political leader, but not a "compassionate conservative." Even though he passed the party leadership to Wilhelm Molterer after the electoral misfortune of 2006, he remained an important figure in the ÖVP until the party's even greater defeat in 2008.

Considering the political developments prior to, during, and after Schüssel's leadership, "rollercoaster" is more than a description of his personal fortunes and misfortunes, but a general characteristic of Austrian politics in the recent past (and probably the near future).

Notes

1. Fritz Plasser and Peter A. Ulram. "Electoral Change in Austria," in *The Changing Austrian Voter*, vol. 16, Contemporary Austrian Studies, ed. Günter Bischof and Fritz Plasser (New Brunswick, NJ: Transaction, 2008), 54-78.

2. Fritz Plasser et al., "(Dis-)Kontinuitäten und neue Spannungslinien im Wählerverhalten," in *Wahlkampf und Wählerentscheidung: Analysen zur Nationalratswahl 1995*, ed. Fritz Plasser (Vienna: WUV-Verlag, 1996), 155-210.

3. Fritz Plasser et al., "Breaking the Mold: Politische Wettbewerbsräume und Wahlverhalten Ende der neunziger Jahre," in *Das österreichische Wahlverhalten*, ed. Fritz Plasser et al. (Vienna: WUV-Verlag, 2000), 55-116.

4. Fritz Plasser and Peter A. Ulram, "Die Erdrutschwahlen 2002 in Österreich," in *Wahlen und Wähler: Analysen aus Anlass der Bundestagswahl 2002*, ed. Jürgen W. Falter et al. (Wiesbaden: VS Verlag, 2005), 572-94.

5. Fritz Plasser et al., "Was Wähler(innen) bewegt: Parteien-, Themen- und Kandidatenorientierungen 2006," in *Wechselwahlen. Analysen zur Nationalratswahl 2006*, ed. Fritz Plasser and Peter A. Ulram (Vienna: WUV-Verlag, 2007), 155-94.

6. Fritz Plasser, *Parteien unter Stress: Zur Dynamik der Parteiensysteme in Österreich, Deutschland und den USA* (Vienna: Böhlau, 1987), 244; Peter A. Ulram, *Hegemonie und Erosion: Politische Kultur und politischer Wandel in Österreich* (Vienna: Böhlau, 1990), 118ff. and 180ff.

7. Fritz Plasser and Peter A. Ulram, *Das österreichische Politikverständnis: Von der Konsum- zur Konfliktkultur?* (Vienna: WUV Verlag, 2002), 29-31.

8. Oscar W. Gabriel and Katja Neller, "Kandidatenorientierungen und Wahlverhalten," in *Wahlen und Wähler: Analysen aus Anlass der Bundestagswahl 2002*, ed. Jürgen W. Falter et al. (Wiesbaden: VS Verlag, 2005), 213-43, here 222.

9. Kenneth Hacker, "Political Image," in *Encyclopedia of Political Communication*, ed. Lynda Lee Kaid and Christina Holtz-Bacha (Thousand Oaks, CA: Sage, 2008), 322-325, here 324.

10. Anthony King, "Do Leaders' Personalities Really Matter?" in *Leaders' Personalities and the Outcomes of Democratic Elections*, ed. Anthony King (Oxford: Oxford UP, 2002), 1-43, here 8.

11. Frank Brettschneider, *Spitzenkandidaten und Wahlerfolg: Personalisierung—Kompetenz—Parteien, Ein internationaler Vergleich* (Wiesbaden: Westdeutscher Verlag,

2002); Kenneth Hacker, ed., *Presidential Candidate Images* (New York: Rowman & Littlefield, 2004).

12. Hacker, *Presidential.*

13. Brettschneider, *Spitzenkandidaten und Wahlerfolg*, 143-44.

14. Emmerich Talos, ed., *Schwarz-Blau: Eine Bilanz des "Neu-Regierens"* (Vienna: Lit-Verlag, 2006).

15. Hans Mathias Kepplinger and Marcus Maurer, *Abschied vom rationalen Wähler* (Freiburg: Alber-Verlag, 2005), 180.

16. Anthony King, "Conclusions and Implications," in *Leaders' Personalities and the Outcomes of Democratic Elections*, ed. Anthony King (Oxford: Oxford UP, 2002), 210-21, here 220.

17. Fritz Plasser, "Assessing the Americanization of Austrian Politics and Politicians," in *The Americanization/Westernization of Austria*, vol. 12, Contemporary Austrian Studies, ed. Günter Bischof and Anton Pelinka (New Brunswick, NJ: Transaction, 2004), 235-54.

18. Ian McAllister, "The Personalization of Politics," in *The Oxford Handbook of Political Behavior*, ed. Russell J. Dalton and Hans-Dieter Klingemann (Oxford: Oxford UP, 2007), 571-88.

19. Kees Aarts, et al., eds., *Political Leaders and Democratic Elections* (Oxford: Oxford UP, 2009, forthcoming).

20. Plasser et al., "Was Wähler(innen) bewegt," 191.

21. Fritz Plasser et al., "Erdrutschwahlen: Momentum, Motive und neue Muster im Wahlverhalten," in *Wahlverhalten in Bewegung: Analysen zur Nationalratswahl*, ed. Fritz Plasser und Peter A. Ulram (Vienna: WUV-Verlag, 2003), 97-158, here 143.

22. Brettschneider, *Spitzenkandidaten und Wahlerfolg*.

23. Plasser et al., "Was Wähler(innen) bewegt," 191.

24. Plasser et al., "Breaking the Mold."

Schüssel and the Media: An Ambivalent Relationship

Günther Lengauer

The first televised pictures of the new coalition government between the conservative Austrian People's Party (*Österreichische Volkspartei*, or ÖVP) and the right-wing populist Austrian Freedom Party (*Freiheitliche Partei Österreichs*, or FPÖ) headed by Chancellor Wolfgang Schüssel on 4 February 2000 were more than critical and anything but a good start. In front of the Office of the Chancellor, on the Ballhausplatz in Vienna, thousands of strident demonstrators gathered to protest the swearing-in of the ÖVP-FPÖ coalition. Consequently, the designated members of the new government had to take a subterranean passage to get to the inauguration ceremony at the president's residence, the *Hofburg*. Additionally, during the preceding weeks the largest Austrian newspaper, *Neue Kronen Zeitung*, with a daily readership of about three million people and, thus, more than 40 percent of the population at that time, had heavily criticized Wolfgang Schüssel for planning this coalition between *Schwarz* and *Blau*[1] with headlines such as "Public Anger Hits Schüssel"[2] (26 January 2000). On 13 January, the chief editor of the *Neue Kronen Zeitung*, Hans Dichand, wrote an editorial under the pseudonym CATO: "The majority of the population that opposes the ÖVP-FPÖ coalition is disregarded by Schüssel. How can this thrive?"

Not only CATO and his *Kronen Zeitung* journalists cultivated a distant relationship with Chancellor Schüssel in their journalistic treatment of him. During his chancellorship, Wolfgang Schüssel was also disparagingly labeled (ambiguously referring both to the title of his favorite book as well as his shortness) as "The Little Prince" (*der kleine Prinz*) as many as ninety times in the Austrian media (newspapers, magazines, radio, and television). Moreover, Chancellor Schüssel's relationship with the Austrian media faced an acid test and was seriously dulled even before the pictures of the demonstrations where aired; in fact, this occurred years before he became chancellor. On 3 July 1997, the daily quality paper *Salzburger Nachrichten* ran "Wolfgang Schüssel Lies" as its editorial headline on the front page referring to the so-called "breakfast affair" (*Frühstücksaffäre*). At that time, he was state secretary and was accused of having seriously insulted the president of the German Central Bank, Hans Thietmeyer, and Danish Prime Minister Poul Nyrup Rasmussen during an off-the-record breakfast conversation with journalists on the sidelines of the European Union Summit in Amsterdam. Initially, the Austrian journalists and witnesses of Schüssel's verbal slander intended not to publish the story. The German news magazine *Focus*, however, reported the breakfast affair. Wolfgang Schüssel persistently denied the accusation, and Ronald Barazon, chief editor of the *Salzburger Nachrichten*, countered with his editorial as other Austrian journalists subsequently did. In an early biography of Wolfgang Schüssel, author Peter Pelinka states, when referring to this incident, that Schüssel's relationship with the media consequently "was clouded for a long time."[3] This early dispute may partially account for further developments in his personal ambivalence to the media and his accented guardedness with respect to journalists. Possibly the breakfast affair also contributed to the nickname Schüssel was given by his political opponents as well as by Austrian journalists: "The Silent Chancellor" (*Der Schweigekanzler*). First, Eva Glawischnig, a Green Party (*Die Grünen*) member of parliament (MP), used this term in a parliamentary session on 29 March 2001 in reference to Chancellor Schüssel's silence concerning recurrent breakdowns in the nearby Czech nuclear power plant in Temelin, which was cited in a report of the Austrian Press Agency.[4] As a point of culmination, the term "Silent Chancellor" was selected as the "Word of the Year" in 2005 by a scientific jury and thereby outperformed expressions such as "bird flu" or "tsunami." It became a well-known saying and an often cited short-cut for Chancellor Schüssel's communication strategy that was alleged by journalists as well as political opponents to be defensive. The linguistic jury substantiated its choice with "the contradiction between the communicative expectancy of the chancellorship and the reversed public impression referring to the apparent incommunicative attitude of the head of the government."[5]

During the nearly seven years of Schüssel's era as chancellor, he was called *Schweigekanzler* no less than 472 times in the Austrian media: 303 times in newspapers, 89 times in news magazines, 37 times by the Austrian Press Agency, 28 times in special interest magazines, and only 15 times on ORF, the Austrian public broadcasting corporation. The critical connotation of *Schweigekanzler* primarily referred to his reluctance to discuss friction with and turbulence caused by his coalition partner, the FPÖ, and by provocative statements of namable representatives of the FPÖ. For instance, he did not comment on Jörg Haider's visit to Saddam Hussein in Bagdad in 2002 and did not take a direct stand on the uprising within the FPÖ in March 2005. At that time, Schüssel refused invitations to political TV programs and interviews to discuss this coalition crisis; instead, he attended the non-political talk show *Vera* on 17 March, speaking with the host about his private life, his sixtieth birthday, and sports.[6] Two weeks later, the crisis of the FPÖ, Schüssel's coalition partner, escalated and cumulated in the secessional foundation of the Alliance for the Future of Austria (*Bündnis Zukunft Österreich*, or BZÖ) by Jörg Haider.

Additionally, during his chancellorship Schüssel was repeatedly criticized for not commenting on incidents in the nearby Czech nuclear power plant in Temelin or troubling statements made by members of parliament from his subsequent coalition partner, the BZÖ (namely Siegfried Kampl and John Gudenus), referring to the alleged "prosecution of Nazis after World War II," the Holocaust, and the existence of gas chambers. Throughout his political career, Schüssel has mostly been characterized as a tight-lipped but philosophic and excellent maneuverer of power as well as a "Teflon chancellor" by journalists, pundits, and even by some of his political allies. The last negative climax of the journalistic contest with Chancellor Schüssel happened during the 2006 electoral campaign. In the course of a broad nursing policy debate in Austria, on 19 August 2006 journalist Hans Weiss accused Chancellor Schüssel of having employed an illegal foreign nurse for his mother-in-law. Thus the journalist laconically wrote in a letter to the editor of the newspaper *Der Standard*: "She was good and friendly as well as cheap (about Euro 2 per hour). Probably not quite legal, but, well, let's forget it!"[7] An inglorious culmination and absolute low-point of this discussion was a fake interview with "Mrs. Maria," the alleged illegal nurse in Schüssel's home, in the Austrian news magazine *News* on 14 September 2006.[8] This supposed investigative interview turned out to be a complete hoax. "Mrs. Maria" turned out not to be the actual nurse employed for Schüssel's mother-in-law, and finally all allegations had to be dropped.

Despite Schüssel's negative and conflictual experiences with the media, he is closely bound to journalism, which becomes clear when we look at his biography. Schüssel's father Ludwig was a sports journalist for the *Neue Freie Presse*,[9] and Wolfgang Schüssel himself gained professional experience in journalism. During his study of law, he worked for the Austrian public radio station *Ö3*.[10] Consequently, Wolfgang Schüssel cannot only be characterized as a victim of investigative and critical political journalism, for he also had insight into the media's logic and knew how to utilize the media and journalists for his political objectives. His alleged defensive communication strategy may more accurately be characterized as selective and strategically calculated. During the 1999 election campaign which led to his chancellorship, the musically talented Wolfgang Schüssel presented a traditional songbook in a very media-effective way by singing and playing with his party colleagues.[11] In order to demonstrate solidarity with his coalition partners, he organized non-political events such as a pilgrimage to Mariazell, a cycling tour with his government team, and a trip to the zoological garden to which he also invited journalists. In a political context, he implemented a regular meeting with the press after the weekly council. There the chancellor and the vice-chancellor presented themselves behind glass lecterns demonstrating their effectiveness and openness and the unity of the coalition. At his first appearance at the European Union Council after the Union had imposed diplomatic sanctions on Austria due to the government participation of the right-wing, populist FPÖ, Chancellor Schüssel drew the media attention only negligibly: for the first time, he wore a tie instead of a bow tie which had been his trademark until then. By doing so, he drew the media attention away from protests and the critical situation of the EU sanctions. During the 2002 election campaign, he presented himself as a cellist and pianist or even as an iceman. Additionally, the ORF public broadcasting station came under fire because the chief editor of the *ORF-Sommergespräche*, an interview program with party leaders, even brought the guest's chair for a fitting to the office of the chancellor before the program was aired. Chancellor Schüssel also published a gardening guide that was presented in a well-attended press conference. To summarize, Chancellor Schüssel was not only in the crosshairs of the media, he and his spokeswoman Heidi Glück also knew how to exploit and utilize the Austrian media for his personal and political image-building.

The following discussion not only gets to the bottom of the myth of the *Schweigekanzler* and his image performance *in* the media during his chancellorship, but also focuses on his policy performance *for* the media. Thus Schüssel's relationship with the media is not solely based on informal and personal experiences and irritations, but is also grounded in a very professional context referring to the media policy that was pursued, implemented, and also unregarded by the government during Schüssel's chancellorship. However, first we draw our attention to the media portrayal of Chancellor Schüssel. Was it all as critical as his experience with journalists and the media may suggest? Did Schüssel really live up to his reputation of being a *Schweigekanzler*? Was the portrayal of the chancellor in the largest newspaper, *Neue Kronen Zeitung*, really highly critical and oppositional? These questions will be answered in the following sections of this article.

Chancellor Schüssel in the Austrian Media

As we have already learned, Chancellor Schüssel was frequently labeled as *Schweigekanzler*. However, the empirical evidence tells another story. When we look at the sound bites of politicians in the Austrian TV newscast *Zeit im Bild 1*[12] with the largest audience share during his chancellorship (a regular viewership of about 20 percent), we can conclude that Wolfgang Schüssel was the political actor given the most time to speak for himself on the prime time news. During the seven years of his terms in office, he spoke for no less than five hours and fifteen minutes, which is equivalent to the total length of about nineteen editions of the Austrian prime time news *Zeit im Bild 1*. In 2000 and 2001, he started with a significant "chancellor bonus" (*Kanzlerbonus*)[13] as far as his speech time on Austrian television is concerned (see Figure 1).

Figure 1
Airtime of Party Chairmen in the *Zeit im Bild 1*, Sound Bites in Seconds, 2000-2006

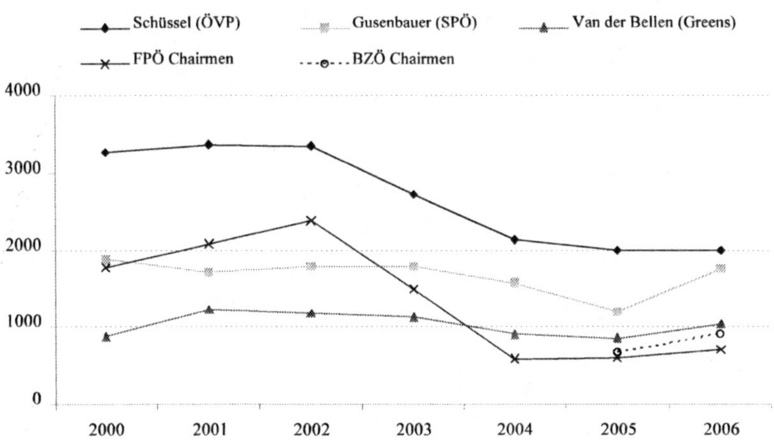

Source: Author's own compilation and calculation on the basis of APA-MediaWatch data.

Throughout the period of his chancellorship, Schüssel was the party chairman with the longest sound bites on the prime time news of the ORF. In total, Schüssel was able to claim 0.7 percent of the total airtime of the news outlets for himself throughout his seven years of chancellorship. The Chancellor concentrated 7.1 percent of all sound bites of all public actors (politicians, experts, and so forth, but excluding ORF journalists) on himself. Schüssel talked about 60 percent longer than the second most present Austrian politician, Alfred Gusenbauer, who was also in power as SPÖ chairman for the whole period under examination. The sound bites of Schüssel's junior coalition partner (the current chairman of the FPÖ or BZÖ) were significantly shorter during the whole period of his chancellorship. However, towards the end of his chancellorship in 2006, Schüssel's sound bite advantage eroded significantly.

Table 1
Top Ten Ranking of Politicians in the Prime Time News Show *Zeit im Bild 1*, 4 February 2000-11 January 2007

Rank	Politician	Sound Bites in Hours	Sound Bites in Percent of All Public Actors*
1	Wolfgang Schüssel (Chancellor, ÖVP)	5.2	7.1
2	Alfred Gusenbauer (Chairman, SPÖ)	3.3	4.5
3	Heinz Fischer (President since 2004)	2.5	3.4
4	Alexander Van der Bellen (Chairman, The Greens)	2.0	2.7
5	Jörg Haider (Founder, BZÖ)	1.9	2.6
6	Karl-Heinz Grasser (non-party Treasury Secretary)	1.8	2.4
7	Susanne Riess-Passer (Chairman, FPÖ 2000-2002)	1.6	2.1
8	Thomas Klestil (President until 2004)	1.3	1.8
9	Peter Westenthaler (Chairman, BZÖ since 2006)	1.1	1.5
10	Herbert Haupt (Chairman, FPÖ 2002-2003)	1.1	1.5

* Statements of the anchors and sound bites from other *Zeit im Bild 1* journalists are excluded.

Source: Author's own compilation and calculation on the basis of APA-MediaWatch data.

Between his inauguration on 4 February 2000 and his retirement on 11 January 2007, Chancellor Schüssel was allowed and willing to speak as long as both SPÖ Chairman Gusenbauer and Greens Chairman Van der Bellen taken together. Contrary to his *Schweigekanzler* image,

Wolfgang Schüssel clearly dominated the Austrian prime time news on television throughout his chancellorship, even though he lost some of his early advantage by the end of his second term in office. By 2006, his leading position was significantly diminishing, and his party, the ÖVP, additionally fell from favor with the voters in the 2006 elections and lost its number one position in parliament. However, not only Schüssel himself lost ground in terms of the share of airtime on television news, but all members of his party, and his governmental coalition lost in terms of media presence measured in aired sound bites. Especially during the second term of Schüssel's chancellery, the representatives of the opposition caught up significantly on airtime (see Figure 2).

Figure 2
Airtime of Austrian Party Politicians in the Prime Time News Show *Zeit im Bild 1*, 4 February 2000-11 January 2007, in Percentage of Cumulative Airtime of Party Politicians

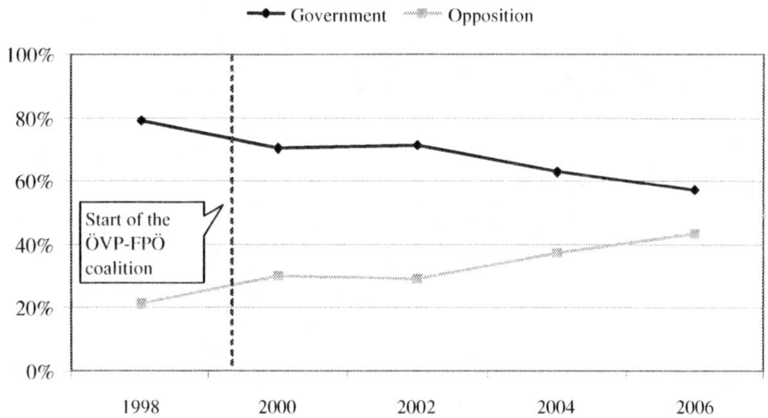

Source: Author's own compilation and calculation on the basis of APA-MediaWatch data.

At the beginning of Schüssel's chancellorship, his coalition gained no less than about 70 percent of all political sound bites in the *Zeit im Bild 1* on ORF. This ratio almost balanced out at the end of his term. This decrease in media presence and agenda-setting power is not so much solely due to a drop in Schüssel's media appeal, but to the whole coalition's appeal which was becoming more passive in terms of media presence. Nonetheless, the government as well as Chancellor Schüssel obviously lost media charisma, especially during the second term of Schüssel's chancellorship. The *Kanzlerbonus* in the *Zeit im Bild 1* diminished. These sound bite rankings published by the Austrian media analysis institute *APA-MediaWatch* regularly bring the political parties and actors to the scene that seemingly missed out on television presence, regardless of the actual composition of the governmental coalition. Consequently, the underdogs regularly protest against an alleged governmental bias and political imbalance in the ORF coverage via press releases.[14] Additionally, the ORF is constantly under political pressure and has to deal with protests relating to its policy regarding whom it invites to participate in political talk shows or interviews. The dimension of political intervention on the public service broadcaster will be discussed in detail in a subsequent section of this article. However, what can be stated here is that this accusation of political imbalance of the ORF with regard to the airtime of politicians is analytically short-sighted. Figure 3 illustrates that the dominance of Chancellor Schüssel's media presence was even higher in the almost exclusively private-owned newspapers than on the public broadcasting network.

Figure 3
Austrian Party Chairmen in the Press, Number of Mentions, 2000-2006

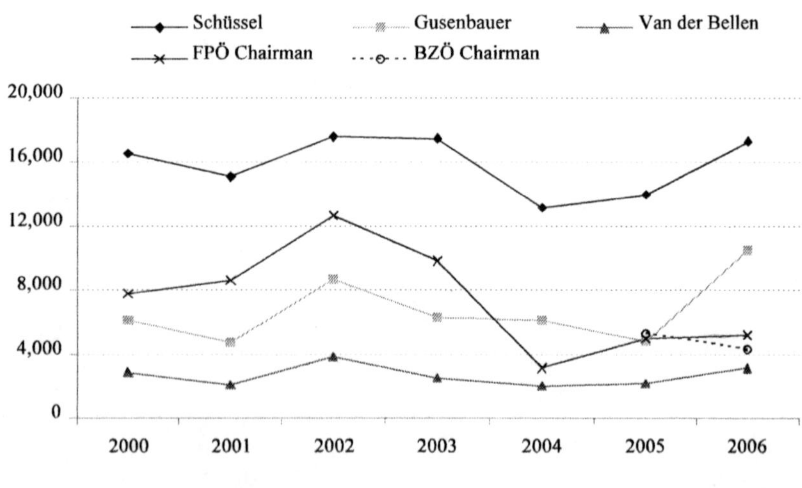

Source: Author's own compilation and calculation on the basis of APA-MediaWatch data.

Similar to the airtime ranking on television news, Chancellor Schüssel also was the most dominant political actor in Austrian newspapers during both his terms in government. Schüssel is almost as present as all other party leaders taken together. He is twice as visible in the newspaper coverage as the changing FPÖ chairmen and SPÖ Chairman Gusenbauer, who are second and third in this long-term ranking. Just as on television, in newspapers we can observe a significant and stable *Kanzlerbonus* referring to the chancellor's presence within the political coverage. Schüssel was anything but an "invisible" or "silent" player in the media. He was by far the most visible and most cited political actor in the political coverage between 2000 and 2006.

As far as Schüssel's media agenda-setting strategy on issues is concerned, we can confirm that he lived up his reputation as a politician who does not want to face the domestic lows in politics.[15] Schüssel's sound bites in the *Zeit im Bild 1* mostly referred to European Union policies (19 percent of his sound bites) which equals about one hour of airtime. Second, he also referred to election campaigning issues (8 percent of his airtime). The domestic policy issue Schüssel talked about the most on Austrian TV was fiscal policy (budget and tax reform) occupying 4 percent of Schüssel's total airtime (23 minutes). Contrastingly, he publicly avoided extensive statements about critical domestic issues such as neutrality (*Neutralität*) (only 0.7 percent of his airtime), the Eurofighter jet controversy (0.7 percent) or the sign dispute (*Ortstafelstreit*) (1 percent). Thus, in his total period of chancellorship he only spent two minutes talking and answering questions about Austrian perpetual neutrality (*Neutralität*) or the disputed purchase of jet fighters (Eurofighter) and three minutes talking about the question of bilingual place-name signs in the Austrian province of Carinthia (*Ortstafelstreit*) on television news.

The beginning of his chancellorship in the year 2000 had been considered the most critical in terms of his media portrayal and the journalistic evaluation of the coalition with the FPÖ. However, this supposedly above-average critical image of Chancellor Schüssel in 2000 cannot be empirically proven for the ORF's *Zeit im Bild 1*. There Schüssel was portrayed slightly more negatively than positively, but his image on television news was similar to Alexander Van der Bellen's, the Greens chairman, and even considerably better than Alfred Gusenbauer's image.[16] Similar are findings referring to Schüssel's coverage on the front page of the *Neue Kronen Zeitung*. Earlier analyses of pundits repeatedly concluded that Schüssel was governing against the background of a severe critique of the coalition with the right-wing, populist FPÖ by the *Neue Kronen Zeitung*. This might hold true for the election campaign in 1999 and the period of the coalition talks in early 2000, but as the following empirical evidence outlines, it cannot be asserted for the terms of his chancellorship.

Initially, the *Neue Kronen Zeitung* heavily and outspokenly criticized Schüssel's strategy to revoke the long lasting Grand Coalition (*Große Koalition*) between the ÖVP and SPÖ and to find a coalition agreement with the FPÖ. During his chancellorship, the *Neue Kronen Zeitung* altered its course and portrayed the chancellor in a more moderate and even favorable way. As we have already concluded for all newspapers and the television news, Schüssel also was the most prominent political actor on the front page of the *Neue Kronen Zeitung* during his terms as chancellor. During the seven years, he was mentioned ninety-two times in the main headline on the front page of the *Neue Kronen Zeitung*. His main political opponents, SPÖ Chairman Gusenbauer or Jörg Haider, were mentioned only half the time in the main headlines of the paper during the same period. Hence, a distinctive *Kanzlerbonus* on this quantitative level can also be diagnosed for the coverage of the *Neue Kronen Zeitung*. On a qualitative level, we can also see that Schüssel's portrayal in the largest Austrian paper was far from being hyper-critical. A quarter of all references to Schüssel in the front page headlines were positive, and only a tenth of all Schüssel headlines were negative in tone. Thus, positive evaluations clearly outnumbered critical statements referring to the chancellor on the front page of the *Neue Kronen Zeitung*. In nearly 20 percent of all headlines, Schüssel was mentioned in non-political and, consequently, less critical settings (playing soccer, attending high-society events, and so forth) with mostly favorable pictures. Additionally, he was often portrayed as a vigorous statesman representing Austria in state visits.

A closing of the ranks between Schüssel and the *Neue Kronen Zeitung* occurred in the course of the European Union sanctions against Austria resulting from the coalition between the ÖVP and FPÖ. The *Neue Kronen Zeitung* showed solidarity and supported Schüssel's rigid standpoint on the EU sanctions or the discussion about the EU membership of Turkey and criticized the European Union. Schüssel was only criticized for his positions on *Neutralität*, the Eurofighter deal, the Temelin question, and, in the beginning, for the coalition with the FPÖ.

Schüssel's media performance during the most recent election campaign in 2006 was also characterized by a significant *Kanzlerbonus* in terms of the visibility of the party front runners. Schüssel was mentioned and portrayed in 24 percent of all politically relevant reports during the final six weeks of the election campaign in newspapers, news magazines, and the *Zeit im Bild 1*. In second place were his challenger Alfred Gusenbauer and BZÖ front runner Peter Westenthaler with a visibility rate of 15 percent each. FPÖ party leader Heinz-Christian

Strache was mentioned in 11 percent of all reports, and the Greens chairman Van der Bellen in 7 percent.[17]

Chancellor Schüssel's Media Relationship

In a study by Fritz Plasser et al. that investigated the relationship between journalism and politics in Austria, journalists were asked in 2003 how they assessed the development of the relationship between politics and journalism.[18] More than seven out of ten leading Austrian journalists answered that the relationship has become more conflictual over the last few years, and only 7 percent noticed a more cooperative relationship between journalists and politicians in Austria.[19]

Table 2
Relationship between Journalists and Politicians in Austria, in Percentage of Respondents (n=95)

Over the last few years, the relationship between journalists and politicians has become . . .	Broadcasting Journalists	Newspaper Journalists	News Magazine Journalists
more conflictual	73	71	69
Unchanged	18	20	19
more harmonious	5	9	8
don't know	4	0	4

Source: Source: Plasser et al.[20]

This perceived trend of an intensifying conflict between journalists and politicians (from the journalistic perspective) is similarly confirmed by newspaper, magazine, television, and radio journalists. The most pessimistic are chief editors and department heads. More than 90 percent of these leading Austrian journalists diagnose an intensifying conflictual relationship with political actors over the last few years. This may be partly due to the fact that these leading figures most frequently are the addressees of political complaints and intervention. Additionally, for Austrian journalists this pessimistic evaluation is also linked to a deficit in the culture of debate of political elites. Their refusal to accept criticism, their reluctance to respect critical journalistic inquiry, and their uncooperative behavior towards the media are the most often cited problems that journalists identify. A notable reason for this adversarial behavior is that journalists not only recognize a tendency towards professionalization of public relations (PR) instruments, spin doctoring, and control from the political side, but also the political and governmental turnaround in the year 2000 with the governmental inauguration of the right-wing populist FPÖ and Jörg Haider. As many as 45 percent of the interviewed Austrian journalists identified the governmental change in the year 2000 as a main reason for increasing tensions. Additionally, more than one-quarter (26 percent) of all journalists also diagnosed the negative attitude of the FPÖ toward the media.[21] From the journalists' perspective, this "atmospheric caesura"[22] between journalists and governmental elites led to a highly polarizing friend-or-foe schema in the government's approach to the media. In the journalists' perception, Schüssel's government brought a more adversarial and a more conflictual spirit into the relationship between politics and journalism in Austria. Intensifying atmospheric disruptions can also be identified—from the journalistic perspective—on the level of perceived political intervention and attempted exploitation. Every fourth journalist assessed intensified attempts of political interference as a significant atmospheric disturbance of the professional relationship between media and politicians.

Table 3

Attempts of Politicians to Exert Influence on Journalism (n=95)

Over the last few years, attempts to exert influence on Austrian journalism by politicians have been . . .	Percentage of Journalists
on the increase	62
Unchanged	30
on the decline	6
don't know	2

Source: Plasser et al.[23]

Almost two-thirds of all interviewed journalists attested to an increasing level of political interference and political pressure over the last few years. Only 6 percent diagnosed a decline of political exertion of influence on Austrian journalists. In the perception of the interviewed journalists, a relevant point of origin for this increase was also the governmental change in the year 2000. The discussion about political influence and intervention on journalism mainly concentrated on public service television broadcasting and radio stations of the ORF. A broad and lasting public discussion about media politics and political influence on the ORF has been provoked by Armin Wolf, the late news anchorman of the ORF's *Zeit im Bild 2,* in May 2006. In his acceptance speech for a journalism award, he denounced "nearly unrestrained exertion of political influence on the ORF." After the governmental change in the year 2000 from the "balance of horror" (referring to the political influence of both Grand Coalition partners, the SPÖ and ÖVP), "only the horror remained" (referring to the ÖVP).[24] Subsequently, both ORF internal and ORF external circles (platform "SOS ORF," initiative "derFreiRaum," ex- and opposition politicians, journalists, media experts, and so forth) voiced public criticism on political pressure and intervention by the ORF. Right at the outset of the ÖVP-FPÖ coalition, Gisela Hopfmüller, a prominent and experienced political journalist at the ORF, concluded that "the current political pressure on the ORF is 'very intense.' It ranks among the most acute phases I have experienced so far."[25] On a single Sunday, the editorial teams of the ORF listed no less than twenty-two phone calls from FPÖ chairman Peter Westenthaler.[26] The former ÖVP politician and political scientist Heinrich Neisser concluded in a recent analysis that "unprecedentedly, political claims to power referring to the ORF have been articulated blatantly [...]. The ORF is regarded as a political domain and politicians envision themselves as hosts."[27]

Consequently, journalists also diagnosed an increasing level of tension and political pressure since Schüssel's inauguration, particularly since the participation of the FPÖ in the governing coalition. In this context, journalists mainly state two strategies that political actors employ to put pressure on the media. The first is a defensive and passive strategy to control the news and involves the refusal of commenting on unwelcome issues and claiming the right to authorize print interviews or to dismiss invitations to live studio interviews. The journalists most strongly associated Schüssel and Haider's teams with these strategies. "In this manner fresh quotes are eliminated, questions are discarded and others are replaced—from the press officers and politicians, not from the journalists!"[28] Almost half of the Austrian journalists identify such a strategy as one of the main practices for putting pressure on the media.[29] Second, journalists also identify more active and offensive forms of political interference (for example, phone calls with complaints about the coverage or threats of lawsuits or other severe consequences). About three out of ten journalists regard this strategy as frequently applied by political elites.

Against this background, Austria's freedom of the press was ranked sixteenth on a worldwide scale of countries by Reporters Without Borders in 2006.[30] Accordingly, the level of press freedom in Austria is comparable to countries like Spain or Hungary from a transnational and comparative perspective. In the early years of Schüssel's chancellorship in 2002, Austria was only ranked twenty-sixth. Another international organization that monitors the levels of press freedom in the world

(Freedomhouse) also confirms a moderate improvement of press freedom throughout Schüssel's chancellorship; however, it also recurrently laments the high concentration on the Austrian press market and number of lawsuits against journalists.[31]

Chancellor Schüssel's Media Policy

Similar to his relationship to journalism, Chancellor Schüssel's record of media policy between 2000 and 2006 may be characterized as ambivalent. Regulatory initiatives also encountered a policy of non-decisions and non-interference. The Schüssel era with regard to media policy mainly concentrated on establishing a framework supportive of competition in the Austrian media landscape.[32] The central instruments were efforts to continue the deregulation of the media markets and prevailing maxims of an economic-technical view on the media and their policy.[33] Privatization and the creation of a dual broadcasting market were central objectives of the government between 2000 and 2006. During the years of the consensual Grand Coalitions between the SPÖ and ÖVP in the 1980s and 1990s, indecisions was interpreted as a specific and dominant feature of Austrian media policy.[34] This may be mainly due to the fact that media policy decisions were conditional on the consensus among the social partners.[35] "Consequently and against this background, Austrian media policy is impeded, and political actors appear more reactive than actively formative."[36] This led to a tradition of non-decisions attributed to the avoidance of conflicts. From this typically Austrian perspective, the Schüssel years in the chancellery were relatively active years of media policy. After years of stagnation regarding Austrian media policy, the Schüssel government caught up on decisions in the year 2001.[37] On 5 July 2001, Parliament passed a resolution ("media package") including the ORF Act, the implementation of a broadcasting regulatory and supervisory body (*KommAustria*), the Private TV Act, and the amendment of the Private Radio Act. The ORF Act contained its re-organization as a foundation regulated by public law and specifications of the public value, whereas the Private TV Act and the Private Radio Act established a basis for nationwide private terrestrial television and radio stations in Austria. Austria was the last European broadcasting market that was opened to private stations. In February 2002, the first private license for nationwide terrestrial TV was assigned to the ATV Privatfernseh GmbH.

Both coalition partners (the ÖVP and FPÖ/BZÖ) were cardinally supportive of the commercialization of the television and radio markets in Austria. "In their basic approaches to an intensified deregulation and broader market liberalization of television and radio, there dominated more ideological conformity between the ÖVP and FPÖ than between earlier coalitions of the ÖVP and SPÖ."[38] However, deregulation does not necessarily mean depoliticization. The ORF Act of 2001 was announced as a step to depoliticizing the Austrian public service broadcaster. It contains a clause that no political mandataries or party employees are allowed to become members of the foundation council. Austrian media analyst Andy Kaltenbrunner states that this is only a "quasi depoliticization" of the ORF: "More than ever the ORF Act 2001 benefits [...] the [actual] government."[39] Additionally, the implementation of the generally acclaimed *KommAustria*, the regulatory and supervisory body of the Austrian broadcasting, was criticized because it is still subordinated to the Office of the Chancellor and the Ministry of Infrastructure and, thus, potentially bound by governmental and political instructions. Another political instrument of media policy is the public media funding (*Presseförderung*), which had also been reformed in 2004 under Schüssel's tenure. The *Presseförderung* is an instrument enabling the viability of non-profitable papers, thus ensuring a high level of plurality on the press market. However, the Schüssel government decreased the funding by 8 percent between 2002 and 2006.[40]

Besides these media policy decisions, the Schüssel era in terms of media politics is also characterized by a number of non-decisions. Above all, the Schüssel government waived the right to restrict press mergers and to prevent further market concentration. Austria remains the European country with the highest press market concentration.[41] In 2001, the Antitrust Court approved the merger of the *News* and *trend/profil* publishing houses that ran (and run) established and competing Austrian news magazines. In the radio market, the Schüssel government facilitated further concentration by softening restrictions on cross-media ownership of private radio stations. On this, Kaltenbrunner concludes: "The new governmental constellation between the ÖVP and FPÖ has not hindered this development anyhow [...]."[42]

Finally, effective media policy applied by the Schüssel government in particular and Austrian governments in general is not only limited to formal channels. On this issue, Kaltenbrunner assesses: "It seems that media policy is also personnel policy."[43] Throughout Schüssel's chancellorship, personnel decisions in the ORF also played—as throughout former coalitions—a significant role, and critics charged that the ORF was politically "redyed" (*Umfärbung*) by the ÖVP-FPÖ/BZÖ coalition. In a number of key journalistic positions, ÖVP or FPÖ/BZÖ affiliated persons served. In December 2001, at the outset of Schüssel's chancellorship, Monika Lindner, the candidate supported by the ÖVP, was elected as director general of ORF and the conservative Werner Mück became ORF chief editor with far-reaching authority to set the agendas of the ORF's news programs. An associate of the FPÖ, Walter Seledec, was also appointed as an ORF chief editor in 2002. Additionally, in 2005 the conservative journalist Andreas Unterberger was appointed chief editor of the official government newspaper *Wiener Zeitung*. In this regard, Schüssel's media policy was not significantly different than that of his predecessors.

Conclusion

The relationship between Chancellor Schüssel and the Austrian media and their journalists is mainly characterized by ambivalence in many respects and by distanced skepticism on both sides. His relationship to journalism was highly disrupted by a series of unfavorable assessments and alleged affairs. This resulted in a distant relationship right from the start of his chancellorship.

First, the essence of his media policy has to be characterized and summarized as highly ambivalent. On the one hand, regulatory initiatives such as the ORF Act or the Private TV Act, the amendment of the Private Radio Act, or the implementation of the supervisory board *KommAustria* signaled a comparably active role in political decision making during his era. On the other hand, Schüssel's media policy is also appropriately characterized by the term "deregulation" instead of "de-politicization." The de-politicization of the Austrian media landscape was postulated by Schüssel's government; however, the ORF Act of 2001 and the creation of *KommAustria* did not bring political influence and greediness to an end, and Schüssel's personnel policy also did not foster and signal an extensive process of de-politicization. Schüssel's media policy mainly concentrated on deregulation by establishing a competition framework supportive of the Austrian media landscape.

The relationship between journalists and Chancellor Schüssel was dominated by mutual suspiciousness and skepticism. Journalists were not friendly with Chancellor Schüssel, for he seemed inapproachable. However, Chancellor Schüssel was not just in the crosshairs of the media; he also knew how to exploit and utilize the Austrian media for his efficient public image-building. Schüssel's allegedly defensive communication strategy has to be interpreted more precisely as a calculatedly selective and strategic attitude towards the media. Partly as a result of this strategy, journalists recognize an increasingly conflictual relationship between journalists and politics during Schüssel's chancellorship. The media elites identify a tendency of political parties to professionalize PR as well as an "atmospheric caesura" leading to a highly polarizing friend-or-foe schema triggered by the governmental turnaround in 2000. Consequently, Chancellor Schüssel was repeatedly as well as disdainfully labeled *Schweigekanzler*, Teflon Chancellor, or the Little Prince in the media. However, the empirical evidence presented in this article conveys a more ambivalent picture and exposes some of these labels as myths. The image of *Schweigekanzler* cannot be sustained as far as Chancellor Schüssel's media presence is concerned. Over the course of the two terms of his chancellorship, he was the most visible political actor in the press as well as on TV. Hence he was anything but an "invisible" or "silent" player in the media coverage. Before the coalition between the ÖVP and FPÖ was sworn in, the *Neue Kronen Zeitung* heavily opposed this change in government. In this context, it was repeatedly said that Schüssel was successfully governing against the resistance of the *Neue Kronen Zeitung*. This is not supported by the empirical findings. In the course of the EU sanctions against Austria in 2000, the *Neue Kronen Zeitung* had started to report in a more favorable tone about Schüssel's chancellorship and partially even supported his policies. Schüssel, his government, and the media embraced an ambivalent relationship based on a polarized friend-or-foe schema in the game of published and public political discourse—obviously and at least partially for the benefit of both.

Notes

1. Black (*Schwarz*) is the party color of the ÖVP, and blue (*Blau*) is the party color of the FPÖ.

2. "Volkszorn trifft Schüssel jetzt voll," *Kronen Zeitung*, 26 January 2000, p. 2.

3. Peter Pelinka, *Wolfgang Schüssel: Eine politische Biografie* (Vienna: Überreuter, 2003), 151.

4. "Nationalrat: Opposition prangert Störfälle in Temelin an," *Austria Press Agency*, 26 January 2000.

5. Rudolf Muhr, "Begründung der Wahl des österreichischen Worts 2005," 12 December 2005, http://www-oedt.kfunigraz.ac.at/oewort/2005/index2005.htm, accessed 9 Febraury 2009.

6. Armin Wolf, "Opfer und Täter zugleich," in *Politik und Medien, Medien und Politik*, ed. Peter Filzmaier et al. (Vienna: Facultas, 2006), 51.

7. "Der Pflege-Kanzler," *Der Standard*, 19 August 2006, p. 39.

8. "Schüssels Pflegerin spricht," *News*, 14 September 2006, p. 48.

9. Joachim Riedl, *Der Wende-Kanzler* (Vienna: Czernin, 2000), 57.

10. Pelinka, *Wolfgang Schüssel*.

11. Wolfgang Schüssel et al., *Rot-Weiß-Rotes Liederbuch* (Vienna: ÖVP, 1999).

12. In April 2007, it was renamed *Zeit im Bild 19:30 Uhr*.

13. This is more specifically explained as the advantage of being the chancellor in power.

14. Examples include "Cap Criticizes the Striking Privilege of the ÖVP in the ORF Newscasts" (SPÖ, 4 November 2005); "ORF Gravitates More and More to Austrian Governmental News" (BZÖ, 13 June 2007).

15. Pelinka, *Wolfgang Schüssel*; Josef Cap, *Kamele können nicht fliegen: Von den Grenzen politischer Inszenierung* (Vienna: Molden, 2005).

16. MediaWatch Institut, *Forschungsbericht 2000: Mediadaten zur österreichischen Innenpolitik* (Innsbruck: MediaWatch, 2001), 90-91.

17. Günther Lengauer et al., "Redaktionelle Politikvermittlung in österreichischen Wahlkämpfen, 1999-2006," in *Wechselwahlen: Analysen zur Nationalratswahl 2006*, ed. Fritz Plasser (Vienna: Facultas, 2007), 115.

18. Fritz Plasser, et al., "Politischer Journalismus in der Mediendemokratie," in *Politische Kommunikation in Österreich*, ed. Fritz Plasser (Vienna: Facultas, 2004), 237-308.

19. Ibid., 291.

20. Ibid.

21. Ibid., 292.

22. Ibid., 291.

23. Ibid.

24. Cited in "Hemmungsloser Einfluss der Politik auf den ORF," *Kurier*, 18 May 2006, p. 31.

25. Cited in Hans Heinz Fabris et al., *Bericht zur Lage des Journalismus in Österreich: Erhebungsjahr 2000* (Salzburg: ipk Salzburg, 2001), 8.

26. Ibid., 8.

27. Heinrich Neisser, "Aufforderung zur Perspektive," in *Der Auftrag: Öffentlich-rechtlicher Rundfunk—Positionen—Perspektiven—Plädoyers*, ed. derFreiRaum (Vienna: Sonderzahl, 2006), 12.

28. Wolf, "Opfer und Täter zugleich," 60.

29. Plasser et al., "Politischer Journalismus in der Mediendemokratie," 296.

30. Reporters Without Borders, *Worldwide Press Freedom Index 2006* (Paris: Reports Without Borders, 2006).

31. Freedomhouse, Freedom of the Press: Austria (2004), 28 April 2004. UNHCR Refworld, http://www.unhcr.org/refworld/docid/473450ef23.html, accessed 9 February 2009.

32. Fabris et al., *Bericht zur Lage des Journalismus in Österreich*.

33. Hans Heinz Fabris, *Bericht zur Lage des Journalismus in Österreich: Ein Qualitätsmonitoring. Erhebungsjahre 2002/2003* (Salzburg, 2003), 17.

34. Andrea Grisold, *Regulierungsformen am Mediensektor: Der Fall Österreich* (Frankfurt: Lang, 1996).

35. Andy Kaltenbrunner, "Medienpolitik," in *Schwarz—Blau: Eine Bilanz des "Neu-Regierens,"* ed. Emmerich Tálos (Vienna: LIT, 2006), 118.

36. Andy Kaltenbrunner, "Keine Brüche im Umbruch: Die Kontinuitäten österreichischer Medienpolitik in einem bewegten Medienmarkt," *Österreichische Zeitschrift für Politikwissenschaft* 2 (1998): 105.

37. Fabris, *Bericht zur Lage des Journalismus in Österreich.*

38. Kaltenbrunner, "Medienpolitik," 118.

39. Ibid., 123.

40. RTR/KommAustria, *Presseförderung* (Vienna: RTR, 2006).

41. Thomas Steinmaurer, *Konzentriert und verflochten: Österreichs Mediensystem im Überblick* (Innsbruck: Studienverlag, 2002).

42. Kaltenbrunner, "Medienpolitik," 134.

43. Ibid., 117.

Making Omelets and Breaking Eggs? Schüssel's Leadership in Government and Party

David Wineroither

Introduction: Governmental Influence and Prime Ministerial Power

Both the range of governmental influence and the level of prime ministerial power in Austria have been described as low. The government's ability to govern is limited by a remarkable number of veto players in the political system.[1] Furthermore, a recent survey revealed that the chancellor was considered a rather weak political leader, ranking nineteenth out of twenty-two countries that were compared.[2] In fact, such "results" reflect some long-standing patterns in Austria, which is a country governed by many grand coalitions with a consociational political culture and strong networks of neo-corporatism (*Sozialpartnerschaft*). However, the creation of the coalition government between the Austrian People's Party (*Österreichische Volkspartei*, or ÖVP) and Freedom Party of Austria (*Freiheitliche Partei Österreichs*, or FPÖ) in February 2000 meant the end of this system. Austria saw a sharp turn towards a majoritarian democracy. Tellingly, the expert survey mentioned above did not include Wolfgang Schüssel's term from 2000 to 2007.

In light of the context just decribed, this article has two aims: to investigate the development of governmental influence and power of the chancellor during the Schüssel years, and to reveal the relationship between the two as the outcome of Schüssel's political leadership style, or more precisely, his personal ambitions.

Alleviating the Problem of Perceptibility in Studies of Executive Leadership

While the strengthening of competition and conflict significantly contributes to the clarification of power relations between political players/actors as observed by voters, the power of prime ministers can remain obscure. If we explore the Schüssel chancellory under the aspect of power and influence, we are confronted with two sorts of knowledge deficits: a general deficit that pertains to the difficulties of cabinet studies internationally and a specifically Austrian one that was attached to the dominant features of party state and consociationalism in the Second Republic's political life up until 2000. The general deficit implies two challenges. First, despite major efforts, there is still a lack of knowledge about the decision-making process in the core executive ("black box"[3]), especially in the cabinet; the secret nature of the most important forums of decision making (council of ministers, intra-party and intra-coalition committees)[4] is also problematic. The second challenge has three indirect aspects that restrict a flow of valuable information. Because of factionalization, the ÖVP learned how to amalgamate antagonistic interests internally, and the negative electoral consequences that were caused by insufficient teamwork among party leaders between 1987 and 1995 increased internal loyalty and reduced overt disagreement. Next, in contrast to Margaret Thatcher and divergent from Gerhard Schröder's case, Schüssel incarnates the antithesis of "spatial leadership" and "outsider" images.[5] Finally, the legendary Austrian discrepancy between powers distributed by the constitution and those performed in actual politics distorts political responsibilities.

Studies of the political executive branch reveal it has followed different paths in its attempt to overcome these restrictions. What they have in common is their assumption that prime ministers act to remain in office. Four analytical strands can be distinguished. First is the neo-institutional context. Prime ministerial ability to effect resolution is measured against the reluctant potential of veto players. Studies analyze the effects of personal reputation and negotiating skills (for example, through a manipulative setting of choices).[6] Second, rational choice approaches work under the premises of methodological individualism and self-interested utility-maximization. They generate cooperative and non-cooperative game-theoretic applications.[7] This field of study creates formal models of coalition building and termination.[8] Special attention is given to the agenda setting potential of political actors.[9] Third, principal agent models open a dual perspective insofar as individual and collective political actors (head of state, prime minister, cabinet) may be representing a principal and an agent at the same time.[10] Research inspired by principal-agent or accountability design occasionally perform systematic analysis of dependences, loyalties, and self-determination at different places in the scheme of political representation.[11] Fourth are expert and elite interviews biased by subjective interpretation and selective remembrance.[12] None of these attempts, though, puts a premium on explaining variation in prime ministerial power over time. This article proceeds by searching for those mechanisms that define how Schüssel's leadership style influenced his power as chancellor through political polarization.

Shifts from Consensus to Majoritarian Democracy

The Majoritarian Turn in the Year 2000: Schüssel's Targets and Policy Consequences

As a valid frame for the government's policy, the coalition agreement of the ÖVP and FPÖ in the beginning of 2000 symbolized a "rejection of the old consociational democracy."[13] Although Schüssel became politically socialized as chief secretary of the ÖVP's League of Austrian Business (*Wirtschaftsbund*), he opposed "big government" and was only cursorily rooted in the realm of social partnership[14]; he rejected "big spending" as an unjustified burden to subsequent generations. As chancellor, and with more success in his first term (2000-2003), he gave priority to a balanced budget over lowered taxes. Last but not least, allowing the right-wing populist FPÖ under Jörg Haider to enter the government was his only option to secure his position as party chairman. Thus the formation of the new coalition in February 2000 corresponded to Schüssel's preferences in the polity, policy, and, as will be pointed out later in this article, also in the politics dimension. According to some party leader's involved in the coalition negotiations after the ÖVP's triumphal victory in the 2002 general elections, Schüssel showed no clear predisposition towards any of the three possible partners—the Social Democratic Party of Austria (*Sozialdemokratische Partei Österreichs*, or SPÖ), the FPÖ, the Greens (*Die Grünen*)—but eventually favored maintaining the ÖVP-FPÖ coalition for policy reasons.[15]

The rise of conflict democracy strengthened the executive branch. In the words of Arend Lijphart, "The prime characteristic of the majoritarian model of democracy [...] is concentration of power in the hands of the majority. The consensus model is characterized by non-concentration of power, which can take the two basic forms of sharing of power and division of power."[16] Veto player analysis with reference to the post-2000 years shows that power sharing and the dispersion of power in Austrian consensual democracy had relied almost solely on inter-party negotiation, mostly between the SPÖ und ÖVP camps.[17] However, under the new absence of consociationalism, most of their potential vanished. This development was demonstrated by Herbert Obinger for economic and social policy, Emmerich Tálos and Bernhard Kittel for social policy, and Marius Busemeyer on the basis of the pension reform(s).[18] The "Myth of *Sozialpartnerschaft*" had been replaced by a "multiformity of political networks, actor set-ups and modes of interaction of various interest groups."[19]

Schüssel did not show any ambition to copy the electoral formula of success utilized by Bruno Kreisky,[20] chancellor from 1970 to 1983, which was to send distinct signals to centrist swing voters, including policy favoring a limitation on the scope of political reforms. However, there is some evidence of response to the veto power of voters, manifest in the almost lightning speed with which reforms were implemented at the beginning of the legislative turn (Andreas Khol's "culture of timeliness"[21]), though there were far fewer reforms in the year of a general election (Finance Minister Karl-Heinz Grasser's "time of harvest has come"[22]). These "electoral cycles" ought to be classified as moderate overall and were focused on the federal level; anticipated or suffered losses in provincial elections were put aside. Indeed, the unpopularity of welfare retrenchment imposed by the federal government could neither be made responsible for the devastating defeat in the Carinthian provincial election (2004), nor for the loss of the status as strongest party in Salzburg (2004)[23] and Styria (2005), which was caused by incompetence and scandals in each area's *Land* organizations. On the contrary, the disastrous losses of its coalition partner FPÖ (2000-2005) in regional and local elections contributed to bitter internal disputes and accelerated the process that led to the resignation of Vice-Chancellor and FPÖ chairwoman Susanne Riess-Passer and others in the summer of 2002 as well as the split with Haider and his supporters in the spring of 2005.

The Philosophy of "Change": Blaming SPÖ-Led Governments

Reversal of its coalition partner, the course of majoritarian democracy, and a comprehensive reform agenda provided substantial ground for the ÖVP effectively to put the blame on the SPÖ for the performance of past governments. Attacks centered on the issue of former deficit spending and claims that the SPÖ was incapable of cooperating in government. For Khol, a former leader of the ÖVP's parliamentary group, the attainment of a balanced state budget served as justification for the existence of the FPÖ experiment.[24] As a consequence of the role change from governing party to opposition as well as adverse public sentiments in domestic and foreign policy (the so-called "sanction" of the other fourteen European Union [EU] member states), voters' belief in the SPÖ's ability to solve problems declined substantially on a number of important issues, which were paralleled by gains of the ÖVP.[25]

Demoscopic studies that were conducted during the time of coalition bargaining in 1999-2000 reveal major dissatisfaction on the part of many Austrians with the performance of the "grand coalition" (1987-2000). Public critique paid modest attention to the (high) level of influence exerted by the trade unions, the chambers of employees and commerce, and their obstructive effect on political reforms. Instead, public attention was fixed on quarrels between the coalition partners, nepotism (*Postenschacher*), and reform gridlock.[26] Whereas Khol's "speed kills" philosophy showed the will of the new government to dissolve reform deadlock (efficiency argument), competent handling of the "smaller" coalition partner fell to the chancellor himself (stability argument).[27] Schüssel's attitude towards other political leaders in the government and the coalition parties was characterized by two aspects: loyalty and collegiality. With respect to the former, Schüssel relied on an established team, defended troubled ministers relentlessly, and supported them in times of crisis (especially Education Minister Elisabeth Gehrer). His behavior was opposite that of Haider, who rarely backed his colleagues in the cabinet against harsh criticism from within his own party. Indeed, the number of disgraced FPÖ ministers reached a historic high. With respect to collegiality, though Schüssel displayed polarizing leadership on policy, he acted carefully within the cabinet to foster collegiality and even harmony. The chancellor "invested a lot in establishing and maintaining personal relations," remembers Riess-Passer.[28] This portrayal of harmony was not supposed to be disturbed by public disagreement, and the two coalition leaders remained silent on their current political intentions during their joint appearances at the so-called *Pressefoyer* (their regular meetings with the media) if they conflicted over the basics of an issue.[29]

Control over the new, unfamiliar, and partly unstable coalition partner was mediated through the official coalition agreement that both parties had signed. Supervision and control through the mutual appointment of junior ministers, which used to be a common procedure during the grand coalition era in Austria and in many German governments, were widely omitted (one for each party in the Ministry of Finance and Economics in the cabinet Schüssel I).[30] The climate in the coalition differed remarkably from—in the words of Khol again—the "icy atmosphere" and "frightening disputes over minutes" during the "grand coalition" period.[31]

The Distribution of Power in the Executive Branch

Schüssel and the ÖVP

Ever since it was founded in April 1945, the ÖVP had been one of the most factionalized parties in Western Europe.[32] However, the slightly less traditional component of oligarchic structure began to overlay the influence attached to the three main leagues and the provincial party organizations.[33] When Schüssel was first elected ÖVP chairman in April 1995, he could finally profit from the harmful effects of the lack of cohesion and solidarity in the 1987-1995 years.[34]

Party heavyweights developed more realistic expectations of their party chairman and closed ranks against the then coalition partner SPÖ. Schüssel's reasonable competence as a campaigner and his brilliant qualities as a bargainer helped him consolidate his leadership. The time of intrigues and indiscretions, even among the party's key figures, had gone.[35] The tight relationship between former party whip Khol and Schüssel is particularly notable because the former had aspirations to assume the leadership of the party. He was "today a rival, tomorrow a loyal follower."[36] Yet the intra-party standing of the party headquarter's general secretariat did not improve significantly until Schüssel became chancellor.[37] To sum up, a trend of reinforced oligarchization, cooperation, and loyalty combined with his success in the 2002 general elections to give Schüssel "more intra-party power than any of his predecessors since the 1950s,"[38] at least in his second term as chancellor (2003-2007). This includes Josef Klaus, who was chancellor between 1964 and 1970 and who presided for four years over a single-party majority government.

Collective party leadership dominates coalition negotiations. Only divisive issues such as distribution of portfolios, the operating principles of the cabinet, and personnel decisions were resolved by the respective party chairman in face-to-face talks.[39] The bulk of previous decisions were made in a negotiation round whose participation did not reflect any party statutes. Membership was given to the leaders of the provincial *Land* organizations, the chairmen of the six leagues, the president of the parliament, the party whip, and the party chairman. As Khol noticed, this particular composition depicted the party's "old party executive before the reform of party regulations." Eventually, all decisions taken invariably were endorsed in the official executive body.[40]

The polarization of domestic politics between government and parliamentary opposition (SPÖ and Greens) facilitated the retention of voting discipline within the ÖVP's parliamentary group.[41] Party discipline during the Schüssel years reflected a dominant influence of party group leadership and cabinet members and left little room to maneuver for ordinary Ministers of Parliament (MPs).[42] Party leadership could rely on manifold *ex-ante* screening and *ex post* monitoring tools in order to establish and maintain desired voting behavior. Above all, it was the prime source for the proliferation of secured mandates.[43] The authority of party whips *vis-à-vis* MPs was described as generally ample.[44] Khol, who was leader of the parliamentary group from 1994 to 2003, served the ÖVP as ideological "mastermind" (evidenced by his contributions to the concept of civic society, *Bürgergesellschaft*, and the new ÖVP-FPÖ-government, the *Wenderegierung*). His successor Wilhelm Molterer, the vice-chancellor, minister of finance, and party chairman (2006-2008), had held the post of general secretary (1993-1994) and was a cabinet member for almost a decade (1994-2003). Both were long-term confidantes of Schüssel, belonged to the inner leadership circle, and were always inclined to support their party chairman. Schüssel's good relationship with Khol was undiminished when Schüssel declined Khol's request to take over the Department of the Interior in 2000. The chancellor did not want to lose his superb leader of the parliamentary group.[45] Indeed, Khol wore his nickname "taskmaster" with pride. After the end of the Schüssel chancellory, MP Ferry Maier in a much-noticed and telling phrase, expressed his criticism of the imposition of leadership mentality in the parliamentary group: "Fold your hands and keep your trap shut!"

More streams of opposing voices came from the *Land* organizations and a number of powerful governors, albeit accentuation of political competition in federal politics did not make entering the national stage of politics more attractive. A governor's power surpasses a chancellor's power and is usually more secure.[46] Lower Austria's Erwin Pröll, who was very influential in the federal party and all powerful in his provincial party organization with its nearly quarter of a million members, looked at the election of Schüssel as party chairman skeptically. For many years, the media presented him as a potential and promising candidate for the party chair or—until 2004—the Austrian presidency. However, in 2008, Pröll is still governor. After 2000, he was occasionally a scathing reviewer of governmental policy, but never acted as the chancellor's rival. The governor's public critique of Chancellor Schüssel was less boisterous than the one provincial party leaders in the SPÖ had addressed to their chancellors in the 1987-2000 period.[47] In return, in a *quid pro quo*, Schüssel limited use of his authority to the challenge of consolidating his position on the top of the federal party organization. He consistently refrained from interference in any regional party matters such as the leadership conflict in the Tyrolean branch in 2001.[48]

However, regional party leaders were informed and consulted early at all times. The usual method of communication was the telephone.

Former FPÖ party leader and Vice-Chancellor Riess-Passer admired the fact that her ÖVP counterpart could put down the receiver and knew he would "get it done at the right time."[49] Even so, many decisions mirrored hierarchies in influence between the federal and *Land* organizations and among the latter as well. For instance, Reinhold Lopatka from Styria managed the 2002 election campaign and, as the federal party's general secretary, the 2006 election campaign both times together with his colleagues from Upper and Lower Austria, thereby representing the three most powerful *Land* organizations. Briefing and, if necessary, persuasion of other party heavyweights was carried out by Schüssel along with Khol, Wilhelm Molterer, Elisabeth Gehrer, and Reinhold Lopatka. This small panel was a forum for sometimes controversial discussions. As a former general secretary, Lopatka recalls that an allocation of responsibilities in this circle could be assessed within a few minutes.[50] Khol describes Schüssel as a "great team player" who was well aware he could not govern without support of the leaders of the *Land* party organizations and those of the party leagues.[51]

Schüssel made a few extremely important decisions. He pursued a call for early elections in autumn 1995; in the middle of the 1999 general election campaign, in order to mobilize hesitating sympathizers to vote for the ÖVP, he announced that his party would refuse to enter any government if it were taken over by the FPÖ on election day (for Khol it is the "privilege of the party chairman" to declare such matters). The Grasser Coup 2002 (the FPÖ finance minister was offered this post in a future ÖVP-led government), again during the election campaign, was the "the best guarded secret in the party," and nobody else was consulted. It was not until January 2007, after the electoral defeat in October 2006 and in the final days of coalition negotiations with the SPÖ, that Schüssel failed in a similar attempt: the single-handed issue of presenting Grasser as forthcoming vice-chancellor, prolonging his term as finance minister, and implicitly, the ÖVP's front-runner for the next general elections was declined by at least eight members of the party executive committee.[52] Unusually, the proposal was not approved by the quartet of Schüssel, Molterer, Gehrer, and Khol. Rather, it was the result of face-to-face talks between Schüssel and Molterer. Only Governors Pröll and Josef Pühringer (Upper Austria) were informed before the decisive meeting of the party executive.[53]

The FPÖ in 2000: An Attractive Coalition "Bride"

Once in government, the FPÖ experienced a series of difficulties typical of right-wing populist parties. This includes a thin staffing level,[54] disclosure to the public of programmatic inconsistence, and the formation of increasingly antagonistic party wings (party in office versus party on the ground). A comparative view across Europe shows that this kind of party often self destructs after elections, especially in coalitions with conservative partners who adopt right-wing paroles and policies.[55] Moreover, the often authoritarian and charismatic party leadership blocks the ability of party committees to resolve intra-party conflict. After February 2000, "scapegoating" increasingly focused on the party's own cabinet members. Finally, the vast majority of functionaries and voters shared unrealistic expectations for electoral rebound and policy performance.[56] Somewhat paradoxically, these expectations had to be disappointed, in part, because the FPÖ in opposition was successful in influencing government policies in some areas and shaping political discourse during the 1990s.[57] The FPÖ's electoral alliance, consisting of heterogeneous voter groups, was loosely constituted.[58] Tendencies for structural "realignment" favoring the FPÖ in the long run could neither be reinforced nor preserved while the party was in office.[59] Haider himself did not close his eyes to the electoral risks of entering a coalition, but at the same time, as Riess-Passer put it, was "the biggest stickler of being in the government," for he feared a continuing decline in support for the ÖVP would cost the party a common majority.[60]

The content of the manifestos of the two parties was highly compatible in the 1990s. This was particularly true for the important area of social and economic policy.[61] Having said that, nevertheless, the rising popularity of Haider among blue-collar voters in the 1999 election culminated in the FPÖ's superseding the Social Democrats in this group of voters. The FPÖ's attraction for the working class helped to sustain and enlarge the majority the ÖVP and FPÖ held together in the national assembly (*Nationalrat*) since 1983. "[N]eocapitalist principles," on the other hand, "do not conflict with nationalist feelings," and the same was true for attitudes of hostility towards foreigners and minorities.[62] The ÖVP and FPÖ's plans to devote more money to support families were congruent as well (see the introduction of *Kinderbetreuungsgeld* on 1 January 2002).

The great exception to all this compatibility existed in matters of European affairs, especially efforts that intended to strengthen EU integration (for example, the Nice Treaty) and the ongoing project of the EU's (eastern) enlargement. However, the content of the coalition agreement was instructive in that the FPÖ "apparently had subordinated its policy goals to office-seeking ambitions."[63] In the scenario of intensifying conflict over European matters, Schüssel ultimately acted intransigently. Like Scandinavian prime ministers in confrontation with their EU coalition partners, the Austrian chancellor was willing to take manifest risks of a coalition break-up in order to see the "centerpiece" of EU enlargement protected.[64]

The Chancellor's Role in the Cabinet

The Austrian chancellor's role in the cabinet was predominantly described as "*primus inter pares*,"[65] while only Kreisky was acknowledged to have represented a "chancellor democracy."[66] Official duties granted to the position in the Austrian constitution are chairmanship of cabinet meetings (Art. 69) and a right of ministerial nomination and dismissal (Art. 70). There is no general competence to set the guidelines of governing. However, as in Germany, where a chancellor possesses such formal competence (*Richtlinienkompetenz*), it may not be adequate for the level of power he exerts over his cabinet. In a similar fashion, Wolfgang C. Müller found Austrian evidence for "prime ministerial" as well as "cabinet" and "party government."[67]

As mentioned earlier in this article, Schüssel was a dedicated practitioner of a cooperative style of governance. Indeed, in the first cabinet formed after the 1999 general elections, both parties had equal ministerial representation, whereas the 2002 Peoples Party's triumph and the FPÖ's fiasco changed the proportion to three to one. The FPÖ's "*annus horribilis*" in 2005, when the party split and the smaller faction (*Bündnis Zukunft Österreich*, or BZÖ) continued its role in the government,[68] further cheapened the ÖVP's coalition partner.

"Inner cabinets," which in some countries (such as the Federal Republic of Germany and Great Britain) reinforce prime ministerial power while in others (such as Belgium) exert an oppositional effect, seemed to have been absent under Schüssel's leadership.[69] The appointment of ministers and junior ministers from different parties, a widely used device of mutually controlling Austria's grand coalitions, almost entirely disappeared in the Schüssel I cabinet and enjoyed confined revitalization in the 2003 remake.[70] Ministerial autonomy was recognized on the basis of principles and content as stipulated in the coalition agreement. According to the Austrian tradition, the agreement of the year 2000 presented a comprehensive document, but dedicated above-average room to policy intentions. It concomitantly reduced the chancellor and his ministers' room to maneuver.[71] Lopatka confirms that ministerial autonomy, which is sufficiently appreciated in the Austrian constitution, is "very respected" in the ÖVP and "was always respected by the chancellor."[72] A statement by Riess-Passer, however, signals the borders of ministerial autonomy: in case of severe disagreement between ministers, she says, Schüssel and she did not hesitate to intervene.[73]

The sequences of governing coordination differed substantially from those of the Helmut Kohl era in Germany. The Austrian process could be characterized by a lower degree of informality. Negotiation rounds of frequently altered composition, so central to the Kohl system, played no role.[74] According to Austria's Andreas Khol, the two leaders of the coalition parties created the agenda of the upcoming cabinet meeting, thereby starting the process of subsequent coordination: "Still, during the term of the grand coalition the chancellor alone decided the agenda which always led to conflicts because the smaller partner depended on his good will to have petitions discussed in the cabinet meeting."[75] In coordinating governmental politics, Schüssel relied on a small circle of party heavyweights that merged into a bigger, but accessible, round in the preliminary discussions of the cabinet meetings, which broadly overlapped with the party's executive committee. The "Monday round" assembled Khol (first president of the *Nationalrat* since 2003), Lopatka (since 2003), Gehrer, the so-called "coordination minister" at the time, and probably also Molterer: "That was the circle—a reduced party executive committee."[76] These talks were paralleled by an increasing number of bilateral contacts between cabinet members.[77]

The coordination session of the government was preceded by the preliminary discussion of each coalition partner. It was attended by all cabinet members, the party whip and president of the *Nationalrat*, and the general secretary of the federal party and those of the six leagues, as well as the leagues' chairmen.[78] For Lopatka, the institutionalized preliminary discussion of cabinet meetings in the ÖVP witnessed many debates and, therefore, accomplished an "integral function" of coordinating executive politics.[79] The sessions of the coordination committee took place on the day before the formal cabinet meeting and represented the "actual council of ministers where discussions are still taking place, questions are still being asked, where one minister or another still admits that she or he is not convinced about something."[80] Participants included not only cabinet members, but also party whips, chiefs of cabinet, and the administrative directors of the parliamentary group. In the official cabinet meeting, in a procedure that deviates from the practice of the Franz Vranitzky cabinets (chancellor between 1986 and 1997), both chancellor and vice-chancellor began with a political address that summarized the coordination session and ended with in the request of ministerial statements outside the agenda.[81] Any ambiguities or unresolved issues were discussed in Tuesday morning's "chancellor breakfast" (*Kanzlerfrühstück*), where chancellor and vice-chancellor tried to revise the agenda eye to eye, sometimes consulting the ministers involved.[82]

In 2000, the ÖVP-FPÖ government distinguished itself from previous cabinets in that the coalition committee no longer "above all was designed in setting emergencies but served as a coordinating and controlling institution."[83] Khol counts ten to fifteen meetings taking place between 2000-2002. These were kept secret. The party whips, general secretaries, and chairman assembled at Khol's home at meetings conceived as a means to neutralize Haider.[84] The informal FPÖ leader, however, had refrained from attending meetings long before the summer of 2002.

With the important exception of the Ministry of Internal Affairs, the ÖVP in 2000 extended its ministries and most portfolios from the grand coalition period. The FPÖ ministers, on the contrary, struggled to establish themselves in traditional SPÖ departments.[85] This distribution basically followed the suggestions of the "portfolio allocation model" (parties claim portfolios to facilitate clientelism). The one significant exception related to the chancellor's "blame avoidance" strategy: FPÖ Chairwoman Riess-Passer was given responsibility for administration and civil service and was the prime counterpart for the influential union of civil servants (GÖD), which is dominated by the ÖVP-affiliated Group of Christian Unionists (FCG).[86] At the final stage of wage bargaining, the FCG chairman, according to a tried and true pattern, sought to get his opponent's resistance overruled by the chancellor's support. Schüssel declined by noting his lack of a constitutional competence.[87]

Conclusion: Chancellor Democrat, Premier-President, or Indispensable Coordinator?

A final assessment of the relationship between the power of the Austrian government and the influence of Chancellor Schüssel is provided by a comparison between the concepts of chancellor democracy and coordination democracy in the light of the "presidentialization" hypothesis.

Chancellor democrats and "presidentialized" premiers are portrayed by definition as exceptionally strong political leaders. The process of "presidentialization" is driven by the growing informal quality of executive politics and by direct communication between leaders and voters through the media. This is less central to the concept of chancellor democracy. The "presidentialized" type often seeks to build alliances across party political frontiers, and some try to avoid polarization.[88] This is not a feature of "chancellor democracy." One's relationship with one's own party typifies the one real drastic difference with the heirs of Germany's Konrad Adenauer, the progenitor of all chancellor democrats, who valued tight control instead of independence and strategic flexibility. Advocates of coordination democracy argue that increasing fragmentation and complexity of decision-making and implementation processes have produced or made necessary a certain form of leadership. Unlike the two other approaches, coordination democracy considers governmental activism as part of the wider political system: the chancellor, then, appears to lead surrounded by veto players (*Mitregenten*), is forced into joint decision making (*Politikverflechtung*), and is restricted by "path dependency." Securing effective and efficient governing, therefore, requires more or less permanent coordination and cooperation.[89] (See Table 1.)

How can we describe Schüssel's executive leadership? Let's start with the concept of "chancellor democracy." Notable, first, is the ambivalent quality of his power in his party: on the one hand, he was unrivaled and, no doubt, played a leadership role on the terrain of EU politics; in a "strategic masterly performance" (Khol) he ended thirty years of "red" chancellors, and he made few but very important decisions (see the list mentioned before). Bids for election dates and coalition aspects were essential to his style of politics. On the other hand, his personal popularity as evaluated in opinion polls was low. Except in 1996 (European parliament elections) and 2002 (general elections[90]), all federal elections results were disappointing for the ÖVP; cooperation in the cabinet was enforced by ministerial autonomy and equal representation of the FPÖ (2000-2003); demands of *Land* party organizations and the six leagues had to be satisfied in the appointment of cabinet members (except for Plassnik, who became minister for foreign affairs in 2004 and had been Schüssel's chief of staff); unlike the Gusenbauer SPÖ (Alfred Gusenbauer was chairman of the SPÖ since 2000) over the course of the BAWAG-ÖGB scandal in 2006 (BAWAG was the bank of the Austrian Trade Union, *Österreichischer Gewerkschaftsbund*), the ÖVP under Schüssel did not introduce any incompatibility rule (conflict of interest and roles) for being member of the parliament and top official in chambers and unions. The one important exception is the president of the chamber of commerce and critic of the new majoritarian course, Christoph Leitl, who never became a member of the *Nationalrat*. He was another candidate for the party chair in 1995 and since then stayed outside Schüssel's leadership team[91]; under Schüssel's leadership, comprehensive organizational innovations were never implemented, and programmatic reforms were never initiated.

Such ambivalence, too, is apparent in the colossal 2002 victory. The campaign's central slogan "*Wer, wenn nicht er*" ("Who else could do the job?") was intended to focus voters' attention on choosing a chancellor. In the last two months before the election, however, his advantage over opposition leader Gusenbauer (SPÖ) dropped some sixteen points, giving him a lead of no more than 7 percent. A moderate turnaround favoring Schüssel took place in the final two weeks of the campaign, and he dominated in the TV debate between the parliamentary parties' front-runners a few days before the election.[92] Schüssel benefited from what Scott Feld and Bernard Grofman call the "benefit of the doubt."[93] The real breakthrough occurred courtesy of the Grasser coup. Again, one might argue that the young finance minister's popularity overshadowed the chancellor's, though it was the chancellor who took the risk of the decision to offer this important post to an active politician representing another party, who had the intra-party authority to make this attractive offer to Grasser and who succeeded in convincing him.

Overall, the elections can be characterized as a plebiscite on the architecture of power relations in the political system, only it was a mediated one about the fate of individual political leaders and not about any of the parties' policy offers.[94] The dominant impact of the issue of power relations would also explain the unique ÖVP gain among blue-collar voters, although laborers were generally the prime target of financial cutbacks since 2000. Sensationally, the ÖVP more than doubled its share of votes.[95] For years later, many of them preferred the SPÖ (minus 12 percent for the ÖVP).[96]

Can coordination democracy contribute to our understanding of Schüssel's executive leadership? With respect to intra-party and cabinet leadership, the answer is yes; Schüssel acted according to the premise of "coordination democracy." With respect to governmental leadership, the answer is "no" because the majoritarian track of decision making attempted to neutralize potential as well as numerous formal and informal veto players.

Finally, we incorporate the aspect of "presidentialization." This international phenomenon, as pointed out by Thomas Poguntke and Paul Webb, subsumes a not necessarily simultaneous, but to a high degree interdependent, increase in the significance of political leaders in the party (party face), in the government ("executive face" including cabinet, parliamentary party group, and bureaucratic structures), and in elections (electoral face).[97] Schüssel hardly acted and performed according to these standards: the personalization strategy in the 2002 campaign was successful, but failed in 2006 (electoral face); there was no attempt to monopolize communication of governmental politics to the media. In sharp contrast to the great communicator among Austrian chancellors, Kreisky, Schüssel's style provoked critics to label him "*Schweigekanzler*"[98] ("the silent chancellor"). Also uncommon were the frequent exchanges and appointments of policy experts, and the same applies to spontaneous agenda setting for the purpose of weakening the position of the cabinet. Eventually, Schüssel rarely presented himself in the guise of a non-party and nonpartisan "moderator" of politics. The "presidential" style of organizing majorities by including oppositional MPs with the purpose of replacing the need to rally his own supporters was extrinsic to his understanding of politics (executive face). The scope of organizational reforms in the party was limited, the official executive committees and boards remained an essential forum of discussion and decision-making, and his appointment authority stayed restricted by traditional forces (party face).

As noted above, Schüssel's relationship to his party marks the fundamental difference in the concepts of chancellor democracy and "presidentialization." Schüssel's case and examples from Great Britain, Australia, and Germany indicate a varying extent of openness towards the evolution of "presidential" features dependent on the party familial background: prerequisites are more favorable in social democratic parties (Tony Blair, Gerhard Schröder), have mixed effects in secular-conservative parties (Margaret Thatcher, John Major, John Howard[99]), and are adverse in Christian democratic parties (Kohl, Angela Merkel, Schüssel).[100] Whereas the last repeatedly (Schüssel) and relentlessly (Kohl) achieved solidarity with their parties and attacked preceding social democratic administrations, Blair practiced a double "blaming" of conservative governments and "Old Labour." Schüssel never used the threat to resign to steer certain policy-outcomes, unlike Schröder who did so several times.[101] (See Table 1.)

Table 1

Leadership Styles and Prime Ministerial Power (Case Studies)

	Schüssel	Kohl	Blair-Schröder
Level of Dominance			
• Cabinet	low to moderate	high	moderate
• Party	moderate	Moderate	low to high
Electoral Vulnerability	low	high	high
Scope of Governance	moderate to high	low to moderate	low to moderate

Despite many similarities between Kohl and Schüssel's "executive leadership," some essential differences exist. Kohl's systematic and almost holistic approach in establishing intra-party networks based on loyalty and dependencies and his offer of protection to allies and fighting against opponents were entirely absent in the ÖVP. This was also the case concerning his personal conflicts and feuds with critics (for example, former General Secretaries Kurt Biedenkopf and Heiner Geissler).[102] Kohl met open opposition and rivals both as party leader and Christian Democratic Union/Christian Social Union of Bavaria (*Christlich Demokratische Union Deutschlands*, or CDU/*Christlich-Soziale Union in Bayern e.V.*, or CSU) front-runner (CSU chairman Franz Josef Strauss became candidate in 1980). Under Schüssel, party management and governmental leadership seemed to be two separate things.[103]

Presidentialized party leaders and premiers face a higher risk of electoral vulnerability (see Table 2 below.) They typically lack the ability to celebrate political comebacks (as did Vaclav Klaus in the Czech Republic and Victor Orban in Hungary), or remain in office without being an asset for their parties in electoral campaigns (Germany's Kohl, with the exception of the 1990 elections). Schüssel's personal ratings remained rather poor throughout most of his chancellorship, and it appears as more than a coincidence that Schüssel's incumbency was shorter than that of two other ÖVP chancellors (Leopold Figl and Julius Raab), while the length of his term on the top of the party and as a minister rank him first.

Table 2
Leadership Styles and Prime Ministerial Power (Concepts)

	Premier Presidential	Chancellor Democracy	Coordination Democracy
Level of Dominance			
• Cabinet	high	high	low to high
• Party	low to high	moderate to high	low to high
Electoral Vulnerability	moderate to high	moderate	low to moderate

Schüssel is a rare example of a prime minister with a failed re-election bid who nevertheless stayed in a central political position (deputy leader in the *Nationalrat*), though not leader of the opposition. During the short-lived "grand coalition" in 2007-2008, SPÖ politicians often accused him of obstructive leadership of the party and of blocking the SPÖ's attempt to keep promises it had made in the election campaign. Whether these reproaches were justified or not shall not be a matter decided here. In fact, charges of this nature indirectly shed light on one aspect of the heritage of Schüssel's dual leadership: his cooperation in the party and the cabinet on one hand, and conflict in expanding the decision-making authority against potential veto players on the other hand. The Schüssel years definitely contributed to the weakening of the internal cohesion of both partisan and corporatist actors as demonstrated in the recent failures of the *Krankenkassenpaket* (a reform intended to provide public health insurance agencies with financial aid) and *Pensionsautomatik* (converting annual increases of pensions into a technocratic "one best policy" matter). This new feature of Austrian politics will not make executive leadership more likely to succeed, though one must ask, will it enforce a distinctive leadership approach?

Notes

1. Manfred G. Schmidt, *Demokratietheorien*, 3rd ed. (Opladen: Leske und Budrich, 2000), 352-53. Schmidt constructed this index in continuation of André Kaiser, "Types of Democracy: From Classical to New Institutionalism," *Journal of Theoretical Politics* 9 (1997): 419-44.

2. Eoin O'Malley, "The Power of Prime Ministers: Results of an Expert Survey." *International Political Science Review*, 28.1 (2007): 7-27, here 14. See also Anthony King, "'Chief Executives' in Western Europe," in *Developing Democracy: Comparative Research in Honor of J.F.P. Blondel*, ed. Ian Budge and David McKay (London: Sage, 1994), 150-63.

3. See, for instance, Wolfgang C. Müller, "Inside the Black Box: A Confrontation of Party Executive Behavior and Theory of Party Organizational Change," *Party Politics* 3 (1997): 293-313.

4. Waldemar Schreckenberger, "Informelle Verfahren der Entscheidungsvorbereitung zwischen der Bundesregierung und den Mehrheitsfraktionen: Koalitionsgespräche und Koalitionsrunden," *Zeitschrift für Parlamentsfragen* 25 (1994): 329-46.

5. Anthony King, "The Outsider as Political Leader: The Case of Margaret Thatcher," *British Journal of Political Science*, 32 (2002): 435-54.

6. See, for instance, Francesco Cavatorta and Eoin O'Malley, "Finding a Party and Losing Some Friends: Overcoming the Weaknesses of the Prime Ministerial Figure in Italy," *Contemporary Politics* 10.3 (2004): 271-86.

7. See, in particular, John D. Huber and Nolan McCarty, "Cabinet Decision Rules and Political Uncertainty in Parliamentary Bargaining," *American Political Science Review* 95.2 (2001): 345-60.

8. Michael Laver and Kenneth Shepsle, "Coalitions and Cabinet Governments," *American Political Science Review* 84 (1990): 873-90.

9. Eoin O'Malley, "Setting Choices, Controlling Outcomes: The Operation of Prime Ministerial Influence and the UK's Decision to Invade Iraq," *British Journal of Politics and International Relations* 9 (2007): 1-19.

10. Kaare Strom, "Delegation and Accountability in Parliamentary Democracies," *European Journal of Political Research* 37.3 (2000): 261-89; Mark Thatcher and Alec Stone Sweet, "Theory and Practice of Delegation to Non-Majoritarian Institutions," *West European Politics* 25.1 (2002): 1-22.

11. Wolfgang C. Müller, "Political Parties in Parliamentary Democracies: Making Delegation and Accountability Work," *European Journal of Political Research* 37.3 (2000): 309-33.

12. O'Malley, "Prime Ministers"; Jean Blondel and Ferdinand Müller-Rommel, eds., *Governing Together: The Extent and Limits of Joint Decision-Making in Western European Cabinets* (London: Macmillan / St. Martin's, 1993); Wolfgang C. Müller, "Models of Government and the Austrian Cabinet," in *Cabinet Ministers and Parliamentary Government*, ed. Michael Laver and Kenneth A. Shepsle (Cambridge: Cambridge UP, 1994), 15-34.

13. Michael Minkenberg, "The Radical Right in Public Office," *West European Politics* 24.4 (2001): 1-21, here 14.

14. See, for instance, the characteristic title of the book *More Private, Less State*: Johannes Hawlik and Wolfgang Schüssel, *Mehr privat—weniger Staat: Anregungen zur Begrenzung öffentlicher Aufgaben* (Vienna: Signum Verlag, 1983).

15. Interviews with Reinhold Lopatka, Andreas Khol, and Josef Pühringer in April 2008.

16. Arend Lijphart, *Patterns of Democracy: Government Forms and Performance in Thirty-Six Countries* (New Haven, CT: Yale UP, 1999), 185.

17. George C. Tsebelis, "Decision Making in Political Systems: Veto Players in Presidentialism, Parliamentarism, Multicameralism, and Multipartyism," *British Journal of Political Science* 25.2 (1995): 289-325, here 293.

18. Herbert Obinger, "Vetospieler und Staatstätigkeit in Österreich. Sozial- und wirtschaftspolitische Reformchancen für die neue ÖVP-FPÖ-Regierung," *Zeitschrift für Parlamentsfragen* 32.2 (2001): 360-83; Marius R. Busemeyer, "Pension Reform in Germany and Austria: System Change vs. Quantitative Retrenchment," *West European Politics* 28.3 (2005): 569-91; Emmerich Tálos and Bernhard Kittel, *Gesetzgebung in Österreich: Netzwerke, Akteure und Interaktionen in politischen Entscheidungsprozessen* (Vienna: Facultas, 2001).

19. Tálos and Obinger, "Gesetzgebung in Österreich," 227. See also Emmerich Tálos and Christian Stromberger, "Verhandlungsdemokratische Willensbildung und korporatistische Entscheidungsfindung am Ende? Einschneidende Veränderungen am Beispiel der Gestaltung des österreichischen Arbeitsrechtes," *Österreichische Zeitschrift für Politikwissenschaft* 33.2 (2004): 157-74, especially 171.

20. See Stephen A. Padgett, "Social Democracy in Power," *Parliamentary Affairs* 46.1 (1993): 101-20, especially 109. Interviews with Lopatka, Khol, and Pühringer.

21. Andreas Khol, *Die Wende ist geglückt: Der schwarz-blaue Marsch durch die Wüste Gobi* (Vienna: Molden, 2001), 177.

22. Budget speech in the *Nationalrat* in October 2004. See also Herbert Obinger and Emmerich Tálos, *Sozialstaat Österreich zwischen Kontinuität und Umbau: Bilanz der ÖVP/FPÖ/BZÖ-Koalition* (Wiesbaden: Verlag für Sozialwissenschaften, 2006), 210.

23. See Peter A. Ulram and Franz Sommer, "Hausgemachte Siege—hausgemachte Niederlagen: Die Landtagswahlen in Salzburg, Kärnten und Vorarlberg 2004," *Österreichisches Jahrbuch für Politik 2004*, ed. Andreas Khol et al. (Vienna: Oldenbourg 2005), 69-80.

24. Khol, "Die Wende ist geglückt," 21. See Reimut Zohlnhöfer, "The Politics of Budget Consolidation in Britain and Germany: The Impact of Blame Avoidance Opportunities," *West European Politics* 30.5 (2007): 1120-38.

25. See Fritz Plasser et al., "Erdrutschwahlen: Momentum, Motive und neue Muster im Wahlverhalten," *Wahlverhalten in Bewegung. Analysen zur Nationalratswahl 2002*, ed. Fritz Plasser and Peter A. Ulram (Vienna: WUV-Universitätsverlag, 2003), 97-157, especially 99.

26. Alexander Janda and Franz Sommer, "Vor und nach der 'Wende': Demoskopische Trends und Regionalwahlen als Messfühler der neuen politischen Landschaft," *Österreichisches Jahrbuch für Politik 2000*, ed. Andreas Khol et al. (Vienna: Oldenbourg, 2001), 59-76, especially 62.

27. See Khol, "Die Wende ist geglückt," 180.

28. Interview with Susanne Riess-Passer.

29. Ibid. Anonymous interview with a former member of Schüssel's personal cabinet.

30. See Dong-Hun Kim and Gerhard Loewenberg, "The Role of Parliamentary Committees in Coalition Governments: Keeping Tabs on Coalition Partners in the German *Bundestag*," *Comparative Political Studies* 38.9 (2005): 1104-29, especially 1123.

31. Interview with Khol.

32. Wolfgang C. Müller and Barbara Steininger, "Party Organization and Party Competitiveness: The Case of the Austrian People's Party, 1945-1992," *European Journal of Political Research* 26.1 (1994): 1-29, here 2.

33. See already Wolfgang C. Müller and Wilfried Phillipp, "Wie oligarchisch sind Österreichs Parteien? Eine empirische Analyse 1945-1992," *Österreichische Zeitschrift für Politikwissenschaft* 21.2 (1992): 117-46.

34. Wolfgang C. Müller and Delia Meth-Cohn, "The Selection of Party Chairmen in Austria: A Study of Intra-Party Decision-Making," *European Journal of Political Research* 20 (1991): 39-61.

35. Interviews with Khol and Lopatka.

36. Reinhard Olt, "Aufbruch, Ausbruch, Durchbruch, Umbruch—die ÖVP in der Ära Schüssel," *Zukunftsfest. 60 Jahre Österreichische Volkspartei*, ed. Andreas Khol et al. (Vienna: Molden, 2005), 145-66, here 145. Interview with former Vice-Chancellor and ÖVP Chairman Erhard Busek (1991-1995).

37. Wolfgang C. Müller, "Die Österreichische Volkspartei," *Politik in Österreich: Das Handbuch*, 3rd ed., ed. Herbert Dachs et al. (Vienna: Manz, 2006), 341-63, here 352.

38. Wolfgang C. Müller et al., "Party Responses to the Erosion of Voter Loyalties in Austria: Weakness as an Advantage and Strength as a Handicap," *Political Parties and Electoral Change*, ed. Peter Mair et al. (London: Sage, 2004), 145-78, 167.

39. Andreas Khol, "Koalitionsabkommen in der Regierungspraxis 1994 bis 2007," *Österreichisches Jahrbuch für Politik* 2006, ed. Andreas Khol et al. (Vienna: Oldenbourg, 2007), 141-55, especially 146-48.

40. Interview with Khol.

41. Wolfgang C. Müller and Marcelo Jenny, "'Business as usual' mit getauschten Rollen oder Konflikt- statt Konsensdemokratie? Parlamentarische Beziehungen unter der ÖVP-FPÖ-Koalition," *Österreichische Zeitschrift für Politikwissenschaft* 33.3 (2004): 309-26.

42. For the theoretical background, see Roderick D. Kiewiet and Mathew D. McCubbins, *The Logic of Delegation* (Chicago: U of Chicago P, 1991).

43. Müller, "Political Parties in Parliamentary Democracies," 323-25 See also Marcus Kreuzer, "Electoral Mechanism and Electioneering Incentives: Vote-Getting Strategies of Japanese, French, British, German, and Austrian Conservatives," *Party Politics* 6.4 (2000): 487-504, here 490.

44. Wolfgang C. Müller et al., "Die Rolle der parlamentarischen Fraktionen," *Die österreichischen Abgeordneten: Individuelle Präferenzen und politisches Verhalten*, ed. Wolfgang C. Müller et al. (Vienna: WUV Universitätsverlag, 2001), 183-260, especially 239-40.

45. Khol, "Die Wende ist geglückt," 128.

46. See Franz Fallend, "Landesregierung und Landesverwaltung," *Politik in Österreich: Das Handbuch*, ed. Herbert Dachs et al. (Vienna: Manz, 2006), 974-89, especially 979-81; Wolfgang C. Müller, "Parties and the Institutional Framework," *Political Parties in the New Europe: Political and Analytical Challenges*, ed. Kurt Richard Luther and Ferdinand Müller-Rommel (Oxford: Oxford UP, 2005), 249-92, especially 253.

47. See Herbert Dachs, "Politische Parteien in Österreichs Bundesländern—zwischen regonalen Kalkülen und bundespolitischen Loyalitäten," *Der Bund und die Länder: Über Dominanz Kooperation und Konflikte im österreichischen Bundesstaat*, ed. Herbert Dachs (Vienna: Böhlau, 2003), 69-138, especially 86-91.

48. Ibid., 108-09.

49. Interview with Riess-Passer.

50. Interview with Lopatka.

51. Interview with Khol.

52. Interview with Khol. For more information, see David Wineroither, "Bundespräsident und Bundeskanzler: Konsens, Konflikt oder Neutralität?," *Österreichisches Jahrbuch für Politik 2006*, ed. Andreas Khol et al. (Vienna: Oldenbourg, 2007), 603-23, especially 620-21.

53. Interview with Pühringer.

54. See Kurt Richard Luther, "The FPÖ: From Populist Protest to Incumbency," in *Right-Wing Extremism in the Twenty-First Century*, ed. Peter H. Merkl and Leonard Weinberg (London: Franc Cass, 2003), 191-219, here 210-11.

55. Günther Pallaver and Reinhold Gärtner, "Populistische Parteien an der Regierung—zum Scheitern verdammt? Italien und Österreich im Vergleich," in *Populismus: Gefahr für die Demokratie oder nützliches Korrektiv?*, ed. Frank Decker (Wiesbaden: Verlag für Sozialwissenschaften, 2006), 99-120.

56. Reinhard Heinisch, "Die FPÖ—Ein Phänomen im internationalen Vergleich: Erfolg und Misserfolg des identitären Rechtspopulismus," *Österreichische Zeitschrift für Politikwissenschaft* 33.3 (2004): 247-62, especially 257-59.

57. See, for instance, Ruth Wodak and Anton Pelinka, eds., *The Haider Phenomenon in Austria* (New Brunswick, NJ: Transaction, 2002).

58. Anthony J. McGann and Herbert Kitschelt, "The Radical Right in the Alps: Evolution of Support for the Swiss SVP and Austrian FPÖ," *Party Politics* 11. 2 (2005): 147-72.

59. Müller et al., "Weakness as an Advantage," 149.

60. Interview with Riess-Passer.

61. See John D. Huber and Ronald Inglehart, "Expert Interpretations of Party Space and Party Locations in 42 Societies," *Party Politics* 1.1 (1995): 73-111.

62. Hilde Weiss, "A Cross-National Comparison of Nationalism in Austria, the Czech and Slovac Republics, Hungary, and Poland," *Political Psychology* 24.2 (2003): 377-401, here 396; Wolfgang Schulz and Hilde Weiss, "Ausländerfeindlichkeit und Neoliberalismus als Elemente populistischer Politik? Zum Wandel der Einstellungen der ÖsterreicherInnen zwischen 1998 und 2003," *Österreichische Zeitschrift für Politikwissenschaft* 34.4 (2005): 395-412, here 408.

63. See Wolfgang C. Müller, "EU-Mitgliedschaft und Regierungshandeln," in *"Europäisierung" der österreichischen Politik? Konsequenzen der EU-Mitgliedschaft*, ed. Heinrich Neisser and Sonja Puntscher Riekmann (Vienna: Facultas, 2002), 101-31, especially 117-18.

64. See David Arter, "The Prime Minister in Scandinavia: 'Superstar' or Supervisor?," *Journal of Legislative Studies* 10.2/3 (2004): 109-27, especially 124.

65. Manfried Welan and Heinrich Neisser, *Der Bundeskanzler im österreichischen Verfassungsgefüge* (Vienna: Hollinek, 1971), 98.

66. Manfried Welan, "Die Kanzlerdemokratie in Österreich," in *Um Parlament und Partei: Alfred Maleta zum 70. Geburtstag*, ed. Andreas Khol et al. (Graz: Styria, 1976), 169-80.

67. Müller, "Models of Government and the Austrian Cabinet"; see similar Peter Gerlich et al., "Potentials and Limitations of Executive Leadership: The Austrian Cabinet since 1945," *European Journal of Political Research* 16.2 (1988): 191-205, especially 203.

68. Walter Hämmerle, "Die Spaltung der FPÖ: Annus horribilis für das freiheitliche Lager," in *Österreichisches Jahrbuch für Politik 2005*, ed. Andreas Khol et al. (Vienna: Oldenbourg, 2006), 239-52.

69. Anonymous interview.

70. See Michael F. Thies, "Keeping Tabs on Partners: The Logic of Delegation in Coalition Governments," *American Journal of Political Science* 45.3 (2001): 580-98.

71. See Laver and Shepsle, "Coalitions and Cabinet Government."

72. Interview with Lopatka.

73. Interview with Riess-Passer. "The bulk of departmental decisions is made by the respective ministers within their jurisdiction without any interference from the cabinet, the chancellor (or vice-chancellor), or the party." (Müller, "Models of Government and the Austrian Cabinet," 31).

74. Schreckenberger, "Informelle Verfahren," 335.

75. Khol, "Koalitionsabkommen in der Regierungspraxis 1994 bis 2007," 153.

76. Interview with Khol and Lopatka.

77. Anonymous interview.

78. Khol, "Koalitionsabkommen in der Regierungspraxis 1994 bis 2007," 150.

79. Ibid.

80. Interview with Riess-Passer.

81. Khol, "Koalitionsabkommen in der Regierungspraxis 1994 bis 2007," 151.

82. Interview with Riess-Passer.

83. Wolfgang Rudzio, *Informelles Regieren: Zum Koalitionsmanagement in deutschen und österreichischen Regierungen* (Wiesbaden: Verlag für Sozialwissenschaft, 2005), 59.

84. Interviews with Riess-Passer and Khol.

85. According to various interviews, the incoming FPÖ ministers usually became acquainted with their new leadership tasks within a couple of months. However, Riess-Passer (interview) refers to one FPÖ minister whose department had to be carried along by a ÖVP cabinet member responsible for a similar portfolio.

86. See Susanne Riess-Passer, "Die Aufgaben- und Verwaltungsreform: ein großer Wurf der Bundesregierung," in *Österreichisches Jahrbuch für Politik 2001*, ed. Andreas Khol et al. (Vienna: Oldenbourg, 2002), 419-32.

87. Interview with Riess-Passer.

88. Karlheinz *Niclauß, Kanzlerdemokratie: Regierungsführung von Konrad Adenauer bis Gerhard Schröder* (Paderborn: Schöningh, 2004).

89. Wolfgang Jäger, "Von der Kanzlerdemokratie zur Koordinationsdemokratie," *Zeitschrift für Politik* 35.1 (1988): 15-32; Fritz W. Scharpf, "The Joint Decision Trap: Lessons from German Federalism and European Integration," *Public Administration* 66.3 (1988): 239-78.

90. See Plasser and Ulram, eds., "Wahlverhalten in Bewegung."

91. Already a study of Karlhofer had established that in 2001 no less than 56 percent of the ÖVP's MPs were declared stakeholders of institutions of the *Sozialpartnerschaft*, whereas this applied to only 32 percent in the SPÖ parliamentary group. See Ferdinand Karlhofer, "Work in Progress? Anmerkungen zum Umbau der Sozialpartnerschaft," in *Österreichisches Jahrbuch für Politik 2001*, ed. Andreas Khol et al. (Vienna: Oldenbourg, 2002), 321-34, here 326.

92. See Fritz Plasser et al., "Kampagnedynamik, Mediahypes und Einfluss der TV-Konfrontationen 2002," in *Wahlverhalten in Bewegung: Analysen zur Nationalratswahl 2002*, ed. Fritz Plasser and Peter A. Ulram (Vienna: Signum, 2003), 19-54, especially 29.

93. Scott L. Feld and Bernard Grofman, "Incumbency Advantage, Voter Loyalty, and the Benefit of the Doubt," *Journal of Theoretical Politics* 3.2 (1991): 115-37.

94. For media coverage, see Günther Pallaver and Clemens Pig, "Medienzentrierter Wahlkampf: Themen und Kandidaten in der Wahlkampfberichterstattung 2002," in *Wahlverhalten in Bewegung: Analysen zur Nationalratswahl 2002*, ed. Fritz Plasser and Peter A. Ulram (Vienna: Signum, 2003), 55-96, especially 61-62.

95. See Plasser et al., "Erdrutschwahlen," 123-31.

96. See Fritz Plasser et al., "Was Wähler(innen) bewegt: Parteien-, Themen- und Kandidatenorientierungen 2006," in *Wechselwahlen: Analysen zur Nationalratswahl 2006*, ed. Fritz Plasser and Peter A. Ulram (Vienna: Signum, 2007), 155-94, especially 158-59.

97. Thomas Poguntke and Paul Webb, eds., *The Presidentialization of Politics: A Comparative Study of Modern Democracies* (Oxford: Oxford UP, 2005).

98. Thanks to Fritz Plasser for this suggestion.

99. Mark Bennister, "Tony Blair and John Howard: Comparative Predominance and 'Institution Stretch' in the U.K. and Australia," *British Journal of Politics and International Relations* 9 (2007): 327-45.

100. Christopher K. Ansell and M. Steven Fish, "The Art of Being Indispensable: Non-charismatic Personalism in Contemporary Political Parties," *Comparative Political Studies* 32.3 (1999): 283-312.

101. See John D. Huber, "The Vote of Confidence in Parliamentary Democracies," *American Political Science Review* 90.2 (1996): 269-82, especially 279; Michael F. Feldkamp, "Chronik der Vertrauensfrage des Bundeskanzlers am 1. Juli 2005 und der Auflösung des Deutschen Bundestages am 21. Juli 2005," *Zeitschrift für Parlaments-fragen* 37.1 (2006): 19-28.

102. Clay Clemens, "Party Management as a Leadership Resource: Kohl and the CDU/CSU," *German Politics* 7.1 (1998): 91-119, here 102.

103. Interview with Busek and anonymous interview.

Governing with Right-Wing Populists and Managing the Consequences: Schüssel and the FPÖ

Kurt Richard Luther

Introduction

On 22 April 1995, Wolfgang Schüssel became the third leader in six years of the *Österreichische Volkspartei* (ÖVP). It had a relatively poor record of achieving its electoral and governmental goals. Since 1970, the party had come second in all national elections to the *Sozialdemokratische Partei Österreichs* (SPÖ) and from 1986 had suffered a seemingly inexorable erosion of its vote share to the benefit of the *Freiheitliche Partei Österreichs* (FPÖ). After seventeen years in opposition, it had in 1987 finally returned to government, albeit as the SPÖ's junior coalition partner. During Schüssel's twelve-year leadership—the longest of any ÖVP chairman—the party obtained 42.3 percent of the vote at the 2002 election, its best result for nearly twenty years. Moreover, by the time of his resignation on 9 January 2007, Schüssel could look back on virtually seven years as federal chancellor, towards the end of which the ÖVP had been able to operate as though it were the sole governing party.

Such success had seemed impossible in the early 1990s, when the party's prospects appeared blocked by two significant constraints. Internally, its exceptionally factionalized structure had long militated against the kind of organizational adaptation arguably required to improve the party's electoral record and thus enhance its potential to win back the chancellorship. Externally, the pattern of party competition had severely limited the ÖVP's coalition options. For one, since Jörg Haider's assumption of the FPÖ leadership in 1986, the SPÖ and ÖVP had operated a policy of *Ausgrenzung*, that is, excluding the FPÖ from national office. This meant that, although the ÖVP and FPÖ had a numerical parliamentary majority throughout this period,[1] the ÖVP had effectively been tied into the role of the SPÖ's junior coalition partner. Moreover, the ÖVP's prime policy goal had since 1987 been EU accession, which required a two-thirds parliamentary majority, so until the requisite legislation was passed (on 11 November 1994), the ÖVP was doubly dependent on a "grand coalition" with the electorally stronger SPÖ.

Crucial to Schüssel's achievement of his office and policy goals was his willingness to break the mold of the party's external relations. This involved adopting a much more confrontational approach to the ÖVP's traditional coalition partner, the SPÖ, and to Austria's neo-corporatist system of social partnership. Above all, however, it required a willingness to countenance the hitherto excluded option of a coalition with Haider's FPÖ. Governing with a party that had since 1986 been pursuing right-wing populist vote maximization was highly controversial at home and abroad. Schüssel's greatest challenge, however, was managing the consequences of the decision he made to pursue his policy and office goals in a coalition with the FPÖ. The twin tasks he faced were governing with such an unpredictable partner and dealing with the tensions caused by it within his own party. This analysis of how he dealt with these internal and external pressures will be subdivided into three sections: the years leading up to the formation of Schüssel's first government on 4 February 2000, the lifetime of that administration, and the second Schüssel government, which lasted from 28 February 2003 until 11 January 2007.

Preparing to Break the Mold: 1995-1999

Internal Constraints and External Preferences

In 1986, the ÖVP garnered an historic low of 41.3 percent of the national vote, and at the elections of October 1990 and 1994 that dropped even further—to 32.1 percent and 27.7 percent respectively—leaving the ÖVP just five points above the FPÖ. According to Kenneth Janda, electoral defeat is the "mother of party change,"[2] but the ÖVP failed to respond to any of these losses with significant organizational reform, limiting itself instead to criticizing frequently and then replacing its chairmen. Successive ÖVP leaders had been aware that the party's peculiar internal structure severely constrained its capacity to respond to the rapidly changing political environment and thus undermined the national party's potential to realize two of the main goals pursued by political parties, namely vote maximization and office.[3] The main stumbling block to extensive organizational reform has been the entrenched power of the three functional Leagues that have together always not only provided the overwhelming majority of the ÖVP's indirect membership, but also been closely linked to Austria's extensive system of social partnership: the Austrian Farmers League (*Österreichischer Bauernbund*, or ÖBB), the Austrian Business League

(*Österreichischer Wirtschaftsbund*, or ÖWB) and the Austrian Workers and Employees League (*Österreichischer Arbeiter- und Angestelltenbund*, or ÖAAB).[4] As Wolfgang Müller and Barbara Steininger have argued by reference to George Tsebelis' nested games theory,[5] from the perspective of the leaders of the Leagues, it was rational to resist organizational reform. For one, it threatened their intra-party office and power. Moreover, the Leagues were motivated above all by policy goals, which could be pursued via Austria's neo-corporatist channel of decision making, even in conditions such as those that existed from 1970 to 1987, when the party was excluded from national office, let alone when it was the junior coalition partner.

As incoming ÖVP leader, Schüssel had a greater incentive to revive the ÖVP's national vote and regain the chancellorship. His policy priorities included European integration, as well as privatization of state enterprises and a considerable liberalization of Austria's economy (no doubt shaped by having been the ÖWB's General Secretary from 1975-1991). Given that major organizational reform of the ÖVP was not an option, Schüssel's maximization of his policy, vote, and office goals relied mainly on altering the party's external relations. He had two main strategic alternatives and until 1999 sought to keep both open. The first was heading up an ÖVP-SPÖ coalition. Even assuming the requisite electoral plurality could be won, this was unlikely to deliver fully Schüssel's economic policy preferences because they were not shared by the SPÖ and would probably also be undermined by the policy and procedural constraints of social partnership. A second alternative was forming a government with Haider's FPÖ, again on the basis of a plurality of votes. This appears initially not to have been his preferred option. Although the FPÖ had long opposed social partnership, it was markedly Euroskeptic and considered by many both within and without the ÖVP to be not only an unreliable, opposition-oriented partner, but also beyond the political pale, not least in view of its xenophobia and relativization of Austria's Nazi past.

Yet the ÖVP was never uniformly opposed to governing with the FPÖ. This had from the outset been favored by former ÖAAB leader Alois Mock, for example, who had led the ÖVP from 1979 to 1989, and was probably opposed most consistently by the influential ÖBB. A coalition with the FPÖ was most clearly ruled out during the leadership of Schüssel's predecessor, Erhard Busek, which commenced a fortnight after Haider's reference of 13 June 1991 to the "orderly employment policy of the Third Reich," as a result of which Haider was forced to resign the governorship of Carinthia. Shortly after Schüssel became chairman, his conservative competitor for the leadership and subsequent close ally, ÖAAB member Andreas Khol, characterized the FPÖ as "beyond the constitutional arch" (*außerhalb des Verfassungsbogens*).[6] Yet behind the scenes, there were numerous tentative discussions between (intermediaries of) the two parties about possible cooperation and even occasional direct meetings between Schüssel and Haider.[7] For its part, the FPÖ had shortly after the 1994 election secretly decided that if it were to obtain sufficient votes at the next general election (scheduled for 1998), it would seek to enter government. It therefore welcomed Busek's departure and started to take steps to make itself appear to be a credible governing party. In August 1995, for example, Haider publically rejected nostalgic Pan-Germanism (*Deutschtümelei*),[8] and for the first time in ten years, the FPÖ started to develop detailed position papers, not only on immigration, but also, for example, on savings, taxation, industrial, and pension policies.[9]

Schüssel's First Attempt at the Chancellorship

Within months of becoming party leader and vice-chancellor, Schüssel started adopting a more confrontational line *vis-à-vis* the SPÖ. With the ÖVP now ahead in the polls, in October 1995 he refused to compromise on his proposed spending cuts and forced a premature election. It appears Schüssel's preference was to use the ÖVP's predicted plurality to assume the chancellorship in a coalition with the SPÖ. In a departure from the post-1986 consensus, however, he refused to rule out a coalition with the FPÖ. The SPÖ's highlighting of that possibility and its claims that Schüssel planned to cut pensions helped ensure that, while the ÖVP's vote rose marginally (to 28.3 percent) at the election of 17 December, the SPÖ's grew by three percentage points (to 38.1 percent). Assuming he could have wrested the role of government *formateur* from the SPÖ (as he was to do after the 1999 election), Schüssel could again theoretically have formed a government with the FPÖ. Such a mold-breaking coalition still lacked political viability, however. Rather than increasing the ÖVP-FPÖ parliamentary majority from five to the hoped-for ten, the election has decreased it to three. The FPÖ had slipped from 22.5 percent to 21.9 percent and as yet had made little progress with its new strategy of presenting itself as a credible governing party. Schüssel's toying with an FPÖ coalition had also alienated significant numbers of ÖVP partisans and many party functionaries, with the result that he could not be sure of the requisite intra-party support.

Snatching Victory from the Jaws of Defeat

Once the SPÖ-ÖVP coalition had been reconstituted on 12 March 1996, Schüssel persisted with a two-pronged strategy towards the FPÖ. On the one hand, he continued quietly to encourage it to make changes that would reduce intra-ÖVP resistance to a possible coalition. The FPÖ duly adopted a number of market-oriented economic and fiscal policies. These were reasserted in its 1997 new program, where this traditionally anti-clerical party also stated "[t]he preservation of the intellectual foundations of the West necessitates a Christianity that defends its values" and maintained it was "an ideal partner of the Christian churches."[10] This went down especially well with the Catholic-conservative wing of the ÖVP, with which Khol had long been associated. On the other hand, normal competition was maintained. This included attacking the FPÖ *inter alia* for its Euroskepticism and demagogy, as well as trying to undermine its capacity to win votes on the immigration issue by supporting the 1997 Integration Package and the 1998 Naturalization Act, which tightened up policy in this area. Yet the FPÖ continued to gain votes, while the ÖVP suffered numerous losses.[11]

Schüssel's leadership predictably came under internal pressure, but there was no clear alternative. Most in the ÖVP attributed the party's ongoing electoral decline in large measure to its junior coalition status and deeply resented both this and the SPÖ's alleged high-handedness. Indeed, in early 1997 an incandescent ÖVP nearly terminated the coalition after SPÖ Finance Minister Viktor Klima approved not only the government-agreed privatization of the SPÖ-dominated Bank Austria, but also the latter's takeover of the ÖVP-dominated Creditanstalt. A few internal voices maintained that the only way out of the SPÖ's politically damaging embrace was cooperation with the FPÖ, which would, they argued, demystify it and thus undercut its electoral support. Yet most continued to regard the FPÖ as uncoalitionable and saw no alternative to playing second fiddle to the SPÖ as long as the ÖVP remained behind it in the polls. Until that changed, Schüssel clearly had no incentive to precipitate premature elections again. Instead, he continued to seek to enhance his party's programmatic distinctiveness *vis-à-vis* the SPÖ. The ÖVP increased its emphasis on neo-liberal economic policy and budget consolidation, confronted SPÖ-oriented labor organizations, and even challenged Austria's foreign policy consensus by questioning the continued relevance of neutrality. Schüssel also sought to capitalize politically on the role his position as foreign minister gave him during Austria's first European Union Presidency (July to December 1998).

At the election of 3 October 1999, the SPÖ lost 5 percent of the vote but remained the strongest party (33.2 percent). The FPÖ leapt to 26.9

percent, while the ÖVP not only recorded another historic low (26.9 percent), but for the first time ever came third, albeit by only 415 votes. After the September polls predicted an even worse result, Schüssel sought to rally ÖVP voters by stating that, were the party to come third, he would lead it into opposition.[12] Instead, he now pursued tactics that were so crucial in making his reputation as a shrewd and ruthless can-do politician, capable of snatching victory from the jaws of defeat, that it is worth detailing them here.

Notwithstanding the ÖVP's calamitous result, Schüssel had opportunities he could exploit. Internally, a shell-shocked ÖVP was divided over its response. Externally, the SPÖ was constrained by its self-imposed injunction against collaborating with the FPÖ, while Schüssel was willing to do so and there had already been behind-the-scenes discussions between the two parties. The political initiative was not Schüssel's, however, but the SPÖ's, which was the party entrusted with the task of forming a government. The ensuing 124 days constituted the second-longest period of coalition-building in the Second Republic's history.[13]

For two months, Schüssel openly engaged in exploratory talks with both parties. Though he had no intention of allowing the ÖVP to go into opposition, he had at that stage not identified his preferred coalition, even to some of his closest allies.[14] Uncertainty regarding his intentions only strengthened his position *vis-à-vis* his interlocutors. On 13 December, Schüssel obtained a unanimous party executive decision to replace his pre-election "irrevocable" commitment to opposition with an agreement to enter coalition negotiations with the SPÖ while keeping all options open.[15] The same day, the FPÖ executive committee decided the FPÖ would in the coming weeks compile its own government program. By then, ÖVP-FPÖ negotiations were apparently quite advanced.[16] As in 1995, Haider gave a public declaration designed to assuage those convinced his attitude regarding the Nazi past made his party unfit to govern,[17] and the FPÖ released documents seeking to demonstrate it had a credible policy agenda.[18] Formal SPÖ-ÖVP negotiations started on 17 December, and though both parties agreed to keep them confidential, enough points of contention leaked out to ensure that by early January 2000 intra-ÖVP opposition to renewing a coalition with the SPÖ grew, *inter alia* from the leaders of the provincial parties of Styria, Burgenland, and Lower Austria, but also from the ÖWB and ÖAAB. Many supported the option of going into opposition and allowing the SPÖ to form a minority government, but some (including the ÖAAB and the Styrian branch) were openly advocating an ÖVP-FPÖ coalition. Others (including the Viennese, Tyrolean, and Upper Austrian parties, as well as most of the ÖBB) were still opposed to that option, and there were even murmurings that if such a government were formed, the ÖVP might split.

Schüssel needed to be seen as giving serious consideration to a coalition with the SPÖ and on 16 January obtained the approval of the leaders of the Leagues and of the provincial parties for him to complete the negotiations, the draft agreement of which was approved on 17 January by the SPÖ executive committee. At the last minute, however, he made a series of policy, portfolio, and procedural demands of the SPÖ, almost certainly knowing it would be unable to accept them. On 21 January, the negotiations duly collapsed. Despite having no presidential mandate to do so, on 24 January Schüssel announced he and Haider would be commencing coalition negotiations. On 1 February, the day after the Portuguese EU Presidency's publication of a threat to impose diplomatic sanctions should the FPÖ enter government, the two parties revealed they had reached agreement. Extremely important for Schüssel's chances of overcoming internal resistance to collaborating with the FPÖ was that the ÖVP was to regain the chancellorship and Haider would not enter the government.[19]

Viewed as a whole, Schüssel's post-election behavior lends weight to the hypothesis that he had by December at the latest decided upon governmental collaboration with the FPÖ. That would imply that his brinkmanship *vis-à-vis* the SPÖ was designed above all to help overcome internal resistance to that decision. Externally, it served to present the SPÖ and President Klestil with a *fait accompli*. These events also illustrate well two of Schüssel's main leadership strengths, namely his capacity to utilize environmental crises to achieve his policy and office goals and his willingness to employ high-risk tactics to secure them, even in the face of internal and external resistance.

The First Schüssel Government (2000-2003)

With his government sworn in on 4 February 2000, Schüssel had achieved his pre-eminent office goal and now needed to manage the ÖVP's internal and external relations in a manner that consolidated his position and realized his policy objectives. That task appeared to have been complicated by the unforeseen international sanctions against the new government. At Klestil's insistence, Schüssel and Haider had on 3 February signed a preamble to their government program, committing themselves *inter alia* to European Union membership and to principles of tolerance, but this could neither avert the sanctions, nor prevent them from galvanizing mass anti-government demonstrations in Vienna and elsewhere.

Internal Relations

The ÖVP was delighted at having regained the chancellorship and relegated the SPÖ to the opposition for only the second time since 1945. Yet there was also near universal dismay amongst ÖVP activists that their party—which they regarded as the embodiment of pro-European sentiment and governmental responsibility—was being reviled internationally for having facilitated right-wing extremist entryism. A significant proportion of the party still regarded collaborating with the FPÖ as anathema and was unconvinced this coalition could either reverse the ÖVP's electoral decline, or realize its various policy preferences. In the event Schüssel's determination to face down the sanctions and his call for a closing of ranks (*Schulterschluß*) against allegedly unjustified external intervention into Austria's domestic affairs stymied the intra-party criticism he had always expected he would face. Moreover, the lifting of the sanctions in September 2000 and the ÖVP's spectacular eleven percentage point gain at October's Styrian *Landtag* elections appeared to vindicate his position. To be sure, internal distaste at collaboration with the FPÖ persisted throughout both Schüssel governments, but he had survived the crucial first few months.

More was, of course, needed to secure long-term support in a party that has always been extremely decentralized, with resource distribution weighted in favor of the Leagues and (to a lesser extent) the provincial parties.[20] First, Schüssel needed to ensure an equitable representation of the Leagues in the key party and governmental posts at his disposal. He was himself identified with the ÖWB and throughout his chancellorship had two key ÖWB confidants: Waltraud Klasnic, who was from 1996 to 2005 governor of Styria and leader of the Styrian party, and Martin Bartenstein, his economics minister and since 1992 Styria's deputy party leader.[21] The requisite ÖAAB incorporation was undertaken *inter alia* by giving the caucus leadership and the position of third president of the parliament to two of its senior members.[22] Former ÖBB Director Wilhelm Molterer retained the Agriculture Ministry, and Maria Rauch-Kallat, leader since 1988 of the Women's League, was appointed the ÖVP's general secretary. Second, as the ÖVP's politically most sensitive internal decisions typically require ratification by the party executive, membership of which comprises mainly ex-officio rather than elected representatives and is thus not within the leader's gift, Schüssel invested considerable effort in networking designed to ensure these bodies returned the decisions he wished. He maintained close contacts with key provincial party actors, chief among whom was Erwin Pröll, governor of Lower Austria and leader of its mighty provincial party, who had initially opposed collaborating with the FPÖ. Moreover, Schüssel made sure the key component elements of the party were linked to the ÖVP's informal decision-making systems. Foremost amongst these was his "kitchen cabinet." Its regular Monday meetings made day-to-day decisions on government business and ensured a two-way information flow with the Leagues, not least through the caucus, the internal organization of which is based around League membership. The kitchen cabinet embraced Schüssel's two deputies (one each from the ÖBB and ÖAAB)[23] and caucus leader Khol, who were all close confidants, as well as the general secretary.

Last but by no means least, Schüssel used such communication channels to convince in particular the Leagues of the benefits provided to them by the coalition. Individual functionaries and activists benefited from selective incentives such as the provision of positions, but also from the solidary incentive of belonging to the chancellor party. Moreover, while the pragmatic policy prioritization of the Leagues had hitherto conflicted with Schüssel's greater emphasis upon vote maximization and office holding, they now mainly worked to his advantage. At the risk of oversimplification, internal support was secured above all by the provision of collective or policy incentives, though the disparate material interests of the Leagues meant Schüssel could not satisfy all of them equally. The greatest support came from the ÖWB, which was enamored of the government's emphasis on neo-liberalism, privatization, and achieving a zero budget deficit. Big business in particular welcomed the coalition's willingness not only to ignore the wishes of the social partners—which the ÖWB had long held to constitute an unacceptable break on necessary reforms—but also to overrule them, not least since this meant reducing the power of organized labor.[24] Collective incentives in the form of a more generous subsidy regime were also provided for the ÖBB, which, despite its initial opposition to collaborating with the FPÖ, was soon on board.

The situation with the ÖAAB was more difficult. Soon after taking office, the government started ruthlessly to sideline or remove as many SPÖ partisans as it could from positions in the state bureaucracy, as well as in (privatized) state enterprises and other para-state organizations, such as the Austrian Federal Railways and the Austrian Highways Agency, ASFINAG. While some such positions went to FPÖ partisans, the majority were available for those of the ÖVP, many of whom were ÖAAB members. For the ÖAAB as a whole, however, such selective incentives were canceled out by negative consequences of the government's neo-liberal policies and its pursuit of civil service reform for workers and salaried employees. Both led to job losses and resentment from within the ÖAAB's ranks at what was considered the prioritization of the interests of capital over those of labor. Though these were policies to which Schüssel was personally committed, it appears he used the fact that the relevant portfolios were held by FPÖ ministries to try to deflect some of the ÖAAB's criticism onto his coalition partner, claiming that maintaining the coalition for which the ÖAAB had long argued required certain policy sacrifices.[25] For now, Schüssel appeared able to keep the ÖAAB more-or-less on board.

External Relations[26]

The formation and actions of the ÖVP-FPÖ coalition led to a significant polarization of Austrian politics. The ÖVP's relationship with the SPÖ was considerably worse than it had ever been. The SPÖ still considered the FPÖ beyond the political pale and could not forgive Schüssel for how he had outmaneuvered the SPÖ to take the chancellorship, to which it felt entitled as the electorally strongest party. Moreover, in pursuit of its neo-liberal policy agenda, but also in order to extend its political power, the coalition rode roughshod over Austrian social partnership and systematically sought to eradicate as much SPÖ influence as possible from the civil service and state-controlled economy. Though the international sanctions initially complicated aspects of day-to-day government business (especially when it pertained to foreign affairs), their broader impact was to undermine the opposition parties. Their failure to denounce them permitted Schüssel to accuse them of national disloyalty and to bind the coalition parties closer together. Indeed, Schüssel demonstrated his defiant commitment to the coalition by regular joint appearances with FPÖ Vice-Chancellor Susanne Riess-Passer.

On paper, the coalition partners appeared fairly evenly matched. The ÖVP held the ministries of Foreign Affairs, Education, Internal Affairs, Agriculture, and Economics and Labor. The FPÖ's portfolios included those of Finance, Justice, Defense, Social Affairs, and Transport. Yet it very soon became clear to Schüssel that the FPÖ's ministerial team was of markedly uneven quality. Within a month, the Justice Minister resigned, and in October 2000, the widely-ridiculed Minister of Social Affairs had to be replaced. Four months later, the Minister for Transport resigned, and his replacement only lasted thirteen months. This quick turnover appeared to vindicate critics' assertions that the FPÖ was unfit to govern, and it created public relations problems for Schüssel. Within the coalition, however, it strengthened the ÖVP's position, bearing out Schüssel's expectation that the FPÖ would turn out to be the less effective governing party. The ÖVP had served in government for the preceding fourteen years, and its ministers (barring the interior minister) were able to capitalize upon considerable levels of civil service support. By contrast, not one FPÖ minister had a prior record of holding national executive office and—with the partial exception of the ministers of Defense and Finance—all found themselves in charge of ministries staffed by civil servants among whom the number of FPÖ partisans was vanishingly small. Furthermore, the ÖVP could draw on the policy expertise of their Leagues and the social partnership institutions with which they were associated, but the FPÖ had no access to such support for policy development and implementation.

As stipulated in the coalition agreement, the ultimate forum for coordinating relations between the governing parties was the coalition committee. It was here that Schüssel had intended government strategy be harmonized and the politically most sensitive decisions made, since Haider's membership would ensure he share governmental responsibility despite not being a minister himself. However, Haider frequently absented himself from meetings at which unpopular decisions were scheduled to be made and in February 2002 finally left the committee altogether. Notwithstanding the fact that Riess-Passer had in May 2000 formally taken over the FPÖ's leadership from Haider, the latter remained its *de facto* leader. Schüssel's inability to bind Haider within the coalition committee made it very difficult for Schüssel to identify and maintain a consistent coalition line. The main venues for coalition coordination were now the well-established weekly pre-cabinet meetings between him and the vice-chancellor and the broader preparatory meeting (*Ministerratsvorbesprechung*) including all government ministers and the caucus leaders that convened shortly thereafter. In general, these coordination mechanisms operated in quite a businesslike and efficient manner, and Schüssel made considerable efforts to lavish praise upon the performance of Riess-Passer and the telegenic Karl-Heinz Grasser, neither of whom were associated with the FPÖ's more right-wing radical elements.

Whether by accident or design, this increased the gap between the FPÖ government team on the one hand and Haider and the wider FPÖ on the other. In part, that distance was a function of the fact that only about half the FPÖ ministers were well-rooted in their party and some were not even party members. Yet there were more fundamental problems. For one, the FPÖ never fully mastered the transition from a party of populist vote maximization to one of governmental responsibility.[27] The basic orientation of most grassroots functionaries and even of some Members of Parliament (MPs) was oppositional, and many were thus unwilling to accept the exigencies of incumbency. Accordingly, once the discipline of the international sanctions was gone and Haider himself started to vacillate between supporting and attacking the government, they, too, felt free to voice their dissatisfaction. Second, there were significant policy differences between Schüssel and the FPÖ. To be sure, there was complete agreement on matters such as a fixed child payment for all parents (the co-called children's check), the extension of employee redundancy rights, and circumventing neo-corporatist decision-making. One area of conflict concerned EU enlargement. However, the main disagreement (both within the FPÖ and between it and the ÖVP) was over the government's economic policy and in particular over what many considered Schüssel's excessive pursuit of a zero budget deficit. Though this necessarily also became closely identified with Grasser, it was never wholeheartedly endorsed by the FPÖ. Indeed, this dispute highlighted the extent to which the FPÖ had—in the interests of coalescing with the ÖVP—adopted a number of neo-liberal policies fundamentally at odds with other elements of its programmatic profile, including its emphasis on social policy and tax reform designed to defend the "little guy." As economic growth declined, unemployment increased, and the government's tax take rose to an all-time high (in part to secure the zero deficit via increased taxation rather than via spending cuts), these tensions become more acute.

The upshot of such policy differences and the FPÖ's deep internal divisions over the switch from protest to incumbency was that Schüssel was confronted by a seemingly unending series of coalition crises. The tactics he used to deal with them included largely ignoring both the FPÖ's dissenting voices and the acts of political provocation by Haider and others in the FPÖ.[28] This response caused critics of the coalition to describe him as a "silent chancellor" (*Schweigekanzler*), who chose to close his eyes to the predictable consequences of his decision to collaborate with a right-wing populist party. It also frustrated Haider, who felt increasingly sidelined, and further alienated many FPÖ dissidents, for whom Schüssel's unwillingness to compromise on, in particular, his economic policy priorities appeared high-handed.

Matters came to a head in the summer of 2002 in the so-called "Knittelfeld crisis," named after a Styrian town in which FPÖ grassroots functionaries staged a revolt against their ministers.[29] The catalyst was the government's insistence on sticking to the zero deficit goal and delaying the planned tax reforms intended to reduce the burden of taxation on the middle classes, while simultaneously confirming the purchase of an expensive new generation of interceptor jets. Disavowed in this way, Riess-Passer and her cabinet team resigned, whereupon Schüssel promptly terminated the coalition.

At the elections of 24 November 2002, the SPÖ made a modest recovery (to 36.5 percent) and the Greens also increased their vote share (from 7.4 percent to 9.5 percent). The greatest beneficiary by far of the FPÖ's catastrophic fall to merely 10 percent of the vote was Schüssel's ÖVP. Its 42.3 percent share constituted the largest percentage increase ever enjoyed by an Austrian party and was the ÖVP's best result since 1983. This significantly enhanced the reputation as an astute political operator that Schüssel had acquired after the 1999 election (see above), not least within the euphoric ÖVP. For one, the FPÖ's self-destruction that had triggered the election was regarded by many as a testament to the efficacy of Schüssel's strategy of bringing the FPÖ into governmental responsibility. It had also brought about the ÖVP's long-awaited electoral revival. Moreover, the fact that the ÖVP had managed to win over approximately half of the FPÖ's 1999 voters was attributed in large measure to Schüssel's election campaign, one of the apparently most successful elements of which was the co-called "Grasser coup," that is, his persuading Grasser to agree serve as a non-partisan minister in the government Schüssel hoped to form after the election.[30]

The Second Schüssel Government (2003-2007)

Coalition Building

The 2002 election had fundamentally transformed Schüssel's external position. As leader of the largest party he was now in the driver's seat of the coalition-building process, was guaranteed the chancellorship, and could in principle form a majority government with any of the three other parties. Internally, he had been greatly strengthened by the scale of the party's victory, but again faced strongly divergent coalition preferences. Schüssel was committed to continuing to break the mold of consensual politics, which implied renewed collaboration with the FPÖ. However, its conduct in the outgoing administration had re-invigorated internal support for a coalition with the SPÖ. This included the leaders of the two largest provincial parties (Josef Pühringer of Upper Austria and Pröll of Lower Austria), as well as ÖWB President Leitl. They were supported externally by President Klestil and by the social partners, who wanted neo-corporatist consensualism restored. Schüssel's need to balance internal and external considerations helps explain why the coalition-building process was again unusually long.[31] In public, he once more kept all options open, but a coalition with the SPÖ was never likely. The last negotiations had left a legacy of very bad blood, and the parties shared virtually no substantive agreement, especially on economic and social policy.[32] Moreover, an ÖVP-SPÖ coalition implied reviving the consensual social partnership structures and would also require the greatest portfolio concessions. Though on 21 January 2003 the SPÖ's executive committee voted in favor of formal coalition negotiations, these thus never materialized.

While many had foreseen this outcome, Schüssel retained his capacity to surprise, offering exploratory talks to the Greens, derided in the ÖVP's campaign as irresponsible lefties. Despite their unpreparedness and post-election commitment to stay in opposition, the Greens attended. On 13 December, their executive approved the talks' continuation and on 5 February sanctioned formal negotiations.[33] They ultimately failed (on 16 February), however, *inter alia* because of differences on social, pension, education, defense and traffic policy. An ÖVP-Green coalition had always been unlikely and vehemently opposed by ÖVP conservatives, including the ÖBB. Some have suggested Schüssel entered negotiations for tactical reasons, including to put pressure on other negotiation partners, to be seen as having explored even the most unlikely options before again collaborating with the FPÖ, or to set a marker for potential future cooperation. Yet insider reports suggest the negotiations were serious.[34] Moreover, it is worth noting they were welcomed by many of the ÖVP's young and educated urban members, for whom an ÖVP-Green coalition offered the potential for an intellectually attractive alternative to renewed collaboration with the FPÖ.

The latter is what eventually emerged, however. As early as 25 November, the FPÖ executive had voted in support of reviving the coalition, and at initial soundings on 5 December, the FPÖ immediately indicated a willingness to make major policy concessions. On 20 December, the ÖVP supported the FPÖ candidate's election as Third President of Parliament, and on 28 January, the FPÖ caucus for its part supported the ÖVP's provisional budget. Five days after the ÖVP-Green negotiation failed, the FPÖ's executive committee voted for formal negotiations with the ÖVP. These were successfully completed within a week, and the new government was installed on 28 February 2003.

Internal Relations

Internal resistance to again collaborating with the FPÖ had persisted. Even at the party executive meeting of 20 February approving Schüssel's proposal to enter formal negotiations with the FPÖ, for example, Pröll and Pühringer voted against, while Leitl and Tyrolean party leader Herwig von Staa abstained. Schüssel's distribution of the ÖVP's cabinet ministries hinted that he wished to build internal bridges. Tyrolean ÖAAB leader Günther Platter became defense minister and Josef Pröll, nephew of the Lower Austrian governor and since 2001 director of the ÖBB, became minister of agriculture. However, these developments also indicate how the 2002 election had enhanced Schüssel's intra-party authority. Despite objections, the Finance Ministry went to Grasser, who had resigned from the FPÖ and was now wholly dependent on Schüssel. Schüssel's confidants Gehrer and Bartenstein remained in post, as did Foreign Minister Benita Ferrero-Waldner, a faithful Schüssel lieutenant.[35] Rauch-Kallat, who had loyally served Schüssel as general secretary, was promoted to health minister. The new general secretary was Styrian Reinhold Lopatka, who had won his national spurs as the aggressive manager of the 2002 election campaign, while Schüssel loyalist Molterer now chaired the caucus. Molterer played a key role in the party's informal internal communication and decision-making networks, including the kitchen cabinet. Yet the flow of communication between the ÖVP's government team and the party's constituent units was to be more top-down than it had been hitherto. In sum, Schüssel enjoyed greater personal political control over the ÖVP's now enlarged ministerial team and appeared less willing to allow his policy preferences to be constrained by the party.

Schüssel's determination that his new government push forward his neo-liberal agenda was welcomed by the ÖWB, which supported his spending cuts, tightening of unemployment benefit rules, and instituting privatization and reform programs, not least when they pertained to SPÖ spheres of influence such as the nationalized industries (VOEST) and the Austrian Federal Railways. Yet there was also unhappiness in some parts of the ÖVP about the consequences of the government's confrontational style. These included the unusual sight of industrial unrest in response to the coalition's 2003 proposals regarding the railways and pension reform. Indeed, within two months of the government's formation, Leitl (acting as president of the Austrian Chamber of Commerce) joined with the SPÖ-oriented Trades Union Federation—a fellow social partner institution—to call for the government's pension reform proposals to be withdrawn. The ÖVP-FPÖ government's relentless neo-liberal emphasis increasingly brought Schüssel into conflict with the ÖAAB, the leadership of which has always overlapped with the civil service union. The ÖAAB was in the vanguard of protests against the 2003 and 2004 pensions reform bills. It obtained some modifications, but remained convinced its interests were under attack.

Schüssel also faced internal dissatisfaction from provincial parties. After an 8.4 percent gain in the Lower Austrian *Landtag* elections of March 2003 (which benefited Governor Pröll), the electoral trend changed markedly. The FPÖ's ever more rapidly declining vote increasingly benefited the SPÖ rather than the ÖVP. In September 2003, for example, the Upper Austrian ÖVP saw its vote increase by 0.7 percent, while that of the SPÖ soared by 11.3 percent. It attributed the scale of its defeat largely to the government's aggressive stance in respect of its controversial pension reform proposals, which had dominated Austrian politics during the preceding months, and to the announcement just weeks before the election of the contentious proposed privatization of the VOEST. Politically, the most painful consequences of analogous defeats at many other elections[36] were the losses of the governorships of Salzburg and Styria, which left the ÖVP with only four (of nine), the lowest share in its history. Such results contributed significantly to one of the main intra-party trends in Schüssel's second government, namely a growing distance between the chancellor and his party. There was a perception on the ground that he had become out of touch and was exhibiting a lack of concern about the negative impact of his government's policies and confrontational style on provincial parties' political fortunes. Inextricably linked with this was his chosen coalition partner, which was again proving unreliable, lacking in competence, and prone to public pronouncements that were highly embarrassing. Indeed, one national-level ÖVP functionary maintains that frustration at the ongoing problems with the FPÖ "was the main motor of intra-party dissatisfaction within the coalition … and was present until the very end … by which time nobody wanted … this coalition partner … anymore."[37]

There are two main reasons why internal dissatisfaction did not generate a challenge to Schüssel's leadership. First, his government continued to provide incentives to key intra-party power brokers. In particular, it was still delivering on the policy preferences of two of the three Leagues (the ÖWB and ÖBB), who thus had no interest in risking internal change. Second, he had acquired a reputation as a formidable political operator, which meant that notwithstanding the ÖVP's string of electoral defeats and the fact that from 2003 until March 2006 it was consistently behind the SPÖ in the polls, there was a belief Schüssel would somehow again be able to pull the political chestnuts out of the fire. The ÖVP's underestimation of the SPÖ threat was based, in part, on a disdain for SPÖ leader Alfred Gusenbauer, but also on a hope that the expected economic revival would come in time for the election of autumn 2006. In early 2006, unemployment did indeed start to decline, and when a major financial scandal centered on the bank of the SPÖ-oriented Austrian Trade Union Federation (BAWAG) broke in March, it appeared the ÖVP would get its last-minute reprieve.

Yet to the surprise of most ÖVP supporters, the party lost the 2006 election and with it the chancellorship. Schüssel soon resigned the chairmanship in favor of Molterer, but rather than withdrawing from politics, he assumed the latter's position as caucus chair. This fueled speculation that notwithstanding the party's electoral defeat, parliamentary arithmetic, and the FPÖ's oppositional orientation, he might yet attempt a political comeback. This was unlikely to be successful, however. His second government's problems collaborating with Austria's right-wing populists strengthened those within the party favoring a return to grand coalition government, a goal achieved in 2007. Molterer's gamble of July 2008 to precipitate early elections with a view to regaining an ÖVP plurality failed to pay off at the election of 28 September 2008. The ÖVP leadership then passed to Josef Pröll, whose strategy was to resume a more consensual line and form a coalition with the SPÖ. The pragmatic Leagues were thus again able to obtain policy objectives via the re-instituted system of social partnership, and the ÖVP's stasis-inclined structure once again militated against internal change.

External Relations

Schüssel entered his second administration from a position of strength that one might assume would permit him to dominate the ÖVP's external relations. The cabinet over which he presided included eight ÖVP nominees, but merely three FPÖ ministers. In the coalition agreement, the FPÖ had effectively capitulated on all the issues that had been the subject of its internal "Knittelfeld rebellion" (including EU enlargement, delayed tax reform, and budget consolidation) and had signed up to what amounted to an acceleration of Schüssel's neo-liberal policy preferences. Moreover, Schüssel's potential to force through that agenda appeared to have been enhanced by the scale of his party's electoral victory, which in turn reinforced his determination not to be constrained by Austria's consensual extra-parliamentary system of social partnership.

Yet even at the outset, there were signs that governing with the FPÖ might again prove challenging. For one, Riess-Passer's resignation of the FPÖ leadership had left the party rudderless. Haider having refused to step up to the plate, there were three interim leaders before a party congress of 12 December 2002 confirmed provisional leader Herbert Haupt, the outgoing social affairs minister. Though uncontested, he could only muster 87.8 percent of the delegate vote. A related second sign of the problems to come was the FPÖ's disunity over re-entering government. November's caucus vote for entering coalition negotiations had been unanimous, but support amongst the grassroots members remained weak. At the party executive meeting of 28 February approving the coalition agreement, two members had voted against the proposal. More ominously, the FPÖ leadership felt unable to accede to internal pressure for an extraordinary party conference to ratify the agreement and left this to a meeting of the party directorate. Only 119 of the 240 members attended, and of these, eleven voted against. Third, Haider was even less tied into the coalition than before. Having refused to resume the party leadership, he had declared (albeit neither for the first nor the last time) his irrevocable intention to withdraw from national politics. He had thus not participated in the coalition negotiations and remained a potent and potentially disruptive force within the FPÖ.

The FPÖ grassroots' populist orientation and hostility to much of the government's agenda endured throughout Schüssel's administration and were manifested in numerous policy fields. How they were to impact Schüssel's management of the coalition was well illustrated in the government's very first major project: the 2003 pension reform. In late March, Schüssel obtained his coalition partner's agreement to a white paper submitted for public consultation. Within days, Haupt had felt obliged to respond to the enormous backlash from within the FPÖ by proposing (without prior consultation with Schüssel) that the reform be subjected to a popular referendum. Schüssel managed on 29 April to get the bill through cabinet (where, as with all cabinet decisions, it required unanimous support), but at a subsequent meeting of the FPÖ executive, four of the nine provincial party leaders rejected it. Haupt then called on President Klestil (with whom Schüssel's relations had long been poor) to host a roundtable comprising the government and social partners to hammer out a compromise. It was unsuccessful, but after a number of additional meetings, many hosted by Schüssel in the Federal Chancellery, the cabinet passed its final draft pension bill on 4 June. This was approved by the parliamentary budget committee with the votes of the FPÖ and ÖVP, yet the very next day, eight of the FPÖ's eighteen MPs declared they would not support the bill in the plenary vote unless there were further reforms. Further compromises were found, and the bill passed on 11 June, but the process had clearly demonstrated that Schüssel could not rely upon the FPÖ leadership to deliver the support of the wider party for coalition policy.

Following another case of poor intra-coalition liaison in September 2003 (this time in connection with the proposed VOEST privatization) and the FPÖ's disastrous showing at that month's elections in Tyrol and Lower Austria (-11.6 percent and -11.6 percent respectively), the FPÖ replaced its coalition coordinator. Haupt also symbolically terminated his regular post-cabinet press conference appearance alongside Schüssel. Such symbolic responses could not resolve the FPÖ's four fundamental and interrelated structural problems, which together greatly complicated Schüssel's management of coalition relations. First, the 2002 Knittelfeld crisis had caused many of the more pragmatic elements of the FPÖ to leave the party, and protest-orientated elements were now being further strengthened by a succession of very poor election results.[38] Second, the FPÖ did not have a clearly identifiable and effective national leadership with whom Schüssel could negotiate. From the outset, Haupt was constantly under internal pressure, not least from Haider, who undermined him at every opportunity. Determined to resist pressure to resign, on 28 June 2003 Haupt engineered a vote of confidence in the party executive, but in October 2003 had to concede the appointment of an executive party leader. This was Haider's sister, Ursula Haubner, an Upper Austrian politician who on 3 July 2004 also replaced Haupt as leader (with only 79 percent of party congress delegate votes). Haubner reintegrated Haider into the national leadership, which gave Schüssel greater clarity over intra-party power relations, but Haider remained an unpredictable partner.

Third, the FPÖ's ministerial team was overall not well rooted in the party. The Justice Ministry initially remained in the hands of Dieter Böhmdorfer, Haider's personal lawyer, who was not a party member, and on 25 June 2004 passed to Karin Gastinger (née Miklautsch), another Haider nominee and non-party member. The social affairs minister was the luckless Haupt, who on 26 January 2005 was replaced by Haubner and who in October 2003 had already had to forfeit the vice-chancellorship to Transport Minister Hubert Gorbach. The latter was a business-oriented pragmatist from the small Vorarlberg branch that was used to governing with the ÖVP and who was for many in the FPÖ's grassroots organization far too quiescent. Fourth, while members of the FPÖ's cabinet team were detached from the party's grassroots, FPÖ MPs were exposed to constant pressure from their provincial parties to reflect grassroots opposition to government policy. Schüssel had in place a body comprising the caucus leaders, their administrative directors, and the heads of the offices of the chancellor and vice-chancellor that was charged with ensuring the passage of agreed upon legislation. However, he could not be confident of his coalition partner's capacity to deliver the requisite parliamentary majorities.

It is, thus, understandable that he did not object when on 4 April 2005 (after secret prior consultation with him) Haider established the League for the Future of Austria (*Bündnis Zukunt Österreich*, or BZÖ). It immediately guaranteed the government's majority and was to ensure that for the remainder of the government's terms Schüssel could act as though he headed a single-party government. For one, the BZÖ's capacity to counter his policy priorities was undermined by the claim made at its foundation that its distinctivess lay in governmental responsibility. Second, contrary to assurances Haider had given Schüssel, large parts of the FPÖ did not defect to the BZÖ, which in the polls was thereafter mainly just below the 4 percent share of the vote necessary for parliamentary representation. Accordingly, Schüssel knew it could not afford to precipitate elections. For Schüssel's supporters, the BZÖ constituted the ultimate confirmation of his strategy of collaborating with Austria's right-wing populists, since it appeared to have separated the FPÖ's more pragmatic forces from its incorrigible protest elements.

Relations within the coalition were now much easier for Schüssel, but his longer-term prospects for maintaining his office and policy goals were less encouraging. The ÖVP remained behind the SPÖ in the polls, and the BZÖ's electoral survival continued to be in doubt. Effectively ejected from governmental responsibility, the FPÖ had, by contrast, been freed to resume all-out populist vote maximization and by the summer of 2006 regained the albeit weak position it had enjoyed in the polls prior to the foundation of the BZÖ. Despite hopes that the BAWAG affair might rescue its fortunes, at the election of 1 October 2006, the ÖVP came in second to the SPÖ (by 34.5 to 35.5 percent). The BZÖ scraped in on 4 percent, while the FPÖ obtained 11 percent, the same as the Greens.[39] ÖVP losses were greatest amongst workers alienated by policies such as the pension reform. They were partly attributable to poor mobilization of the ÖVP's vote, especially where internal resentment against Schüssel had been greatest. Others criticized the ÖVP campaign's focus on the chancellor who, though respected as a fearsome strategist and tactician, was not popular. Moreover, the SPÖ had been successful in its three-year campaign to portray him as the embodiment of "social coldness," a label predicated upon the government's neo-liberal policies, but which his rather aloof style also did little to counter.

Between them, the ÖVP, FPÖ and BZÖ had a parliamentary majority (94 of 183 seats), but personal relations between the FPÖ and BZÖ ruled out this coalition combination, as did internal ÖVP opposition. Schüssel stayed on long enough as party leader to take charge of the ÖVP's coalition negotiation team. He faced in SPÖ *formateur* Gusenbauer someone as keen to be chancellor as he had been in 1999, but with only one politically realistic coalition option, namely an SPÖ-ÖVP government. Schüssel's reputation for unexpected coalition maneuvering provided a tactical advantage in the coalition negotiations in which he managed to achieve for the ÖVP an unexpectedly good outcome. Despite having lost the election, the party retained the Foreign Ministry and the key ministries of Finance and the Interior, both traditionally held by the SPÖ in grand coalitions. Moreover, the coalition agreement did not contain any radial change to the ÖVP's neo-liberal policy agenda. On 11 January 2007, Gusenbauer replaced Schüssel as chancellor, but weakened from the start by the concession he had made in the coalition negotiations, he was to prove the Second Republic's shortest-lived incumbent.

Conclusion

Schüssel can be regarded as a political entrepreneur motivated in particular by holding the highest political office and liberalizing economic policy. Unable to adapt the ÖVP's organization to his ends, his pursuit of these goals focused above all on altering the external constraints he faced. He had two major external options: replacing the SPÖ as the strongest party, or governing with the hitherto excluded right-wing populist FPÖ. He will be remembered for deciding to govern with the FPÖ and for his challenge to the decision-making style and economic policy consensus of postwar Austrian politics, but also for a leadership style characterized by ruthless exploitation of external and internal opportunities to achieve his goals.

Some of the external tactics he employed were successful. These included those adopted in the coalition negotiations after the 1999, 2002, and 2006 elections, as well as his decision to face down the international sanctions against his government. Others failed, including his 1995 attempt to win the chancellorship, as well as his 2006 election campaign. Moreover, while the FPÖ's self-destruction in 2002 and the formation of the BZÖ seemed at the time to have vindicated his prediction that bringing the right-wing populists into government would fatally undermine them, by 2008 the picture looked somewhat different. The combined FPÖ and BZÖ vote was even higher than that of the FPÖ in 1999. Internally, his tactics embraced informal networking, but above all relied upon the provision of a combination of selective and collective incentives to key power brokers such as the ÖVP's Leagues. Though the party remained divided throughout over both Schüssel's decision to govern with the FPÖ and his confrontational political style, he was able to establish and maintain sufficient internal authority to permit him to pursue his policy goals. Paradoxically, this was in part due to the inherently conservative nature of the party's internal structure, something that had originally constituted a hindrance to his office, policy, and vote goals.

A number of implications for the broader party system resulted from Schüssel's decision to bring the FPÖ in from the cold. It caused a considerable increase in political polarization. Indeed, the enduring bad blood between the ÖVP and SPÖ was one of the factors undermining the viability of the Gusenbauer government. Though both the SPÖ and ÖVP invested considerable effort in the early months of Walter Faymann's government in order to appear more conciliatory, it remains to be seen if consensus has really been restored. Second, Schüssel certainly initially liberated the ÖVP from the SPÖ's embrace and expanded his party's coalition possibilities, including in the direction of the Greens. On the other hand, the founding of the BZÖ freed the FPÖ to resume a strategy of populist vote maximization and generated personal animosities between these two parties that at least for some years undermined the ÖVP's prospects of forming a government with Austria's populist, radical right. Indeed, the overall shift in party strengths since 2006 means that the ÖVP is again left with few alternatives to the role of junior partner in a coalition with the SPÖ, an position which the ÖVP's still unreformed internal structure makes it difficult for an ÖVP leader to break out of.

Having said that, although the ÖVP's electoral defeats have to date not provoked the kind of organizational change predicted by Janda's thesis that such events are the "mother of party change",[40] they did in the late 1990s allow a strong political entrepreneur to change the party's external relations. In an age of greater electoral volatility, political entrepreneurs are more likely to encounter opportunities to alter their respective party's external competitive environment. To be able to capitalize on them, however, they will need to manage effectively both the internal and external consequences of their decisions.

Notes

1. Together, the ÖVP and FPÖ caucuses had the following number of seats in the 183-member National Council: 1986: 95; 1990: 93; 1994: 94.

2. Kenneth Janda, "Towards a Performance Theory of Change in Political Parties," Paper presented at the *World Congress of the International Sociological Association*, Madrid, 1990, 5.

3. Wolfgang C. Müller and Kaare Strøm, *Policy, Office, or Votes? How Political Parties in Western Europe Make Hard Decisions* (Cambridge: Cambridge UP, 1999).

4. Wolfgang C. Müller, "The Development of Austrian Party Organizations in the Post-war Period," in *How Parties Organize: Change and Adaptation in Party Organizations in Western Democracies*, ed. Richard S. Katz and Peter Mair (London: Sage, 1994), 51-79; Kurt Richard Luther, "Must What Goes Up always Come Down? Of Pillars and Arches in Austria's Political Architecture," in *Party Elites in Divided Societies: Political Parties in Consociational Democracy*, ed. Kurt Richard Luther and Kris Deschouwer (London: Routledge, 1999), 43-73.

5. Wolfgang C. Müller and Barbara Steininger, "Party Organisation and Party Competitiveness: The Case of the Austrian People's Party, 1945-1992," *European Journal of Political Research*, 26 (1994): 1-29.

6. Andreas Khol, "Die FPÖ im Spannungsfeld von Ausgrenzung, Selbstausgrenzung, Verfassungsbogen und Regierungsfähighkeit," in *Österreichisches Jahrbuch für Politik '95*, ed. Andreas Khol et al. (Oldenburg: Verlag für Geschichte und Politik, 1996) provides interesting clues about the foundations of possible future cooperation with the FPÖ. See also Andreas Khol, *Die Wende ist geglückt: der schwarz-blaue Marsch durch die Wüste Gobi*, 3rd ed. (Vienna: Molden, 2001).

7. Interviews conducted by the author with relevant actors. See also Lothar Höbelt, *Defiant Populist: Jörg Haider and the Politics of Austria* (West Lafayette, IL: Purdue UP, 2003) 107.

8. See *Wirtschaftswoche*, 17 August 1995; *Profil*, 21 August 1995, 27-33 and Haider's televised interview of 20 August 1995 with the state broadcasting company (*ORF-Sommergespräch*).

9. These appeared in publication series of the party academy (*Freiheitliche Akademie*) such as the *Reihe Vertrag mit Österreich* and the *Freie Argumente*.

10. Program of the Austrian Freedom Party, adopted 30 October 1997, Chapter V, Article 2.

11. Notably in Burgenland and Vienna in 1996 (-2.2 points to 36 percent and -2.8 points to 15.3 percent respectively); in Upper Austria in 1997 (-2.5 points to 42.7 percent); in Carinthia and Salzburg in March 1999 (-3.1 to 20.7 percent and -1.8 to 36.8 percent) and in Vorarlberg in September 1999 (-4.2 to 45.7 percent).

12. Exit poll data suggests this helped mitigate ÖVP losses: Fritz Plasser et al. ed. *Analyse der Nationalratswahl 1999* (Vienna: Zentrum für Angewandte Politikforschung, 1999).

13. At 129 days, the longest was that which in March 1963 resulted in ÖVP leader Alfons Gorbach's short-lived second administration.

14. Interviews by the author with an ÖVP functionary.

15. Asked to justify Schüssel's abandonment of his promise, Khol cited Francis Bacon's dictum, "Truth is the daughter of time" (*Die Wahrheit ist eine Tochter der Zeit*).

16. Interviews by the author with relevant high-level party actors.

17. "Speech on the State of the Republic" (*Rede zur Lage der Republik*) held on 12 November in the roof foyer of the Imperial Palace's Redouten Hall, in which he said he could no longer accept any brown shadows (*braune Schatten*) and personally apologized for any statements made in respect of National Socialism that "might well have been insensitive or given to misunderstanding" (Transcription provided by Haider's office). Haider also made numerous media appearances both at home and abroad.

18. The first (on 28 October) was entitled "Freedom Party Positions for the Future of Austria" (*Freiheitliche Positionen für die Zukunft Östererichs*).

19. The author's interviews with FPÖ actors suggest this was not a consequence of the EU's threatened sanctions, but of Haider's earlier decision to keep out of the cabinet until the FPÖ's hoped-for second term. After the FPÖ's victory at the Carinthian *Landtag* election of March 1999 (33.3 to 42.1 percent), Haider had been elected governor and undertaken to remain in post the full five years. Unconfirmed speculation suggests the Carinthian ÖVP's vote for Haider's candidacy was supported by Schüssel because he hoped this would keep Haider from taking national office after the 1999 general election.

20. Indeed, Müller has argued that "[p]ushing the point to an extreme, the party as distinguished from the Leagues can be reduced to the party chairman, the general secretary, the leader of the parliamentary Fraktion and the staff of the party headquarters" ("Development of Austrian Party Organizations," 57). See also Müller and Steininger, "Party Organization," and Wolfgang C. Müller and Delia Meth-Cohn, "The Selection of Party Chairmen in Austria: A Study in Intra-Party Decision Making," *European Journal of Political Research* 20.1 (1991): 39-65.

21. There were limits to Schüssel's inclusiveness. By all accounts he had a rather distant relationship to ÖWB president and deputy chairman of the Upper Austrian party, Christoph Leitl. Schüssel's erstwhile competitor for the party leadership and from 2000 president of the Austrian Chamber of Commerce, Leitl was known to favor both coalition with the SPÖ and social partnership.

22. These were Khol and Werner Fasslabend (ÖAAB president since January 1977) respectively.

23. Molterer (his deputy since 1995) and Elisabeth Gehrer (his deputy since 1999 and Minister for Education, Science, and Culture).

24. Emmerich Tálos, ed., *Umbau in Schwarz-Blau (-Orange): Eine Bilanz* (Vienna: Lit Verlag, 2006).

25. Interview by the author with central party office staff. Vice-Chancellor Riess-Passer was in charge of the public services and Finance Minister Karl-Heinz Grasser of the budget.

26. For an analysis of the FPÖ's strategy and behavior in the coalition, see Kurt Richard Luther, "Strategien und (Fehl-) Verhalten: Die Freiheitlichen und die Regierungen Schüssel I und II," in *Umbau in Schwarz-Blau (-Orange): Eine Bilanz*, ed. Emmerich Tálos (Vienna: Lit Verlag, 2006), 19-37, upon which some of the following draws.

27. Kurt Richard Luther, "The FPÖ: From Populist Protest to Incumbency," in *Right-Wing Extremism in the Twenty-First Century*, ed. Peter Merkl and Leonard Weinberg (London: Frank Cass, 2003), 191-219.

28. These included Haider's visit to Saddam Hussein, timed to coincide with Riess-Passer's official visit to Washington and a July 2002 meeting he held—and deliberately leaked to the press—with representatives of Belgian and Italian radical right parties.

29. On the Knittelfeld crisis, see Kurt Richard Luther, "The Self-Destruction of a Right-Wing Populist Party? The Austrian Parliamentary Election of 2002," *West European Politics* 26.2 (2003): 136-52.

30. For analyses of the 2002 election, see Günter Ogris et al., *Nationalratswahl 2002: Analyse des Wahlergebnisses und des Wahlkampfes* (Vienna: SORA, 2002), and Fritz Plasser and Peter Ulram, eds., *Analyse der Nationalratswahl 2002: Muster, Trends und Entscheidungsmotive* (Vienna: Ludwig Bolzmann Institut, 2002).

31. At ninety-six days, it was the then third longest in the Second Republic's history.

32. Schüssel made this abundantly clear by releasing his "Economic Policy Agenda 2010"of 4 December, which identified his proposed priorities for a new government. These included a savings package with a reduced role for the state in public service provision, as well as cuts in the social system, education, and health. For the SPÖ caucus leader's view of the ÖVP-SPÖ talks, see Josef Cap, "Die Sondierungsgespräche mit der ÖVP—Chronik eines geplanten Scheiterns," in *Österreichisches Jahrbuch für Politik 2003*, ed. Andreas Khol et al. (Vienna: Verlag für Geschichte und Politik, 2004), 103-12.

33. The vote was 21:8, with opposition coming above all from the left-wing Vienna branch.

34. Interviews by the author with relevant ÖVP and Green actors.

35. In October 2004, she was to replace Austria's outgoing EU Commissioner, ÖBB man, and sometime Schüssel critic Franz Fischler, and in turn to be substituted by Ursula Plasnik, Schüssel's former cabinet chief, who had no power base within the ÖVP, but was instead dependent on Schüssel.

36. September 2003 in Tyrol: ÖVP +2.7 percent, SPÖ +4.7 percent; March 2004 in Carinthia: ÖVP -9.1 percent, SPÖ +5.5 percent; and in Salzburg: ÖVP -0.9 percent, SPÖ +13.1 percent; June 2006 in Vorarlberg was an exception (+9.2 percent versus the SPÖ's +1.6 percent), but followed in October by the Burgenland election (ÖVP +1.0 percent, SPÖ 5.7 percent) and the disastrous Styrian election (-8.6 percent versus the SPÖ's +9.3

percent). In addition, at the May 2005 presidential election, ÖVP candidate Ferrero-Waldner lost to SPÖ candidate Heinz Fischer.

37. Interview with the author.

38. In addition to the aforementioned results in Lower Austria and Tyrol, they included Salzburg (March 2004): -10.9 percent; European Parliament (June 2004): -17.1 percent, and Vorarlberg (September 2004) -14.6 percent.

39. On the 2006 election, see Günter Bischof and Fritz Plasser ed. *The Changing Austrian Voter*, vol. 16, Contemporary Austrian Studies (New Brunswick, NJ: Transaction, 2008), and Fritz Plasser and Peter A. Ulram, eds., *Wechselwahlen: Analysen zur Nationalratswahl 2006* (Vienna: facultas.wuv, 2007).

40. Janda, "Towards a Performance Theory of Change," 5.

The Politics of Asymmetry: (Non) Corporatist Policy Making, 2000-2006

Ferdinand Karlhofer

Introduction

From its establishment in the late 1940s through the turn of the twenty-first century, *Sozialpartnerschaft* enjoyed a high reputation in Austria's political system. This was clearly the case until the 1980s and even, albeit with certain qualifications, in the 1990s, when the chamber system—traditionally the main pillar of social partnership—faced a severe crisis. Social partnership owed its prestige in the public to its role as a reliable and calculable mechanism for interest intermediation, thus decisively contributing to the country's economic development. Although there have always been close ties between chambers and the trade union federation on the one side, and political parties on the other, the functioning of corporatist policy making remained untouched from government changes. Called into being under the Grand Coalition of the Austrian People's Party (*Österreichische Volkspartei*, or ÖVP) and the Social Democratic Party of Austria (*Sozialdemokratische Partei Österreichs*, or SPÖ) (1945-1966), social partnership had its golden age under the single party government of the ÖVP (1966-1970) followed by the SPÖ (1970-1983). Even when the Freedom Party of Austria (*Freiheitliche Partei Österreichs*, or FPÖ), a party all along critical against corporatism, joined a coalition with the SPÖ (1983-1986), this had no effect on the interest system.

Quite different were the premises in 2000. For the first time, a program of a government explicitly aimed at changing the rules regulating relations between government and interest groups surfaced, all the more surprising because the terms of reference had been decided without any consultation of the social partners. It was the starting point for a series of disputes between government and associations, in particular, the labor organizations, the Austrian Trade Union Federation (*Österreichischer Gewerkschaftsbund*, or ÖGB) and the Federal Chamber of Labor. The tried and successful pattern of negotiation based on consensus and compromise was abruptly canceled. As a result, the polarized politics that surfaced in the government of the ÖVP and FPÖ (and later the Alliance for the Future of Austria [*Bündnis Zukunft Österreich*, or BZÖ]), in particular with the cabinet of the Schüssel I Administration, revised what had until then been the most resilient pillar of the political system.

Considering the situation just a few months before 4 February 2000, both the speed and the intensity of change were surprising. A few days before the election of October 1999, the presidents of the four big associations (Economic Chamber, Chamber of Agriculture, Chamber of Labor, and ÖGB), in a startling press conference, expressed their reservations about the FPÖ possibly taking office for it might lead, as they argued, to a "demolition of social partnership." Yet immediately after the election, the social partners went their separate ways and resigned from joint action. Events in the year 2000 conveyed the impression that the authority ascribed to social partnership had never existed.

A couple of questions arise in this context. Why did the consensus of elites, a characteristic of social partnership, not apply before and after the formation of the government? Was the weakening of the corporatist negotiation system a deliberate act of the government, or did it just continue a process that had begun previously? Finally, what will the future of Austro-Corporatism be?

Addressing these questions this article proceeds in three stages. Section one provides an overview of the profile of Austrian corporatism. The second section deals with the interests and motives of the ruling parties between 2000 and 2006. In section three, the broader context of the recent changes in the relations between government and interests is discussed. The article concludes with a look at the ÖGB crisis caused by currency speculations of the union-owned BAWAG bank and its implications on corporatist politics.

The Profile of Austro-Corporatism

In the literature on corporatism, Austria has been classified a special case.[1] It also ranks first (followed by Norway and Sweden) on Alan Siaroff's scale of *integrated economies*, with integrated economy defined as "a long-term co-operative pattern of shared economic management involving the social partners and existing at various levels such as plant-level management, sectoral wage bargaining, and joint shaping of national policies in competitiveness-related matters (education, social policy, etc.)."[2]

The capacity to meet the criteria of a highly integrated economy is closely attributed to Austria's extraordinary extensive chamber system covering virtually all people in employment except for public officials. The chambers are established as self-governing statutory corporations with compulsory membership. Their broad functions can be categorized as 1.) those of an autonomous nature, such as services to members, 2.) the function expressed as the right to give opinions on draft laws in the legislative process, and 3.) quasi-public and judicial functions in which the chambers are represented on the decision-making apparatus of the State (commissions, committees, advisory panels, courts, insurance institutions, and so forth), as well as those in which they perform direct State functions (constituting foreign trade delegations and the like).[3] All things considered, the chambers have far-reaching competences including control over the social security system, involvement in social and economic legislation, and participation in public administration. In combination with the Works Constitution Act (*Arbeitsverfassungsgesetz*), the chamber system forms the basic framework for corporatist politics in Austria.[4]

Most relevant as corporatist actors in Austria are its chambers, volunteer organizations, and political parties. The Economic Chamber (*Wirtschaftskammer*) and the Chamber of Labor (*Arbeiterkammer*) are the interest representations for business and labor, covering about 300,000 employers and 2.5 million employees, respectively. Both chambers are, in an international perspective, special cases. Economic chambers with compulsory membership exist in most European countries, yet the Austrian chamber is the only one which is exclusively entitled to conclude collective bargaining agreements with labor organizations. Chambers of labor exist, apart from Austria, in Luxembourg and in two German provinces (Saarland and Bremen). The outstanding feature of the Austrian chamber, however, is its by far higher financial endowment (compulsory membership fees amount to 0.5 percent of the gross income), allowing for extensive activities in service, education, and research.

In addition to the chambers, there are voluntary associations for business and for labor: the Austrian Federation of Industry (*Industriellenvereinigung* (IV)) and the ÖGB. In this mixed system of organizations, the chambers represent the steady pillar, all the more so because there is no competition between statutory and voluntary associations. As for the Chambers of Labor, they exist in close relationship to the ÖGB whose functionaries are at the same time delegates to the chamber's assembly. From the very beginning, the chamber has been an instrument of the union, attending to expertise and services, thereby providing most helpful "external" support for union power, both organizationally and financially. On the employers' side, representation is slightly different because the Economic Chamber covers the whole business community, while the IV is confined to industrial enterprises. In practice, however, the IV has control over the Chamber's industry division.

The three big chambers (for business, labor, and agriculture) are governed by political factions on the basis of periodical elections. The ÖVP holds the majority in the Economic Chamber and in the Chamber of Agriculture, while the SPÖ is dominant in the Chamber of Labor. Akin, the Trade Union Federation is composed of political factions, with the SPÖ holding the majority and the ÖVP being the strongest minority. The Federation of Industry is formally independent, but is informally closely related with the ÖVP.

The interdependency between associations and political parties finds its expression in the composition of legislative bodies at all levels. In the late 1970s, more than 50 percent of the members of the Austrian National Council (*Nationalrat*) were at the same time high-ranking functionaries (including presidents) of the big labor market organizations. Since then, the number has decreased significantly (to 15 percent by 2000). The presidents of the three big chambers waived their seats in the late 1990s; the president of the Federation of Trade Unions followed in 2006.[5]

To sum up, chambers and party influence are certainly not exclusively Austrian properties. It has, rather, been the comprehensiveness of the chamber system and the scope and intensity of the parties' influence that have given rise to the attributes of the Austrian political system being expressed by the terms *Kammerstaat* (chamber state), *Verbändestaat* (state associations), and *Parteienstaat* (party state).

The Year 2000: Interests and Motives of the Ruling Parties

The question regarding which of the two parties played the key role in paving the way for the coalition is not central in this context. Certainly of importance, though, was that the FPÖ had to make substantial concessions in order to erase doubts about its ability to govern, while the ÖVP could not resist seizing the opportunity of a political turn. Clearly, the ideological differences between the two parties were large. On the other hand, in several policy fields, such as family, social, economic, and security policy, their positions were considerably less divergent than had been the case between the ÖVP and SPÖ. All above, the cutback of the welfare state after three decades of social democratic hegemony was a matter of great concern both for the

ÖVP and the FPÖ. Regarding social partnership, however, interests and motives of the new partners in government were quite divergent.

The FPÖ's attitude towards social partnership was essentially determined by its relationship to the SPÖ. In countless elections in the past fifteen years, a good deal of the party's increase in votes came from the Social Democratic *Lager*, causing persistently fierce competition between the two parties. In the national election of 1999, the FPÖ became the strongest party among skilled workers, the SPÖ's traditional core electorate. The fact that the SPÖ, since the mid-1980s had been denied a coalition with the party due to its problematic behavior in dealing with the Nazi past, reinforced the FPÖ's hostile and exacerbated attitude.

In election campaigns, the FPÖ frequently took advantage of grievances against the *Kammerstaat* caused by extensive personal privileges and the excessive incomes of functionaries. Surprisingly, despite its outstanding successes with political elections, the FPÖ failed to achieve comparable results in chamber elections, not even in the elections of the Chamber of Labor which was, it should be noted, the primary target of the party's attacks. Not even when the chambers were urged by the government to hold (coercive) ballots among their members on the question of whether or not they wanted to maintain the chamber system, the FPÖ's efforts were crowned with success—a vast majority in all chambers voted in favor of the status quo. Not much different, the party failed to make use of discontent among ÖGB members; an FPÖ separatist trade union named Free Austrian Trade Union (*Freie Gewerkschaft Österrreichs*), founded in 1997, recruited merely a handful of members and vanished quietly from the scene after a couple of years.

The FPÖ's inability to catch up among labor organizations the same way it did in the political arena made its self-perception of being the "new labor party" incomplete and inconsistent. Due to its outsider status in labor organizations, the FPÖ's options for exerting influence were low, and the same was the case with regard to social partnership. As a party in government, though, weakness in the corporatist system turned to strength in politics, at least to some extent. The FPÖ had much less reason to be considerate of members' interests and loyalties than the ÖVP had. Thus, for instance, holding conflict-laden portfolios such as the reform of administration (implying the impairment of civil servants' rights) was less challenging; what is more, any resistance of the employees' representation could be easily communicated as delaying tactics to the public.

Quite different was the interest profile of the FPÖ's coalition partner, the ÖVP. Subdivided into, among others, three big leagues

(*Bünde*) for employers, employees, and farmers, all of them strongly represented in the respective chambers, the ÖVP can be regarded a "corporatist" party *par excellence*. Its leagues are, at the same time, political groups in the chambers and subdivisions of the party.[6] Legal entities of their own (as a rule, joining the ÖVP takes place via joining a league), the leagues have direct access to the membership fees. As a result, any conflict with a social partner organization is potentially an internal conflict tangling with the balance of power within the party, too. As already mentioned, several issues such as administrative reform or bargaining rounds in the public sector, accompanied by unusually controversial negotiations between the minister in charge (FPÖ) and the Union of Public Service Employees (dominated by the respective ÖVP league) would have been unthinkable under a homogenous ÖVP government.

Industrial Relations and Political Turn

As stated at the beginning of this article, the relations between government and social partners escalated immediately after the coalition took office, resulting in an abrupt suspension of corporatist practices. Significantly, the coalition pact had held out the prospect of a "reform of social partnership" with regard to several issues (labor market service, reform of the pension system, gender equality), even explicitly providing for the involvement of the social partners.

In practice, however, there was a tendency to ignore the principle of parity in the treatment of business and labor interests from the very beginning. This exclusion occurred in a threefold way:

Social bias: Most of the relevant government bills for labor and employment law changes aimed at a cutback of employment rights, thus severely challenging trade unions and the Chamber of Labor. Most provocative was certainly a passage in the coalition contract which read "change of all provisions disproportionately burdening business."

Break with the rules of the game: Contrary to the announcement of the coalition pact, the government did not involve the social partners in social and economic policy-making processes. Right-leaning social policy had always been a field where the corporatist actors were used to negotiate a consensual solution which was (mostly) adopted by government and parliament. Due to that, social partnership was frequently criticized for predetermining the parliament's autonomy. Yet despite controversy, it secured social peace and contributed to the economic upturn enjoyed for over half a century. With the government leaving no room for negotiation, this function could no longer be performed.

Inclusion and exclusion: The coalition was obviously strongly influenced by business interests. In contrast to previous practices, business associations—Economic Chamber, Federation of Industry—still enjoyed privileged access to policy makers, while labor organizations increasingly were excluded. The unequal treatment of interest groups appeared to drive a wedge between business and labor organizations.

The rationale of social partnership had always been that none of the partners exploits its actual position, but all seek to come to a compromise—ideally a win-win situation for all actors involved. Now, by contrast, the trend seemed to go in the direction of redistribution—a zero-sum game in which only one wins at the cost of others. As a result, tripartite relations change for the worse: unions and the Chamber of Labor are no longer accepted as equal partners in the game; their role as actors in economic and social policy is downgraded and restricted to partial aspects of the objective.

Irritating for labor organizations, in this context, must have been less the fact that an anti-corporatist party was in government, but that the ÖVP as a corporatist party supported the new policy.[7] A striking example of the ÖVP's changed position was the transfer of the "labor" portfolio from the Ministry of Social Affairs to the Ministry of Economy. So far, there had been consensus that the separation of economy and labor reflected a distinct role assignment for the respective ministers. Commenting on the changes in connection with the reallocation, the Economy Minister (ÖVP) stated he wanted "to overcome the cliché that there was an antagonism between employers and employees"[8]—a position implicitly questioning the trade union which derives its *raison d'être* from conflicting interests in industrial relations.

Several passages in the coalition pact indicated a strengthening of business against labor. These passages related to the redefinition of the health and safety executive's role (focus on service rather than on control), shift of the rights of co-determination from the sectoral to the plant level (thus weakening trade union influence), emphasis of the service character of the chambers, and reorganization of the electoral law for chambers.

As regards the Chamber of Labor, the government parties soon delivered the threat that, if the chamber continued to oppose government policy, they would cut the Chamber's membership fee from 0.5 to 0.3 percent of the members' incomes, thereby forcing it to undertake a drastic reduction of its services.

As far as changes of the corporatist structures were at stake, consent to the envisaged changes was not to be expected from trade unions and the Chamber of Labor, simply because they could not accept restrictions for their sphere of influence. Apart from this, the principle of the chambers governing themselves had always been interpreted broadly; not only had legal changes of the chambers' competences and structures never been undertaken without their consent, but alterations had principally been made solely on their own initiatives. The "reform of social partnership" as envisaged in the coalition pact broke with tradition because political regulation was given priority over the social partners' autonomous status.

In light of this reprioritizing and the general political turn of 2000, the rules for the corporatist negotiating system were abruptly redefined, too. Both in aim and practice, the government suspended the so-far generally accepted consensus about seeking a balanced configuration of interest groups. The government's turn did not necessarily put an end to the bipartisanism between business and labor. Yet, as a matter of fact, it was to be expected that the aggravated relationship between government and labor organizations would have a negative effect on the established negotiation culture.

Labor on a Collision Course with the Government

Although the corporatist pattern had already declined in the years preceding the 1999 election, the government change in 2000 marked a severe break in the relations between associations and the state. Their new relationship, at least in the first years after the political turn, had little in common with the traditional understanding of social partnership. Due to its excellent performance throughout the Second Republic, Austro-Corporatism had always enjoyed a high reputation. Self-governance of the chambers, the embeddedness of associations in policy-making structures, and an underlying assumption of parity between capital and labor had been the basic principles of its mode of operation. All three elements were now fundamentally disputed. When the center-right coalition took office in February 2000, the "reform of social partnership" was declared a priority objective. Government policy aimed at reducing the social partners' influence; contrary to the past, their expertise was sought less, and the chambers' formal right to give an opinion on a draft law was frequently bypassed. In general, legislative action tended to override the principle of parity at the expense of labor, thereby making the latter a fierce opponent of the government.

In reaction to the government's policy, the ÖGB changed gradually from a formerly pronounced consensual style to a confrontational one.

In October 2001, a ballot vote among the 1.4 million union members took place. To many observers, even to union leaders, the ballot appeared risky, since it was the first one of its kind in the union's history. In the end, the turnout of 57 percent, in which more than 90 percent voted in favor of a more militant union policy, was surprisingly high. From then on, the ÖGB had a strong mandate for action which, however, was not exercised immediately.

As a matter of fact, the vote impressed both the government and the employers' side and gave rise to a temporary revival of social partnership; for example, within a startling short time, a joint solution for the long discussed reform of severance pay was found. On the whole, however, the unequal treatment of labor and employers' organizations by the government continued. In spring 2003, the dispute between the government and the ÖGB hit its peak when the government presented a draft law concerning severe cuts in the pension system. Since the government had refused to consult the social partners (notably labor) before drafting the legislation, the ÖGB mobilized with almost half a million workers protesting against the reform plans. Though inviting the union, among others, to a roundtable discussion,[9] the government remained adamant and pushed the bill through parliament. With a total of 10.4 million hours lost and a relative duration of roughly three hours and sixteen minutes per employee in employment, the strike activities of 2003 exceeded the postwar peak of 1950.

Table 1
Strikes in OECD Countries, 1993-2002*

Country	Strikes	Country	Strikes	Country	Strikes
Spain	252	Ireland	77	Netherlands	18
Canada	187	Australia	77	Germany	5
Denmark	174	United States	45	Switzerland	3
Italy	130	Sweden	30	**Austria**	**1**
Finland	115	United Kingdom	25	**Austria 2003**	**41**
France	92	Portugal	23		

*Working days lost per 1, 000 employees, annual average 1993-2002.
Source: Informationsdienst des Instituts der deutschen Wirtschaft Köln, October 2004.

The outcome of the strike was ambivalent. On the one hand, the ÖGB clearly lost in its conflict with the government. Yet both the ballot and the protest actions indicated a metamorphosis of the Austrian trade union movement. Until a couple of years previous, the ÖGB had been committed to a strictly cooperative negotiation strategy, which in doubtful cases was pursued even against the members' expressed wishes. Over the years, the membership had gradually fallen from over 60 percent in the mid-1960s to less than 40 percent in the late 1990s. Yet now, with the background of continuous conflict with the government, the identification with union goals was on the rise again, thus bringing the loss of members to a halt—though just temporarily, as it turned out.

Obviously, strong pressure from the party's rank and file and their expectations, emanating from the ballot vote of 2001, significantly contributed to the alteration of the ÖGB, which now puts an emphasis on mobilization and campaigning. For some time, it was unclear whether the union would—under altered political conditions—resume its "vote and seat" on the negotiating table. There were strong indications, however, that its former role of being the most loyal and faithful partner in the corporatist system was a thing of the past. Like the associations of business and farmers which had already been oscillating between corporatism and lobbyism for several years, the ÖGB, too, was likely to accentuate its members' interests rather than the commonweal, thus inevitably leading to less calculability of the actors involved.

The Broader Context of Change: Power Shift and Fragile Consensus

Even though the momentum for the rapid changes of relations emanated from the government, it must be recalled that the scope for mutual concessions had already narrowed. In retrospect, a striking loss of authority of the corporatist associations occurred. In particular, on the economic chamber's side an increasing number of sectoral groups tended to refuse macro-level collective bargaining agreements, many of them striving against coercive chamber membership. In response to discontent and adopting an attitude of *laissez-faire*, the federal chamber repeatedly accepted particularist groups stepping out of line and refusing to conclude bargaining agreements with the union. In general, internal troubles on both sides—centrifugal tendencies on the employers' side, at the same time, a steady loss of members on the ÖGB's side—inevitably had an impact on corporatist relations. For either side, it became increasingly difficult to find the balance between optimal goal achievement as a corporatist actor on the one side, and member-oriented pressure politics on the other. Like it or not, the associations changed the tune, from time to time escalating, although—what is worth mentioning—never risking the collapse of the negotiation system. Yet the system had already become fragile before Wolfgang Schüssel came to power.

Obviously, aside from the political turn, other forces at work were responsible for the declining demand for corporatist policy-making. First and foremost, the opening of the Austrian market—a process that started in 1973 when Austria signed a free trade agreement with the European Community and found its completion with the entry into the European Union in 1995—contributed to it. The logic of corporatist action was no longer demand-side but supply-side oriented, that is, acting in accordance with the imperative of backing the country's competitiveness.[10] The coalition which came to power in 2000 put the focus from the very beginning on a genuinely "anti-corporatist" goal: zero budget. Later on, the government committed itself to the Brussels consensus on macroeconomic stabilization policies, thereby, once again, foiling the corporatist logic of operation.[11]

Second, in the 1990s the Austrian chamber system suffered from a severe loss of legitimacy which, in the end, challenged its future existence. Basically, the chambers, as organizations with compulsory membership, are not faced with density problems, as free associations are, since there is no exit option for members. Thus it is not associability but the turnout in elections that must serve as an indicator of organizational stability. It was the turnout that decreased in all chamber elections, most dramatically in the Chamber of Labor which, between 1984 and 1994, registered a decline from 64 to 30 percent. In order to cope with the crisis, all chambers started extensive reform processes which, all things considered, put the focus on the improvement of services for members.[12] By the late 1990s, the crisis was overcome, members' confidence was regained, and turnout increased again. One consequence, however, was a gradual shift from the "logic of influence" towards the "logic of membership" (following the terminology introduced by Philippe Schmitter and Wolfgang Streeck[13]), making the chambers less reliable actors in terms of social partnership.

Third, the extension of actors in decision-making bodies (think tanks, policy advisers) have had an effect on the formerly almost exclusive position of corporatist actors in a number of policy fields.[14]

Fourth, the policy style in Austria has markedly shifted from consensus democracy to conflict democracy.[15] Certainly, the year 2000, with the relations between government and the social partners (strictly speaking, the labor side) souring from one day to the other, marked an unprecedented rupture in the history of the Second Republic. However, the basics of consensus democracy had become unstable long before the political turn.[16]

Given the international drive of continuing decentralization with the center of gravity of industrial relations shifting from the macro- to the meso- and the micro-level, the foundations of corporatist policy-making have eroded thoroughly.[17] With some time lag, the "winds of change" have been blowing in Austria, too. During the 1990s, social partnership came increasingly under stress, mainly due to the limited scope for action coming along with Europeanization and economic structural change. The process of interest concentration and problem solving was more and more complicated as a result of the divergent interests and orientations of the social partners. It became clear that Austro-Corporatism, in a historical sense, had already passed its zenith. Notably, the Parity Commission on Prices and Wages, formerly the core of social partnership, no longer existed; at least, it has not been convened since 1998.

The associations, without withdrawing from the negotiating system as such, set out to extend their strategic repertoire. Namely, the employers' motives have become ambivalent. While the Economic Chamber has still a self-interest in cooperating with labor organizations, the Federation of Industry regards itself, meanwhile, as a lobby organization rather than a social partner.[18] (The latter, having had a strong influence on the center-right government, was supposed to be the *spiritus rector* of the turnaround in social and economic policy).[19]

Corporatism appears to be no longer the one and only way for interest representation; instead, a parallelism of both corporatist and lobbyist practices has become the rule. The trend in Austria seems to confirm the paradigm shift mirrored in recent comparative research on interest groups: the increasing differentiation of societal interest intermediation pluralizes corporatist arrangements, thereby confronting the actors with an increasing diversity of interests, interest representation, collective action, and political strategies.[20] As a matter of fact, there is no continuous pattern of interest intermediation in Austria; rather, the boundaries between "corporatist" and "pluralist" forms of interest representation have become indistinct.[21]

Latest Developments: Union Crisis and Collective Bargaining

In 2006, the ÖGB experienced an unprecedented shock after the union-owned BAWAG, one of the largest banks in Austria, suffered heavy losses in currency speculation. Since, as a result, the ÖGB faced debts of close to two billion Euro, the bank had to be sold in order to avert union bankruptcy. The BAWAG debacle caused unrest within the ÖGB and a severe union crisis affecting both the identity and credibility of the organization, particularly because high-ranking union leaders had been informed about the shady dealings. As a first consequence, the union president and the secretary of finance were forced to resign (the president, in addition, had to withdraw from parliament). In January 2007 at a union congress, substantial changes were passed aiming at, among others things, more transparency and control in the union structure.[22]

The ÖGB crisis is still far from being overcome; confidence among members is deeply shaken (more than 40,000 members were lost in 2006) and can be rebuilt only gradually. Clearly, the ÖGB has been weakened in the course of the BAWAG affair, and it is doubtful that it will regain its old strength as a player in the political arena. Surprisingly, however, and contrary to widespread expectations, the system of collective bargaining has not really been affected by the union troubles. The same applies to cooperative relations with employers—in September 2006, right at the height of the union crisis, the social partners concluded an agreement (Bad Ischl Declaration) aiming at a reform of the *modus operandi* for future cooperation. Since then, the social partners have agreed upon several position papers and opinions delivered to the (new) government.[23] In retrospect, the six years of center-right government under Chancellor Schüssel were not a heyday of Austro-Corporatism. Yet, all things considered, its basic structures have remained intact so far.

Notes

1. Cf. the overviews by Carlo Dell'Aringa and Manuela Lodovici, "Industrial Relations and Labor Policies in European Countries," in *The Future of Industrial Relations: Global Change and Challenges*, ed. John Niland et al. (London: Sage, 1994), 389-92; Oscar Molina and Martin Rhodes, "Corporatism: The Past, Present, and Future of a Concept," *Annual Review of Political Science* 5 (2002): 305-08.

2. Alan Siaroff, "Corporatism in Twenty-Four Industrial Democracies: Meaning and Measurement," *European Journal of Political Research* 36 (1999): 175-205.

3. Jim Sweeny, *Employer and Employee Chambers in German Speaking Countries* (Aldershot: Avebury, 1996), 58-59.

4. Jörg Flecker and Christoph Hermann, "The End of the Austrian Way? From State-Led Coordination to 'Negotiated Liberalism'," paper presented at the 26th Conference of the International Working Party on Labour Market Segmentation, Berlin, 8-11 September 2005. Constitutional experts tend to classify the Austrian social autonomy (*Sozialautonomie*) as a distinct case in international perspective (cf. Peter Pernthaler, "Kammern und Pflichtmitgliedschaft in Österreich aus der Sicht des öffentlichen Rechts, " in *Kammern und Pflichtmitgliedschaft in Österreich*, ed. Peter Pernthaler et al. (Vienna: Verlag des ÖGB, 1994), 19-91.

5. Ferdinand Karlhofer, "The Long Shadow of Corporatism: Scope and Limits of Think Tank Activities in Austria," *German Policy Studies* 2 (2006): 359.

6. Cf. Ferdinand Karlhofer, "The Present and Future State of Social Partnership," in *Austro-Corporatism: Past, Present, Future*, vol. 4, *Contemporary Austrian Studies*, ed. Günter Bischof and Anton Pelinka (New Brunswick, NJ: Transaction, 1996), 119-46.

7. We have to bear in mind that Wolfgang Schüssel was for a long period of time in his political career (1975-1991) general secretary of the ÖVP *Wirtschaftsbund*, one of the core players of social partnership.

8. *Der Standard*, 10 February 2000.

9. "[...S]ome commentators suggest that such consultations may have been offered by the government for the sole reason of appeasing the social partners, and, in the case of the unions, to prevent further industrial action" (cf. "Annual Report, Austria 2003," European Industrial Relations Observatory Online, http://www.eiro.eurofound.ie/2004/country/austria.html (accessed 28 Oct. 2008).

10. Cf. Franz Traxler, "Sozialpartnerschaft am Scheideweg: Zwischen korporatistischer Kontinuität und neoliberalem Umbruch," *Wirtschaft und Gesellschaft* 22 (1996): 13-33.

11. Markus Marterbauer, "Veränderte Rahmenbedingungen und Präferenzen in der Wirtschaftspolitik," in *Sozialpartnerschaft: Österreichische und Europäische Perspektiven*, ed. Ferdinand Karlhofer and Emmerich Tálos (Vienna: LIT Verlag, 2005), 57-78.

12. Cf. Anton Pelinka and Christian Smekal, *Kammern auf dem Prüfstand: Vergleichende institutionelle Analysen institutioneller Funktionsbedingungen* (Vienna: Signum, 1996); Werner Muhm, "Die Arbeiterkammerorganisation im geänderten wirtschaftlichen, gesellschaftlichen und politischen Umfeld," *Wirtschaft und Gesellschaft* special volume (2002): 5-14.

13. Philippe C. Schmitter and Wolfgang Streeck, *The Organization of Business Interests: Studying the Associative Action of Business in Advanced Industrial Societies* (Cologne: Max Planck Institute for the Study of Societies, 1999).

14. Karlhofer, "The Long Shadow," 24-25.

15. Anton Pelinka et al., "Von der Konsens- zur Konfliktdemokratie? Österreich nach dem Regierungs- und Koalitionswechsel," in *Die Zukunft der österreichischen Demokratie: Trends, Prognosen und Szenarien*, ed. Anton Pelinka et al. (Vienna: Signum, 2000), 439-64.

16. Fritz Plasser and Peter Ulram, "Überdehnung, Erosion und rechtspopulisitische Reaktion," *Österreichische Zeitschrift für Politikwissenschaft* 21 (1992): 147-64.

17. Cf., e.g., Wolfgang Streeck, "Nach dem Korporatismus: Neue Eliten, neue Konflikte?" MPIfG Köln, Working Paper No. 4 (2005).

18. Karlhofer, "The Long Shadow," 371-72.

19. An evaluation of six years of center-right government (2000-2005) came to the conclusion that, in retrospect, despite a couple of far-reaching changes, in particular with regard to the privatization of the state-owned industry, major alterations in the institutional framework of interest representation remained undone. See Felix Butschek, *Industrialisierung: Ursachen, Verlauf, Konsequenzen* (Vienna: Böhlau, 2005), 195.

20. Cf. Thomas von Winter, "Lobbyismus: Forschungsstand und Realität," paper presentated at the conference "Lobbyismus in Deutschland: Fünfte Gewalt—unkontrolliert oder einflussreich?" University of Leipzig (2003).

21. Emmerich Tálos and Bernhard Kittel, *Gesetzgebung in Österreich: Netzwerke, Akteure und Interaktionen in politischen Entscheidungsprozessen* (Vienna: WUV, 2001), 231.

22. Cf. Ferdinand Karlhofer, "BAWAG und die Folgen," in *Österreichisches Jahrbuch für Politik 2006* (Vienna: Verlag für Geschichte und Politik, 2007), 23-40.

23. See the overview given in the official website, Die Sozialpartner Österreich, http://www.sozialpartner.at (accessed 28 Oct. 2008). The record includes, among others, a proposal on "Growth and Full Employment."

Unremarkably Remarkable, Remarkably Unremarkable: Schüssel as Austria's Foreign Policymaker in a Time of Transition

Reinhard Heinisch

Within [the constraints of European Council meetings] Wolfgang Schüssel was the omnipresent stage director, who determined the mise-en-scène, set the tone and manipulated the script as and when he saw appropriate. Schüssel's influence was apparent from the very beginning, when the Presidency first outlined its ideas about the agenda at the end of April [of 2006]. It was typical of the chancellor's style that he chose to ignore the Council's rules of procedure [...] As a result, the tone was, and to a large extent remained, Schüssel speak rather than Council Secretariat speak [...]. The section on Justice and Home Affairs was not "Justice and Home Affairs," let alone an "Area of Freedom, Security, and Justice," but "Europe Protects" [...]. In the weeks that followed, the chancellor continued to ride roughshod through the post-[Council of] Seville procedures [...]. Schüssel also tried to determine the wording of the Conclusions at several crucial points [...]. Suffice to say, that as far as these two topics were concerned, it was the chancellor who defined the terms of the debate throughout. [...].

> Rules of procedure are not and never have been a constraint. Nor is it the cautious advice of senior officials. On the contrary, fonctionnaires, whether in Vienna, Brussels or elsewhere, exist to serve their political masters, not to restrain them. Previous presidents in office have depended heavily on the advice of their permanent representatives in Brussels. Although Gregor Woschnagg has been a senior member of the chancellor's entourage at the European Council since 2000, he was in the final analysis just another fonctionnaire, with little if any influence where it mattered [...].[1]

Peter Ludlow's account of the "Schüssel Presidency" of the European Union in 2006 is a telling indication of the style and manner of

Schüssel the man and the politician. It evokes the image of a masterful tactician, whose prodigious strategic talent has been echoed in newspaper commentaries both at home and abroad when he was credited with "defanging" the notorious Freedom Party of Austria (*Freiheitliche Partei Österreichs*, or FPÖ) leader Jörg Haider.[2] Ludlow's observations also portray a person who plays his cards close to the chest, relies on a small coterie of confidantes, and appears sometimes dismissive of the input from outside the inner circle. What emerges is the picture of a politician who follows his own instincts against both the apparent better judgment of others and even the political mainstream. Yet, despite a certain smugness often associated with the smartest student in class and in spite of a reputation for appearing cool and technocratic, Schüssel has also demonstrated a keen sense of the popular, if not to say, the populist political message. In situations when he has nothing to say, however, he prefers to remain silent, waiting for others to make a move and expose vulnerabilities. The Austrian weekly *Profil* qualified this taciturn streak as "silence as a tactic."[3]

This essay does not present a point-by-point account of Schüssel's foreign policy from 1995 to 2006, but seeks instead to provide a general analysis of the man and his decision making. Specifically, it argues that, as the architect of Austria's external relations, Schüssel represented a political departure from his predecessors. His unquestionable commitment to Austria's future in an integrated Europe aside, Schüssel's foreign policy was to remain largely an extension of his domestic political ambitions and objectives. First, as a political entrepreneur, his main objective lay with breaking Social Democratic political dominance, even if that meant engaging in policies that alienated Austria from its international partners. Second, as Conservative party leader tempted by the opportunity of chancellorship, he pursued what many foreign critics would regard as a *mésalliance* and a breech of political taboo. Thirdly, as chancellor faced with domestic opposition, he would time and again recognize the political value of confronting "Brussels," even at the expense of being politically isolated when pursing Austrian objectives in the European Union (EU). Fourth, through his silence when others railed against Europe or by making subtle gestures himself, Schüssel helped exacerbate a populist discourse in which the European Union came to be viewed increasingly negatively by a large share of the Austrian public. The argument here is not that Schüssel necessarily ought to have acted differently. Rather, it needs to be recognized that he was willing to go further in the interest of party/political expedience than his two predecessors.

In doing so, one may argue, Schüssel leaves behind an ambiguous legacy. On the one hand, his imprint on European politics was larger than that of any other Austrian government leader with the exception of Chancellor Bruno Kreisky in the 1970s. In the process, Schüssel undoubtedly displayed, at times, tactical brilliance and confronted "Europe" with the shortcomings of its own policy decisions. By the same token, we must recognize that, during Schüssel's tenure as foreign minister and chancellor, the nation and its foreign policy went through a profound transition when Austria was facing the twin challenges of political integration and economic globalization. More than anybody else, Schüssel would have been well-placed to mitigate latent Austrian tendencies toward self-isolation and existing fears of external threats; instead, his center-right government, time and again, instrumentalized such sentiments to mobilize political support.

Unremarkably Remarkable and Remarkably Unremarkable

The quiet tactician Schüssel, often likened to a "poker player,"[4] appears as one of the most remarkable Austrian politicians in recent history. Not since the chancellorship of Bruno Kreisky in the 1970s did an Austrian head of government have so much freedom to maneuver and leave his imprint on national politics. By 2008, Schüssel was even treated in the international media as a serious candidate for the new post of president of the European Council. Apart from neutering the Freedom Party, his achievements entailed leading his own Austrian People's Party (*Österreichische Volkspartei*, or ÖVP) back to power in 2000 after thirty years either in opposition or as a junior partner in an unloved coalition. Despite his party's worst results in a national election, Schüssel played his cards so well that after nearly four months of negotiations, he was able to assume the chancellorship while forcing the stronger Social Democrats into opposition. Subsequently in 2002, Schüssel presided over the biggest gain of an Austrian party in national elections when support for the Conservatives soared from 27 percent to over 40 percent.

Other credentials of Schüssel "the poker player" include his success at outmaneuvering his colleagues in fourteen EU member states that had imposed bilateral sanctions on his government for coalescing with the Freedom Party. The chancellor withstood both the enormous domestic pressure accompanied by massive demonstrations and largely hostile media reporting as well as international isolation and condemnation. Shortly after Austria's EU partners ended their sanctions, a handshake between Schüssel and his German and French counterparts, two of his most ardent critics, at an EU summit were as much a symbolic gesture intended to show improving bilateral relations as a signal of begrudging respect for the Austrian chancellor's political stamina under fire.

Remarkable as the these episodes may be, it seems puzzling that the same Schüssel had previously served as a singularly unremarkable and, at times, even tactless foreign minister, when, for example, he insulted the head of the German Bundesbank and the Danish foreign minister by thoughtless remarks. In nearly five years as head of the Austrian foreign ministry, he failed to leave his mark on the country's international policy and was often remembered more for being at odds with the Austrian head of state, President Klestil, and Austria's EU Commissioner, Franz Fischler, both members of Schüssel's own party.

Under similarly difficult political conditions for the ÖVP, even Schüssel's famously staid and staunchly conservative predecessor, Alois Mock, had managed to implement his vision of a new, post-1989 comprehensive integration policy, which he pursued with single-minded determination.[5] His goal of anchoring Austria as much possible in the Western alliance system, thus throwing overboard the Social Democratic foreign policy priorities of the 1970s, may not have been to everybody's liking, but at least it represented a clear and consistent new roadmap of where the country was to be headed. Such independent policy contours never emerged under Schüssel as foreign minister, whose tenure coincided with Austria's entry into the European Union. Neither he, nor the government as a whole, distinguished themselves during these first years of EU membership, more often than not failing to achieve support for Austrian policy objectives in Brussels.

It is also puzzling that someone who has often been labeled a master tactician was capable of such profound misjudgments both in domestic and international politics. For example, as soon as Schüssel had taken over the party in 1995, he gambled on provoking new elections, assuming he had caught his coalition partner, the Social Democratic Party of Austria (*Sozialdemokratische Partei Österreichs*, or SPÖ), in a moment of weakness. The latter, however, subsequently won one of their most resounding electoral triumphs in years, emerging in the end far stronger in the coalition government than the People's Party. Likewise, the election in 2006, which ended Schüssel's tenure as chancellor, was a political upset when the SPÖ unexpectedly inched ahead of the Conservatives because he and his party had badly misread the mood of the people.

As will be discussed below, the chancellor's misinterpretation of the political tealeaves was also apparent in international relations. Although credited for getting Austria and his government out of the sanctions in 2000, Schüssel, more than anybody else, has to bear the responsibility for maneuvering the country into that situation. Five years as foreign minister had apparently not provided him with the standing and trust in the eyes of his European counterparts so as to avert the embarrassing affair altogether. He was neither kept abreast of what was about to unfold, nor did he correctly judge the international consequences of his decision to form a coalition with Haider's Freedom Party. Even after the boycott, Austria's bilateral relations with several fellow member states remained at an unprecedented low point. It is indeed remarkable that, under Schüssel's leadership, a small, neutral country like Austria failed to have thoroughly good relations with several of its equally democratic neighbors. Despite Schüssel's unquestionable political accomplishments, he therefore remains a political figure full of contradictions both in terms of his policies and qualities.

The Accidental Foreign Policymaker

As Ludlow observes correctly, if we are to understand Schüssel's foreign policy, "we have to get back to Schüssel the head of government, if not Schüssel the man."[6] Neither by his biography nor by any of Schüssel's public pronouncements earlier in his political career do we detect an affinity with, or a particular interest in, international relations. To Schüssel, foreign policy seems incidental in that he obtained the post of foreign minister in 1995 along with becoming vice-chancellor and party leader. The logic of maintaining a carefully calibrated balance of power within the governing SPÖ-ÖVP coalition ensured that Schüssel obtained a cabinet portfolio with sufficient gravitas. More importantly, it afforded the Conservatives independent access to the international stage, supplying them with crucial information during Austria's sensitive integration process into the European Union. From the standpoint of political symbolism alone, it was critical for the People's Party not to leave this arena to the chancellor and the Social Democrats.

Wresting this cabinet post from the SPÖ in 1985 had been something of feat for the Conservatives because of the central importance accorded to it by the Austrian Left. In the subsequent decade, Schüssel's predecessor, Alois Mock, shaped this portfolio to such an extent that many of the objectives of the Austrian Conservatives became *de facto* the national foreign policy priorities. However, after developing medical problems and seeing his dream of Austria's integration into the European Union come to fruition, Mock reluctantly retired in 1995. At the same time, an ongoing internal conflict in the People's Party between the Catholic conservative wing and the reformist liberals had come to a head, resulting in the ousting of yet another politically unlucky party leader. This time it was Erhard Busek, the party's foremost exponent of urbane liberalism, who was forced to step aside. Yet he doggedly resisted pressures by the ultraconservatives to have one of their own become the new party leader and threatened to run once again as a candidate for leadership, thus possibly denying a significant majority to the eventual successor. The impasse was resolved when, to everybody's surprise, Busek nominated Minister of Economic Affairs Wolfgang Schüssel as the new party leader.

In the cabinet since 1989, Schüssel seemed an unlikely choice.[7] For one, he appeared too liberal to be a credible personification of the party's new edgier conservative profile. Secondly, as a long-term top functionary in the Economic Federation, he represented business interests in the party and, indirectly, in Austria's famously consensual neocorporatist system. Therefore, he seemed hardly the man to lead the ÖVP into a bold new direction in tune with the rising confrontational mood of its members. Instead, the new party leader was initially seen as yet another compromise candidate reflecting the smallest common denominator between the party's varying factions.

Given the centrality of foreign policy to the ÖVP, it is nonetheless remarkable that the person chosen to succeed someone of Mock's stature utterly lacked the corresponding international credentials. There was, indeed, little in the new party leader's background to suggest that he was particularly well-suited to be Austria's new foreign minister. It is, however, a measure of Schüssel's talent as a politician not only to have already had a long career within the party, holding significant party offices at least since 1975, but to emerge as the compromise candidate in such a divided organization. Traditionally counted among the liberal Viennese camp and in style and appearance relatively unconventional, he had nonetheless enjoyed the support and protection of the conservative Mock.[8]

Foreign Policy and Austrian Party Politics

In the 1970s under Chancellor Bruno Kreisky, Austrian foreign policy emerged from the Soviet shadow and became bolder and more globally oriented so that its practice of passive neutrality gave way to a period of active neutrality. The country's position between the major blocs and the general climate of détente in the 1970s provided many opportunities that Kreisky skillfully understood to enhance Austria's position relative to its power resources.[9] However, by the early 1980s, Vienna's relations with Washington became increasingly strained. Most importantly, the international environment had changed, constraining Austria's room to maneuver compared with what it had been in the 1970s. Vienna's support for leftist movements in Latin America and other parts of the world were regarded as unwelcome by the Reagan Administration, and Austria's close economic ties to Eastern Europe became the subject of increased scrutiny.[10] With Kreisky's resignation in 1983, Austria returned to a more regional orientation.[11]

The new direction of a "realistic foreign and neutrality policy" commensurate with the Austria's true capabilities and immediate (mainly economic) interests was implemented to its fullest when the foreign ministry came under ÖVP control in 1987. In part, this had been the price for persuading the Conservatives to join the Social Democrats in government. As Paul Luif observed, Conservative Party leader Alois Mock was one of the first Austrian politicians to adopt a "global approach" to European integration,[12] which meant that the country should seek full membership in the European Community/European Union, instead of a selective participation in Europe's internal market.

The ÖVP's thrust toward Europe affected all other political parties in that it pushed the traditionally Euro-skeptical Social Democrats into the pro-European camp so as not be outdone by their principal rivals. In turn, the smaller opposition, such as the Greens (*Die Grünen*) and, especially, the Freedom Party, came to adopt negative attitudes to integration, hoping to attract those voters who disapproved of the government's policy toward Brussels—in the case of Haider's FPÖ, it actually meant a complete reversal of their earlier position.

Generally speaking, Austria's policy toward integration was a muddled affair in the sense that it seemed both precipitous and oddly obstinate at the same time. Although Austria had not debated the possibility of full membership as late as the 1986 elections, the country plunged itself into this process only a short time thereafter, submitting the so-called "letter to Brussels" on 17 July 1989. Nonetheless, the document contained a lengthy list of reservations and exceptions, making it seem it was the European Community that wanted to join Austria.[13] Most crucially, each of the three applications (to the three communities of the European Community) contained a reservation concerning Austria's neutrality (in contrast to Sweden and Finland), which became the subject of prolonged negotiations.[14] The Janus-faced approach to Europe had its roots in the insular mentality of a population accustomed to a position of relative geopolitical detachment and geographic isolation after almost fifty years spent existing between two powerful military blocs.[15] Austria's ambivalent attitude toward European integration, compounded by an "image and identity crisis"[16] because the country had lost its cherished role as a bridge between East and West, is well-documented and need not be revisited.[17] What is important here are the ramifications of Austria's somewhat insular mentality for the Schüssel era and the rise of Austrian populism in the 1990s and beyond.

Besides pushing for integration, the Conservatives were also the architects of Vienna's policy during the conflict in the former Yugoslavia, which was unfolding on Austria's doorstep. On the question of recognizing the independence of Slovenia and Croatia, the ÖVP quickly moved ahead suggesting that "*Austria would have to be* [their] *advocate and interpreter in the West.*"[18] In their commitment to the cause of Slovenian and Croatian independence, the People's Party not only risked public confrontations with its Social Democratic coalition partner,[19] but also stern rebukes by Paris and Moscow, as well as a serious confrontation with Belgrade—the latter accused Austria of fomenting separatism. As in the case of European integration, the Austrian Social Democrats eventually converged more or less on the position adopted by Foreign Minister Mock. In retrospect, however, it is noteworthy that Mock and his party abandoned their avowed "realistic" foreign policy in favor of an activist, if not to say interventionist and idealist, course in the Yugoslav conflict.

From Nation State to Member State—Schüssel as Party Leader and Foreign Minister

When Schüssel took the reigns of both his party and the foreign office, he found a situation in which the Conservatives had been largely in the driver's seat on foreign policy, but were otherwise in acute danger of shrinking to mid-size status. The Social Democrats could, despite all setbacks, still count on the bonus of being the chancellor's party while the FPÖ benefited from growing anti-European and anti-internationalist sentiments. Austria's largest and most powerful newspaper, *Neue Kronenzeitung*, began converging on the anti-European line of the Freedom Party, calling, for example, the former ÖVP Minister and then EU Commissioner Franz Fischler "unpatriotic" and the European Union a threat to Austria's identity.[20] Presenting itself as the *Europa-Partei* was no longer an attractive enough rationale to lure sufficient voters to the ÖVP. If anything, the party's avowedly pro-European stance conflicted with a new kind of Austrian patriotism and the emerging politics of identity.

Under Mock, foreign policy had been largely independent of the day-to-day domestic political calculus. Instead, it was based on the clear principle that Europe was paramount and Austria's integration into the emerging Union the overriding objective of the party and the country. Under Schüssel, the Conservatives' emphasis shifted in subtle but perceptible ways, although the ÖVP remained the relatively most pro-European of Austria's parties. Now, however, it presented itself less as Europe's voice in Austria and increasingly as Austria's advocate in Europe. At the time, the European Union was slowly turning into a popular target in national politics because of a series of conflicts between Vienna and Brussels. Specifically, several uniquely Austrian arrangements had run afoul of EU regulations, and the government was additionally chided by the European Commission for the slow pace of implementing the large body of community law. Unfamiliarity with the political process at the European Union level as well as ineffectiveness in both forging cross-national alliances and reading the political signs early enough meant that Austria saw itself outmaneuvered and overruled when key interests were at stake. This created the public impression that the "big countries were ganging on the little Alpine republic." From unilaterally wanting to restrict transalpine road traffic to maintaining the nationally popular anonymous bank accounts, Austria saw itself pressured by the European Commission to comply with treaty obligations.[21]

An even more sensitive matter concerned Austria's integration into the so-called *Euro* zone. The comprehensive austerity measures required to meet the convergence criteria and, thus, qualify for the planned single currency were politically costly to Social Democrats and Conservatives alike. The voters reacted with anger to a scenario in which they were first promised major economic benefits from accession in 1995 and subsequently confronted with a series of social cutbacks in the name of participating in the single market.[22] Other "European" issues such as the outbreak of mad-cow disease, first in the United Kingdom and later elsewhere in Europe, the dismantling of border checkpoints in compliance with the Schengen Agreement, and the looming question of enlarging the European Union into Eastern Europe all added to an anti-EU backlash that was bound to hurt the ÖVP as the most openly pro-European party.

Membership in the European Union presented not only problems, but also provided political party advantages by offering Austrian policymakers an additional platform in an important new setting. Soon after accession, Foreign Minister Schüssel and the Austrian government became fully engaged in the European Union decision-making processes and were trying to take advantage of the international political limelight. This occurred first in the context of the negotiations for the new Amsterdam Treaty and then during Austria's first EU Council Presidency in 1998. Especially the latter case had been intended to showcase, a year prior to the national elections, both the accomplishments of the government and Austria's readiness for membership. It was also meant to turn around the public's mood about "Europe." However, despite extensive preparations for the first presidency of a new member state, conflicts between the two political parties and attempts between the chancellor and the vice-chancellor to upstage one another diminished potential political party benefits.[23]

For Schüssel, who was not only foreign minister but, more importantly, vice-chancellor and party leader, domestic questions and party-political concerns were taking center-stage regardless of how they would be perceived in Brussels and by Austria's political partners. In fact, when ÖVP officials began making ominous statements linking Czech and Slovenian EU membership with extraneous but populist issues, it became clear that opposition to "Europe" could serve as a welcome source of political mobilization for the Austrian center-right. As a precondition for EU accession, the Freedomites and also some Conservatives demanded that the Czech Republic rescind the "Beneš Decrees" and Slovenia the so-called "AVNOJ Mandates" to redress the grievances of ethnic Germans expelled after 1945. The campaign by right-wing politicians in Austria fed on popular anti-Slavic sentiments, exacerbating latent negative attitudes in the population about the enlargement process. Another issue affecting Austrian-Czech relations was the dispute over the Czech nuclear power plant at Temelin, the closure and dismantling of which Austria's public demanded as a precondition for approving Prague's accession to the Union. This was a particularly sensitive matter for Schüssel's party because the Austrian border state of Lower Austria was governed by one of the ÖVP's most powerful and influential politicians, Governor Erwin Pröll.

Although Austria and the ÖVP's official rhetoric continued to present the Alpine nation as a supporter and friend of the quick integration of its southern and eastern neighbors into the European Union, the country's *de facto* policy was more obstinate.[24] As a result, Vienna gradually acquired the image of a troublemaker, whose true intention was to slow down or even thwart Eastern expansion. In due course, this foreign policy was notably criticized by East European politicians such as Polish Foreign Minister Wladyslaw Bartoszewski, who accused Vienna of a lack of leadership and a failure to continue the "direction of Kreisky and Busek."[25] We may, therefore, agree with Helmut Kramer that apart from Austria's formal role during the EU presidency in 1998 when Vienna did support the launching of accession negotiations, "the contribution of Austria and the Austrian government to the expansion of the "common European house," which was to receive not only "an additional floor but also a new foundation", can be qualified as "disappointing."[26]

Austria's tacit skepticism of enlargement was even more remarkable given that its economy not only benefited enormously from this development, but that Austrian businesses explicitly embraced expansion. In time, they became the largest international investors in countries such as Slovenia, Slovakia, Hungary, and Bulgaria—Jan

Stankovsky estimates that Austrian GDP grew by an additional 3 percent due to the economic stimulus from enlargement.[27]

There were other policy areas in which Austria played a more constructive and internationalist role. In 1994 the country had joined the Danish-led Standby Force High Readiness Brigade for UN Operations (SHIRBRIG). Subsequently, it participated with small troop contingents in the International Force (IFOR)[28] and the Stabilization Force (SFOR) in Bosnia and later in the Kosovo Force (KFOR). This commitment of 750 men was a novel departure for Austrian foreign policy and domestically rather controversial.[29] Vienna also followed an invitation by the West European Union (WEU) and the Western European Armament Group (WEAG) for full membership. These measures were designed to integrate Austria's defense and armament industry into the emerging European security and defense architecture. The Austrian expertise in the Balkans was especially valued by the European Union, which entrusted experienced officials such as Wolfgang Petritsch[30] and Erhard Busek[31] with important international missions. Vienna also actively supported EU instruments such as the Stability and Association Pact (SAP) with the countries of the Western Balkans in order to facilitate their integration into Europe. Outside the European theater, Austria's foreign policy continued to follow a tradition of pursuing humanitarian and social objectives, especially in the area of human rights[32] and the elimination of landmines (Ottawa Process).[33] In this, Austrian policy relied increasingly on cooperation with non-governmental organizations (NGOs) and benefited from Vienna's location as an important seat of international organizations such as the United Nations and the Organization of Security and Cooperation in Europe (OSCE).

The most controversial foreign policy initiative that Conservatives undertook was the push toward membership in the North Atlantic Treaty Organization (NATO), the discussion of which had been spearheaded by Mock and others in the party. In 1997, the ÖVP officially adopted this step as a foreign policy objective despite objections by some quarters in the party. Initially, it seemed an attainable goal in the sense that the suddenly shifting conception of Austrian neutrality appeared to lead to its complete lapse, thus making accession to NATO possible. However, after some initial hesitation, the Social Democrats rejected the idea. This and the growing influence of populism on matters of foreign policy made NATO membership a politically costly agenda. A subsequent ballot initiative launched in 1996 in favor of Austria's permanent neutrality was signed by 6.2 percent of the eligible voters. However, even this low number was sufficient—along with polls showing that 60 percent of Austrians regarded neutrality as part of the country's identity—to convince Schüssel to abandon the quest for NATO membership. Austria's Left in particular regarded the Western alliance not only as too expensive a security option, but, in many cases, an instrument of U.S. hegemony. This negative perception prevailed even after nearly all of Austria's neighbors had joined NATO and other traditionally neutral countries had abandoned their respective policies (such as Finland in 1995 and Sweden in 2002).

Instead, Austria joined the NATO-led Partnership for Peace (PfP-plus), which represented a minimal consensus between the coalition partners. This was a disappointing outcome in light of an earlier overly ambitious joint declaration by SPÖ-ÖVP to pursue "policies in the spirit of European solidarity and for the purpose of permanently guaranteeing the security of the Republic [...] and the full participation in the effective European security structures."[34]

Summing up, Austrian foreign policy in the mid- to latter half of the 1990s had entered a period of transition and ambivalence. After Austria had managed to be an active and useful member of the international community during the decades of its rather exceptional position between the two blocs, the geopolitical changes after 1989 and the country's insertion into the complex multilevel European system resulted in a prolonged period of insecurity. After the all-important national goal of EU membership had been realized, Austria's ambivalence about its role in the new Europe manifested itself fully in the ambiguity of its actions.

The changes in the external environment were complemented by domestic political processes that saw the decline of the major political parties, which had dominated national politics and foreign policy decision making since the end of the Second World War. Simultaneously, new political actors such as the FPÖ under Jörg Haider and the Greens, a new populist political style, and new issues such as the politics of identity and the fear of globalization gained in importance. As a consequence, the country's level of activity in and commitment to international affairs was increasingly affected by a domestic political discourse shaped by populist voices on the far-right and anti-international tabloids. In those foreign policy areas that were judged as politically "safe" because the causes seemed popular or sufficiently "harmless" or because they were occurring largely "below the radar screen" of the general public, Austria remained fairly active. In other areas that were regarded as controversial and politically costly, the party-political calculus often prevailed. As a result, Austria became a less predictable international partner.

Foreign Minister Schüssel was the face of Austria's ambivalent foreign policy at the time and did not particularly endear himself to his international colleagues. While he can, for the most part, not be held responsible for the difficulties the country experienced with confronting the new geopolitical realties, he certainly did little to mitigate the situation or demonstrate any special leadership. He was neither willing nor able to communicate to the country the importance of the nation not appearing in the international community as a freeloader that was benefiting from the enhanced security and market opportunities while demonstrating an unwillingness to make contributions commensurate to the available resources.

Neither on the basis of Schüssel's background nor his interests was he the best person to manage Austria's succession successfully. In fact, his double role as chancellor and party leader even added to the problem in that he had to weigh carefully any position he took on foreign policy with the long-term political interest of his party. His goal of extricating the ÖVP from the unloved coalition with the Social Democrats and reversing the political fortunes of the Conservatives were paramount for Schüssel the party leader. Had he only been foreign minister, he might have been better placed to be a forceful advocate of a more active foreign policy without fearing to damage the party. As the ÖVP moved to the right and the overlap in the domestic agenda with the Freedom Party grew, foreign policy was no longer an important enough factor to restrain the party leader from forging a coalition with an aggressively nationalist party, the FPÖ, which was widely regarded as an international pariah.

Austria as International Pariah—Schüssel Becomes Chancellor in 2000

The single most important development in Schüssel's first term as Austrian chancellor and arguably the most difficult period for Austrian foreign policy since the end of Allied occupation in 1955 was the international quarantine after the ÖVP formed a government with Haider's Freedom Party. Already the strong showing of the FPÖ in the 1999 elections had dominated the international headlines. At the time, the most negative reaction by a foreign government came from Israel.[35] In front of international journalists in Luxemburg, Israeli Foreign Minister David Levy made unmistakably clear that any participation by the FPÖ in a future government would change the bilateral relations between Austria and Israel.[36]

France, too, expressed growing concern about the situation in Austria. Already in November 1999 during the Istanbul summit of the Organization of Security and Cooperation in Europe, French President Jacques Chirac indicated to the Austrian delegation that the inclusion of the FPÖ in a future Austrian government would have "far-reaching consequences."[37] At the time, according to French diplomatic sources, Vice-Chancellor Schüssel assured the French that this would not happen. Already once before in February of 1999, the Conservatives had rejected the notion that they intended to form a partnership with the Freedomites. This fact gave rise to speculations that Chirac felt betrayed by his fellow conservative counterpart in Austria because the Gaullist French President had always resisted the political temptation of cooperating with the extremist right in his own country.

The rocky negotiations between the SPÖ and ÖVP during December and January continued to make headlines, and numerous international voices sought to deter Schüssel from contemplating a coalition with Haider. Following an international Holocaust Conference in Stockholm on 21 January 2000, the mostly Social Democratic government leaders expressed their solidarity with outgoing Chancellor Viktor Klima and informally discussed possible measures against Austria in the event of a Freedom Party government. A second thrust to thwart a Schüssel-Haider government in Vienna came from the French President. While Schüssel rejected the international calls as unwarranted interference in national politics, Haider continued to mock his international critics, aggravating the situation.[38]

Before the final round of negotiations between the ÖVP and the FPÖ on 1 February, the United States along with Israel and most other Western democracies threatened consequences for their bilateral relations with Vienna. In response to the international concerns, the ÖVP-FPÖ pact included a preamble, of which President Klestil was officially introduced as the author, but evidence suggested that, in fact, Schüssel had drafted most of the statement himself.[39] In this lengthy declaration signed by Schüssel and Haider entitled "Responsibility for Austria—A Future in the Heart of Europe," the new government expressed its commitment to the protection of human rights, the principles of democracy, and the abolition of discrimination and intolerance. It stated that Austria was bound by EU treaty commitments to the principles of liberty, democracy, human rights, and the rule of law. It also declared the government's continued support for the European Monetary Union and EU enlargement, promised a self-critical scrutiny of the Nazi past, and accepted Austria's responsibility under the Nazi regime.

A catalogue of measures against Austria emerged in conference calls involving groups of three or four.[40] Initially, Luxembourg Prime Minister Claude Juncker hoped the sanctions would be presented to the Austrians at an EU Council meeting. Instead, EU Council President and Portuguese Prime Minister Antonio Guterres announced them on the afternoon of 31 January, indicating they were to go into effect after the center-right government had taken office. Chancellor Klima, Foreign

Minister Schüssel, and President Klestil were informed, but Austria was not consulted in the negotiations by the other fourteen EU nations. The measures were as follows: 1) the governments of the fourteen would not promote or accept any bilateral official contacts at the political level with an Austrian government integrating the FPÖ, 2) there would be no support (promotion or acceptance) in favor of Austrian candidates seeking positions in international organizations, and 3) Austrian ambassadors in EU capitals would only be received at a technical level. Although Austria's bilateral relations with the other EU members were effectively downgraded to a technical level, the sanctions were not imposed by the European Union as such and, thus, did not legally affect Austria's participation in EU institutions. Had this been the case, the smooth operation of the Union would have been jeopardized, which both the EU and its members wanted to avoid.

From the beginning there was a strong indication that, internationally, the views about Austria and the sanctions were more divergent than the public protestations of unity and the harshness of the measures made it appear.[41] Besides Israel, which immediately recalled its ambassador, a range of other countries in Eastern Europe and the Americas expressed support and understanding for the international boycott. The United States temporarily called its ambassador back to Washington "for consultations," but adopted what Secretary of State Madeleine Albright, dubbed a "wait and see" attitude.[42] The East Europeans were more cautious in their approach because, as applicant countries, they wanted to remain in the EU leaders' good graces. However, they did not wish to provoke Vienna into vetoing or seriously delaying their accession. Thus Austria's smaller neighbors Slovakia, Slovenia, and Hungary did not join the boycott, whereas the Czech Republic and Poland did. As a result, the relations between Vienna and Prague deteriorated even further. Nonetheless, the President of the Czech Parliament Vaclav Klaus sent a letter of solidarity to Schüssel, denouncing Brussels. Meanwhile, Hungarian Prime Minister Viktor Orban demonstratively invited the Austrian chancellor to Hungary.

In the negotiations prior to forming a government and in the run-up before the sanctions were announced, Schüssel displayed his characteristic knack for turning long odds into a political advantage. He remained steadfast, relying on a close circle of supporters in the party and ignoring the enormous criticism that came from abroad, the media, the Austrian president, and quarters in his own party. For one, he recognized that the international pressure could give him much needed political leverage at home and increase the political legitimacy of his embattled government. The actions by the EU14 directed at Schüssel's administration were perceived by most Austrians, even those critical of the

ÖVP-FPÖ government, as an affront against the entire country and an illegitimate interference in national sovereignty. Thus the boycott served as a source of cohesion and public mobilization for Schüssel's government while making life difficult for the opposition, which had to be careful not to appear unpatriotic when criticizing the center-right coalition.

Second, the international pressure also allowed Schüssel to domesticate the Freedomites and commit them to a policy that was *de facto* more pro-European than their rhetoric. Most crucially, the worldwide negative reactions to Haider sealed his fate in national politics, and he withdrew to his home state of Carinthia where he had been the elected governor. From there, he tried to dominate his party but, as time would show, with decreasing effectiveness.[43] Within three years, his party splintered, and Haider came to preside over what was a diminished split-off from the Freedom Party. In retrospect, it is profoundly ironic and somewhat paradoxical that the sanctions actually increased both Schüssel's leverage and room to maneuver.

Internationally, the quarantine was undoubtedly a blow to Austria and Schüssel's prestige. As the chief architect of the new government, the boycott was primarily directed at him. But the measures also contained a series of weaknesses that Schüssel was willing to exploit and turn to his advantage. For one, the sanctions were legally hard to justify, for they had no real basis in either the common EU law or international law.[44] Austria had neither breached any agreements, nor been found guilty in any tribunal. The formation of the center-right government reflected the national electoral will and was entirely consistent with Austrian law. Second, the measures were politically problematic and hastily conceived. On the one hand, there was no clear agreement on the goal and purpose of the sanctions, and it seemed only a matter of time before the united front would splinter. The smaller countries and the more sovereignty-conscious nations such as Denmark and the United Kingdom appeared increasingly uneasy. On the other, the sanctions contributed to the image problem of the European Union as a place in which political correctness ran amok and big nations bullied smaller ones if the latter had dared vote for the "wrong" party. The sanctions were also tactically ill-conceived because, in the long run, they put the onus of action on the EU-14 and not Austria. If the latter simply did nothing, the others were forced to act because the sanctions could not be maintained indefinitely. That created a dilemma because many member states did not have the stomach to impose harsher and perhaps more effective measures whose legitimacy would have been even more doubtful. At the same time, lifting the sanctions without Austria making any concessions was considered a humiliating defeat. The EU-14 had to face the fact that there was no readily apparent face-saving exit strategy. Nonetheless, the formal goal of changing the composition of the Austrian government was insofar unattainable as Schüssel had overriding domestic priorities that he wanted to implement regardless of the international pressure.

The international quarantine had also unintended consequences negatively affecting the public perception and media coverage, not just in Austria,[45] but also abroad.[46] Stories abounded that Austrians, either individually or as groups, had been treated poorly in different European countries because of overeager officials or because the meaning of the measures had been misunderstood. What is more, the grotesque diplomatic contortions necessary to pretend that everything was "business as usual" to ensure the smooth decision-making process of the European Union, such as refusing officially even to discuss the issue, contrasted unfavorably with the rather puerile gestures to avoid at all cost any contact with Austrian delegations at various EU gatherings. Arranging photo opportunities, seating orders at dinners, group photos, and handshakes became nightmares for protocol officials.[47] Some of these actions were directed against Schüssel personally. One such form of humiliation included wearing buttons[48] mocking the Austrian chancellor, refusing handshakes, and suspending bilateral institutional relations.[49] In many ways, the tokenism of these acts symbolized also the helplessness of the EU-14 to effect real change in Austria, but provided instead ample reason for ridiculing the measures.

After various Austrian attempts, including a so-called "charm offensive" by the new Foreign Minister Benita Ferrero-Waldner as well as mediation attempts by President Klestil and the new SPÖ leader Alfred Gusenbauer, had failed to resolve the issue, Schüssel decided to raise the stakes and bring greater pressure to bear by revealing a lengthy catalogue of counter-measures.[50] Most critical among these was the announcement that the Austrian government would hold a national referendum on the sanctions and exercise its veto-option to block legislative progress in EU institutions. Chancellor Schüssel traveled to Brussels in July 2000, forcing a meeting with Commission President Romano Prodi. Simultaneously, the Austrians intervened with the Commission charging that, in a flagrant violation of the EU Treaty, Austrian students and civil servants had been subject to discrimination in member countries, notably in Belgium. Parallel measures were aimed at legal action against the EU-14 and included proposing a "objective framework" for resolving similar cases in the future.[51]

Taking a more aggressive stance toward the European Union carried little risk for the Austrian government given the anti-European sentiments of the population. While polls in Austria signaled that the attitudes towards the European Union had plummeted during the first half of 2000, surveys taken in all EU member countries showed that the overwhelming majority of Europeans did not support the measures.[52] In this context, a growing number of politicians, both in EU institutions and among member states, began searching for a way out. In view of the upcoming elections in Italy and motivated by concerns about a backlash against the European Union, the government in Rome was eager to mediate, as documented by an exchange between Foreign Minister Lamberto Dini and his Austrian counterpart Ferrero-Waldner, which was leaked to the Italian press.[53] Politicians in Greece, Ireland, Denmark, Finland, and subsequently also the United Kingdom, the Netherlands, and Sweden had either gone on record questioning the usefulness of the sanctions or voiced opposition to their continuation.[54]

An important first step in the resolution of the crisis and a vindication for Schüssel was the "acquittal" of the ÖVP on 6 June 2000 in the ongoing proceeding to revoke its membership in the European People's Party. The mechanism chosen to study the case and review the record of the Austrian Conservatives was to become the model for an international approach to assess the entire case against Austria.[55] The formula that was eventually adopted centered on a so-called committee of sages, who would investigate the political nature of the Freedom Party in terms of whether it conformed both to the letter and the spirit of Article 7 in the Treaty of Rome. Schüssel had initially resented the idea of Austria having to undergo an external review, but in the end recognized its political usefulness.

From 28 through 31 August 2000, former Finnish President Martii Ahtisaari, the German expert on international law Jochen Frowein, and the former Spanish Foreign Minister and previous EU Commissioner Marcelino Oreja met with a variety of representatives of all Austrian political parties, major interest groups, and principal institutions. The three sages gave Austria an unambiguously positive verdict although it was critical of aspects of both the FPÖ and Austrian asylum procedures. In its judgment of the government's political practice as well as Austria's legal protections of minorities and existing programs to fight xenophobia, racism, anti-Semitism, and discrimination, the report contained much praise.[56] It also concluded that the sanctions had outlived their usefulness and were counterproductive.

On 8 September, Ahtisaari, Oreja, and Frowein handed their findings to French President Chirac in his capacity as EU Council president. Since the substantive conclusions had already been leaked[57] to the media, the French had no alternative but to release the official report immediately to the public. Four days later, a communiqué of the fourteen released in Paris stated that the bilateral measures between the

EU-14 and Austria had been removed and that the quarantine had been "useful." Because the measures were lifted without a follow-up procedure, the Austrian "government hailed the decision as a triumph."[58] Nonetheless, the experience continued to overshadow Austria's foreign policy during the entire first chancellorship of Schüssel.

At the time of the boycott of the EU-14, Austria also had to chair the OSCE and successfully oversee the return of Yugoslavia to the international organization.[59] Yet, apart from such successes, Austria's relationship with its European partners remained difficult. In issue after issue, from enlargement to transit traffic, Austrian neutrality, and eventually the question of Turkey's accession to the European Union, the Alpine nation was either out of step with the majority of its European partners or embroiled in political conflict.

Between Euro-Skepticism, Populism, and Business as Usual—Schüssel's Chancellorship 2000-2002

Despite concerted efforts by the Schüssel government to create an image of normalcy and "business as usual" in the relations with its European partners, the effect of the international boycott lingered. During an official visit by the Austrian Chancellor to Berlin in November 2000, his German counterpart signaled distance and was unwilling to exchange little more than superficial pleasantries. France, Sweden, and Belgium continued to avoid any gestures that could be seen as more than the minimum necessary required by the standards of bilateral contacts among EU members. A noticeable improvement both in the atmosphere and substance of relations came with the smaller EU members such as Greece, Finland, Denmark, and Ireland. Generally, however, the climate between the Austrian government and its international counterparts benefited from the resignation of the FPÖ leader so that both Chancellor Schüssel and his foreign minister could dismiss his continued verbal outbursts as those of a provincial politician that one should ignore.

The international sanctions against Austria were a painful but useful learning experience for all parties concerned. In some respect, the measures demonstrated to Austrians and also to Haider that a Freedom Party-dominated government would face tremendous international opposition. The European Union, on the other hand, found itself confronted with questions about its own democratic character and was forced to admit that "nationality is even more 'sticky' than it may have seemed."[60] In response, the fifteen member states of the European Union decided at their summit in Nice in December 2000 to amend the EU Treaty in the sense that the Union could intervene in the future if there arose the "danger" of a serious breach of treaty principles (by, for example, setting up a Committee of Wise Persons to report on the case). In this way, the Austrian delegation successfully promoted and supported the principle that the member state in question must be heard before there was any action taken.[61]

Despite the stated commitment to European integration by the center-right government, FPÖ officials took every opportunity to criticize the European Union for everything ranging from its handling of mad cow (BSE) and foot-and-mouth disease to rulings against Austria on transit traffic and anonymous savings accounts. High-ranking party members routinely attacked EU officials, specifically the commissioner on enlargement, Günter Verheugen, referring to him as a "coward"[62] and Austrian EU Agriculture Commissioner Franz Fischler, calling him a "traitor."[63]

EU enlargement ended up in the crosshairs of the FPÖ. The accession by the Central and Eastern European countries was unpopular in Austria. Haider demanded that "integration can only take place without a significant detriment to Austrian interests."[64] The complexity of the integration process, its uneven economic impact, and the humiliation of the sanctions all played their part. Moreover, campaigning against "Europe" diverted attention from the Freedom Party's disastrous domestic political performance and provided a way to distinguish itself more clearly from its coalition partner. Thus the Freedom Party continually brought up new issues and made certain demands designed to raise Austria's political leverage while slowing down the enlargement process. For example, Freedomite officials insisted that "enlargement must cost less" and announced that Austrian contributions between 2004 and 2006 would be lower than demanded by the European Commission.[65] FPÖ politicians also continued to insist that Prague rescind the "Beneš Decrees" if the Czech Republic did not want Austria to block the accession process. With respect to the controversial Czech nuclear power plant at Temelin, the Conservatives appeared to support the hostile rhetoric of the Freedomites.

Wolfgang Schüssel, who had not forgotten the criticism that came from Prague and Ljubljana for his *mésalliance* with Haider, appeared initially in no mood to placate the mutual sentiments. Particularly surprising were statements by the Austrian Chancellor in which he implied the internationally highly respected Slovene President Kucan was still "with one leg in the old (Communist) regime" [of former Yugoslavia], to which the latter replied in an interview, "I am not offended but have certainly gained a new impression of Chancellor Schüssel."[66] As in the case with the Czech Republic, there were similar demands made of Slovenia that it, too, shut down its nuclear reactor at the plant in Krško. As a result, Austria's relationship with its two Slavic neighbors, the Czech Republic and Slovenia, reached a nadir between 2000 and 2001. Finally, relations with Germany also continued to be poor, although that had more to do with the difference in political philosophy between the leftist Social Democratic-Green coalition in Berlin and the center-right government in Austria.

Whether it was out of a lingering feeling of personal humiliation at the hands of his international counterparts, tactical calculus, or a combination of the two, Schüssel's foreign policy with respect to Europe became bolder and tougher in the sense that his statements and several of his initiatives were made with a view to the domestic audience, or in coordination with the domestic political calendar. In this, the chancellor was oddly helped by the climate created by the preceding sanctions. The European Union was reluctant to reengage Austria in such a negative manner and tolerated some of the noises coming from Vienna. Repeatedly, Schüssel let matters escalate, despite knowing that Austria was internationally isolated on particular issues, only to pull back at the last moment.

With tiny Slovenia, it was Ljubljana's explicitly conciliatory policy toward its bigger Austrian neighbor that brought about an improvement in relations. The same cannot be said about the situation between Vienna and Prague, where the issue of the Temelin nuclear reactor appeared intractable. While the Czech Republic had invested several hundred million dollars and thirteen years of construction, Austria regarded itself as, what the *Economist* labeled "a self-proclaimed nuclear free zone obsessed with the idea that Temelin would become another Chernobyl."[67] There was broad agreement across all political camps in Austria that the project had to be stopped, so there was widespread dismay when EU Commissioner for Enlargement Günter Verheugen announced that nobody could dictate energy policy to an applicant provided the plant met all (national) safety standards (there was no single EU standard at the time). Border boycotts (for which the regional government closed the schools so students could participate), demonstrations, and fiery speeches by politicians formed the climax of a wave of anti-Czech protests.

Recognizing the futility of Austria's demands and fearing real political damage, Schüssel eventually reached for the political olive branch that Prague offered by agreeing to a joint dialogue about a safety review and mutual consultation. Labeling it the "Melk process" was classically Schüssel in that it made it appear this was not only an Austrian initiative, but also launched in Melk, Lower Austria, and, thus, in that (ÖVP governed) region of the country which was most opposed to Temelin. Eventually, Prague agreed to some additional safety measures, which, however, did not become part of the Czech treaty of accession. Vienna's initiative to get the Czech Republic to rescind the so-called Beneš Decrees and recognize the claims of expelled Germans went nowhere. However, Austria did succeed in negotiating (along with Germany) the longest possible exemption (seven years) from having to open its labor market to workers from the new EU member states, which, in terms of Austrian *Realpolitik*, was much more important for the government than the symbolism of the anti-German decrees.

The Schüssel government was haunted by the still unresolved issue of international truck traffic through Austria, which continually brought the country into conflict with Brussels and its powerful neighbors Germany and Italy. The comprehensive arrangement worked out in 1998 under which Austria was to spread its road toll evenly across the entire length of the affected transit route was nixed after the governor of the province, a member of Schüssel's Conservative party, refused to implement it. The subsequent tug-of-war between Vienna and both the European Community and the European Council, in which Austria found itself isolated and outvoted multiple times, was an acrimonious issue for all sides concerned. The matter also led to verdicts by the European Court of Justice against Austria for being in breach of its treaty obligations. Pressured by strong local opposition and popular demands, the Schüssel government was unable to agree to a compromise solution, which also would have implied accepting a disproportionably high share of the environmental burden and cost. Austria eventually struck back by bringing its own court case against the European Commission and threatening the European Council with blocking a part of the accession negotiations with the new member states.

Whereas the details and merits of the case cannot be reviewed here, the transit dispute with the European Union exposed the continuing weaknesses inherent in the Austrian approach to policymaking in the European arena, especially the initially noticeable lack of anticipation, initiative, and imagination. In general, there was little Austrian input in the early stages of opinion and policy formation at the European level. Instead, Austria waited for a consolidated policy position to emerge, which it then sought to block, deflect, or wear down in protracted negotiations. This issue also draws attention to a bigger underlying problem: Austria has not really had any stable partners or allies at the European level. Unlike the Scandinavians, the Benelux countries, or the Mediterranean member states, Austria does not have an automatic cohort of sympathetic neighbors to which to turn for support. Attempts to launch initiatives to develop such interest-based natural partnerships remained largely without effective results. For example, an intended "strategic partnership" with Austria's neighboring EU accession countries had to be renamed "regional partnership" and yielded as little of substance as did the Central European Initiative or the Danube Cooperation Process.[68]

However, the dispute over the trans-Alpine truck traffic also shows that the Schüssel government became savvier over time and learned to extract concessions by taking advantage of the fragmented and shifting interests arrayed against it in multiple policy arenas. Nonetheless, this was an area in which important national objectives were at stake and where Austria legitimately felt it had to resort to all available means to stand its ground. Yet it is another example of how Vienna seemed unable to make itself heard and advance an arguably reasonable agenda on the basis of already existing international agreements without acrimony and friction. The complaints, threats, and lawsuits as well as verbal exchanges on all sides accompanying this process are indicative that, in its dealings with Europe, Austria was still far from being able to work smoothly behind the scenes.

In the transit controversy as in the conflict over enlargement and the Czech nuclear plant, the Schüssel government (along with nearly all other Austrian parties) was willing to play "Europe" off against domestic interests and thus contributed to an "us versus them" populist discourse in which the "others" and Brussels were portrayed as ganging up on a small country. From an official side, there was neither sufficient effort to explain the kind of obligations Austria had incurred as a result of membership, nor an attempt to convey what facts had persuaded other member states to arrive so often at a decision different from that of Vienna. Instead of seeking to mitigate the existing tensions, the latter were instrumentalized for the purpose of domestic party politics by reinforcing latent myths about Austrian exceptionalism.

Political Calculus and the Troublesome Freedom Party

The coalition with the conflict-prone Freedomites did offer some tactical advantages to Schüssel in that it made the Conservatives appear more statesmen-like, professional, and pro-European. At the same time, the existence of the FPÖ reminded others that worse could follow if Schüssel were not to succeed with his political project. For this, the Conservative party leader was willing make sacrifices, if need be, also in Austria's international relations. Ever since the Conservatives had moved to the right, they sought to undo much of what they regarded as an excessive Socialist imprint on Austria's social and economic system. Both the ÖVP and the FPÖ were also eager to reduce severely the influence of the SPÖ on the state and the public sector, over which the Social Democrats had accumulated significant power after three decades in the government. By and large, the policy changes introduced were not the "slash and burn" neoliberalism that critics alleged, but were in line with conservative reforms elsewhere. However, the new political agenda, especially in social policy, was such that its implementation would have been impossible without close cooperation between the Conservatives and the Freedom Party. Schüssel also recognized that many of the reforms implied greater hardship for core Freedomite voter groups. Therefore, to maintain his alliance with the FPÖ and keep his domestic reform project on track, the chancellor was willing to tolerate regular Freedom Party outbursts about international and EU matters.

In general, the ÖVP learned to reign in the Freedomites on the foreign policy questions where it mattered or to use them in a sort of "good cop/bad cop" manner. In some instances, the Conservatives appeared to support the rhetoric of the Freedomites, while, as in the case of the conflict with Prague over Temelin, one ÖVP cabinet minister along with the tacit approval of the EU Commission had worked out an agreement with the Czech government that no longer demanded the dismantling of the plant. In other instances, politically thankless issues were left for FPÖ-led ministries such as the vastly unpopular decision to purchase expensive fighter planes. Within the Schüssel cabinet, the Freedomites faced the added difficulty of remaining internationally isolated even after the sanctions had ended. When, for example, German Chancellor Gerhard Schröder briefly visited his Austrian counterpart, Vice-Chancellor and FPÖ leader Susanne Riess-Passer was not even invited to the luncheon and the photo-op. Such missed opportunities robbed the latter of valuable public relations while allowing the chancellor and his foreign minister, Benita Ferrero-Waldner, to dominate the international stage.

The coalition with the Freedomites also resulted in significant political drawbacks for Chancellor Schüssel. Its precarious internal situation made the government perpetually unstable. Internationally, the Freedom Party was a constant embarrassment and served as a reminder that Austria's international relations would not be fully normal as long as this coalition existed.[69] FPÖ officials regularly put the Schüssel administration into an awkward position by offering revisionist accounts of Austrian history when, once again, portraying the country as a victim of history.[70] For example, the government was generally praised for concluding a Euro 420 million restitution settlement with some 149,000 surviving forced laborers of the Nazi regime itself. Yet several Freedomite officials left little doubt how they regarded this accord—an FPÖ member of Parliament referred to it as "protection money" to safeguard "Austrian trade relations with the U.S."[71] Anti-Jewish remarks also accompanied Haider's third visit to Saddam Hussein, which was in itself an embarrassment, always prompting stern U.S. protests.

Eventually, the tension between the two coalition parties over Europe became a significant strain in the government as well as within the Freedom Party between the leadership and the base. To the extent that the FPÖ's poor overall political performance resulted in a string of electoral defeats in regional elections and declining poll numbers, campaigning against "Europe" became an ever more important source of Freedom Party cohesion and mobilization. The FPÖ's stance on Europe was also the one policy area that allowed the party to appeal to its diverse coalition of voters, uniting modernization losers, hardcore right-wingers, welfare chauvinists, blue-collar workers, and cultural traditionalists. Thus being able to pare the Freedom Party down to a manageable size must have seemed an irresistible option to Schüssel.

After early elections in the fall of 2002 which had been prompted by the turmoil within the FPÖ, Schüssel was able continue the coalition with a much diminished partner. The chancellor's room to maneuver increased further after the Freedom Party fragmented in the spring of 2005, at which point the ÖVP carried on with a group of former Freedomite members in government. The latter had formed a new political party dubbed the Alliance (for the) Future (of) Austria (*Bündnis Zukunft Österreich*, or BZÖ). As a result, the coalition partner was less and less able to affect foreign policy decision making other than by threatening to bring down the government and effectively commit political suicide.

The Center-Right's Embrace of Foreign Security Policy

A policy area in which the center-right government brought about steady and substantive change was that of national security policy. Although many of the initiatives were by themselves too insignificant to raise much public attention and, in some respects, represented merely the logical extension of earlier policies, their cumulative effect amounted to Austria's integration into the European security and defense architecture. Nonetheless, the country stopped short of outright membership in NATO. As in the rest of Europe, the evolution of security policy in Austria was overshadowed by the events of 11 September and the subsequent wars in Afghanistan and Iraq.[72]

Austria, along with the rest of the European Union, supported the United States after the terrorist attacks of 9-11, but declared its neutrality when the war in Iraq started. Shortly thereafter, this declaration was withdrawn to "avoid the impression of equidistance" between Washington and Baghdad.[73] Subsequently, Austria tried to stay out of the transatlantic quarrels, but refused to grant U.S. war planes the right to fly through Austrian airspace. The widespread hostility in Austria to the U.S. intervention in Iraq only solidified the already prevailing negative views about full membership in the Western military alliance.

As early as May 2000, the government had introduced a new defense doctrine based on the principle of comprehensive security. In 2002, the chancellery updated this concept by talking about "preventive security."[74] In line with new foreign policy focus, Austria sent, for first time, military attachés to Syria and Iran. In 2001, the Schüssel Administration established a new National Security Council which would report directly to the chancellery, thus replacing or superseding the previous assortment of advisory bodies. In the same year, the government also changed the neutrality clauses in Austrian law to allow for the shipment of military materials to combatant countries in the context of the EU's Common Foreign and Defense Policy (CFSP). The strategic partnership between the European Union and NATO as envisioned by the Treaty of Nice resulted in an internal Austrian debate regarding whether the country's concept of neutrality had changed to such an extent that the military could take part in CFSP peace enforcement missions even without an appropriate UN Security Council mandate. Although the government eventually backed down on this question, the mere contemplation of possible Austrian military action outside a UN authorized mission shows how far Austrian foreign security policy had changed within a few years.

Undeterred, the Schüssel II government pursued active Austrian participation in actions and collaboration with EU member states to aid militarily in the defense of a fellow EU country although it was well understood that many of the European armed forces involved would have to rely on NATO assets. Only after fearing losses in regional and national presidential elections in 2004 did Austria support a Finnish initiative designed to weaken Britain's proposal of such unconditional military support.[75] Austria subsequently participated in the newly created European Defense Agency and announced in 2004 that the country would also take part in the European Battle Group with Germany and the Czech Republic. In this manner, Austria could logistically rely on Germany as a lead nation.[76] However, the popularity of neutrality convinced the Freedom Party and, subsequently in 2004, the ÖVP to recommit themselves once again to this cherished Austrian doctrine, although neutrality's real meaning and practicality had become rather questionable by that time.

Austria and the Question of Turkey's Accession to the European Union

During Schüssel's second term, probably no foreign policy position caused more international stir and was more controversial than Austria's stance on the question of Turkish accession to the European Union.[77] Given the cultural, geographic, and political distance between Vienna and Ankara, Austria's active opposition seemed incomprehensible to outsiders because expectations assumed that Greece or Cyprus would be the real obstacles to Turkey's accession. Moreover, Turkish membership was expected to affect positively the EU's defense architecture and, thus, the relationship with NATO and the United States. Conventional wisdom said it would provide the European Union with a significant foothold in the politically sensitive Middle East and serve as a showcase of how the West could integrate a moderate Islamic country into alliances. In short, these were all highly important geopolitical questions that not only extended far beyond Europe, but also affected the political arena of European defense policy and transatlantic relations in which Austria was less than a minor player. Even more remarkably, the Schüssel government spent significant political capital on this issue and maintained its position in the face of a great deal of international pressure, including that brought by the United States.[78]

The simplistic view of Austria's actions, reflected in several international publications, invoked Austria's historical role as an anti-Turkish bulwark and made references to the Ottoman sieges of Vienna in 1529 and 1683.[79] Other international commentators had pointed out that many Christian-conservative politicians such as those in the Austrian People's Party regarded the European Union as a Christian club and did not wish for a Muslim country to join.[80] The reality was more complicated. First, the lingering negative perception of the previous round of enlargement, in the context of which the government had talked tough but was unable to deliver, provided the subtext of the Turkish question. Many in the Alpine nation dreaded the perceived uneven economic impact and the expected high cost of yet another large but poor country acceding to the European Union, for which Austrians assumed their country—as a net payer— would have to pay a disproportional share. Second, the crucial issue of immigration played a role because Austria already contained a substantial Turkish population. The majority of these individuals were guest workers and often not from the fairly westernized Istanbul, but from the more tradition-bound east and, thus, appeared culturally rather distinct from the Austrian mainstream. Following a massive influx of foreigners in the 1990s, especially from Eastern Europe and the Balkans, immigration had become a hot political topic that was driven by ever more populist rhetoric.

Along with the issue of economic competition, the public discourse centered on questions of identity and the cultural compatibility of Turkish immigrants with Austrian and European society. Conservative politicians appeared especially sensitive to the argument that, in an increasingly more culturally heterogeneous Union, the ordinary citizens would feel alienated and, thus, increasingly less attached to the common European project. As a small country with, historically, an ambivalent national identity, Austrians appeared particularly susceptible to these concerns. Always sensitive to the public's mood, the Schüssel government recognized that Austrian approval of its own EU membership would decline further if Brussels went ahead with Turkish accession so shortly after the acrimonious debate on East European enlargement.[81]

There were two additional factors strengthening Vienna's determination to delay or derail Ankara's bid. For one, there was the question of Islam, which was indeed an issue for some in a Christian conservative party and coincided with a curious debate in parts of Austria (and Germany) about the appropriate size of mosques and the height of minarets in relation to Christian houses of worship. Secondly, there was a genuine sense on the part of some in the Austrian civil service that an even more complex European Union would not only become unwieldy and *de facto* ungovernable, but difficult to manage especially for the smaller states with their lesser resources.[82] Sentiments like this gave rise to the question of how much capacity the European Union truly had to absorb further members under current circumstances. As a result, Austria made this an issue and saw to it that the point of the Union's "absorption capacity"[83] be inserted into EU Council documents. Thus, when the European Commission announced that Ankara had fulfilled enough prerequisites to warrant the opening of accession negotiations and the EU Council was expected to give a green light, Austria refused to go along. Vienna kept insisting that Turkey be offered an "alternative" to membership in the form of a "privileged partnership" and resisted pressure to vote in the affirmative. The British EU Presidency, which was determined to deliver a positive verdict on Turkey, was particularly exasperated by the Austrian stance as Foreign Minister Jack Straw readily admitted.[84] Although the Turkish Prime Minister Recep Tayyip Erdogan was waiting to attend the Council meeting to receive personally the EU's go-ahead on 3 October 2005, Schüssel did not budge. Before making any concessions, he appeared at the very least determined to await the outcome of regional elections in Styria on the same weekend, where his party was expecting losses.[85] When the Chancellor finally relented at the end of the summit, the Austrians were able to secure the concession by the Council that accession talks would also begin with Croatia,[86] whose future in the European Union Vienna had always championed.

The fact that the Schüssel government promoted the integration of "Austria's largely Roman Catholic neighbor" so heavily, as CNN put it,[87] as well as that of the other Danube and Balkan countries, indicates the importance not necessarily of religion *per se* but at least of culture and heritage in the approach that Austrian conservatives take concerning European integration. What critics sometimes dismiss as Habsburg nostalgia and *Abendland*[88] rhetoric has served as source of historical and cultural identity for tradition-minded Austrians. From this perspective, it becomes understandable that, at EU gatherings, Schüssel refused to refer to "Macedonia" by its awkward official UN name of FYROM, sought to bring Serbia and Montenegro closer to the European Union, and pushed for moving forward with the Stability and Association Agreement with Bosnia and Herzegovina. No less than three Austrian officials served in top EU positions concerning the Balkans,[89] which is in itself an indication of Austria's expertise about a region with which the country has seen itself connected through dynastic history. Needless to say, Schüssel also consistently "championed Kiev's cause in the European Council"[90]; after all, the Ukraine's westernmost territories were once part of the Hapsburg orbit and, thus, belong to the same *Mitteleuropa.*

At the Zenith of His Power and Influence—Schüssel's Final Years as Chancellor

As the sole master of Austria's foreign policy, the chancellor began his second term with more discretion in shaping Austria's foreign relations than any Austrian politician since Bruno Kreisky in the 1970s. After the Freedom Party in parliament was reduced to less than half of its previous size in 2002 and eventually replaced in the coalition by the tiny BZÖ, Schüssel's free hand in foreign policy became even freer. By the same token, the chancellor's latitude was also never really constrained by the members of his own party, all of whom had accepted that the dramatic reversal of the Conservatives' fortune was in large measure owed to their leader's prowess.

What is more, the two ÖVP foreign ministers during Schüssel's chancellorship were considered political lightweights and unlikely to undertake independent action. Benita Ferrero-Waldner was amiable and popular but, as a previous career diplomat, did not have the backing in the party that her predecessors Mock and Schüssel had enjoyed. In addition, she came across more as a chief of protocol, a post she had held with the United Nations, than as the real architect of Austrian foreign policy. In 2004, Ferrero-Waldner moved on to become European Commissioner for External Relations and European Neighborhood Policy after her failed bid for the Austrian federal presidency. She was succeeded by Ursula Plassnik, who was even closer to the Chancellor.

Married to a Social Democrat, the new foreign minister had entered the ÖVP only when she had accepted her position and, thus, depended entirely on the Chancellor's protective hand. Plassnik had previously served as Schüssel's chief of staff. After a brief stint as ambassador to Switzerland, she was recalled by Schüssel to take over the foreign ministry. In the context of European Councils, observers could not help notice "that the chancellor still regarded her as an official, rather than as a minister, let alone a peer."[91] Other senior foreign policy officials faired little better. "Gregor Woschnagg, [who was Austria's long-serving Permanent Representative to the EU] was obliged to admit to his colleague [...] that he did not have any influence over Vienna's stance."[92]

By his second term as chancellor, Schüssel had been on the international stage for more than seven years and was one of the most experienced members of the European Council. Enjoying the respect typically accorded to elder statesmen, the Austrian chancellor had seen many other European leaders come and go. The culmination and conclusion of the decade in which Wolfgang Schüssel presided directly or indirectly over Austria's foreign policy was the country's second EU presidency in 2006. In this context, Vienna hosted both the Latin American-EU summit and U.S. President George W. Bush. Chaired by the Austrian chancellor, sixty government delegations representing twenty-seven EU and thirty-three Latin American and Caribbean countries visited the capital, which was the largest diplomatic gathering since the Congress of Vienna. The annual EU meeting with the U.S. president was understandably another highpoint during the Austrian presidency, not only because this was the first time in more than two decades that a sitting U.S. head of state visited the country, but Bush also appeared "more disposed to engage the Union in a serious dialogue than his first administration."[93]

President George W. Bush and Chancellor Wolfgang Schüssel meet during the U.S.–EU summit meeting in Vienna on June 21, 2006.

picture credits:
HOPI-MEDIA Medienservice GmbH, Vienna

Schüssel approached the six months of presiding over the European Council with a meticulously prepared, comprehensive, and detailed agenda laid out in a White Book. He was also fortunate in that one of the most intractable issues, the EU's new financial perspective, had been unexpectedly resolved in the final days of the UK presidency. With a view to the domestic audience and the upcoming national elections, Schüssel's program emphasized creating jobs and growth and made specific references to the European social model after what Ludlow termed "six months of abrasive 'Anglo-Saxon' rhetoric."[94] The so-called values debate, which the Austrian government hoped would rebuild confidence in the European project after the French and Dutch "no" votes on the EU's constitutional treaty, stressed classical Austrian themes such as subsidiarity and better regulation. Schüssel also flexed his muscles when other delegations objected to references in the Austrian presidency's draft proposal on enlargement that qualified "absorption capacity" as a "criterion."[95] On this issue, he initially remained adamant and "allowed his critics to bash their heads against what appeared to be a brick wall."[96] In the course of the negotiations, the Austrian chancellor made what appeared to be some tactical concessions and struck a conciliatory note by stressing language that the Council would "honor existing commitments." What mattered both to him and in Austrian public opinion were frequent references to the "present and future perception of enlargement" and assurances that public opinion "must in the future be taken into account when the European Council decides on how far and how fast to go with enlargement."[97]

Generally, Schüssel conducted himself ably and won plaudits for his commanding presence during Austria's EU Presidency. The latter was considered overall a success under difficult circumstances, for the Union was still reeling from internal divisions and seeking to recover from the rejection of the Lisbon Treaty. However, Schüssel's handling of the Council received other than praise; insiders also noted that "his management style placed unnecessary strains on the system" and that his constant assertions of "his own authority undermined the authority of some of his closest" (and ablest) advisors.[98] It was also pointed out that his impatience with normal procedure meant that "on occasions quality was sacrificed" and that he did not get some of the things he most wanted because "his partners resented the pressure" to which they were subjected.[99] In the end, however, the government's performance at presiding over the European Council mattered little to the Austrian electorate whose decision to turn against the Schüssel administration was driven by domestic political considerations.

Conclusion

The strengths and weaknesses of Schüssel in his handling of the EU presidency mirror his contradictory record in Austrian foreign policy. On the one hand, he has shown a great mastery of detail and considerable tactical prowess and tenacity, as well as a keen sense of public opinion and atmospherics. Moreover, he usually appeared personally affable and approachable. On the other, he needlessly provoked others into stiffening their resolve and clung for too long to indefensible positions. He also acquired a reputation of supreme self-confidence bordering on arrogance, making him impervious to the sound advice of others. Thus, despite impressive tactical victories, his record in foreign policy contains some strategic blunders.

Schüssel presided over the Alpine nation's foreign relations in a period of transition and insecurity during which the country was seeking a new role for itself while struggling to define its identity in an integrated Europe and a globalizing world. It was a decade when Austria's foreign policy was also increasingly overshadowed by a populist discourse in which the external environment was perceived as consisting primarily of threats. Three aspects seem particularly noteworthy in this context. First, Schüssel did little to mitigate the negative perception of all things foreign. In fact, both his rhetoric and, more often, his silence even exacerbated these latent tendencies in Austrian public opinion. He was largely unable to communicate effectively the purpose of the country's EU integration and its benefits. Yet, while Schüssel may not have tried hard enough to change Austrian attitudes toward Europe, he needs to be credited with trying to sensitize the European Union more to the perceptions of ordinary Europeans.

Second, during Schüssel's tenure as the architect of Austria's foreign policy, the country often stood alone. Unable to forge lasting partnerships, at odds even with some of its neighbors, and frequently opposed by Brussels and a majority of EU member states, Austria was forced into humiliating retreats after the country had staked out obviously hopeless positions. The international isolation of the Austrian government was worst during the international boycott in 2000. Yet this was also the moment of one of Schüssel's greatest triumphs. There were also other occasions in which either the chancellor's tenacity paid off or the European Union moved closer to the Austrian position. The French and German governments, for example, became arguably more skeptical about Turkish accession, and the European Union signaled it would recognize the particularly sensitive nature of trans-Alpine road traffic and, thus, the need for greater regulation.

Third, under Schüssel, foreign policy took a backseat to a domestic political agenda that intended to break the power of the Austrian Social

Democrats and undo their influence on the national economy. This is not to say that external relations were not very important to the chancellor, but what mattered more was their impact on domestic politics. Schüssel's conservatively accented foreign policy was most visible in foreign security and defense policy, whose expansion contrasted sharply with the complete de-emphasis of development policy. The latter had been an important Social Democratic objective until the 1980s. As former secretary general of the Austrian Economic Chamber, Schüssel undoubtedly welcomed the *anti-dirigiste* bent of European integration. It was a means of delivering Austria from the corset of labor-imposed regulations that he regarded as stifling. In this, the chancellor was undoubtedly a champion of Europe. Nonetheless, Schüssel was no Thatcherite free marketeer. In fact, by being steeped in the Christian Social tradition, he also recognized the limits of any deregulatory agenda in the interest of social harmony and economic security.

To the ÖVP leader, Europe appeared to be a means to other ends, not an end in itself. In this, Schüssel, by his own admission[100] appears different not only from statesmen like Helmut Kohl and Jacques Delors, but also from his predecessors like Erhard Busek and even Alois Mock. Whether, for example, his insistence on "absorption capacity" merely reflects concern about good government, or shows his sensitivity to public opinion, or is in reality an expression of a narrow ethno-cultural understanding of Europe, or combines all three is difficult to say. In any case, the chancellor's own record betrays an ambivalence toward foreign relations that seems to match that of his population.

Yet Schüssel outlasted or outsmarted most of his domestic political opponents and international colleagues. He may not have endeared himself to all, but he undoubtedly earned the respect of many of his peers. We may, therefore, agree with Peter Ludlow when he writes that Wolfgang Schüssel was "undoubtedly one of the most interesting members of the [...] European Council"[101] and as such one of the most impressive and politically successful political leaders in modern Austrian history.

Notes

1. Peter Ludlow, "European Council: Wolfgang Schüssel Leaves his Mark," *Euro-Comment Briefing Note* No 4.5/6 (August 2006): 2-3, 5.

2. Within two years of joining a coalition with the weaker Conservatives (ÖVP) under Schüssel, the Freedom Party was on the brink of disintegration and had lost a third of its electorate, much of which subsequently migrated to the chancellor's People's Party.

3. *Profil*, 30 October 2000, p. 48.

4. Ibid.

5. Mock too, was in a coalition with the stronger Social Democrats and was likewise confronted with harsh international criticism of Austria, in that case, for having elected Kurt Waldheim president.

6. Ludlow, "European Council," 5.

7. Peter Pelinka, *Wolfgang Schüssel—Eine politische Biografie* (Vienna: Ueberreuter, 2003), 126-28.

8. It is also remarkable that Mock and Schüssel represented two opposing wings of the party in that the latter had been a top functionary representing business and employer interests from 1975 to 1991, whereas the former came from the ÖVP's Federation of Workers and Employees.

9. In these years, Vienna became a seat of the United Nations and the permanent host to the Organization of Petroleum Exporting Countries. For most of the decade, Austria remained a focal point of international diplomacy, hosting a staggering array of high-level visitors and important conferences, while Austrian diplomats and politicians, with Kreisky at the center, played a significant role in numerous international initiatives.

10. Washington, for example, feared with some justification that sensitive U.S. technology circumvented stringent export controls by being shipped to Eastern Europe through Austria.

11. John Luchak, "Amerikanisch-österreichische Beziehungen von 1955 bis 1985: Neutralität und der Ost-West-Konflikt," Ph.D. diss., University of Vienna, 1987, 229.

12. Paul Luif, *On The Road to Brussels—The Political Dimension of Austria's, Finland's, and Sweden's Accession to the European Union* (Vienna: Braunmüller, 1995), 191.

13. Aside from the important question of the country's international status as a neutral nation, the Austrian cabinet had insisted on the following additional conditions: Austria's federal character had to remain intact, the economic competition in the Single Market was not to affect Austria's social system, the domestic environmental standards and the "active environmental policy" would have to be maintained, "nationwide family farming" was to be protected, and the lingering dispute over international transit traffic through Austria would need to be resolved outside the accession framework. Heinrich Schneider, "Gerader Weg zum klaren Ziel? Die Republik Österreich auf dem Weg in die Europäische Union," *Österreichische Zeitschrift für Politikwissenschaft* 23.1 (1994): 5-20, here 5.

14. Initially, the European Union opposed these reservations conveying its opinion to Austria officially in an *avis* issued on 31 July 1991. Brussels feared that Austria's neutral status could conflict with article J(8)2 of the European Union Treaty requiring unanimity for a resolution on joint action related to the common defense policy. Austria's neutrality also threatened plans concerning the integration of the West European Union (WEU) into the European Union. In long negotiations with Brussels, Austria subsequently reduced the concept of neutrality to the "military core" (Herbert Hausmaninger, *The Austrian Legal System* [Vienna: Manz, 1998], 84), which the European Union eventually accepted in 1994.

15. It also reflected the tensions, especially manifest in the run-up to the 1989 national elections, between the two government parties as labor interests remained both profoundly skeptical of the EU/EC's deregulatory agenda and wedded to the concept of Austrian neutrality.

16. Helmut Kramer, "Strukturentwicklung der Außenpolitik (1945-2005)," in *Politik in Österreich—Das Handbuch,* ed. Herbert Dachs et al. (Vienna: Manz, 2006), 807-37.

17. Christian Schaller, "'Ja' oder 'Nein' zu 'Europa'? Die österreichische Debatte im Vorfeld der Rekonstruktionsversuch," in *EU-Referndum. Zur Praxis direkter Demokratie in Österreich*, ed. Anton Pelinka (Vienna: Signum Verlag, 1994) 49-85; Heinrich Schneider, *Alleingang nach Brüssel: Österreichs EG-Politik*. (Bonn: Europa Union Verlag, 1990); Reinhard Heinisch, "Salvation and Villain: The Role of Europe in Austrian Politics and the Rise of the radical Right," *Politique européenne* 14 (Autumn 2004): 165-87; Paul Luif, *On The Road to Brussels*; Reinhard Heinisch, *Populism, Proporz and Pariah—Austria Turns Right: Austrian Political Change, Its Causes and Repercussions* (Huntington, NY: Nova Science, 2002).

18. Kramer, "Strukturentwicklung der Außenpolitik," 827.

19. Mock, Alois, ed., *Das Balkan-Dossier: Der Aggressionskrieg in Ex-Jugoslawien—Perspektiven für die Zukunft* (Vienna: Signum, 1997).

20. Kramer, "Strukturentwicklung der Außenpolitik," 831.

21. Reinhard Heinisch, "Austria—Confronting Controversy," in *The European Union and the Member States,* eds. Eleanor E. Zeff and Ellen B. Pirro (Boulder CO: Lynne Rienner, 2001).

22. Fritz Plasser and Peter Ulram, "Meinungstrends, Mobilisierung und Motivlagen bei der Volksabstimmung über den EU-Beitritt," in *EU-Referndum: Zur Praxis direkter Demokratie in Österreich*, ed. Anton Pelinka (Vienna: Signum Verlag, 1994): 87-119.

23. Otmar Höll and Sonja Puntscher-Riekmann, eds., *The Austrian Presidency of the European Union: Assessment and Perspectives* (Laxenburg: Laxenburg Working Papers, 1999).

24. Gerald Hinteregger, "Wo ist die Ost-Kompetenz Österreich's?" *Europäische Rundschau* 26.4 (1998): 3-24; Michael Gehler, *Der lange Weg nach Europa: Österreich vom Ende der Monarchie bis zur EU*, vol. 1, Darstellung (Innsbruck: Studienverlag, 2002); Helmut Lang, *Die österreichische EU-Rastpräsidentschaft 1998* (Frankfurt: P. Lang Verlag, 2002).

25. Kramer, "Strukturentwicklung der Außenpolitik," 831.

26. Ibid., 831-32.

27. Jan Stankovsky, "EU-Erweiterung: Chances und Herausforderungen für die österreichische Wirtschaft," in *Europäisierung der österreichischen Politik—Konsequenzen der EU-Mitgliedschaft*, ed. Heinrich Neisser and Sonja Puntscher-Riekmann (Vienna: WUV, 2002), 319-67, here 320.

28. This transport regiment consisting of 250 soldiers was deployed near Sarajevo and represented the first such mission by the Austrian Army. It was especially sensitive for Austria as a neutral country that the overall command lay with a U.S. and, thus, NATO commander.

29. Helmut Kramer and Vedran Dzihic, *Die Kosovo-Bilanz—Scheitert die internationale Gemeinschaft?* (Vienna: LIT Verlag, 2005).

30. Petritsch was the EU's chief negotiator during the Rambouillet Conference in 1999 designed to defuse the Kosovo crisis.

31. Busek became special EU coordinator for the Stability Pact with Southeastern Europe.

32. Following the UN World Conference on Human Rights in Vienna in 2002, Austria played a leading role in the "Network Human Security," which seeks to enhance the cooperation between governments, NGOs, and international scholars in the area of human rights.

33. Austria was entrusted with the development of a proposal for a convention on the prohibition.

34. Paul Luif, "Wandel der österreichischen Neutralität—Ein sicherheitspolitischer Trittbrettfahrer," *Working Paper* 18 (Vienna: ÖJIP, 1998), 363.

35. The relations between Austria and Israel had been especially sensitive ever since the Waldheim affair in 1986 when Tel Aviv had recalled its ambassador from Vienna. After Tomas Klestil became president in 1992 and after both he and Chancellor Vranitzky had expressed remorse and regret for the nation's role in the Holocaust, bilateral relations were normalized. Nonetheless, Israel continued to monitor the activities of Haider and the FPÖ very closely.

36. *Der Standard*, 11 Oct. 1999.

37. Margaretha Kopeinig and Christoph Kotanko, *Eine europäische Affäre: Der Weisen-Bericht und die Sanktionen gegen Österreich* (Vienna: Czernin Verlag, 2000), 17.

38. He described the French President Jacques Chirac as someone "who had made every mistake one could possible make" (*Kleine Zeitung*, 30 Jan. 2000). Later he was also to call Chirac "a pocket Napoleon" (*Der Standard*, 27 Feb. 2000). During the same event in January, Haider referred to the Belgian government as "corrupt," having "tolerated pedophiles" (ibid). One day later, he gave an interview to the Italian daily *Corriere della Sera,* in which he was quoted as warning against the EU's enlargement and implicitly linking Austria's position on Slovenia's accession to the European Union with that country's settlement of the claims of expelled ethnic Germans (*Der Standard*, 31 Jan. 2000).

39. Kopeining and Kotanko, *Eine europäische Affäre*, 23.

40. Heinrich Schneider, "Österreich in Acht und Bann: Ein Schritt zur politisch integrierten Wertegemeinschaft," *Integration* 23.2 (2000): 120-48; Kopeinig and Kotanko, *Eine europäische Affäre.*

41. While Belgian Foreign Minister Louis Michel (cf. Ian Black "Europe Rallies Against Haider Coalition," *The Guardian*, 4 Feb. 2000) vowed to "smash this government as quickly as possible" and President Chirac declared to maintain the sanction's regime as long as an "extremist, xenophobic party is in the government," EU Commission President Romano Prodi sent a telegram congratulating Schüssel and expressing his concern but also his hopes for "constructive cooperation" (Kopeinig and Kotanko, *Eine europäische Affäre*, 25).

42. "An Interview with the Secretary of State," *The NewsHour with Jim Lehrer*, PBS, 7 Feb. 2000.

43. Reinhard Heinisch, "Success in Opposition—Failure in Government: Exploring the Performance of the Austrian Freedom Party and other European Right-wing Populist Parties in Public Office," *West European Politics* 26.3 (2003): 91-130.

44. Peter Pernthaler and Peter Hilpold, "Sanktionen als Instrument der Politikkontrolle—der Fall Österreich," *Integration* 23.2 (2000): 105-19.

45. Some 66 percent of Austrians stated they were outraged by the sanctions. Naturally, the ratio was highest among conservative (82 percent) and freedom voters (84 percent) while relatively lowest among Green (47 percent) and Social Democratic supporters (37 percent). About one third (35 percent) did not believe in a quick end of the international boycott. However, only 19 percent wanted Austria to leave the Union, although that percentage (43 percent) was noticeably higher among FPÖ sympathizers (*Der Standard*, 4 March 2000).

46. See for example: "In the meantime, the EU's decision to speak as one, against one of its own, is having its own fallout. It has given birth to a new Euroskepticism" [...] The Change in the mood is a direct response to the heavy-handed tactics of the EU leadership in Brussels" (*The Washington Post*, National Weekly Edition, 14 Feb. 2000, 26B). "Haider and the Hypocrites: The Inclusion of a Slick and Sickening Fascist in the Democratically Elected Government of Austria has Provoked a Peculiar Season of Over-Reaction and Under-Reaction" (*New Republic*, 21 Feb. 2000). "[...T]he best antidote the EU member states could offer against Jörg Haider would be to make good on their own recent lofty rhetoric, supplementing their existing anti-immigration statutes with a genuine commitment to combating xenophobia at home" (*Civilization*, April/May 2000: 44). "'The Perils of Austracism' [...] It is time the European Union ended its absurd isolation of Austria. Divorce in haste, repent at leisure [...] it is embarrassing, because the fourteen are already starting to squirm. They must now either climb down or risk getting into an even bigger mess [...]" (*Economist*, 17 June 2000: 20).

47. When, for example, the Austrian Minister of Social Affairs, Elisabeth Sickl, spoke at the EU's first ministerial meeting after the boycott was launched, the French and Belgian ministers walked out. Subsequently, also the senior Italian official (Italy had sent no minister at all) left demonstratively, resulting in the cancellation of the ministerial photo opportunity and planned social agenda. At the EU summit in Freira, Portugal, there was an embarrassing discussion about who would be standing next to whom when the official photograph was taken. Then, at the Lisbon Council meeting, all the other countries shunned the hotel in which the Austrian delegation stayed for fear one might run into FPÖ politicians in an elevator or corridor. A request by the Austrian Chancellor to discuss the boycott in the formal meetings was rejected by the EU-14.

48. At an EU meeting, delegates appeared wearing a button with a crossed-out bow-tie, the trademark of the Austrian Chancellor, who subsequently switched to regular ties.

49. Upon learning that the Austrian Minister of Defense was a member of the FPÖ, his Belgian counterpart Andre Flahaut protested at the Council meeting in Sintra, Portugal, and subsequently ordered all bilateral military contacts between Austria and Belgium suspended. German Defense Minister Rudolf Scharping expressed support for his Belgian counterpart and criticized especially the ÖVP for "having broken their promise to go into opposition." (*Der Standard*, 28 February 2000).

50. The government's catalogue included all the following. 1) Organizing opinion surveys in all member countries coordinated by an Austrian survey research institute, the results of which greatly strengthened the position of the Austrian government because the poll suggested majorities in each of the 14-EU countries favored an end to the sanctions. 2) The Austrian foreign ministry, through its embassies and consulates, began an increased information campaign about the political situation in Austria and the government's policies. The government also announced it was compiling a comprehensive report on the state of racism, anti-Semitism, and anti-foreigner sentiments in Austria. 3) The provincial governments were asked to reach out especially across their borders to neighboring regions. 4) The government also sought to organize special "Austria days" in each of the fourteen member countries, particularly in Paris, London, and Madrid. These events coincided with visits by the Austrian foreign minister to maximize media attention. For the fall of 2000, the government planned a special "international media action day." 5) The government's plan also foresaw activating special international elite networks of "friends of Austria," such as Austrians living abroad or members of Austria clubs and various cultural societies. 6) A host of measures aimed at preventing EU institutions from conducting business as usual. Austria thus continued to demand that the sanctions be placed on the agenda of Council meetings. Moreover, the Austrian chancellor traveled to Brussels in July, forcing a meeting with Commission President Romano Prodi.

51. *Profil*, 31 July 2000.

52. There was only one nation, France, in which a relative majority (42 percent vs. 40 percent) felt that the ÖVP-FPÖ government represented a danger to democracy and human rights in Austria. In thirteen of fourteen member nations, as well as in Switzerland, more than 50 percent of the people surveyed felt the boycott should be lifted (but vigilance maintained). These sentiments were most pronounced in the small countries of Greece (74 percent), Denmark (73 percent), Switzerland (71 percent), and Finland (68 percent), where the concern about outside intrusion was traditionally high. Among the big four member states, the populations of Germany (72 percent) and Italy (65 percent) were noticeably more supportive of an end to the sanctions than those in the UK (51 percent) and France (46 percent) (*Der Standard*, 14 June 2000).

53. *Profil*, 21 Aug. 2000, p. 23.

54. *Profil*, 10 July 2000, p. 26; *Profil*, 31 July 2000, pp. 30-31.

55. Kopeining and Kotanko, *Eine europäische Affär*, 31.

56. The report's conclusions were as follows (excepts): "The legal situation of applicants for asylum is similar to that in other European Union countries. In our assessment the current government continues Austria's traditionally open policy towards refugees. [...] As in other European Union countries such a refugee rate creates problems of social integration. We have however not discovered any indications that the new Austrian government has deviated from the principles followed by its predecessors." (Martti Ahtisaari et al., *Report*, adopted in Paris on 8 Sept. 2000, sec. 40, p. 14, http://www.mpil.de/shared/data/pdf/report.pdf (accessed 22 Nov. 2008). "[...] It can be stated that the policy of the Austrian government as to immigration shows a commitment to common European values" (Ahtisaari et al., *Report*, sec. 51, p. 17). The three wise men acknowledged also the existence of "areas with certain problems," which included "extremely short periods for appealing asylum decisions" (a practice amended after a ruling by Austria's Constitutional Court in 1998), the great reliance on charitable organizations to care for refugees, detaining applicants "even without the realistic possibility of returning them to a third country or their country of origin," and "holding a relatively high number of minors in detention" (Ahtisaari et al., *Report*, sec. 14, p. 14). The report dedicated an extensive part of the document to an "evaluation of the political nature of the FPÖ" and concluded it was a "right-wing populist party with extremist expressions" (Ahtisaari et al., *Report*, sec. 92, p. 27), but that "[w]e have gained the impression that the overall performance of the Ministers of the FPÖ in government since February 2000 cannot be generally criticized" (Ahtisaari et al., *Report*, sec.104, p. 30). About the sanctions, the wise men's committee clearly stated that they had outlived their purpose: "It is our opinion however that the measures taken by the XIV Members States, if continued, would become counterproductive and should therefore be ended. The measures have already stirred up nationalist feelings in the country, as they have in some cases been wrongly understood as sanctions directed against Austrian citizens" (Ahtisaari et al., *Report*, sec. 116, p. 33).

57. The were media reports that Frowein and Ahtisaari may have favored a harsher verdict concerning Austria and that there had been disagreements about the final version of the report. In order to create a *fait accompli*, Oreja allegedly leaked the report to the media (Kopeinig and Kotanko, *Eine europäische Affäre*, 33).

58. See "EU Lifts Sanctions Against Austria," 12 Sept. 2000, http://www.CNN.com/2000/WORLD/europe/09/12/vienna.eu.02/index.html (accessed 15 Nov. 2008).

59. Anselm Skuhra and Michael Merlingen, "Der österreichische Vorsitz der OSZE—Ein Rückblick," in *OSZE-Jahrbuch*, ed. Institut für Friedensforschung (Hamburg: U of Hamburg P, 2001).

60. Gerda Falkner, "The EU 14's "Sanctions" Against Austria: Sense and Nonsense," *European Community Studies Review* 14.1 (2001): 14-20, here 15.

61. See the proposal by the Austrian Delegation concerning Articles 7 and 46 of the EU Nice Treaty Negotiations, CONFER 4782/00 ANNEX 2 Brussles, 6 September 2000.

62. *Der Standard Online*, 14 April 2002.

63. *Der Standard Online*, 8 April 2002.

64. *Profil*, 25 Sept. 2000, p. 33.

65. *Der Standard Online*, 2 Sept. 2002.

66. *Profil*, 27 Oct. 2000, p. 64.

67. *The Economist*, 2 Sept. 2000, p. 44. It should also be pointed out that the plant was not without controversy in the Czech Republic itself and was built to a standard not as advanced as that in Western Europe. Points of Austrian criticism were the containment shell of the reactor bloc and the heat exchange system, which, in the case of an accident, were said to allow internal contamination to reach the outside world.

68. Lázló Kiss et al., "Die Regionale Partnerschaft: Subregionale Zussammenarbeit in der Mitte Europas," *Österreichische Zeitschrift für Politikwissenschaft* 32.1 (2003): 57-75.

69. While government representatives were also noticeably absent from internationally well-attended events held in memory of the victims of Fascism (for example, a Mauthausen commemoration in May 2001, the anniversary of the Lidice massacre), FPÖ officials nonetheless found time to attend pan-Germanic manifestations and right-wing vigils. A high-ranking Freedom official even likened Austria's postwar occupation to the Nazi regime, referring to the Allies as "tyrants" (*Der Standard Online*, 11 July 2002, http://derstandard.at/ (accessed 15 Nov. 2008).

70. For examples, see Max Preglau, "Rechtsextrem oder Postmodern? Über Rhetorik, Programmatik und Interaktionsformen der FPÖ und der FPÖVP-Koalition," unpublished manuscript (Innsbruck: U of Innsbruck, 2002).

71. *Der Standard Online*, 1 Jan. 2002, http://derstandard.at/ (accessed 15 Nov. 2008).

72. Specifically after the attacks in Madrid on 11 March 2004, Vienna stated that in cases of terrorism and in solidarity with other European nations, it would make its military resources available since such threats involved non-state actors and therefore did not affect the country's constitutional restrictions on neutrality.

73. Anselm Skuhra, "Österreichische Sicherheitspolitik," in *Politik in Österreich—Das Handbuch,* ed. Herbert Dachs et al. (Vienna: Manz, 2006), 838-61, here 856.

74. Ibid., 855.

75. Paul Luif, "Österreich," in *Jahrbuch der europäischen Integration 2003/2004*, ed. Werner Weidenfeld und Wolfgang Wessels (Baden-Baden: Nomos, 2004), 367-70, here 369.

76. Anselm Skuhra, "Österreichische Sicherheitspolitik," 857.

77. "EU 'on Precipice' over Turkey," CNN, 3 Oct. 2005, http://www.cnn.com/2005/WORLD/europe/10/03/eu.turkeytalks0800/index.html (accessed 15 Nov. 2008).

78. "EU warns Austria on Turks," *The Guardian,* 1 Oct. 2005.

79. Rainer Hermann, "Feiertag für Chauvinisten" *Frankfurter Allgemeine Zeitung*, 3 Oct. 2005, http://www.faz.net/s/RubDDBDABB9457A437BAA85A49C26FB23A0/Doc~

E57B43A0062B14EFDB26D7638D3EE98FB~ATpl~Ecommon~Scontent.html (accessed 15 November 2008).

80. "Schüssels kroatische Karte," *Berliner Zeitung*, 5 Oct. 2005.

81. "Austria Repeats Turkey Objections," BBC News, 1 Oct. 2005, http://news.bbc.co.uk/2/hi/europe/4299626.stm (accessed 15 Nov. 2008).

82. In the context of a different research project, this author conducted structured interviews with Austrian civil servants in preparation for the second Austrian EU Presidency in the context of which ministerial officials complained repeatedly that they already had to attend some eighty bilateral and multilateral preparatory meetings which were a strain on a small civil service.

83. Peter Ludlow, "Dealing with Turkey—The European Council of 16-17 December 2004," *EuroComment Briefing Note* No. 3.7 (Feb. 2005): 1-56, here 39.

84. UK Foreign Secretary Jack Straw in meetings with his Austrian counterpart stated: "It is a frustrating situation but I hope and pray that we may be able to reach agreement." (Vincent Boland and Daniel Dombey, "Straw Holds Out Hope for Turkey's EU Entry Talks," *Financial Times*, 2 Oct. 2005, http://www.ft.com/cms/s/0/e7750a02-3369-11da-bd49-00000e2511c8.html [accessed 15 Nov. 2008.])

85. The Conservatives not only lost 8.7 percent and the governorship in Styria, but also expected heavy losses in the upcoming votes in Burgenland and Vienna.

86. Membership talks with Croatia had been suspended after the chief prosecutor of the international war crimes tribunal on former Yugoslavia ruled that Zagreb was failing to help track down an indicted war criminal General Ante Gotovina. The European Union made the question of cooperation with the tribunal in The Hague a condition for starting entry talks.

87. "EU 'on Precipice' over Turkey," CNN, 3 Oct. 2005, http://www.cnn.com/2005/WORLD/europe/10/03/eu.turkeytalks0800/index.html (accessed 15 Nov. 2008).

88. Referring to an exclusive Christian/Western "occidental" conception of Europe.

89. Stefan Lehne is Javier Solana's Balkan coordinator, Albert Rohan serves as Stability Pact Coordinator Ahtisaari's number two, and Erhard Busek had previously been the EU's Special Coordinator of the Stability Pact.

90. Peter Ludlow, "The Austrian Presidency of the EU," *EuroComment Briefing Note* 4.1 (Dec. 2005): 1-31.

91. Ludlow, "European Council," 5.

92. Ibid., 2-3.

93. Ludlow, "Austrian Presidency," 25.

94. Ibid., 5.

95. Ludlow, "European Council," 59.

96. Ibid.

97. Ibid., 60.

98. Ibid.

99. Ibid.

100. Cf. *Datum*, July 2008: 27-31.

101. Ibid., 67.

II. POLICIES AND POLICY CHANGES

Wolfgang Schüssel and Austrian Foreign Policy

Otmar Höll[1]

Introduction

Two decades after the end of the Cold War, two major processes characterize the still ongoing transformation of the global and European political landscape. First is the process of globalization and, strongly interlinked with it, an ever increasing socioeconomic and political interdependence of all states, as well as new and challenging security threats. Second is the continuing emergence of an international system of cooperation that will be more multilateral than those witnessed during the last century. For a small state like Austria, which since the end of World War II has tried hard to come to grips with the uneasy task "to balance between autonomy and dependence" as Peter Katzenstein put it,[2] full membership in the European Union (EU) was the logical and necessary step forward to avoid economic and political marginalization in a globalizing world. So when Austria joined the supranational Union in 1995, a completely new chapter of its foreign relations had been opened.[3] It had become "part of a greater political whole," as then-Federal President Thomas Klestil said in his speech on the Vienna Heldenplatz on 1 July 1998; a new era of foreign policy under completely different political frameworks had begun.

So when Wolfgang Schüssel took over the Foreign Ministry from Alois Mock on 4 May 1995,[4] the international environment as well as the fundamental constraints of Austrian foreign policy had changed completely in legal and political terms. That makes it difficult to compare Schüssel's foreign policy to those of the two other remarkable "eras" of Austrian foreign policy under Bruno Kreisky and Alois Mock.[5] A great part of Austria's former national "foreign policy" was now transformed into "European domestic policy."[6] What made Austria's voice and impact in the international arena more important—having become a recognized member of a global economic and political group—became less visible at home: increasingly, Austrian foreign policy and, to some extent, security policy have been merged into a "common" policy of the Union, which means discussing new ideas and initiatives first in Brussels with representatives of the other members rather than at an early stage with the public at home. EU membership and the Partnership for Peace agreement (PfP) with the North Atlantic Treaty Organization (NATO) in February 1995 (and PfP "plus" in November 1996) predictably had an additional impact on downgrading the substance of Austria's (previously "permanent") neutrality, which had served the country well during the long period of the Second Republic. In this period, both abolishing the status of neutrality and eventually seeking NATO membership were seriously and controversially discussed by political elites, with some repercussions in the media and in the general public, but these issues are not likely to pop up again in the foreseeable future.

Schüssel, who was not a "born" foreign affairs professional like Kreisky or Mock whose brains *and* hearts were intertwined with this specific field of politics, suffered no disadvantage due to this fact. As a highly intelligent and pragmatic professional, he quickly learned how to make optimal use of the complicated, sometimes obstinate, institutional setting of the Austrian Foreign Ministry and to profit from the sophisticated knowledge of those collaborators and advisors he carefully chose. He had no specific mission or long-term vision for a particular Austrian foreign policy besides the European approach. The non-European world or the United Nations were of minor interest for him. His understanding of how to deal with foreign policy was mainly limited to strategic considerations: to represent Austrian interests abroad as well as possible and to act in a highly efficient and solution-oriented manner. His era was full of ups and downs; when he became chancellor in 2000, like others before him, he dominated Austrian foreign policy after he had stepped down as foreign minister. So we can say that his "era" of foreign policy lasted from 1995 until 2006, when his time in the Chancellery ended. Will this "Schüssel era" of foreign policy prevail as being worth remembering in the critical assessments of future historians? On this question there is some doubt; some say that Wolfgang Schüssel will be remembered as a politician who framed and shaped Austria in the first years of the twenty-first century, especially as Austrian chancellor, but not in the same way as he did while serving as foreign minister.

The First Phase: Continuity and Adaptation (1995-2000)

When in 1995 Austria joined the European Union, its institutional structures had already been evolving for more than four decades, which required Austria to undertake a high amount of institutional, strategic, and political adaptation of its internal political and administrative fabric. In adjusting the domestic decision-making structures to EU membership, Austria had to tackle three major problems: first, the coordination of EU-related governmental policy and governmental decision-making processes; second, the involvement of the nine federal provinces (*Bundesländer*) into decision-making processes (Austria is a federal state); and third, cooperation with and scrutiny by parliament.

However, this process had already begun in a broad way before accession to the European Union and resulted in a compensation agreement between the Federal State and the nine provinces for the losses of competencies due to EU membership,[7] giving the social partners the legal right to obtain all relevant information related to the EU accession process. It also resulted in the adaptation of decision-making processes and institutions in the ministries and the revision (down-grading) of Austria's status as a permanently neutral country.[8] Since then, Article 23f (1) allows participation in economic sanctions, among other things. Later, new functions were extended to include the more far-reaching Petersburg tasks. From 1995 until February 2000, the chancellor and the minister of foreign affairs hailed from different parties, the SPÖ and ÖVP, which usually complicated things. Therefore, the two parties arranged a system of complete formal equality between the political parties in the Coalition Agreement of 1996. Thus coordination of EU-related ministerial policy and decision making was done jointly—although often reluctantly—by the Chancellery and the Foreign Ministry. Also, the provinces were strongly involved into the decision-making processes, and cooperation with and scrutiny by the Parliament was adopted.[9]

When Wolfgang Schüssel took over the Foreign Ministry, he somehow "inherited" the foreign agenda from his predecessor, Alois Mock, and only gradually got more and more involved in its complex matter. His foreign policy activities during the first two years followed the previous path set by Mock. Schüssel, leader of the Austrian People's Party (*Österreichische Volkspartei*, or ÖVP) since 1997 and now vice-chancellor, was charged with a heavy working load and chose Benita Ferrero-Waldner as his state secretary for the Foreign Ministry, to share at least some of the "daily work." He took part in the meetings of the General Affairs Council and the European Summits and showed an impressive record in quickly understanding, participating in, and handling multilateral negotiation processes.

As a new member of the Union, Austria in this period broadened its foreign economic relations. Austria was a partner in EU cooperation agreements with politically and economically interesting partners in many parts of the world, including Asia and Latin America, and was a stake-holder in the so-called European agreements in the Central and Eastern European regions. In 1996, Austria acceded also to the Lomé IV Agreement with African, Caribbean, and Pacific States. Austrian representatives were actively involved in the preparations and negotiation meetings that led to the highly important Amsterdam Treaty of October 1997 (in force since May 1999). Austrian proposals focused especially on the topics of the environment, fundamental rights, and equal treatment.[10]

The Highlight: First Presidency of the Union

Austria in the second half of 1998 was the first country of the three who had become EU member states (together with Finland and Sweden) in the fourth enlargement round to take over the presidency of the Union.[11] Especially for small states, assuming the presidency of the European Union is a complicated and prestigious matter. Depending on the pillars of the Union, the respective policy field, and events in the international environment, presidencies have different rights and roles. Their formal task is to manage the Council's business, to act as the spokesperson of the Council and of the Union as a whole, and to initiate, coordinate, and implement policy, especially in the political fields of the second and third pillar. Austria had to preside over little less than fifty ministerial conferences, and approximately 1,500 technical meetings, which was a heavy workload for a small country. But even more tricky are the political functions for presidencies, like acting as neutral brokers to find consensus or majorities in cases where decision-making processes are blocked. Presidencies also have a symbolic function; they are paramount for the way Europeans perceive the Union, and they have an integrative function for the whole Union. Thus they should try to mobilize interest and awareness in member states for common tasks and in doing so strengthen identification with the Union and bring about socialization of citizens and political elites.

Austria assumed its first presidency at a decisive moment for the Union's integration process. Among other agenda items was the third stage of the Economic and Monetary Union to be prepared, the enlargement process for the next enlargement round of ten or more candidates, and the Agenda 2000 reform package, yet these were only the most prominent tasks.[12] Administration and programming for the Presidency had started rather late, yet it was done efficiently. The priorities of the first Austrian EU Presidency were officially the following:

> Enlargement is by far the best and most effective instrument to strengthen security in the regions. It keeps the nationalist demons at bay. It reinforces the civil society in these countries and stimulates economic and political reforms. It helps to stabilize societies and thus reduce the risk of organized crime and illegal migration. In the long term, the Union will either export stability towards the East, or will import instability. No other country has a higher stake in this than Austria.[13]

The 1998 Presidency was, in fact, a short one, because the six-month period included the summer months July and August which would see only reduced activity in the EU's institutions in Brussels. It ended without any unexpected or major crisis. Starting the preparations for the fifth enlargement round, one of the most central tasks, was well accomplished. Although the Austrian coalition government's position was strongly in favor of enlargement, more than 50 percent of the Austrian population were against it, mainly due to economic fears, as Eurobarometer statistics show. Yet the Austrian coalition government managed to balance domestic and international dimensions and successfully finalized the preparatory work for enlargement, introduced the common Euro currency, and concluded the necessary final decisions on the working capacity of the European Central Bank. Some progress was also made on Agenda 2000, which included reforms of the Common Agricultural Policy and the Structural Policy and advanced negotiations on the highly important provisions for the financial framework for the next seven years' budgetary period from 2000 to 2006. Austria would have liked to move faster on the issue of EU-budget, but had to leave the task to Germany, whose presidency followed Austria's. In spite of some reluctance on the side of member states, an innovative step towards improvement in the security related matters of Pillar Two of the European Union was the topic at the unofficial first meeting of Defense Ministers during the Presidency in Vienna, on the invitation of Austria's then Defense Minister Werner Fasslabend of the ÖVP, which initiated a series of such meetings and contributed to improving progress on the EU's Security and Defense Policy (ESDP). At the informal European summit in the Carinthian city of Pörtschach some weeks later, convened by Chancellor Victor Klima, Tony Blair signaled a significant shift in British views regarding EU defense, which later on in November 1999 led to the well-known French-British initiative of St. Malo. Progress on the ESDP was greatly needed, as the EU's failure to play a constructive and moderating role in the Yugoslav wars in the 1990s had made painfully clear.

Among the most difficult tasks of a Presidency is the proper handling of—more than often unforeseeable—international crises somewhere in the world. In the case of Austria's Presidency, this could have happened in the Western Balkans, the Middle East, or Asia. For a neutral country like Austria, this could have led to some unconventional and troublesome problems. Fortunately enough, the Presidency was a rather quiet and "normal" one, with some challenges like the Rubel and the Kosovo crises. With the support of the Commission, Austria in the opinion of most of the members, succeeded in doing an overall good job, with critical remarks from only some member countries.[14] The critiques focused on the lack of coherent political strategies and courage with regard to challenging tasks, such as the Agenda 2000 and the imminent institutional reform. Others recognized some ambivalent attitudes concerning EU enlargement, where they found that "a special commitment was pronounced in public and seemingly countervailed in action."[15]

Austria's first Presidency of the European Union also produced interesting domestic results. I take it as a proof of the ambivalence hypothesis of mine concerning Austrian foreign policy in the whole of the Second Republic that after the impressively high turnout in the referendum on Austrian EU membership in 1994 (in which two thirds of the Austrian electorate voted in favor of membership) the coalition government of the Social Democratic Party of Austria (*Sozialdemokratische Partei Österreichs*, or SPÖ) and the Austrian People's Party (*Österreichische Volkspartei*, or ÖVP) failed to maintain a high level of open public discourse about European matters. It only was taken up again in the time of the Presidency in the second half of 1998, some time before it started and after it ended. Political discourse about the European Union has unfortunately been dominated by flashy elements rather than by serious strategies and communication about the status quo and by the nature and the perspectives of the European integration process.

Finally, the Presidency undoubtedly resulted in positive effects in domestic politics, especially in terms of achievements in the Austrian administrative structures and the cooperation within and among ministries and the two coalition parties. The intensive workload undertaken in preparation for and during the Presidency and Austria's intensive involvement in the political agenda of the Union led to a downgrading of hierarchical procedures and gave more leeway and also more responsibility to individual politicians, a fact positively recognized by many.

In short, the Presidency made the Austrian bureaucracy and the Austrian politicians fit for the Union, and the Austrian public more aware of the fact that Austria had become part of the European Union and was internationally more recognized and respected than in recent years. In an overall assessment as of today and after another successfully accomplished Austrian Presidency in the first half of 2006, however, one still has to be critical. Neither for the political system nor for the Austrian public opinion were the international experiences and domestic benefits capable of bringing about sustainable and substantial change. "Europeanization" was partly and modestly realized on institutional and administrative levels, but to date can hardly be found on a societal level, where only little knowledge and considerable skepticism still prevail.

This skepticism also holds true for the rest of the decade and thereafter. While on the political macro-level Austrian verbal commitment to the European Union still remained high, on the level of civil society, acceptance of the European Union decreased constantly after some rise as a result of increased information and discussion on European topics during the first Presidency. Keeping a certain distance from the Union may be due to the power of Austrians' traditional, inward-looking, and skeptical mentality,[16] based on a long, ambiguous, and sometimes disastrous process for arriving at a somehow consolidated Austrian national identity. It is definitely also due to the ambivalence of the Austrian political class in relation to EU membership, at least as far as continuity and coherence in their positions is concerned. Whereas Jörg Haider's far-right Freedom Party of Austrian (*Freiheitliche Partei Österreichs*, or FPÖ) at the end of the 1990s was rapidly growing and strongly criticizing the European Union and its enlargement policy with populist and xenophobic slogans, the two coalition parties in power remained reluctant to counter these positions and ambivalent in their communication strategies and positions in the public debate. In the election campaign to the European Parliament in June 1999, which all parties saw as a rehearsal for the coming parliamentary elections in October of the same year, European issues were hard to find. The campaigns of the parties focused mainly on Austrian neutrality, which, because of the wars in Yugoslavia in the first half of the 1990s and the ongoing crisis in Kosovo, was partly understandable. Finally, the discourse shifted in the direction of a shared consensus that there is a need to enhance the European security system independent from NATO. The issue of the Union's enlargement only played a minor role in the campaigns, even by the Freedom Party, which immediately resulted in a 4 percent loss of support for the FPÖ as compared to its results in the last elections.

In drawing a short conclusion on the first phase of the Schüssel era, one could focus on two positive features: first, the continuing legal, organizational, and administrative adaptation of the political and institutional structures of Austria's foreign policy and, second, the successful organization of Austria's first Presidency by the coalition government. Wolfgang Schüssel, who had chosen to become foreign minister while holding the chairmanship in the People's Party not least for strategic reasons and the high visibility of the foreign minister in the media and who led the Ministry together with Benita Ferrero-Waldner as state secretary, did a professional job, continuing in the line of Alois Mock during the first years. In terms of cooperation at the highest political level, the relationship between the two partners of the coalition government, the ÖVP and its senior partner the SPÖ, gradually deteriorated decisively, despite the fact that cooperation and enthusiasm had been clearly evident on both the SPÖ and ÖVP's sides during the whole of 1998 and for some months after successfully ending the Presidency together. The eventual failure to reach consensus on sensitive security-related issues in the so-called "Options Report"—notably on the issue of NATO-membership—(*Optionen-Bericht*) earlier in March 1998 might have contributed to these destructive dynamics, although the evident success of the first presidency in the second half of 1998 was understood as an outcome of a common endeavor.

The Second Phase: From Squeeze to Triumph to Agony

The singular events around the establishment of the Austrian People's Party and the Freedom Party of Austria as a coalition government that came into office on 4 February 2000 were politically exceptional and dramatic. The Israeli ambassador was recalled immediately, and Israeli President Ezer Weizman said in an interview that "the situation in Austria now is exactly the same as it was in Germany seventy years ago."[17] U.S. Ambassador Kathryn Hall was called back to Washington some days later for consultations, and the fourteen other EU members put in effect the "measures against the Austrian government" (later connoted as "sanctions") that they had threatened to install on 31 January. In this letter, which was sent through the Portuguese Presidency, the fourteen other members had warned they would "not promote or accept any bilateral official contacts at the political level with an Austrian government integrating the FPÖ" and threatened sanctions against Austria, including no bilateral visits on the ministerial level, ambassadorial visits only on a technical level, and no support of Austrian applications for international appointments.[18] Street protests followed on the Ballhausplatz in front of the Chancellery and the building of the Federal President, as well as at the ÖVP and FPÖ party headquarters. The amount of attention the Austrian "case" received in print and in visual media all over the world was enormous. The associative thread was usually the same: Austria, from the home country of Adolf Hitler to the Austrian Secretary General of the UN and later Federal President Kurt Waldheim to Jörg Haider (often quoted as an admirer of Adolf Hitler and of Nazi Germany), and finally to police cordons and protesters against the government on the Vienna streets.

All this happened, however, because the ÖVP, acting in complete accordance with the Austrian Constitution and general parliamentary rules, established a coalition government with the FPÖ.[19] Obviously, Wolfgang Schüssel was the mastermind behind the scenes. This coalition was the unexpected outcome of the national elections of autumn 1999 and of the negotiations that followed regarding building a coalition government between the SPÖ and ÖVP, with the FPÖ as the "lucky third." The result constituted the myth of Wolfgang Schüssel as the "father of all strategists" at home and a person strongly rebuffed, sometimes even hated, abroad.[20]

In the prelude to all that, in the elections of October 1999, the ÖVP and FPÖ ended up as second and third behind the Social Democrats, the FPÖ led by a very close margin of 415 votes more than the ÖVP. In spite of this fact, the ÖVP, represented by Wolfgang Schüssel who had publicly declared its retreat into opposition, was able, based on a tough tactical gamble, to nominate the chancellor. Thus a change of partners in a coalition government would be quite a normal thing, if the FPÖ were not widely recognized as a party on the far right of the political spectrum, with Jörg Haider as its well known "leader" (at that time) and quite some high ranking functionaries known as being close to radical right and even xenophobic positions.[21] I do not want to judge here whether the specific form of reaction taken by the rest of the EU members was wise or prudent.[22] However, on 12 September 2000, the fourteen EU member countries lifted the sanctions after an internationally high-ranking investigating committee ("Wise Men Group") proposed the step. "A dark veil has fallen from the face of Europe," Wolfgang Schüssel was quoted as saying, hailing the decision as "a great success for Austria resulting from our patience and firmness" on national TV.

The lifting of "sanctions" was finally seen as a success for Austria, which in the wake of the painful discussions was good enough to propose for the first time formal rules for the application of sanctions against a Member State (Art. 6 and 7 of the EU Treaty). These provisions were adopted in the Treaty of Nice.

Finally, one can say that the consequences of including the FPÖ in a coalition government with the ÖVP later yielded some positive results for the whole political system in Austria. All other governmental alternatives, like a renewed "grand coalition" or a minority government, would have strengthened the FPÖ and given the party and Haider even more support by protest voters, and eventually the chancellorship for the latter at the next parliamentary elections, because with the FPÖ remaining in opposition the probability that it would end up in first place in the upcoming elections was rather high. As a coalition partner in power from 2000 until 2002, the party's mythos diminished. The early, strategic elections Wolfgang Schüssel provoked in November 2002 changed the whole picture again. The FPÖ lost dramatically, the ÖVP increased its margin to an incredible 42+ percent, and the SPÖ and the Greens ended up with a moderate increase. After the snap election, Wolfgang Schüssel and his now reinforced ÖVP again reinstated a coalition government with the weakened FPÖ, which lasted until 2005. The "third *Lager*" weakened itself further when the newly founded Alliance for the Future of Austria (*Bündnis Zukunft Österreich*, or BZÖ) under Jörg Haider split from the FPÖ. Schüssel then formed a new coalition government with those parts of the BZÖ which seemed fit for governmental duties, while Haider—influential still—remained governor of Carinthia.

Shortly after the "sanctions" where lifted, however, the BZÖ and Schüssel announced Austria's intention to build a "Strategic Partnership"[23] with its neighboring countries, the Czech Republic, Hungary, Slovakia, and Slovenia as well as its "cultural neighbor," Poland. The goal of this venture was to look for common interests and to find common positions of all countries in the region in order to strengthen their joint influence after having become members of the Union. After some critical remarks from the European Union as well as from the neighbors, the name of the group was changed to "Regional Partnership."[24] The group was formally established on 6 June 2001 in Vienna at a meeting of the foreign ministers of the respective partner states. It still is an informal—and presently poorly working—forum for regional cooperation intended to create some added value for the region and for Europe as a whole, but bound to improve the stance of all group members within the European Union.

Coalition building and regional cooperation groups like those among Belgium, the Netherlands, and Luxembourg ("Benelux"), or "the Northern cooperation," including Finland, Sweden, and Denmark, reflect the highly important dimension of "networking" within the European Union in general. It is especially so for smaller states which should have a "natural" interest in building good relations with other members in order to strengthen their influence and receive support in decisions which are favorable to them. In the views of neutral but well informed observers in Brussels (and also of reflexive and critical people in Vienna), Austria on a broad level is not networking very well.[25] Successful networking requires a lot of confidence among the members and trust in the high reliability of the respective country. Undoubtedly, Austria had not met the high expectations of the "older" members and of some of the new members which would allow it to become an initiator of new strategies and measures and a supporter of the integration process of the candidate countries. When compared to its peer-group of smaller and middle states, Austria is not in a very favorable position. Indeed, much depends on "subjective factors"; personal relations and specific personalities—think of Erhard Busek or Wolfgang Petritsch—play an important role. However, it is important to be known as a trusted part of the multilevel networking and communicative processes that are going on all the time. It can be crucial to collect different or similar positions at an early date, persuade those with contrary positions, and negotiate initiatives, find compromises, or package deals. It is of high importance to be known as a responsible and fair actor, especially when the "vital interests" of a country are at stake, and one needs the support of as many members as possible. Networking is cost-intensive and needs a lot of human skills and capacities and a well functioning and well coordinated center, none of which should end immediately after the end of the Presidency period. From the beginning of the accession process until now, the Austrian business sector has done a better job than the political in terms of networking.

A case in point, but a paradoxical one, was the crisis between Austrian negotiators and the European Union at the occasion of negotiations in Brussels to start accession negotiations with Turkey at the beginning of October 2005. Austria threatened to oppose the decision for some days and only gave in after provincial elections in Styria were over and once all members agreed to start accession talks with Croatia. The issue was intensively discussed during these days both in Brussels and in the Austrian media and public, where more than 80 percent of the population in the meantime were against Turkish membership, but more than 50 percent favored Croatian accession. Immediately after Austria gave its approval to starting negotiations, Wolfgang Schüssel announced the installment of the new Minister of the Interior, a woman, Liesel Prokop, which came as a great surprise. The new minister garnered much more media attention in Austria, more than Brussels' decision to start negotiations with Turkey. Behind closed doors, the Austrian chancellor and his foreign minister were more than often congratulated for standing firm on their position in the Turkish case. Once more, Schüssel showed his great talent in strategic thinking and received considerable respect for it, though from the smaller states. In contrast, some of the larger states' representatives felt that their former resentment against Austria and its chancellor was again justified.

When Schüssel had become chancellor in February 2000, Benita Ferrero-Waldner, his former state secretary followed him as foreign minister.[26] Ferrero-Waldner's primary task was first and foremost to get rid of the "sanctions," which she tried bravely and persistently to do. Finally, she was given the nickname "Lady Minister with the fighting smile" (*Kampflächeln*), an appellation she lived even in situations when she was more or less ignored during the months of "sanctions" by her EU compatriots.

It came as a windfall for the right-wing ÖVP-FPÖ government when in January 2001 the United States, the Republic of Austria, Jewish organizations, and a group of lawyers agreed on a package of Austrian measures for victims of National Socialism, which for Austria had been a never-ending story. Not all measures have so far been realized, but an amendment to the National Fund, granting compensation for the loss of Jewish property and improving social laws favoring the victims during this governmental period. Together with the compensation fund act (*Entschädigungsfondsgesetz*) for forced foreign labor during Austria's Nazi period, both funds should close the still existing gaps in restitution.

The Other Highlight: The Second Presidency

The second Austrian Presidency started on 1 January 2006, only three months after the Brussels' enlargement summit. It was a "full-time" Presidency,[27] again occurring at a critical time, since the tensions inside and outside the European Union were on the rising. The process of ratification of the Constitutional Treaty had been blocked when at the end of May and 1 June 2005 two referenda in France and in the Netherlands both ended negatively. The member states voted for a "period of reflection," to analyze the problem and look for possible solutions, although eighteen countries had successfully ratified the Treaty, including Austria. Frustration with the EU elite integration project seemed surprisingly high,[28] so the strategy for 2006 and the priorities of the Austrian Presidency as well were focused more than usual on citizens' vital daily interests and needs. Among others, priority was given to measures on the creation of jobs and economic growth, the environment and energy, and bringing "the EU citizens" back into the center. Based on the multi-annual program[29] for three years from 2004 to 2006, the two Presidency states, Austria and its successor Finland, published a common program for the whole year of 2006. This time, the

Austrian Presidency had to preside over approximately 250 committees and working groups on the level of ministerial officials, and some 2,500 EU meetings in total. All together, some 10,000 people were involved in the organization and technical procedures of the Presidency. These rough statistical figures clearly show how extraordinary the number of negotiating and decision making meetings had increased as compared to the first Presidency.

The Presidency in 2006 had a really tough time. Immediately it started with an outside crisis on 1 January when Russia, because of troubles with the Ukraine over the price of gas, temporarily reduced the gas supply. Not long thereafter, the cartoon controversy between Denmark and the Islamic world came up, and Iran's nuclear program with its impact on the European Union commanded the full attention of Austrian politicians. In cooperation with the Council and the Parliament, the Presidency coordinated important common positions and successfully came to terms with a series of delicate situations. Especially the Foreign Ministry played a pivotal role in coordinating all Brussels institutions and the Presidency; it "had functioned as Europe Ministry and had proven its worth," as Wolfgang Schüssel put it in his final press conference at the end of May. Among other topics, some decisions about a common energy policy were taken, which were incorporated in the conclusions. Provisional measures were taken to increase cross-border energy exchanges of 10 percent among member states, to increase the share of renewables to 15 percent by 2015, and to increase the use of biofuels to 8 percent. Finally, the conclusion of the services directive and some progress in the science and research dimension also contributed to the success of the Presidency. Some critical statements in the media and comments of experts that the Austrian Presidency was more show than practical achievements, cannot counter the fact that Austria made good use of the opportunities the EU Presidency offers, especially for a small state. It provides a wide window to the world and, therefore, enhanced visibility for the leading country.

The constructive and professional organization of the Austrian Presidency provoked the respect of the German foreign minister and the French president, who both hastened to congratulate the chancellor and the foreign minister for an excellently organized Presidency. Unfortunately, at home, information on, communication about, and public opinion regarding the Union improved only in a short term, a trend that did not continue after the end of the Presidency. Recent Eurobarometer data show that acceptance of the European Union has fallen from more than 70 percent in 2002 and far below 50 percent in 2007 to only 36 percent in 2008.[30] Another 36 percent say that EU membership is neither good nor bad, and 26 percent think negatively about the Union. The respective average figure for the EU-27 is 54 percent who believe EU membership is a good thing and 52 percent think their country has benefited from membership. This Austrian development is not only dramatic, but difficult to explain, especially if we consider that 75 percent of Austria at the same time believe their country is doing better economically than any other country, while in the whole of the European Union only 35 percent believe that their countries are doing better than the rest. Asked whether the situation in the job markets are better than in other countries, 72 percent of Austrians answered "yes," as compared to only 34 percent in the overall Union. Thus Austrians see no relation at all between favorable economic development, EU membership, and EU enlargement, which most Austrians will not see happen any more in the future, except in the case of Croatia.

Things become a bit clearer and the Austrian "soul" better understood if we continue to look at some other statistical figures. Compared to 29 percent of the EU-27 who argue that the voice of their country has no influence in Brussels, for Austria the figure is 46 percent, and only 38 percent of Austrians trust the European Union, whereas the EU-27 figure is 50 percent. Almost half of Austrians associate the Union with a waste of money. Interestingly, 45 percent of Austrians believe they know how the European Union works, which is a surprisingly high number. I can only understand the results given here in the light of what I have written before on the traditional shortcomings of information and communication patterns in Austria.

Changes in Substance and Priorities of Austrian Foreign and Security Policy

Changes during the Schüssel era have been numerous, deep-rooted, and sometimes confusing. If we consider the profoundly changed and ongoing transition of the international setting with which Austria has had to cope since the end of the Cold War, many of its political principles and strategies require change as well, or at least adaptation. Neutrality policy, relations to the signatory powers of the State Treaty, neighborly relations especially towards the whole of Western Europe, and active engagement in international organizations ranked high on Austria's foreign policy agenda before the demise of the USSR. While during bipolarity most of Austria's foreign political strategies were reactive, taking cautious advantage of its specific position as a neutral country between the two blocs, intensified globalization and the demise of the bloc system demanded a higher amount of active engagement. Growing economic interconnectedness, increased competition and vulnerability as a result of increased world market integration, and the emergence of regional economic blocs consequently led to the most fundamental and decisive change: Austrian membership in the European Union. Independence or as much autonomy as possible had been one of the most important goals of foreign policy in a wide sense before 1989. These goals were substituted by strategies of membership and accession to the clubs of the well-to-do European countries rather than "dying in isolation." Looking for a broad spectrum of autonomy as a means of political independence for a single small country was replaced by gaining a variety of new options and being actively involved in decision-making processes of a much larger political unit with much higher aspirations. Most other changes and strategies of minor importance are derived from this fundamental decision, and Austria's European dimension has changed from articulating a genuine foreign policy to a kind of domestic policy field. Changes in the administrative structures as well as in the strategic political fields had already started before accession, but continued after 1995.

During the whole of the Schüssel era, a good neighbor policy was still important, but now to a great extent that policy is within the EU frame, the bilateral rest of it is concerned with only Switzerland and Liechtenstein, and/or has been connected with issues of future enlargement, as is the case with "cultural neighbors" Croatia and the Western Balkan countries. Despite some opposition from different sources such as the trade unions, the Chambers of Labor and Agriculture, and some federal provinces (especially from the eastern parts of Austria and especially before provincial elections), the official Austrian position has always been strongly in favor of enlargement. Of all EU member states, Austria has been profiting the most in economic terms, more than Germany, which was highly absorbed with integrating the former provinces of the German Democratic Republic into a reunited Germany. Specific Austrian interests in this respect are issues related to transit traffic (given the country's central geographic position and sensitive ecological landscape), freedom of movement from candidate countries, nuclear safety, ecology, organized crime, and terrorism.

Moreover, Austria has a particular interest in keeping the Balkans stable and developing. More or less democratic governments now exist everywhere in the Balkans, some having further intentions for reforms, some to a lesser extent, but all are in bad economic shape. As a result, high degrees of corruption and organized crime exist, and only little success in the resolution or management of ethnic conflicts has been made. All the countries of the Balkans need a "European perspective," including Bosnia-Herzegovina and Kosovo.

As many small or medium states do, Austria supports, cooperates with, and makes use of the multilateral framework of international organizations and regimes. It is still an active member of the Organization for Security and Cooperation in Europe (OSCE) and supports its activities in the Balkans and the Caucasus. Austria chaired the OSCE in 2000.

Austria to some extent has always been active within UN structures, but with changing intensity. For Wolfgang Schüssel, the United Nations was no major field of action, but it has been a more important arena under the leadership of Benita Ferrero-Waldner and Ursula Plassnik; Austria's successful candidacy for the Security Council during the period of 2009-2010 is strong proof of that. Contrary to the first and second terms in the early 1970s and 1990s, Austria now will not only play a role as small member of the exclusive club, but will raise its voice as an EU member. In the past, activities were focused on peacekeeping missions; in the more recent past, the United Nations was especially active in the fight against landmines, illegal small weapons production and trade, the drug trade, and human trade, and it has been strongly pushing for the establishment of the International Criminal Court. Moreover, Austria has joined the United Nations in supporting especially all kinds of human rights activities and disarmament, as well as time and again advocating for the general strengthening of international law in international relations.

Neutrality still remains a delicate and tricky issue. Before accession to the European Union, permanent neutrality had already been watered down, and if Brussels' witnesses are serious and do not lie, then more than one high-ranking Austrian politician has told their counterparts there that Austrian neutrality no longer matters. When Wolfgang Schüssel became foreign minister, he declared in a radio interview on 29 April, "I am not willing to abandon Austria's neutrality."[31] Later on, he and other ÖVP and FPÖ politicians declared that regardless of further progress of the Common Foreign and Security Policy (CFSP) in the Union, Austria should apply for membership in the Western European Union (WEU) and the North Atlantic Treaty Organization (NATO). This would put an end to neutrality, of course. The NATO "option" as a idea promulgated in the Options Report was decisive for the termination of negotiations with the SPÖ. In his speech on Austria's National Day in 2001, Chancellor Schüssel said: "Lipizzaner horses, Mozart balls, and neutrality do not fit into the complex reality of the twenty-first century." But things changed again when former Foreign Minister Benita Ferrero-Waldner ran for the office of federal president, for she excluded membership in NATO because of Austria's neutrality. But she wanted a solidarity guarantee within the security framework of the European Union, which would have led to a kind of split neutrality: inside the European Union solidarity, outside neutrality. But again things progressed. In October 2004 when the new Foreign Minister Ursula Plassnik was sworn in, she explained that, for her, neutrality was a matter of fact, and later on she enforced her statement by saying "because neutrality is part of our Constitution."[32] A similar development can be found also with the FPÖ and later on the BZÖ.

Currently, Austrian neutrality is not questioned. I resist discussing the reasons for this surprising development, which Heinz Gärtner has done from a theoretical point of view in 2006. The reasons are abundant. In the context of this article, I wanted to shed some light on the sloppy and *en passant* manner in which serious foreign policy matters sometimes are handled publicly. Does it reflect the rather low level of Austrian political culture? In any case, it is no contribution to a clear, open, and informative debate.

This overview tried to assess Austria's changed views, opinions, and political positions on some of Austria's major principles, strategies, and goals and if and how they have changed since EU membership. To a considerable extent, the changes can be related to Austria's fundamental change from a single small and permanently neutral country to a member of a global political body. It is still neutral, it claims, but to a much lesser extent than before EU membership, and nobody seems to care anymore.

Conclusions

Austria's foreign policy will be facing challenges and options in the near future. During the ten years of the Schüssel era, the global scope of Austrian "national" foreign policy, which was part of its success during the Kreisky era, especially its position as a mediator in international conflicts, has not risen to its former dimensions. Considering the deep and still lasting transformation of the present global international setting with which Austria now has to cope, this fact does not come as a surprise. Many of Austria's traditional attitudes and strategies require fundamental change, or at least proactive and creative adaptation. As a member of the European Union since 1995, it has regained some of its formerly diminished space for maneuvering insofar as new options arise from being part of the European Union. It is up to Austrian political representatives to prepare well, bring, and communicate Austria's national interests and positions to others within the manifold dimensions of common decision making in the Union. In some respects, this could not be efficiently achieved so far, although after some troublesome months in 2000 relations to the other fourteen members are back to normal again.

Finally, Wolfgang Schüssel's foreign policy record is a mixed one. Without any doubt, he succeeded in creating respect and recognition for his professional and efficient handling of and engagement in the two Presidencies and in several multilateral negotiating processes. But he was also blamed by some of his fellow politicians in Brussels and at home for his arrogance and indolence; however, he also was not able (or willing?) to change the chronic lack of information and debate on the Union in Austria and could not substantially improve Austria's ambivalent image in Brussels and among member states.

On the contrary, since national foreign and security policy had become less visible at home, had become to a large extent integrated into a broader European perspective for the above mentioned reasons, and would in the future be decided primarily within EU institutions, the Austrian government under Schüssel's leadership took no sustainable initiative whatsoever. Moreover, the manifold new opportunities membership in the Union provide for member states are not reflected satisfactorily in the political discourse in Austrian public discourse. After almost one and a half decades of membership of the Union, Austria and the Austrian people to a great extent have not really "arrived in Brussels," as many experts rightly put it; ambivalence still prevails.

The ÖVP during the whole of the Schüssel era of foreign policy spoke of itself in terms of being "*the* European party" in Austria and has not changed substantially this image and its communication strategies.[33] Of course, the European Union and its institutional framework are far from being perfect, and a critical—but in general positive—stance and open discussions are paramount and necessary. But in most cases, blaming the European Union for all kinds of political shortcomings in political domestic debates runs counter to the fact that decisions in Brussels have always been taken with Austrian contributions. Austria has become part of the Union, but it still behaves as if "the Union" were the unfriendly, sometimes even hostile, "other."

It may well be that Austrian representatives are not always fully capable of influencing the other members to approve their positions when common decisions are taken. Of course, no single member of the Union, not even the larger ones, are able to get all their particular national agendas approved. The same applies for the smaller states like Austria. But then it is up to those representing Austria to improve their record in lobbying and coalition building with other members, or to make it clear at home why and how Austria cannot get all it wants. Well informed rumor has it that Austrian politicians are not as successful as they could be in lobbying, networking, and coalition building. Moreover, the attitudes of Austria in relation to and in Brussels are far from perfect. Today Austria still ranks among those members which only sloppily carry out their obligations in implementing EU rules into its legal system. More than once Austria took a high risk (to say the least) in accepting an EU infringement procedure, for example, on the issue of the anonymous saving accounts or the attendance of EU students, especially German students of medicine, at Austrian universities. All that negatively influenced the image of Austria in Brussels and contributed to the skepticism of the Austrian public regarding the EU's motives because the information was highly biased and incomplete. Austria's position within the European Union and also the EU's image in relation to Austrian citizens would improve if politicians would fundamentally change some of their traditional nasty attitudes towards the Union. More information in the Austrian public about concrete decisions taken and about the general procedures in Brussels, as well as clear messages about how the Austrian economy as a whole has profited from membership are necessary to improve Austria's standing in Brussels and Brussels' image to the Austrian public.

Austria has not only developed its relationship with the members of the European Union and gained from having done so, but it has also enforced its initiatives in and improved relations with other countries of the world because of its EU membership. Austrian initiatives in the Western Balkans, Franz Vranitzky's mediation mission in Albania in 1997, and the role Austrian foreign policy and several high ranking figures like Erhard Busek, Stefan Lehne, Albert Rohan, Wolfgang Petritsch and others contributed to improving the situation in the Balkans and positively added to Austria's reputation in the European Union and the world. Of course, still much remains to be done to bring the whole region closer to the European Union. The organization of the EU-Latin America Summit during the Austrian EU Presidency opened up new opportunities for Austria in these regions. Finally, the countries of East and Southeast Asia, including Australia and the Pacific States, together build one of the most dynamic mega-regions of today's world, where Austrian economic and cultural interests as well as security needs are at stake and deserve much more attention both now and in the future. I doubt whether Austria is fit enough to lead, given the little factual attention and little resources—in human and financial terms—the Austrian administration is able to provide for these regions.

On the other hand, it is well known that Austria still enjoys high prestige in many regions of the third world, notably in Africa and the Middle East. This prestigious image is due to Austria's well known, small, and non-colonial state and welfare image, but to an even greater extent is a result of its role in the not so distant past. Even today, Austrian developmental and social initiatives during the 1970s within and outside the UN system and its mediating role in the Israel-

Palestinian conflict, among others, are still remembered. Even Austria's neutral status, whose relevance in the north I doubt, but whose relevance in these regions and countries I have to admit, forms a solid basis for improving Austria's international profile and stance as an active player contributing to resolving the most pressing problems of our present world. The fact that Austria acts as a non-permanent member of the UN Security Council during the period of 2009 and 2010 will require Austrian politicians to be more creative.

Foreign and security policy in the future will also have to be more focused on a broad and comprehensive understanding of security and development, especially as relates to international terrorism, and also global problems like the deterioration of the ecological sphere among others.[34] Globalization, besides its consequences for more economic competition and a globally widening gap between the richer developed and the least developed countries, means also the community of states has more and more transnational problems in common, problems that can only be solved cooperatively by many or all states together. Preventative foreign policy, not only on governmental but also on other levels, like civil forms of conflict management and resolution, is a case in point. But third party intervention or mediation in international conflicts is by no means a prerequisite of neutral countries or great powers anymore. There is a growing conviction among politicians, ministerial officials, and civil societies in all parts of the world that social peace and economic development is a necessary condition for sustainable development. The role of Norway (not only) in the Palestinian peace process, for example—problem ridden as Palestine still is today—was highly recognized and reinforced Norway's high international profile as a "like minded country" worldwide. Austria has failed in the past to adapt its administrative structures and its financial means to the changed structures and the urgent needs of the international system, which will also be needed to react efficiently and effectively in favor of Austrian citizens in crisis and emergency situations abroad.

In summarizing and in coming to some conclusion, the considerations above show that with some degree of certainty there will be only modest but important room left for a specific national or "bilateral" part of Austria's foreign policy in the future. Domains for such remnants will be found first and foremost in the fields of culture, in economic issues like tourism, and in neighborhood policies, common environmental or security problems connected to neighboring countries, mediation in international conflicts, and cooperation with some regionally specified areas. In one of these areas, the Regional Partnership in Central Europe, Austria could play at least some role. The possibility for playing a role in the wider regional or even global dimension, like developmental and environmental issues, as well as of security issues of a global reach, exists as well. These issues can best be tackled within multi- and supranational institutions and regimes like the United Nations, the OSCE, the European Union, and global economic institutions. Austria would be well advised to act more creatively within multilateral organizations, which by no means totally excludes its activities on bilateral dimensions.

In an ever changing international environment, all countries must adapt their foreign policies to new and transformed dynamics and events. In the history of humankind, most periods have, in one way or the other, been periods of transition. Today we live in a world in which changes are not only fundamental and manifold, but also highly complex and interdependent; countries and their representatives are supposed to meet rapidly moving targets. The positive aspect of these circumstances is that all states are affected and all of them have to change and to cleverly react to these changes. The challenging part of these circumstances is that Austrians have to change. It remains to be seen whether the hearts and minds of Austria's political elites and Austrians in general are well enough prepared to meet the future, for the future will not wait.

Notes

1. I would like to thank a number of people who were either close collaborators of the Foreign Minister and Chancellor Wolfgang Schüssel, or were well acquainted with his foreign policy, as politicians or experts, practically engaged in Austrian foreign and security policy, some belonging to different parties. They gave me the chance to speak to them about the "Schüssel era" and to learn from their close and direct knowledge and experience. These people are Caspar Einem, Werner Fasslabend, Peter Jankowitsch, Marion Knapp, Ulrike Lunacek, Hans Peter Manz, Eva Nowotny, Thomas Nowotny, Erich Reiter, Albert Rohan, Herbert Scheibner, Peter Schieder, Michael Spindelegger, and Gregor Woschnagg. They definitely contributed a great deal to my understanding, but nevertheless the responsibility for the whole article is completely mine.

2. Cf. Peter J. Katzenstein, *Small States in World Markets: Industrial Policy in Europe* (Ithaca, NY: Cornell UP 1985), 29.

3. As Alois Mock put it in an interview with the Tyrolian daily *Tiroler Tageszeitung* from 31 Dec. 1994 and 1 Jan. 1995.

4. Before Wolfgang Schüssel became Austria's Foreign Minister in May 1995 until February 2000, he had served as secretary of the Austrian People's Party's Parliamentary group (1968-1975), then as General Secretary of the Austrian Economic League (1975-1991); then he became Minister of Economics (1989-1995). On 22 April 1995, he was also elected chairman of the Austrian People's Party; then from January 1997 until February 2000 he acted as vice-chancellor and minister of foreign affairs at the same time. From February 2000 until the beginning of January 2007, he was the federal chancellor of Austria.

5. As for the highly recognized foreign policy era of Bruno Kreisky, cf. among others Otmar Höll, "The Foreign Policy of the Kreisky Era," in *The Kreisky Era in Austria*, vol. 2, Contemporary Austrian Studies, ed. Günter Bischof et al. (New Brunswick, NJ: Transaction, 1994), 32-77. Alois Mock's role in strengthening Austria's orientation towards the European Community and his—reductionist, as some say—role in the Yugoslav secession wars is highlighted in *Austrian Foreign Policy in Historical Context*, vol. 14, Contemporary Austrian Studies, ed. Günter Bischof et al. (New Brunswick, NJ: Transaction, 1994), 8-12, and in Michael Gehler, *Österreichs Außenpolitik der Zweiten Republik: Von der alliierten Besatzung bis zum Europa des 21. Jahrhunderts* (Innsbruck: Studienverlag, 2005). Mock's social democratic counterpart in the late 1980s and early 1990s, Federal Chancellor Franz Vranitzky, a former banker and previous minister of finance with little prior experience in foreign affairs, was also covered by this journal in volume seven (1999). He served from 1986-1997 as Austria's federal chancellor and eventually became an important and successful foreign policy actor. He not only convinced his party, the SPÖ, to re-direct its goal towards the European Community in 1986/87, but also acted as a substitute to the then widely boycotted Austrian President Kurt Waldheim and represented "the other Austria" abroad and at home.

6. Cf. Helmut Kramer, "Strukturentwicklung der Außenpolitik (1945-2005)," in *Politik in Österreich: Das Handbuch*, ed. Herbert Dachs et al. (Vienna: Manz, 2006), 829.

7. Cf. Christian Schaller, "Die österreichische EG/EU-Diskussion in den Ländern," in *Österreichs europäische Zukunft: Analysen und Perspektiven*, ed. Albrecht Rothacher et al. (Vienna: Signum, 1996), 191-94. For further analysis on structural changes, cf. Otmar Höll et al., "Austria: Structural Change through European Integration," in *Fifteen into One? The European Union and Member States*, 2nd ed., ed. Wolfgang Wessels et al. (Manchester: Manchester UP, 2003), 337-54. In the preparation process for accession, a new Council for Integration Policy was founded by the coalition government in 1989, which not only tied up the social partners, but also all nine provinces, the municipalities, and the National Parliament.

8. Previously in 1991, Manfred Rotter had published a critical contribution on permanent neutrality: "Von der integralen zur differentiellen Neutralität," *Europäische Rundschau* 3 (1991): 25-35. Ten years later, Waldemar Hummer in an article spoke about the final end of neutrality; see "Solidarität versus Neutralität: Das immerwährend neutrale Österreich vor und nach Nizza," *Österreichische Militärische Zeitschrift* (*ÖMZ*) 39.2 (2001): 147-66.

9. See: Höll et al., "Austria: Structural Change."

10. For more information, see also Gregor Woschnagg, "The Priorities of the Austrian EU Presidency," in *The Austrian Presidency of the European Union*, ed. Otmar Höll (Laxenburg: Österreichisches Institut für Internationale Politik, 1998).

11. The presidency of the Council of the European Union, which rotates every six months, is responsible for the functioning of the Council of the European Union and its many meetings during this period. There is still no single and elected president as envisaged by the preliminary Lisbon Reform Treaty, but the task is carried out by an entire national government and—what is important for small states—with the support of the Commission. Since 2006, new presidencies cooperate with the last and next one on a common political program.

12. See: Gregor Woschnagg, "The Priorities of the Austrian Presidency", 32-33.

13. See Foreign Minister Schüssel's Speech at the Royal Institute for International Affairs in London, 3 June 1998, "*The Priorities of the Austrian Presidency of the European Union*," (mimeo).

14. Cf. Otmar Höll and Sonja Puntscher-Riekmann, *The Austrian Presidency of the European Union: Assessments and Perspectives* (Vienna: oiip, 1999).

15. This ambivalence could be interpreted as the result of the growing influence the radical right in Austria gained at that time, cf. Höll et al., "Austria: Structural Change," 352.

16. Cf. Wilfried Spohn, "Austria, Europe and the Nation in Austrian National Identity," in EURONAT project, Robert Schuman Centre for Advanced Studies, 2002/EURONET-rep/A, 2- 28.

17. Cf. Batsheva Tsur and News Agencies in the *Jerusalem Post*, 4 February 2000.

18. "Statement from the Portuguese Presidency of the European Union on Behalf of the XIV Member States," 1 Feb. 2000. Cf. also a.o. Otmar Höll, "Österreich unter Beobachtung," in *Österreichisches Jahrbuch für Internationale Politik 2000* (Vienna: Böhlau, 2001); and Anton Pelinka and Waldemar Hummer, *Österreich unter "EU-Quarantäne": die "Massnahmen der 14" gegen die österreichische Bundesregierung aus politikwissenschaftlicher und juristischer Sicht, Chronologie, Kommentar, Dokumentation* (Vienna: Linde, 2002).

19. A very well explained and sound analysis of the context and its impact is given from an Austrian "outsider"; cf. Lonnie R. Johnson, "On the Inside Looking Out: An Essay on Austria's New ÖVP-FPÖ Government, Jörg Haider, and Europe," Working Paper 00-1, Austrian Fulbright Commission, Vienna, June 2000.

20. At the occasion of a speech Wolfgang Schüssel gave in Strasbourg only some days before the "sanctions" were put in place, some members of the European Parliament showed unconcealed hatred, as one of my interview partners told me.

21. Hans Magenschab, a well-known Austrian journalist and later on speaker of former Austrian Federal President Thomas Klestil, published in the daily *Der Standard* from 5/6 February 2005 that he had been a witness at the Istanbul OSCE summit in middle November of 1999 when Wolfgang Schüssel promised Jacques Chirac and some other EU politicians that the ÖVP would not form a coalition government with the FPÖ.

22. My argument, published shortly after the sanctions had been lifted, can be found in Höll, "Österreich unter Beobachtung."

23. The concept of "strategic" partnership aimed at engaging in closer cooperation and searching for common interests and positions with Austria's neighboring countries that were candidates for the European Union in respect to their future membership. Neither in the European Union, nor in the countries mentioned above, did the notion of "strategic" partnership raise positive feelings; the concept had not been elaborated upon and discussed with them. Obviously it was made public too early, probably as a reaction of defiance because of the "sanctions."

24. For more information about the Regional Partnership, see Làszló J. Kiss, "Die 'Regionale Partnerschaft': subregionale Zusammenarbeit in der Mitte Europas," *Österreichische Zeitschrift für Politikwissenschaft* 32.1 (2003): 57-65.

25. Typical examples of poor or missing coalition building were the issues of road traffic and the nuclear power plant Temelin in the Czech Republic. In the first case, Austria cooperated in Brussels, but at home castigated the Union for mismanagement. On the second issue, Austria's behavior politically incriminated relations with the new members in the East.

26. As in previous cases when the Chancellery and Foreign Ministry belonged to the same party, the Chancellor's influence dominates over the Foreign Ministry's and its political main directions.

27. A Presidency in the first half of the year is called a "full-time Presidency" because it covers work over six months, whereas a Presidency during the second half of the year—normally—carries a lighter workload because during summer time (at least July and August) Brussels is "on holiday."

28. Social scientists all over Europe time and again have been urging governments to integrate the EU "demos," the citizens, better into the Union by giving them more and clear information about, communication with, and participation in EU institutions and overall EU political matters, but obviously more or less in vain.

29. Four strategic topics in the European Council's multi-annual strategic program were proposed: to create jobs and enhance growth, to secure and develop the EU's social model, to rebuild confidence in the Union among citizens, and to further establish the European Union as a strong and reliable global partner.

30. Cf. *Eurobarometer* 69 (Spring 2008), http://ec.europa.eu/public_opinion/standard_eu.htm, accessed 29 Dec. 2008. Obviously due to the global financial and economic crisis the appreciation of EU-membership among Austrians rose in almost all dimensions, cf.. http://ec.europa.eu/public_opinion/archives/eb/eb70/eb70_de_nat.pdf..

31. See also Heinz Gärtner, "Die Metamorphose der österreichischen Außen- und Sicherheitspolitik am Beispiel der Neutralität," in *Schwarz-Blau: Eine Bilanz des "Neu-Regierens,"* ed. Emmerich Talos (Vienna: LIT, 2006), 312ff.

32. See the interview with Ursula Plassnik in the Austrian weekly *Der Falter* 8/2005, 23 February 2005.

33. The self understanding of the ÖVP as a the "natural European Party" is well expressed by Wolfgang Schüssel at the occasion of the already above mentioned speech in the London Royal Institute for International Affairs, on 3 June 1998:

> Our history and our self-definition has always been a supranational one, whether you put it in the context of the Holy Roman Empire of German Nation or into the context of the Austro-Hungarian Empire. Thinking and living in a larger European framework and in supranational structures is not an alien concept to us. There is, one would say in today's language, a genetic predisposition, and the historic memory is still alive.

34. For more and extended reflections on Austria's future tasks in its foreign and security policy see Eva Nowotny's the far-sighted essay "Österreichische Außenpolitik vor neuen Aufgaben", in *Themen der Zeit II*, ed. Franz Vranitzky (Vienna: Passagen Publ., 2009), 185-93.

The Schüssel Years and the European Union

Heinrich Neisser

Austria's First Stage as a Member of the European Union (1995-2000)

Austria joined the European Union (EU) on 1 January 1995. Together with two other new member states—Sweden and Finland—it became a full member of a political Union established by the Maastricht Treaty signed on 7 February 1992, entered into force after the ratification process on 1 November 1993. Austria's admission to the European Union was legitimized by a referendum which demonstrated that a very significant majority of Austrians favored this membership. On 12 June 1994, Austria voted for a Europe shaped by the Maastricht Treaty with the highest percentage of any continental European Country: 66.6 percent.

Thanks to its consistent policy of European integration before 1989, Austria joined the European Union in an economically advanced stage. Since 1987, the Grand Coalition, consisting of Social Democrats and Christian Democrats, governed Austria. The coalition partners tried to adhere to the criteria for convergence in the form of austerity programs and tax increases.

Some events gave Austria crucial incentives to participate fully in EU policy making. One of the most important ones was to develop the framework of a common Security and Defense Policy. In November 1998, European defense ministers gathered for the first time in the history of European integration. The ministerial meeting was initiated by the Austrian presidency and was informal in nature. One month later, France and Britain adopted a joint declaration in St. Malo in which they asked the Union to have a "capacity for autonomous action" in the field of defense. The meeting of Tony Blair and Jacques Chirac was the beginning of a new stage heralding a more unified European defense policy. One year later in June 1999 at the European Council's summit in Cologne, the European Union adopted the European Security and Defense Identity and began outlining it by establishing the concept of battle groups.

Austria's admission to the European Union conferred the status of full membership on the country. Austria became an actor in the Union's institutions. It had the possibility of nominating someone as a Commissioner. As member of the Commission, Franz Fischler, the former minister of agriculture in the national government, was nominated. Fischler's portfolio covered agriculture and rural development.

In the European Council, Austria was represented since 1997 by Chancellor Viktor Klima, who became in this year the head of government.[1] He was from the Social Democratic Party (*Sozialdemokratische Partei Österreichs*, or SPÖ). The foreign minister was Wolfgang Schüssel, since 1995 chairman of the Austrian People's Party (*Österreichische Volkspartei*, or ÖVP).

Austria also nominated a member for the Court of Justice and another member for the Court of Auditors. In the advisory institutions of the European Union, Austria was represented by twelve members in each of them.[2]

Special provisions gave Austria the possibility of electing its members of the European Parliament during the first two years of membership. In that transitional period, twenty-one Austrian members of the European Parliament were elected by the Federal Assembly of Austria (*Österreichische Bundesversammlung*).[3] On 13 October 1996, the first direct elections of twenty-one members of the Austrian delegation to the European Parliament took place, based on a system of proportional representation.[4]

The most challenging activity during the first five years of Austria's EU membership was the presidency. Because Austria joined the European Union in 1995, its turn filling the presidency was fixed for the latter half of 1998. Preparations for the Austrian Presidency began shortly after 1 January 1995. Administrative adjustments in the Austrian federal government were necessary, and an assimilation of considerable information and analyses was needed to guarantee that Austrian policy makers would be fully informed about EU policy issues. Thus the Austrian government began to develop and to immerse itself in the dense network of contacts and consultations typical of the European Union.

The agenda of the first Austrian Presidency was quite busy. Its agenda included fighting unemployment, completing of preparations for the monetary Union, directing the enlargement process towards Central and Eastern Europe, developing environmental protection policies, strengthening the EU's international profile, coordinating the fight against international crime, and so forth.

Observers generally viewed Austria as having done a great job in organizing all the meetings, conferences, and summits. As far as the policies are concerned, Austria didn't make great progress on the agenda. On this point of evaluation, political scientist Michael Huelshoff states: "Since the Austrian agenda was so heavily influenced by the agenda it inherited, it is not surprising that the results of its presidency are best characterized as incremental."[5]

By and large, one can say that the first five years of Austria's EU membership were a successful period during the course of which Austria was highly esteemed by the other member states. The situation changed suddenly at the beginning of the year 2000.

The Case of Austria: A New Government Takes Over Responsibility (2000)

How the New Government Came into Office

On 3 October 1999, Austria elected a new parliament. In the *Nationalrat*—the first chamber of the Austrian legislative system—the Social Democratic Party and the Austrian People's Party lost some seats; the Freedom Party of Austria (*Freiheitliche Partei Österreichs*, or FPÖ) and the Greens (*Die Grünen*) won. The Freedom Party of Austria became the second strongest political party, receiving 415 more voters then the Austria People's Party.[6]

The "Sanctions" by Fourteen EU Member States against Austria

The government of Belgium was a driving force in taking measures against a possible coalition government formed by the Austrian People's Party and the Freedom Party of Austria. At the end of January 2000, Belgium sent a note to the Portuguese Presidency of the EU Council demanding joint action by the fourteen EU member states against the coalition government that was in process of forming in Austria.

On Monday, 31 January 2000, the Portuguese Presidency announced measures in case Austria formed a coalition government integrating the FPÖ. This statement, agreed upon by the heads of state and government of fourteen member states of the European Union, notified the Austrian president, federal chancellor, and foreign minister of the following measures:

- the governments of the fourteen EU member states would not promote or accept any bilateral official contacts at a political level from Austrian government integrating the FPÖ;
- there would be no support for of Austrian candidates seeking positions in international organizations;

- Austrian ambassadors in EU capitals would only be received at a technical level.

These measures threatened by the fourteen governments of the member states took effect with the swearing in of the new Austrian federal government on 4 February 2000.

Austria's Role within the European Union during the First Six Months of 2000

This new coalition started its period of governance with a declaration that was absolutely unusual and unprecedented in the Second Republic. The leaders of the ÖVP and the FPÖ had signed a preamble to the governments' program with the title "Responsibility for Austria—A Future in the Heart of Europe." At the beginning, the government underlined its commitment to European values:

> The Federal Government reaffirms its unswerving adherence to the spiritual and moral values which are the common heritage of the peoples of Europe and the true source of individual freedom, political liberty and the rule of law, principles which form the basis of all genuine democracy. The coalition government also declared its commitment to Austria's membership of the European Union as the basis of the cooperation between the coalition parties.

In this respect it declared: "The Federal Government is bound by those principle of liberty, democracy, respect for human rights and fundamental freedoms and the rule of law which, under Article 6 of the Treaty of the European Union, are common to all member states of the European Union."

European countries responded to these measures in different ways. Norway and the Czech Republic expressly agreed with the measures. Other European countries like Switzerland, Slovenia, Slovakia and Hungary declined to endorse them. A number of German federal *Länder* adopted a friendly attitude toward Austria.

The non-European states also reacted in different ways. Israel was the only state to withdraw its ambassador from Vienna. Argentina confined bilateral contacts to a "strictly technical level." The United States restricted itself to recalling its ambassador for periodic reports.

Referring to the above-mentioned measures, the European Commission made a statement on 1 February:

> "At this stage the work of the European institutions is not affected. In this context the Commission, in close contact with the Governments

of the Member States, will follow the situation carefully, maintaining its working relations with the Austrian authorities."

The Austrian government reacted to the joint action by the 14 EU member states with a decisive rejection of these undemocratically instigated sanctions and asked for their immediate withdrawal. In consultation with leading Austrian experts on European and international law, Austria's Federal Ministry for Foreign Affairs made the following assessment of the legal aspects of the sanctions:[7]

1. The statement from the Portuguese Presidency of the European Council "on behalf of XIV member states" exceeded the limit of its competence, since a presidency is not empowered to issue declarations that are not based on decisions by all member states.
2. The declaration violated fundamental legal principles as well as the spirit of the treaties that are the foundation of the Community and the Union.[8]
3. The action against Austria also violated the general loyal principle of *audiatur altera pars* and thereby the principle of fairness and objectivity that is to be expected from other member states within the framework of the European Union. Austria was not even given an opportunity to present its own position.
4. The measures also offended international courtesy.

The Austrian federal government made a lot of appearances on television and radio and in the print media to clarify the distorted image of Austria the sanctions presented. In many information campaigns, Austrian institutions tried to improve the international image of Austria.

Despite of these efforts, Austria was faced with disadvantages and boycott measures. The reduction of bilateral contacts to a purely technical level meant that Austria was not fully included in the decision-shaping process at the EU level. Particular tensions existed between Austria and certain EU partners. Belgium completely froze military cooperation with Austria. Belgium's foreign minister called for a boycott of holidays in Austria. France canceled all events in the 2000 bilateral program of military cooperation that could have had a public effect. Individual school and student exchange programs in France and Belgium were canceled.

Although the Austrian federal government made many efforts to reestablish a dialogue among all fifteen member states, it took several months until the fourteen member states were willing to redefine their attitude. At the informal meeting of foreign ministers on 6/7 May several members indicated that they would be prepared to consider an "exit scenario." The attitude of the European Parliament was also helpful for finding a solution. In a resolution addressed to the Feira European Council of on 19/20 June, the European Parliament asked the Council Presidency "to evaluate relations between the fourteen member states and Austria and to develop, with all the parties in the EU concerned, a procedure that will lead to an acceptable solution."

The Report of the "Three Wise Men" and the Lifting of the Ban

Soon after the Feira European Council, the Portuguese prime minister invited Luzius Wildhaber, the president of the European Court of Human Rights, to nominate three personalities to draw up a report on the Austrian government's observance of common European values, in particular the rights of minorities, refugees and immigrants, as well as "the development of the political nature of the Freedom Party of Austria."

Wildhaber issued a mandate to Marti Ahtisaari, former president of Finland, Jochen Frowein, director of the Max Planck Institute for Foreign Public Law and International Law, and Marcelino Oreja, formerly Spain's foreign minister and member of the European Commission, to draw up a special report. This group was dubbed the "Three Wise Men," and their report took that name. These three investigators held discussions with the Austrian government, the parliamentary parties, the social partners, religious communities, judges, ombudsmen, and representatives of non-governmental organizations. On 8 September 2000, the Three Wise Men delivered their report to the head of the European Council, Jacques Chirac. This report recommended the lifting of the sanctions and stated that "the Austrian government is committed to European values" and that it "has also taken practical measures to improve its compliance with these values and standards." One remark was critical of the measures enacted by the EU-14: "The measures have already stirred up nationalist feelings in the country, as they have in some cases been wrongly understood as sanction directed against Austria citizens." Finally, the report suggested the development of a mechanism within the European Union "to monitor and evaluate the commitment and performance of individual member states with respect to common European values."

The lifting of the sanctions was announced on the evening of 12 September 2000. After seven months and ten days, the French Presidency stated on behalf of the fourteen member states, "The Austrian government has not failed in its commitments to uphold European common values."[9] The debate within the European Union "should be furthered on the way to forecast, monitor, assess and react on similar situations." The report of the Three Wise Men was the end of an affair which was very problematic for Austria. Certainly the measures of the fourteen EU member states become "counterproductive" as the Three Wise Men pointed out in their report.

There is no doubt Austria lost a part of its international prestige, for its political image in Europe was damaged. Another effect of the sanctions was that the attitude of the Austrians changed considerably. In the spring of 2000, only 34 percent of the Austrian population agreed that their country had benefited from membership in the European Union. In the autumn of 1999, that figure was still 45 percent. In comparison with the referendum on membership in 1994 (66.6 percent), the level of approval had dropped by half.[10]

In the year 2008, one can say the EU-14 measures for most Austrians faded into the history of the European integration process. Public opinion in Austria is very critical, but the reasons for that are manifold. The Austrian population feels a great lack of confidence in the institutions and policies of the European Union.

Summing up the general dimension of the confrontation between Austrian and the other fourteen member states in the year 2000, three perspectives indicate the importance of these events for the process of the European integration.

First, it is imperative to understand that the EU-14 measures have not been "sanctions" in the sense of the Treaty on European Union (TEU). Since the Treaty of Amsterdam enforced in 1999, the possibility for adopting sanctions against a member state formally exists.[11] In this situation,

> The Council, meeting in the composition of the Heads of State or Government and acting by unanimity on a proposal by one third of the Member States or by the Commission and after obtaining the assent of the European Parliament, may determine the existence of a serious and persistent breach by a Member State of principles mentioned in Article 6(1), after inviting the government of the Member State in question to submit its observations.[12]

If this body determines that a breach has occurred,

> "[...] the Council, acting by a qualified majority, may decide to suspend certain of the rights deriving from the application of this Treaty to the Member State in question, including the voting rights of the representative of the government of that Member State in the Council."[13]

The TEU contains a concrete and clear procedure for the adoption of "sanctions." No one element of this procedure had been applied in the case of Austria. There was no proposal for making such a decision, no intervention made by the Council, and no accusation of a serious and persistent breach of the EU's principles. There is no doubt: the EU-14 measures have not been "sanctions" in the sense of the TEU because they had no explicit legal basis. Thus they were only a politically motivated statement made by fourteen member states.

Second, the question must be raised whether the Union follows the principle of equal treatment, particularly in its application to big and small member states. To investigate this, a comparison between the Austria federal government in the year 2000 and the participation of the National Alliance (*Alleanza Nationale*, or AN), a post-fascist political party in the Italian government, yields interesting results. In 1994, Italian Prime Minister Silvio Berlusconi formed a coalition government with the AN. At that time, the European Parliament adopted a Resolution on the European Council in Corfu on 4 May 1994 asking "that the Member States of the European Union should it make clear towards the President of Republic of Italy that the Italian government must respect the basic values which have been prevailing for the foundation of the European Community."[14] This was six years before Austria's federal government formed a coalition between the ÖVP and the FPÖ.

More than one year after the formation of the Austrian government of the ÖVP and FPÖ, Silvio Berlusconi won the parliamentary election for Italian prime minister in May 2001. When he formed a government with the neo-fascists of the AN and the North League (*Lega Nord*, or LN), the reaction from the EU side was different. Immediately after the Italian general election on 13 May 2001, Belgian Minister for Foreign Affairs Louis Michel evidenced the same reaction against the "neo-fascists" of the AN and the LN as had been expressed against the FPÖ. Berlusconi and Italian Foreign Minister Lamberto Dini protested harshly against this statement; nevertheless, Michel insisted that sanctions be imposed. Major players in the European Union, however, failed to take up the call, noting that the case of Italy could not be compared with that of Austria. French Foreign Minister Hubert Védrine said that the European Union must be vigilant about the new Italian government. Swedish Prime Minister Göran Persson, at that time the EU Council's president, definitely ruled out sanctions against Italy. By and large, the EU reactions in the case of Italy were much different and much more moderate than in the Austrian affair. It was a double standard applied from the EU side.

Third it must be considered that radical political parties, particularly from the extreme right, exist in many member states (for example, *Le Pen* in France, the *Vlamske Bloc* in Belgium). These parties are elected in national and regional parliaments. There is no rule from the European

Union regarding how those parties should be treated in the constitutional system of the member states. How far political parties can be excluded is an issue for each nation's political system. The European Union has only the ability to influence the democratic quality of the Member States by adopting the sanctions mentioned above.

Austria's Presidency in 2006 (1 January to 30 June)

A major European event of the second Schüssel government was the presidency of Austria in the European Union during the first half of 2006. This special kind of leadership within the Union was the second chairmanship exercised by Austria (the first time was during the second half 1998). The Union's presidency comprises the chairmanship in the European Council and in the Council of Ministers. It changes every six months to another country following an order which is adopted by the Council unanimously; for a list of presidencies, see Table 1. Austria will hold its next presidency in the year 2018.

Table 1
EU Presidencies from 2000-2006

Year	Country with Presidency in First Half of Year	Country with Presidency in Second Half of Year
2000	Portugal	France
2001	Sweden	Belgium
2002	Spain	Denmark
2003	Greece	Italy
2004	Ireland	The Netherlands
2005	Luxembourg	The United Kingdom
2006	Austria	Finland

Essence of the Presidency

The Council of Ministers is the most powerful organ within the institutional framework of the Union. The Council ensures coordination of the general economic policies of the member states and has the power to make decisions and confer on the rules which the Council lays down.[15] The Council consists of representatives from each of the member states at the ministerial level, the foreign minister of the state concerned assumes the title of President of Council of Ministers, and the foreign ministry of his or her country undertakes, with the help of the Council Secretariat, the organization of the Council's business during the six months.

Apart from the Council of the European Union, there is also the European Council, which meets at European Summits several times per year. The European Council brings together the Heads of State or Government of the member states and the President of the Commission. They are assisted by the ministers for foreign affairs of the member states and by the vice-president of the Commission.[16] The European Council provides the Union with the necessary items for its development and defines the general political guidelines thereof.

During the first half of 2006, Austria presided over a large number of bodies: at a political level in the European Council and the Council of Ministers and at the level of officials in around 250 committees on working groups. In course of six months, Austrians chaired some 2,000 meetings. They also represented the EU abroad and spoke on its behalf at summit meetings and international conferences.

Essentially, the EU presidency comprises the European Council and all the committees supporting and working for the presidency. These committees and working parties make up the base of the Council's internal structures and have grown up over the years to number about 400.[17]

Every country that holds the rotating presidency sets own priorities and brings something new in the agenda of EU structures comprising representatives of the other twenty-six member countries. It is part of the presidency's duty to oil the wheels of the community and to strive to reach agreement on as many issues as possible. The presidency is supposed to exert itself to produce compromise proposals whenever there is a deadlock.[18]

The exercise of the presidency requires careful, long-term, plenary planning.[19] Presidencies must draw up programs, and since 2003 they must cooperate in drawing up three- year, multi-annual strategic plans. Moreover, for the member state exercising the presidency, it is very important to react swiftly to unforeseen circumstances.

Today the main question is whether the system of a six month rotating presidency is an appropriate instrument for effective political leadership within the European Union. In the Union of twenty-seven, the single member state has to wait longer before its turn comes around again. Another argument is that the presidency has becoming increasingly complex and onerous. Moreover, an increasing number of policy processes (like co-decision legislative procedures) go beyond the six month period and, in any case, the Council's new multi-annual planning mechanisms have reduced the scope of presidency initiatives.

For all these reasons, a reform of the presidency of the European Union has been discussed in the last few years. The constitutional treaty which couldn't be ratified by negative referenda in France and The Netherlands in the year 2005 contained a new system: the president of the European Council would be elected by a qualified majority for a term of two and one-half years, renewable once. The president would be responsible for leading the European Council and driving forward its work, for ensuring proper preparation and continuity in cooperation with the president of the Commission, and for facilitating cohesion and consensus with the European Council, especially in terms of integrating the work of the General Affairs Council.

Another proposed change involves creating the post of EU minister for foreign affairs who would chair the External Relations Council. This minister should be appointed by the European Council and would also be one of the vice-presidents of the European Commission, with the responsibility for handling external relations.

For all other Council seats, the system of six-monthly rotation of the presidency should be preserved.

Organizational Challenges

The biggest challenges for the member state exercising the presidency are the organizational tasks. The presidency has as its primary responsibility organizing and chairing all meetings of the Council and of the European Council as well. Fulfilling this task requires a lot of human resources and a high level of efficiency, especially in the host country's national bureaucracy. More specifically, the foreign ministry must be able to use an intense network of contacts and consultations that is so common in the European Union.

The administrative focus of the Austrian Presidency 2006 was the "EU Executive Secretariat," which was set up in the foreign ministry and chaired by the secretary general. It was the center for coordinating all the events that occurred during the EU presidency, including 200 working groups of the Council that had to be chaired by Austrian top officials and about 4,000 meetings and conferences that had to be scheduled.

In addition to the regular summits and meetings of the EU institutions, the Austrian Presidency organized two extraordinary events. Together with the European Commission, the Austrian Presidency held a conference on the future of Europe from 27 to 28 January entitled *The Sound of Europe*. The conference took place in the congress center in Salzburg, the city in which Wolfgang Amadeus Mozart was born exactly 250 years ago. The conference participants discussed fundamental questions as to the future of Europe and European values, identity, and culture. More than 300 personalities from the worlds of politics, science, the arts, and the media deliberated on prospects and proposals for making progress on the European project in view of global challenges.

The unease and skepticism people express about Europe was also addressed and the underlying causes discussed.

Another European conference on subsidiarity was co-organized by the Austrian Presidency with the Austrian Parliament and the *Bundesland* Lower Austria on 18 and 19 April 2006 in St. Pölten, which is the capital of Lower Austria. At this conference entitled *Europe Begins at Home*, representatives of the EU member states, the European Commission, the European Parliament, and other EU institutions, together with experts, discussed the subsidiarity principle and the proportionality principle as well as better regulation in the institutions of the European Union. The discussions focused on citizen-based policies and the contribution of the regions and the local authorities, the role of parliaments in the implementation of the principles of subsidiarity and proportionality, and subsidiarity and better regulation.

As far as the organizational challenge of the EU presidency is concerned, Austria's presidency supplied proof of Austria's ability to organize impressive events and to provide appropriate venues for the social life that is part of the work of the presidency country.

Programs of the Presidency

The programmatic orientation of Austria's Presidency was laid down on three levels. First, the key strategic issues had been laid out in the European Council's 2004-2006 multi-annual strategic program. Second, Austria and Finland, who both held the presidency in 2006, used this as the basis for establishing the debated annual operational program for 2006 which set out the main objectives for the Council's work in this year. The annual operational program contained the following general objectives:

- create jobs and growth in Europe,
- secure and develop the specifically European social model,
- rebuild confidence in the European project among EU citizens, and
- further establish Europe as a strong and reliable global partner.

Moreover, the two presidencies were to work closely together in order to ensure that the work of the Council during 2006 contributed to advancing economic and social welfare, protecting the environment, ensuring the freedom and security of Europe's citizens, and strengthening the role of the Union in the world. Third, based on those two programs, the Austrian Presidency presented a "white book" containing the concrete goals and priorities of the Austrian chairmanship. This document contained 123 items and gave special priority to reviving the discussion on the future of the European Union and the search for an answer to the question of how far the EU's borders should extend. The white book dealt with three substantial perspectives: the future of Europe, including the constitutional debate where Austria failed; the internal dimension of EU politics, like growth and employment, services directives, and areas of freedom; and foreign policy, specifically security and law, as related to the summits with Russia, the United States, and Latin America.

The program of the Austrian presidency was presented to several EU institutions. On 9 January 2006, the Commission as a whole visited Vienna and discussed the main problems Austrian Chancellor Schüssel presented in the European Parliament in Strasbourg. He explained the priorities of Austria's Presidency and mentioned in particular the debate about the European Constitution, which must be confirmed with the European Parliament, the European Commission, the national parliaments, and the European public. As mentioned before, this announcement was not effective. The debate regarding the European Constitution had to be continued one year later under the German Presidency.

EU Summits and External Relations

Apart from the regular summits of the European Council, the European Union organizes special summits between the Union's representatives and the political representatives of countries outside the European Union. These summits are organized regularly every two or three years and are crucial for the external relations of the European Union. Under the Austrian Presidency, three special summits are notable: the Latin American summit, the EU-Russia summit, and the meeting between the European Union and the United States as an element of the transatlantic agenda.[20] Each of these meetings had a different importance for the external relations of the European Union.

The Fourth Summit Meeting with Latin America and the Caribbean

This meeting was chaired by the Austrian federal chancellor in Vienna from 11 to 13 May. About sixty foreign delegations attended this summit, making it the largest event during the Austrian Presidency in 2006. There was an open debate among the delegates on multilateral, economic, and social issues. During the summit, meetings took place between the European Union and the Andean Community, the Caribbean Community (Cariforum), Mercosur, Central America, Chile, and Mexico. Moreover, several preparatory meetings of parliamentarians, business executives, and representatives of civil society from both regions gave participants the opportunity to exchange points of view on numerous topics. In concert with the summit, the first business forum for leading business executives from the two regions was also held.

Generally, one can say that this summit was a platform for talking about possible future bilateral agreements. The participating states had been in favor of an effective multilateral system. Finally, the partners of the summit stressed the necessity of a closer regional and internal cooperation on the energy sector.

The European Union and Russia

Relations with Russia were among the top foreign policy priorities of the Austrian Presidency. The relations between the European Union and Russia are not only a major factor in the stability and political development of the European community, but also that of the entire world. The Austrian Presidency followed the strategy that no one, single, serious international problem can be solved without taking into account the Russian position. The main event of the dialogue between the European Union and Russia, prepared by the Austrian Presidency, was the summit in Sochi in late May 2006. The main topics of the EU-Russia summit were energy questions and the possibility of closer cooperation in the fields of economics and research.

Prior this meeting, a conference of Russian Foreign Minister Sergei Lavrov and his colleagues with EU representatives took place in February 2006 in Vienna. This Vienna meeting brought an in-depth exchange of opinions on five areas of foreign policy: closer dialogue and cooperation on the international arena, counterterrorism, non-proliferation and disarmament, crisis management, and civil defense. The Vienna meeting reiterated that regional cooperation and integration play an important role in consolidating security and stability. Austria's Presidency paved the way for the negotiations regarding a new Partnership Agreement which would be necessary when the Partnership and Cooperation Agreement expired on 1 December 2007.

The European Union-United States Summit

U.S. President George W. Bush made an official visit in Vienna on 21 June 2006. The summit between the European Union and the United States was an important part of the transatlantic dialogue. The main topics discussed in that summit were strengthening the economic partnership between the United States and the European Union, the fight against terrorism, perspectives on multilateralism, and climate change. The signing of an agreement containing measures for improving educational exchange, such as mutual recognition of programs of study and the development of joint training programs, evidenced concrete results. The meeting of the European Union and the United States in Vienna was a substantial, but not an outstanding, contribution to the transatlantic dialogue.

Financial Planning

By 1999, a new long-term financial perspective covering a seven-year period from 2000 onward was due to be approved by the Council of Ministers. The financial perspective 2000-2006 expired at the end of 2006. By early 2005, uncertainty still existed about when and how the next financial perspective, from 2007 to 2013, would be agreed upon by the EU member states. The United Kingdom Presidency during the second half of 2005 had exerted much effort on developing a consensus about the financial perspective from 2007 to 2013. In December 2005, EU leaders had reached an agreement, but this was overwhelmingly rejected by the European Parliament in mid-January. The members of

Table 2

Overview of the Financial Framework, 2007-2013, in Billions of Euros at 2004 Prices

Commitment Appropriations	2007	2008	2009	2010	2011	2012	2013	Total: 2007-2013
1. Sustainable Growth	5e+13	52.415	53.616	54.294	55.368	58.876	58.303	382.139
a. Competitiveness for Growth and Employment		9.097	9.754	10.434	11.295	12.153	12.961	74.098
b. Cohesion for Growth and Employment		43.318	43.862	43.860	44.073	44.723	45.342	308.041
2. Preservation and Management of Natural Resource of which: market related expenditure and direct payment	5e+09	54.322 42.697	53.666 42.279	53.035 41.864	52.400 41.453	51.775 41.047	51.161 40.645	4e+11
3. Citizenship, freedom, security and justice	1.199	1.258	1.380	1.503	1.645	1.797	1.988	10.770
a. Freedom, Security and Justice	600	690	790	910	1.050	1.200	1.390	6.630
b. Citizenship	599	568	590	593	595	597	598	4.140
4. EU as a global player	6199	6469	6739	7009	7339	7679	8029	49463
5. Administration*	6633	6818	6973	7111	7255	7400	7610	49800
6. Compensations	419	191	190					800
Total Commitment Appropriations	120.702	121.473	122.564	122.952	124.007	125.527	127.091	864.316
As a percentage of GNI	1.10%	1.08%	1.07%	1.04%	1.03%	1.02%	1.01%	1.048%
Total Payment Appropriations	116.650	119.620	111.990	118.280	115.860	119.410	118.970	820.780
As a percentage of GNI	1.06%	1.06%	0.97%	1.00%	0.96%	0.97%	0.94%	1.00%
Margin available	0.18%	0.18%	0.27%	0.24%	0.28%	0.27%	0.30%	0.24%
Own Resources Ceiling as a percentage of GNI	1.24%	1.24%	1.24%	1.24%	1.24%	1.24%	1.24%	1.24%

* The expenditure on pensions included under the ceiling for this heading is calculated net of the staff contributions to the relevant scheme, within the limit of Euro 500 million at 2004 prices for the period 2007-2013.

Source: European Commission, DG Budget.

the European Parliament criticized both the size of the budget (Euro 862 billion, or 1.05 percent of GDP) and the relatively small share of funds allocated to future-oriented resources such a research and development.

After making several efforts, an Inter-institutional Agreement on the financial framework from 2007 to 2013 was signed on 17 May 2006. The key elements included a multi-annual financial framework for a total of Euro 864 billion (in 2004 prices) and additional flexible amounts and contributions providing for a maximum of some extra Euro 2.4 billion per year; a strengthened commitment to sound financial management of EU funds; and a stronger role for the European Parliament concerning external actions, the budget of the Common Foreign and Security Policy, and the adoption of the new financial regulation.

Policy Development

One of the most important successes of the Austrian Presidency was the final discussion of the Services Directive. This directive was intended to facilitate the provision of cross-border services within Europe. The Services Directive was essential for completing the internal market and reinforcing European competitiveness. Services account for approximately 70 percent of private per capita income and people's jobs in the European Union. The directive had different social and consumer protection implications. Austria had to take particular care to ensure that the directive as formulated would not lead to wage dumping and social dumping.

The debate started in 2004 when Commissioner Frederik "Frits" Bolkestein presented the Commission's Directive on Services in the Internal Market (the so-called Bolkestein Directive). This document contained a very liberalized position on services and was harshly criticized from many sides. Therefore, the original draft was revised and negotiated on the basis of a revised directive which the European Parliament and the Council developed.

After more than two years of debate about and revision of the original draft, the Austrian Presidency (especially Minister for Economics and Labor Martin Bartenstein) would reach a consensus: the Council adopted the Services Directive on 29 May 2006, with only one abstention by Lithuania. The Council's adoption had to be accepted by the European Parliament (in accordance with the co-decision procedure). In mid-November, the Services Directive was approved as law.

The final outcome was a compromise in many ways. One key concession late in negotiations ensured that service providers operating abroad would be required to obey the labor laws of the host country, not their country of origin. This provision was crafted to avoid a so-called "race to the bottom," under which firms from countries with weaker social protection, particularly in Eastern Europe, could drastically undercut competition.

Key provisions of the directive ensure:

- service providers are not required to open a separate office in every country in which they wish to conduct trade, nor will they be required to install local representatives,
- freedom for service sector businesses to establish services in another member state,
- freedom to provide services on the territory of another EU member state,
- each EU member state must create a simple "one stop shop" for service providers from another country to complete all necessary registration and paperwork,
- a strengthening of service users' rights by ensuring the right of non-discrimination,
- the removal of various legal and administrative barriers through forty-two new measures, and
- the simplification of many procedures guaranteed by sixty-five measures.

It is estimated that a least 600,000 extra jobs for workers will be created and greater choices for consumers will result as competition delivers a higher quality of services throughout Europe.

Another community policy field called for very quick action by the European Union. Energy policy became a very sensitive issue when the gas conflict between Russia and Ukraine started. At the beginning of 2006, Russia's refusal to ship natural gas to Ukraine made clear how delicate an issue the energy dependence of the European Union is. In 2006, the Union imported 42 percent of its gas from Russia; this figure demonstrates the Union's dependence on energy from other countries. Almost 80 percent of Russian gas deliveries to Europe flow through Ukraine. Despite its own gas production, which amounts to less than 30 percent, Ukraine is highly dependent on Russia. The energy supply of Europe is, therefore, dependent on bilateral and even multilateral relations and is thus subject to international politics.

Since 1973—the year of the oil crisis—the European Community tried to intensify the cooperation of the member states in energy affairs. In 1992, the Maastricht Treaty announced that the European Community "shall contribute to the establishment and development of trans-European networks in the areas of [...] energy infrastructures."[21] Today the energy policy is an essential element of the internal market.

Several green and white books elaborated strategic goals and measures for a common energy policy. The Austrian Presidency in 2006 focused on three objectives within its energy policy: the increase of energy efficiency, the promotion of renewable energies, and an improvement of the functioning of the internal energy market. A success of the Austrian chairmanship was that the Council of Ministers of Energy Affairs adopted on 14 March 2006 a directive about "energy efficiency and energy services" aimed at reducing energy consumption over the next nine years by 1 percent annually. Another success was a top-level meeting on 15/16 March 2006 in Moscow. This conference was a meeting of the sixty-eight energy ministers in which EU energy ministers and chairpersons of international organizations like the IAEO, OPEC, and the World Bank participated. The Austrian energy minister asked for "energy partnership in a new style." While the European Union is a consumer of energy, Russia a supplier of energy: about 90 percent of Russian exports is energy. During this conference, new pipelines were discussed.

The Austrian presidency also made some progress in the field of environmental policy. Directives regarding the production of batteries as well improving air quality were adopted. Austria devoted particular attention to the issues of air quality and the urban environment. The objectives of the urban environmental strategy were to improve environmental efficiency and the quality of life in urban areas, to ensure a healthy living environment for urban residents in Europe, and to strengthen the ecological contribution to sustainable urban development. The Austrian Presidency's efforts to move the Registration, Evaluation, and Authorization of Chemicals (REACH) directive forward was another Austrian contribution to environmental policy. The key objectives of this directive reallocated responsibilities in the chemical sector and established a European Chemicals Agency in Helsinki.

Final Remarks: A General Assessment

In the debate on the progressive nature of globalization, Europeanization is more and more being understood as a response to globalization. The process of European integration has two aspects: on the one side, it is globalization on a regional scale; on the other side, it is a defensive response to the worldwide trend of growing economic interdependence.[22] Political leadership within the European Union has the power to take advantage of both these aspects. Doing so leads to a process of structural transformation and influences the speed of integration. The current presidency system is unique and gives only limited possibilities to the chairmanship. Nevertheless, the presidency can make a substantial contribution to deepening the European integration process. The Jean Monnet strategy that asserts European unification must be developed step by step is also evident in the current system of the presidency. The Austrian Presidency in 2006 was not an outstanding event, but it was an essential contribution to the process of Europeanization.

The Challenge of Enlargement for the European Union

The last two enlargement rounds have posed many challenges for the European Union. Some of these challenges arise solely from enlargement, but others have different roots which present themselves as being a result of enlargement. The enlargement process east—with ten new member states in 2004 and two new member states 2007—has had significant impact on Austria's position with the Union. When Austria became a member state of the European Union on 1 January 1995, it was located on the periphery of the Union's territory. Since the 2004 enlargement, the Czech Republic, Slovakia, Hungary, and Slovenia—all countries that neighbor Austria—are member states of the European Union. Subsequently, Austria shifted from the geographic periphery to the center of the European Union. Thus Austria has a new perspective regarding its neighbors, and a new concept of a regional partnership has been developed. As a result, Austrian strategic concerns in terms of future EU enlargement have changed. A short analysis of two enlargement rounds reveal the different approaches Austria tried when addressing the relations between the European Union and the West Balkan area and Turkey's application for EU membership.

Austria's Link to the "West Balkan Region"[23]

Austria has traditionally held strong historical, cultural, and business links with the Balkans. During its EU presidency, the Austrian government paid attention to political developments in this area and stressed its commitment to supporting the efforts of countries in the region to develop closer ties to the European Union. Austria was convinced that the future of all the countries in the Western Balkans lay within the European Union. In June 2005, the European Council reaffirmed that all the Balkan states have a "European perspective" and, thus, the possibility to accede to the Union under the condition that they meet the criteria for membership.

Austria strongly supported the strategic priorities of the European Union for the Balkans. The four main goals of the EU's policy included

- the creation of an area of peace, welfare, and stability;

- encouraging countries in the region to cooperate with the European Union with an eye toward future admission;
- support for reconstruction and recovery; and
- support for reform policy.

Within Austrian foreign policy, diplomatic relations with the Balkan countries play a significant role. Austrian diplomats have a special expertise in the Balkan region, and Austrian businesses have a lot of operations in the countries of the Balkans. Austrian companies are the most important foreign investors there. Thus, there are many reasons why Austria's Presidency placed a special focus on Balkan issues. Between November 2005 and June 2006, Austria initiated seven conferences dealing with Balkan issues. In all these meetings, security concerns played an essential role. At the center of the discussion was better cooperation between the European Union and the Balkan states in preventing and combating crime, organized or otherwise, particularly terrorism, trafficking in person, corruption, and fraud.

Austria gave special support to Croatia in its efforts to become a member of the European Union. The former Commissioner Franz Fischler works as a special adviser to the Croatian government on European affairs.

The Application of Turkey: A Special Agreement

The relationship between Turkey and the European Union has its roots 1963 with the signing of an Association Agreement, which eventually led to Turkey's accession to the Union. In 1987, Turkey made a formal application for membership. The reaction of the European Community was negative. The Commission considered Turkey incapable of bearing the constraints and disciplines "applying to member states," and the community was not ready to cope with the problems that Turkey's integration would bring.

The Luxembourg Summit of December 1997 excluded Turkey from the formal enlargement process and denied Turkey full candidate status while at the same time offering enlargement negotiations to eleven other applicants. Despite a Customs Union agreement introduced in 1996, the EU's relationship to Turkey remained distant. In 1998, the European Commission presented a European Strategy for Turkey to "prepare Turkey for accession by bringing it closer to the European Union in every field." This strategy was not a great success, and Turkey didn't welcome it as a positive step towards full integration.

The Helsinki Summit of December 1999 brought much more progress, for the European Union formally granted Turkey the status of candidate country. After that, Turkey was recognized as a candidate country and evaluated on the same criteria as all the other candidates.

Official negotiations began in October 2005, but the parties made slow progress. By the end of June 2008, eight of the thirty-five chapters of the *acquis communautaire* had been negotiated, but not finished, and only one chapter had been concluded. Negotiations of several chapters stopped when Turkey refused to open its harbors to ships registered in Cyprus because Turkey refuses to recognize Cyprus diplomatically.

Austria's position in the case of Turkey has been rather reluctant. As opposed to the position taken by the U.K. Presidency in the second half of 2005, Austria did not support full membership for Turkey. U.K. Foreign Secretary Jack Straw made a clear announcement on 8 September 2005 supporting the full membership of Turkey:

> A stable prosperous Turkey anchored in the European Union would be a powerful symbol indeed that the true divide lies not between civilisations but between the vast majority of civilised people across the world and uncivilised few who use violence and terror to try to destroy the common values and beliefs which bind the rest of us. It will prove that a secular democratic state which shows respect for Islam can live comfortably within Europe.[24]

Given the attitudes of many member states, numerous politicians noted that Austria would be bound to change its position. However, Christian Democratic politicians propagated the idea that Turkey is not "of Europe" and that the European Union had "cultural, humanitarian and Christian values different than Turkey's."

The attitude of the Austrian government to the Turkish application was strongly influenced by public opinion in Austria which was clearly against the full membership of Turkey in the Union. The polls showed a broad majority against it. Therefore, the Austrian government followed the proposal of the German government which favored a "privileged partnership." But the content of this kind of partnership is not clear. As another measure, the Austrian government made a promise to the Austrian people to organize a referendum before Turkey will be a member of the European Union.

During the EU presidency, Austria highlighted the necessity of an analysis of the EU's capacity to accept new member states. The Austrian perspective was that the case of Turkey must be examined not only in regard to the Copenhagen Criteria, but also in terms of the Union's ability to integrate new member states. Moreover, some Austrian politicians pled for a referendum in Austria before Turkey should be admitted into the Union.

Notes

1. The European Council brings together the Heads of State or Government (Art. 4 TEU).

2. The advisory institutions are the Economic and Social Committee and the Council of Regions. See Art. 257 to 265 of the Treaty Establishing the European Community, Consolidated Version 1997, *Official Journal* C 340 (10 November 1997), *EUR-Lex*, http://eur-lex.europa.eu/en/ treaties/index.htm, accessed 26 February 2009.

3. The *Bundesversammlung* is, in accordance with the Austrian Federal Constitution, the joint assembly of the two legislative bodies, the *Nationalrat* and *Bundesrat*. See Art. 38 of the Austrian Federal Constitution.

4. See Heinrich Neisser, "Wahlen zum Europäischen Parlament," in *10 Jahre EU-Mitgliedschaft Österreichs: Bilanz und Ausblick*, ed. Waldemar Hummer and Walter Obwexer (Vienna: Springer, 2006), 97-108.

5. Michael Huelshoff, "The European Council and EU Summitry: A Comparative Analysis of the Austrian and German Presidencies," in *Austria and the European Union*, vol. 10, Contemporary Austrian Studies, ed. Günter Bischof et al. (New Brunswick, NJ: Transaction, 2002), 106.

6. The *Nationalrat* comprises 183 seats. After the 1999 election, the seats have been distributed as follows: sixty-five to the SPÖ , fifty-two to the ÖVP, fifty-two to the FPÖ, and fourteen to the Greens.

7. Waldemar Hummer and Anton Pelinka, *Österreich unter "EU-Quarantäne": Die "Maßnahmen der 14" gegen die österreichische Bundesregierung aus politikwissenschaftlicher und juristischer Sicht, Chronologie, Kommentar, Dokumentation* (Vienna: Linde Verlag, 2002).

8. For text on promoting solidarity among member states, see Art 2. of the Treaty Establishing the European Community, Consolidated Version 1997, *Official Journal* C 340 (10 November 1997), *EUR-Lex*, http://eur-lex.europa.eu/en/treaties/index.htm, accessed 26 February 2009; for text on enhancing mutual political solidarity, see Title V: Provisions on a Common Foreign and Security Policy, Art 11 (2) of the Treaty of Amsterdam amending the Treaty on European Union, Consolidated Version 1997, *Official Journal* C 340 (10 November 1997), *EUR-Lex*, http://eur-lex.europa.eu/en/ treaties/index.htm, accessed 26 February 2009

9. Hummer and Pelinka, *"EU-Quarantäne,"* 254.

10. Michael Gehler, "'Preventive Hammer Blow' or Boomerang?", in *Austria in the European Union*, vol. 10, Contemporary Austrian Studies, ed. Günter Bischof et al. (New Brunswick, NJ: Transaction, 2002), 180-222.

11. Art. 6 (1) of the Treaty of Amsterdam amending the Treaty on European Union stipulates: "The Union is founded on the principles of liberty, democracy, respect for human rights and fundamental freedoms, and the rule of law, principles which are common to the Member States," *Official Journal* C 340 (10 November 1997), *EUR-Lex*, http://eur-lex.europa.eu/en/treaties/index.htm, accessed 26 February 2009.

12. Art.1 (F) of Part One—Substantive Agreements of the Treaty of Amsterdam amending the Treaty on European Union, Consolidated Version 1997, *Official Journal* C 340 (10 November 1997), *EUR-Lex*, http://eur-lex.europa.eu/en/treaties/index.htm, accessed 18 February 2009.

13. Art. 7 (2) in ibid.

14. Resolution on the European Council in Corfu, *Official Journal* C 205 (25 July 1994): 154.

15. See Art. 202 of the Treaty Establishing the European Community, Consolidated Version 1997, Official Journal C 340 (10 November 1997), *EUR-Lex*, http://eur-lex.europa.eu/en/treaties/index.htm, accessed 26 February 2009.

16. Art. 4 of the Treaty of Amsterdam amending the Treaty on European Union, Consolidated Version 1997, Official Journal C 340 (10 November 1997), *EUR-Lex*, http://eur-lex.europa.eu/en/treaties/index.htm, accessed 26 February 2009.

17. Martin Westlake and David Galloway, *The Council of the European Union*, 3rd ed. (London: John Harper, 2004), 223.

18. Ibid., 55.

19. Ibid., 334.

20. Another summit had been held with Japan during the Austrian Presidency. Austria worked for a more intensive dialogue with Japan based on the 2001 EU-Japan Action Plan.

21. Art. 154 (1) of the Treaty Establishing the European Community, Consolidated Version 1997, Official Journal C 340 (10 November 1997), *EUR-Lex*, http://eur-lex.europa.eu/en/treaties/index.htm, accessed 26 February 2009.

22. Peter van Ham, *European Integration and the Postmodern Condition: Governance, Democracy, Identity* (London: Routledge, 2001), 43.

23. The West Balkan states are Croatia, Serbia, Bosnia and Herzegovina, Montenegro, Kosovo, Albania, and Macedonia.

24. See Chris Rumford, *The European Union: A Political Sociology* (Oxford: Blackwell, 2002), 241.

Reinventing Tradition and the Politics of History: Schüssel's Restitution and Commemoration Policies

Günter Bischof and Michael S. Maier[1]

> *"Human beings' ability to rewrite the past to suit the present—and especially to recast our individual complicity with a shameful past—is testament to the creativity and ingenuity of the species. It is a phenomenon whenever one official orthodoxy gives way to another."*[2]

Introduction

During his six years in office, Wolfgang Schüssel's ambivalent political history (*Geschichtspolitik*) was as active, if not more so, than that of any postwar Austrian chancellor. One has to assume that his coalition partner, the Freedom Party of Austria (*Freiheitliche Partei Österreichs*, or FPÖ), was a reluctant partner in most of his initiatives. Little is known to date about actual negotiations inside the government coalition about FPÖ reactions to Schüssel's restitution policies during his first government and his call to the nation to make the "memory year 2005" a *Gedankenjahr*—a year of thoughtful reflection about important anniversaries (1945, 1955, 1995). This essay operates with the working assumption that most of these initiatives in managing Austria's complex recent past and shaping the collective cultural memory of Austrians originated with Schüssel personally and the People's Party (*Österreichische Volkspartei*, or ÖVP) as a project for strengthening Austrian identity and patriotism. Schüssel took close personal interest in the progress of the restitution negotiations and the details of planning the events of the memory year 2005.[3] The FPÖ—with its long history of defying any notion of the past (*Vergangenheitsbewältigung*)—played the silent coalition partner. At times, FPÖ/BZÖ party members ran active interference by making public statements that militated against Schüssel's policies. The contrite Social Democratic Party of Austria (*Sozialdemokratische Partei Österreichs*, or SPÖ) engaged in a serious effort of investigating the "brown spots" ("*braune Flecken*") in its own party history. The principal opposition to Schüssel's politics of history came from the critical intellectual class—mainly situated on the left and from outside the parliamentary opposition.

This essay argues that signal restitution policies of the Schüssel government were a historical turning point, if long overdue, in postwar politics. By March 2000, the Schüssel government set up a task force headed by Maria Schaumayer to investigate and compensate former slave laborers who worked in Nazi industries during the war. Only weeks later, Ambassador Ernst Sucharipa began negotiations with organizations representing Jewish victims to fill "gaps and deficiencies" in Austria's complex postwar restitution legislation, culminating in the "Washington Agreement" of 17 January 2001 and the commitment to pay restitution to victims of "Aryanizations" in 1938, thus bringing legal closure to this long-standing issue.[4]

Vice-Chancellor Schüssel surfed on the international wave of confronting the ugly National Socialist past.[5] He reacted to the sanctions of the European Union against the formation of his government in late January 2000. Schüssel wanted to circumvent his new government's humiliating international pariah status after the formation of the ÖVP coalition government with populist *enfante terrible* Jörg Haider's right-leaning FPÖ. The Schüssel government's initiatives and breakthroughs in restitution policies had been the result of an international wave in the 1990s of nations embracing their historical guilt and moral responsibility for past injustices.[6] Judging from a *Festschrift* published on the occasion of his sixtieth birthday in 2005—with essays written and edited by his fawning party associates and friends—one would never guess that fair restitution policies and a focus on *Geschichtspolitik* were part of Schüssel's political vision.[7]

The later 1980s and 1990s formed an era when Austria's World War II past was rewritten. Ever since the great debate about ÖVP presidential candidate Kurt Waldheim's World War II past, postwar Austria's consensual postwar memory culture proffered by the two principal parties, the ÖVP and SPÖ, had been changing.[8] A younger generation of historians was willing to engage in battle with the postwar myths. They have subjected the official victim doctrine (*Opferdoktrin*) of Austria as a casualty of Hitlerite Germany—the founding myth of the Second Republic—to ever more critical inquiry. An alternative historical narrative of Austrians as perpetrators during World War II has been gaining ground and *eroding* the official "victims doctrine." The long hibernation of the contested space of World War II history ended in Austria in the mid-1980s. In 1988, historians and officials took the fiftieth anniversary of the Anschluß as an opportunity for a closer investigation of Austrians' roles as perpetrators of war crimes during World War II. When the Wehrmacht exhibition (*Wehrmachtsausstellung*) toured Austrian cities in the 1990s, Austrians had to confront the myths of the "clean" German Army and Austrian soldiers' participation in war crimes on the eastern and southeastern fronts. During the 1988 national "memory year," President Waldheim was finally willing to admit that in 1938 and during the war there were "Austrians who were victims and others who were perpetrators." SPÖ Chancellor Franz Vranitzky in a 1991 speech in Parliament again spoke of Austrian "victims and perpetrators" and of Austrian "collective responsibility" for the pain inflicted by the perpetrators. Both Vranitzky and President Thomas Klestil reiterated the new memory formula of Austrian "victims and perpetrators" and acknowledged "Austrian responsibility" for supporting National Socialism during speeches in Jerusalem in 1993 and 1994 respectively.[9]

The 1990s turned out to be a decade when restitution to and reconciliation with victims was an important element in international politics. After the end of the Cold War, the Eastern European nations, after ridding themselves of communism, began confronting their unmastered pasts. On top of this, the administration of U.S. President Bill Clinton made the "unfinished business" of full restitution of Holocaust era assets a political priority and part of its wider campaign for human rights;[10] moreover, American lawyers pushed class action suits against Swiss, German, and Austrian financial institutions and businesses, sparking the appointment of historians' commissions and serious investigations into the uncharted territory of the past.[11] The spillover effects of this international politics of restitution and reconciliation, which probed what Elazar Barkan has called "the guilt of nations," put enormous pressure on the Austrian government to follow suit.[12]

In 1995, the SPÖ/ÖVP grand coalition turned words into deeds. Chancellor Vranitzky's coalition government set up a new National Fund (*Nationalfonds*) to compensate victims of Nazi policies. In 1998, the SPÖ/ÖVP coalition government of Chancellor Victor Klima set up the long overdue Austrian *Historikerkommission* to investigate the massive property thefts and transfers of the World War II era. In both these governments, Schüssel served as vice-chancellor and foreign minister and was part and parcel of the new politics of history admitting to Austrians' offender history (*Tätergeschichte*) in World War II war crimes.

Yet Schüssel also proffered a *Schlussstrichmentalität*—ridding Austria of the long shadows of World War II past, while the massive research project of the *Historikerkommission* reports published in 2003/2004 opened up a wide window into the vast criminal project and deep implication of Austrian *Täter* in National Socialism, along with the spotty and uneven postwar restitution efforts. Never before had historians and legal scholars probed the depth of the Vienna pogroms and property transfers ("Aryanizations" of Jewish property during 1938-1942) so thoroughly as the deeply researched thirty-two volumes of the historians' commission have done.[13]

In the preamble of its 2000 government program, the Schüssel coalition government paid lip service to both Austria's need to confront "the dark chapters of Austrian history" and the 1991 formula pioneered by Chancellor Vranitzky of Austrians being both "victims and perpetrators" during World War II. At the same time, Chancellor Schüssel tended to return to the traditional, overly legalistic "Austria as victim" paradigm. In a number of high profile statements, he stubbornly insisted that "Austria was a victim of Hitlerite aggression in 1938," thus backtracking to the one-sided old postwar *Opferdoktrin* paradigm. Concurrently, however, historical scholarship has ever more deeply fleshed out the dreadful narrative of Austrians' role in Hitlerite war crimes. Critical scholarly and ambiguous official narratives of Austrian World War II memory coexist and are still at war with each other.

Schüssel's launch of the *Gedankenjahr* during 2005 seized the celebration of a number of important anniversaries as a spectacular opportunity for *Geschichtspolitik* and (re)definition of Austria's collective memory culture. Schüssel set up a special office to coordinate the numerous historical exhibits, events, and commemorations, which gave him plenty of opportunity to put his spin on how he wanted to read Austria's postwar past and forge the country's identity. This presented an opportunity to turn the clock backward in confronting Austrians' roles in and lack of contrition over World War II crimes. He prodded Austrians to think about their postwar success story rather than their wartime complicity.[14] This allowed Austrians to bask in nostalgic contemplations of history rather than confront both the homemade era of Austrofascism[15] and the unseemly World War II past. Rewriting the past, reaffirming dear historical myths, was a strategy to control the present.

Indeed, when it came to politics of history the greatest failure of Schüssel's ÖVP party leadership came in his refusal to confront the dual legacies of Austrofascism and Nazism. The ÖVP refused to follow the example of the Socialist Party and investigate its predecessor's roles in bringing down democratic government in 1933 and engaging in post-Anschluss "Aryanization" of Jewish property and investigate the ÖVP's postwar strategy in recruiting and harboring former National Socialist Party members in its ranks.[16] To date, the ÖVP has failed to master its own past and look for the Nazi skeletons in its closet. Schüssel missed a golden opportunity to embark on such a critical historical mission. Taken together, then, Schüssel's *Vergangenheitspolitik* is as ambiguous and tortuous as Austrians' roles in World War II and their belated effort to come to terms with that past.

Restitution and Compensation during the Schüssel Years

After the end of World War II—for half a century—the complex restitution and compensation issue for victims of National Socialism had been an inglorious chapter of Austria's *Geschichtspolitik*, often neglected or intentionally silenced by governments. The international and independent Austrian *Historikerkommission* concluded in its final 2003 report that the entire restitution complex in Austria was continually overshadowed by the *Opferdoktrin* and Austrian governments' persistent refusal to accept any (shared) responsibility for Nazi war crimes. Numerous restitution laws were reluctantly passed by Parliament from 1945 onwards. Yet they made access to material compensation for Nazi victims very difficult and produced enormous resentment in Nazi victims *vis-à-vis* the Republic of Austria. Moreover, the *Historikerkommission* also drew attention to the fact that restitution or compensation acts were—as a form of equilibrium thinking (*Gleichgewichtsdenken*)—often paralleled by laws compensating other victims of war such as German *Wehrmacht* soldiers, "victims of the postwar Allied occupation," and other victim groups, including former Nazi perpetrators and supporters of Hitler's dictatorial regime. The restitution laws included almost every Austrian in the great postwar Austrian victims' collective.[17]

In 1995, on the occasion of the fiftieth anniversary of the Second Republic, the paradigm shift in Austria's *Vergangenheitsbewältigung*, which had started with the Waldheim fiasco of 1986, reached a point of new political sensitivity for the country's wartime culpability. This became manifest in the establishment of the *Nationalfonds*. The National Fund of the Republic of Austria for Victims of National Socialism was set up by the SPÖ/ÖVP grand coalition under Socialist Chancellor Franz Vranitzky in order to express Austria's "particular responsibility" towards the victims of the Nazi regime.[18] It was designed to demonstrate—beyond mere monetary compensation—a high symbolic value, bridging the historical chasm between the Republic of Austria and the long-neglected Nazi victims. As the former ÖVP party whip Heinrich Neisser, who was one of the movers and shakers behind the establishment of the *Nationalfonds*, pointed out, the Fund was basically a "political gesture of reconciliation, recognition and respectfulness."[19] For the first time ever in Austria's postwar restitution and compensation history, lump-sum recognition payments (so-called "gesture payments") of 70,000 schillings (later 5.087 euros) were extended to all surviving victims of Nazi persecution around the world. In cases of social hardship, even larger payments were made.

It has been statistically established that 80 percent of the applicants to the *Nationalfonds* (and its successor, the General Settlement Fund) were Jewish.[20] In a dramatic turning point, victim groups long ignored by the postwar political establishment were recognized for the first time.[21] Both homosexuals and the survivors of euthanasia crimes received compensation and, thus, a late symbolic validation of their persecution by the Nazis. Former slave or forced laborers remained excluded, however.[22] By October 2008, 30,097 humanitarian payments totalling about 153 million euros (approximately 200 million dollars) had been transferred to Nazi victims by the National Fund. There is no deadline for applications, so future payments can still be made.[23]

The *Nationalfonds* is also designed to keep the memory of Nazi war crimes and persecution alive. It has sponsored some 700 commemorative and historical projects around the globe to actively document Nazi war crimes and bear witness to the suffering of victims of National Socialism.[24] Even though a complex unresolved parallel problem—namely paying compensation for losses of or damages to private property after the 1938 Anschluss was left open—the National Fund and the intensive media coverage of its inception and role marked a turning point in Austria's now much more transparent restitution policy. The vaunted *Nationalfonds* undoubtedly played a decisive role in raising public awareness of the Holocaust. Its transparent administration also pioneered the way towards the future trajectory of intensifying restitution and compensation measures.

In the late 1990s, the Republic of Austria also experienced enormous pressure to make amends for past injustices and became caught up in the international trends of what has been called "Holocaust-era assets" issues. After the collapse of communism and the end of the Cold War, a new historical consciousness about historical guilt of state actors emerged. Following the establishment of "truth and reconciliation commissions" in South Africa and Latin American countries, historical commissions were appointed by European governments as well as private corporations to investigate illegal property transfers forced under duress that had taken place under the Nazi dictatorship; moreover, the entire complex of postwar restitution legislation was reviewed. The District Attorney of Manhattan seized four iconic painting by Austrian painter Egon Schiele that were under suspicion of being art looted by the Nazis. These paintings happened to be in the possession of the state-financed Leopold collection in Vienna. Swiss banks had to investigate and pay compensation for "dormant bank accounts" among their assets of Holocaust victims. An intense discussion, which resulted in compensation payments, in Germany about former slave laborers exploited by the Nazi economy increased the pressure on the Austrian federal government to follow suit and turn its attention to forced labor exploited by the Nazi economy in the former *Ostmark*.[25]

Then came the parliamentary elections of October 1999 and the contentious formation of a new government, resulting in the unlikely coalition of the ÖVP and FPÖ led by Chancellor Schüssel. The inauguration of the Schüssel government on 4 February 2000 resulted in an outcry by the international community for giving the "right-wing" Freedom Party of Jörg Haider governmental power. Isolation of the pariah government followed. Austria's *Vergangenheitspolitik*, or rather the lack thereof, more than ever garnered international attention. Sanctions by the European Union and intense protests from around the world against giving the likes of populist Jörg Haider a place in the sun forced Schüssel and Vice-Chancellor Susanne Riess-Passer (FPÖ) to send positive signals concerning Austrian sensitivity towards the controversial chapters of its World War II past and coming to terms with them. The long-standing restitution and compensation issue, where significant progress had been made in the second half of the 1990s by an SPÖ/ÖVP coalition government with Schüssel as vice-chancellor and foreign minister, provided the changing government (*Wenderegierung*) an opportunity to close "the gaps and deficiencies" in Austria's restitution agenda. Dramatic concessions in the restitution arena were designed to salvage and enhance the international image of the new government. In an interview, FPÖ provincial politician and State Secretary Eduard Mainoni called the advances in restitution policies a "win-win situation" for his party.[26]

The record of Austria's postwar restitution policy was not so poor in terms of the amount of payments made. But restitution occurred in fitful starts and was marked by a record of frequent and willful procrastination ("*ich bin dafür, die Sache in die Länge zu ziehen*"[27]). Policy makers had operated with bad faith and had always been reluctant to advertise vigorously their cumulative accomplishments, fearing public abuse and additional demands from the victims. Compared to this record of Austria's previous restitution policies, the brisk pace of the Schüssel/Riess-Passer government in approaching the unresolved questions of restitution and compensation was remarkable and downright frantic. On 15 February 2000, only a few days after the stigmatized ÖVP/FPÖ coalition embarked on their new government, Chancellor Schüssel appointed Maria Schaumayer as his special envoy to conduct bilateral negotiations concerning compensation to former

Nazi slave and forced laborers working on Austria territory. For Stuart Eizenstat, President Bill Clinton's special envoy on Holocaust-era assets issues, the main motive for Schüssel's urgency in this complex problem long brushed aside was quite evident. He noted in his memoirs that Austria's diplomatic isolation by its EU partners put Schüssel on the spot "to demonstrate to the world his sensitivity to Holocaust issues by tackling the forced labor issue [U.S. sponsored] class-action suits had thrust into prominence."[28]

From the very beginning, Chancellor Schüssel gave the publicly much admired Schaumayer his complete personal support. As a former highly successful governor of the Austrian National Bank, she enjoyed a sterling reputation as a public official. Schaumayer also could count on a broad consensus from all Austrian political parties and Parliament. She pursued a clear and very transparent negotiating strategy in her contacts with the governments in Central and Eastern Europe representing the slave laborers. This vigorous public stance produced an unusually high public acceptance rate from the Austrian population on an issue which was usually subject to considerable abuse and the typical Austrian grousing (*Raunzerei*). The gentle yet bold Schaumayer convinced both Schüssel and Eizenstat to take a different approach from the Federal Republic of Germany. To simplify and strengthen the negotiation process, Schaumayer (with the able and keen assistance of Martin Eichtinger, a professional diplomat) advocated the strict separation of the agendas relating to the forced laborers (*Zwangsarbeiter*) from the even more contentious issue of 1938-1942 looted property (*Arisierungen*). The Austrian side aimed for intergovernmental agreements to block the involvement of greedy class action lawyers. Such direct negotiations between governments were designed to end the interminable class action suits by American lawyers such as the redoubtable Ed Fagan.

Central and Eastern European negotiators and representatives of victim's associations directly negotiated with representatives from Austria, including Austrian industry directly affected by the outcome. Moreover, the top experts from the academic community and members of the *Historikerkommission* were invited to add their valuable background knowledge and to participate in the negotiations. In May 2000, only three months after the initiation of these negotiations, a Reconciliation Fund Conference was organized in Vienna to approve the key outcomes of the negotiations. At this unprecedented conference, the various representatives agreed that Austria would pay six billion schillings (more than 400 million dollars at that time) to an estimated 150,000 former *Zwangsarbeiter* who were still alive. Schaumayer, with her great sensitivity and calm temperament, added additional payments to victims. Next to slave and forced laborers who had worked in industry and agriculture, the expanded categories of victims who would be compensated included children, who had been deported with their parents and female forced laborers who had given birth to children in the Danube and Alpine *Gaue* of Hitler's Third Reich.

In July 2000 in record time, the Reconciliation Fund Law was approved by both houses of Parliament with the unanimous vote of all parliamentary parties. During September and October, Schaumayer was able to conclude intergovernmental agreements with five Eastern European countries (Belarus, Poland, the Czech Republic, Ukraine, and Hungary); in November, a separate agreement was signed with Russia. Austria also insisted on receiving a "Statement of Interest" from the U.S. government, designed to achieve "legal closure" in this issue and prevent future private U.S. class action suits.

This dramatic breakthrough in the restitution arena was only the beginning. On 5 October 2000, Schüssel and Eizenstat met again in Vienna to set the course for yet another round of important restitution negotiations. Four months later, only days before the accession of George W. Bush as U.S. president on 20 January 2001, another agreement was signed with the Clinton Administration after very tough negotiations by Ambassador Ernst Sucharipa, the director of Vienna's venerable Diplomatic Academy whom Schüssel had appointed special envoy on "Aryanization" matters. In return for keeping the class action lawyers at bay and achieving "legal closure" in U.S. courts, Chancellor Schüssel agreed to provide immediately 150 million dollars in compensation payments for Jewish apartment leases and commercial property, household goods, and personal valuables "aryanized" mostly by force after the Anschluss in 1938. The *Nationalfonds*, established in 1995 and under the able leadership of Hannah Lessing producing an admirable record in compensation payments, was commissioned to administer also the transactions of this new round of compensation payments. Additionally, it was agreed the General Settlement Fund would cover all the remaining "potential gaps and deficiencies in prior Austrian restitution programs." The Executive Agreement between Austria and the United States signed on 24 October 2000 marked a historical breakthrough in Austria's compensation policies and can be seen as a major accomplishment of Schüssel's *Vergangenheitspolitik*. It not only improved Austria's reputation among the Eastern European countries, but also finally brought Austria in alignment with Western practices of more openly mastering the past. Once the class action suits against Austrian companies were withdrawn in December 2000, the Fund for Reconciliation, Peace, and Cooperation began its work in Vienna.[29]

The payments made to the slave and forced laborers in Central and Eastern Europe were dispersed quickly. One may dispute how significant these funds were, yet to the thousands of retirees who enjoyed these unexpected payments, they were most welcome, especially as they came with an Austrian apology for the past injustices. At last, their suffering was acknowledged. According to the Reconciliation Fund Law, voluntary compensation payments of 20,000 schillings (1,453 euros) were made to former forced laborers in agriculture, and 35,000 schillings (2,543 euros) to forced laborers in the industry. Slave laborers (prisoners of war in *Ostmark* camps) received 105,000 schillings (7,630 euros); an additional amount of 5,000 schillings (363 euros) was paid for childbirth. At its beginning, the Fund was capitalized at more than 439 million euros. Both the Austrian government and the private sector made contributions, at least 50 percent of the funding coming from Austrian businesses. The state-owned industrial sector alone provided some 73 million euros for the funding (about a third of the industrial sector's portion), with large amounts coming from the Austrian State Railways and the electricity industry. By 2005, the Austrian Reconciliation Fund had approved some 132,000 applications and disbursed 352 million euros. The remaining 96 million euros were distributed in a project-oriented manner, benefiting former slave and forced laborers and even their heirs. To keep the memory of these abject era and Austrian culpability alive, 20 million euros were allocated to the newly established Future Fund for Research and Remembrance, set up in 2005 to sponsor research projects with a focus on the Nazi era.[30]

Parallel to this set of quickly concluded negotiations on *Sklaven- und Zwangsarbeiter*, the issues dealing with the restitution for "Aryanized" property turned out to be much more challenging. The seasoned diplomat Sucharipa was confronted with a multiplicity of negotiating partners, namely representatives of the Clinton Administration and Austrian and international Jewish victim organizations, as well as the demanding class action lawyers. After exploratory discussions in Vienna, New York, and Washington, the Framework Agreement Concerning Austrian Negotiations Regarding Austrian Nazi Era Property/Aryanization Issues of 5 October 2000, negotiated between Schüssel and Eizenstat (see above), formed the statutory framework for these negotiations. Numerous rounds of parleys between Sucharipa and Eizenstat studied Austria's former restitution legislation. The agreeable pair began to hammer out a fixed amount deemed adequate for compensations. The agreement was nailed down in Washington on 17 January 2001 in the waning days of the Clinton presidency. The Austrian government adopted the agreement on 23 January 2001.[31] The immediate outcome of the Joint Statement was that the Austrian government transferred an additional sum of 150 million dollars to the accounts of the *Nationalfonds*, earmarked for compensating Jewish victims of "Aryanization" who had lost their tenancy rights, household property, personal valuables, and other effects.[32] For a second time, the National Fund made lump sum payments amounting to 7,639 euros to more than 20,000 deserving applicants. From what was left over from the fund, additional supplements of 1,000 euros were paid out to all applicants or their heirs.[33] According to the second law passed by the Austrian Parliament on the basis of the 17 January 2001 Washington Compensation Agreement, the General Settlement Fund for Victims of National Socialism was established on 28 May 2001. It was designed "to comprehensively resolve open questions of compensation of victims of National Socialism for losses and damages as a result of or in connection with events having occurred on the territory of the present-day Republic of Austria during the National Socialist era."[34]

Again, both the Republic of Austria and Austrian private corporations endowed the General Settlement Fund with 210 million dollars, of which 25 million dollars was earmarked for losses from insurance claims. In contrast to the lump sum disbursements made and completed by the National Fund, the General Settlement Fund is still paying out calculated pro rata payments to more than 20,000 Holocaust survivors or the heirs of eligible claimants. The applications were due to be filed before the deadline of 28 May 2003. This compensation was earmarked for victims whose businesses were liquidated, or who lost real estate, capital assets (bank accounts, stocks, bonds, and mortgages), movable property (unless covered by the National Fund), insurance claims, occupational or educational losses, and any other losses or damages that were not covered under prior restitution or compensation measures. For the purpose of *in rem* restitution of publicly owned property, an Arbitration Panel was set up to adjudicate claims.[35] After "legal closure" was reached with the U.S. government in December 2005 (meaning Austrian companies could not be sued again by class action lawyers), the General Settlement Fund began disbursing "initial payments" of 10 percent and 15 percent of the allotted amount, depending on the legal process.[36] By 13 January 2009, 12,744 advance payments had been transferred.[37] Finally, the Washington Agreement of 2001 also included a set of social benefits for surviving victims of the Nazi persecution, including pension payments and money dedicated the nursing care of aging victims. Taken together, the Austrian government measures passed since the establishment of the *Nationalfonds* in 1995, the Republic of Austria and the Austrian business community allocated restitution and compensation payments amounting to a whopping 1 billion U.S. dollars.[38]

Cynics will argue that Schüssel's accomplishments in restitution policies are a case of "too little, too late." Yet the ever critical tribe of historians of Austrian World War II memory also ought to concede that Chancellor Schüssel played a crucial role in advancing long overdue restitution and compensation programs for Austrian victims of Nazism, especially Jews and Roma and Sinti. There may be personal reasons for his active role. Like hundreds of thousands of other Austrian families, Schüssel's personal family history also has to contend with "brown spots" (*braune Flecken*).[39] Schüssel is unique among Austria's postwar chancellors in inserting himself personally in these negotiations. Schüssel's very active restitution policies, his excellent knowledge of the issues, and his "sure instinct" have received high marks and been valued as one of the "plus factors" of his term in office.[40] No less than Stuart Eizenstat, Clinton's chief negotiating partner on the U.S. side, gave him generous credit for his "inspired leadership" in this delicate and complex issue.[41] Nevertheless, historians will also agree that Schüssel's inspired restitution policies were in response to the "class-action syndrome"[42]—part and parcel of the international Holocaust-era assets debates of the 1990s. Moreover, the circumstances of his accession to the federal chancellorship also did their part to motivate Schüssel to choose an aggressive forward defense. The storm of protests at home and abroad following the participation of the right-wing FPÖ in Schüssel's coalition government made these dramatic advances in restitution policies a matter of shrewd politics. Historians still have few insights into the intergovernmental negotiations between the ÖVP and its polarizing coalition partner, the FPÖ, and have, therefore, chalked up much of the progress in this area to Schüssel's personal leadership. Schüssel deserves credit for delving into the contested field of compensating long-neglected groups of Austrian Nazi victims with almost reckless abandon. By the time the Austrian memory year arrived in 2005, much of Schüssel's restitution agenda had been completed, and he could delve into shaping the meaning of the past with his hyperactive *Geschichtspolitik*.

The Year of Historical Memory 2005

It would be presumptuous to assume that in an essay one could cover the blizzard of memory events in 2005 comprehensively. In the following analysis, some trends and key discourses will be identified that might characterize the direction of Chancellor Schüssel's ambiguous politics of history intended to rewrite the master narrative to his liking and his efforts to shape Austria's cultural memory. An overall assessment would be ill-advised, but parameters for future debates and evaluations of this era may arise from a broad treatment of the memory events. Sufficient historical evidence is already available to embark on such an assessment. A good starting point is the useful preview of the entire program activities along with a glossy "reader" of texts and photos what the year 2005 might signify for prominent Austrians, produced by the Federal Chancellor's Office.[43]

Schüssel set up a special *Planungsbüro* under the leadership of State Secretary Franz Morak, a planning team organized by journalist Hans Haider, responsible for coordination of the blizzard of anniversary activities.[44] At the end of the memory year, the *Planungsbüro* published the comprehensive documentation *2005: Ein Gedenkjahr*—a three-volume set with a printed volume of speeches, 2 DVDs documenting the many memory events of 2005, and a DVD on the controversial memory events named *25 Peaces*.[45] This media-documentation set constitutes a *summa* of what Schüssel and his memory event managers tried to accomplish in 2005. In addition, historian and filmmaker Helene Maimann published a useful volume of key texts published in newspapers and media during the year as a running commentary on the memory activities and their meaning, tending to be critical of the *Gedankenjahr* presumptions of reinventing the past.[46] Even more dismissive of Schüssel's politics of history is the volume of essays by a younger generation of mainly cultural historians, many of them outright contrarians.[47] A special Forum in this journal also tried to summarize the commemorations of 2005 and the "exhibitionism" of Austrian memory culture in the numerous historical exhibits and their catalogues.[48] American historian Matthew Berg was the first scholar outside of Austria to take note of and analyze the intense 2005 memory discourses in Austria.[49]

To his credit, Wolfgang Schüssel takes Austrian history seriously, but also sports uncompromising views on it, steeped in his party's ideology. He involved himself personally in the management of a patriotic consensual narrative of the entire trajectory of post-World War I Austrian history and the staging of memory events—his ultimate objective being the strengthening of the Austrian nation as he sees it. In 2004, he had already gathered prominent historians and philosophers around him at the Federal Chancellery to act as his consultants in preparing for the memory year 2005. Even though there seems to be a debate over "copyright," the idea of making 2005 a year of reflection apparently originated with Helene Maimann in a conversation with her boss Wolfgang Lorenz at the Austrian National Broadcasting Corporation (ORF). Lorenz, one of Schüssel's consultants, mentioned the

Gedankenjahr idea to the Chancellor who apparently swallowed it hook, line, and sinker and claimed the copyright.[50]

The planning bureau was set up in the Federal Chancellery in 2004 to prepare the catalogue of the many 2005 memory events and their hierarchy. Federal ministries and institutions such as the National Library and the various state museums were asked to commemorate the anniversaries with special exhibits. The staging of the memory year was designed to be nationwide, so the *Bundesländer* also were called upon to contribute to the memory blitz with exhibits and memory events.[51] Presenting the program for 2005, State Secretary Morak gave the marching orders. The "*Jubiläumsjahr* 2005" would make a stand (*Standortbestimmung*) on "the positioning of Austria around the question where do we want to find ourselves in the future." Chancellor Schüssel raised the issue of Austrian identity formation from 1945 to 2005 as a basic inquiry for this year of reflection, essentially asking, "Who are we?" Rarely has a nation staged such an extended series of historical commemorations over the course of a whole year. Critics soon began to make fun of Schüssel's ulterior motives (*Hintergedanken*) and the bathos of the "year of historical reflection," the Austro-centric rituals of commemoration, and the presumptions behind the entire "patriotic '*Jubiläumsmaschine*'" of Morak's planning bureau.[52]

The unfolding of the 2005 memory year happened on many different levels, and a comprehensive overview is impossible. Even the *Planungsbüro*'s meticulous recording of every happening failed to track every memory-related occurrence, especially those staged abroad. On the one hand, there were the many *official* commemorations, historical exhibits with their grand openings, and the event series *25 Peaces*. On the other hand, semi-, non-, and anti-official symposia, exhibits, and happenings occurred all over Austria and around the world.[53]

On the official level, the commemorative anniversary celebrations of key historical events were given the highest priority: 27 April 1945 (Austrian Declaration of Independence and formation of the Provisional Renner Government), 15 May 1955 (signing ceremony of the Austrian State Treaty at Castle Belvedere), and 1 January 1995 (Austria joining the European Union). A festive assembly of the Austrian Parliament launched the official inauguration of the memory year 2005. This ceremony was overshadowed by a commemoration of the victims of the recent tsunami catastrophe in East Asia. Chancellor Schüssel seized the opportunity to remind the audience that the East Asian natural disaster reminded him of the "landscape of ruins" left by the war in Austria sixty years ago. Schüssel thus continued the traditional metaphorical diction in his party since Chancellor Julius Raab in the 1950s, seeing World War II as a "natural catastrophe" that had overwhelmed and victimized the passive Austrians.[54] Critics such as contrarian Robert Menasse quickly jumped on Schüssel for this comparison that sent the message that "fascism was a natural catastrophe," engulfing the population like an unstoppable flood.[55]

To be fair, Schüssel's speech in Parliament actually concentrated on both Austria's success story of economic and political reconstruction and bridge-building during the Cold War, and its procrastinations in facing the past. He did mention Austria's historical trail of tears (*historische Wundspuren*) since 1914, including the "expulsion, expropriation, and murder of Jewish citizens," as well as the handicapped, homosexuals, Roma and Sinti, and the persecution of all people of different political and religious persuasions—thus expanding the categories of Austrian victims of National Socialism beyond the traditional Austrian victims collective of civilians, soldiers, and resistance fighters. President Heinz Fischer (SPÖ) stressed that in the spring of 1945 Austrian democracy was restored after the horrors of National Socialist violence. Fischer noted that in 1945 "the red-white-red flag triumphed over the swastika, and democracy over dictatorship."[56]

In February, the ten-year membership of Austria in the European Union was celebrated in a "European Congress" in the Vienna Hofburg—with the stress on both Austria and the European Union profiting from this membership.[57]

The anniversary activities culminated in April and May 2005 around the key historical events of 27 April 1945 and 15 May 1955 as the anchors of postwar memory culture. Within the timeframe of three weeks, the sixtieth anniversary of the Declaration of Austrian Independence was celebrated in the Hofburg, while the fiftieth anniversary of the signing of the Austrian State Treaty was celebrated in the Belvedere Palace. Austria's liberation from the Nazis was at the center of the first anniversary and the country regaining its full sovereignty at the center of the second. Critics note that an undertone of liberation from the four Allies marked the State Treaty celebration, especially among the conservative forces of the country, who had already felt that way in 1955 ("liberation from the liberators").

Fischer's 27 April keynote address concentrated on both the end of Hitlerite Germany and the foundations of postwar democracy and freedom. He reminded his audience of the victims of World War II, including civilians, soldiers, resistance fighters, and Jews (a somewhat hidebound listing of victims). He admonished Austrians not to play off 27 April against 15 May, for both days were crucial foundations in building the postwar "Austrian house." Schüssel also dwelt on the many Austrian victims of the war: civilians, those murdered in concentration camps, victims of religious and political persecution, Jews, Roma and

Sinti, the handicapped, and killed and maimed soldiers and prisoners of war. In his accounting, Austria "strangely" had almost as many victims (400,000) as Nazis (500,000)—thus *low-balling the number of Nazis*—a tactic the ÖVP had consistently employed since the first round of state treaty negotiations in London in 1947 (the *Ostmark* prided itself on some 700,000 registered Nazi party members). Then Schüssel backtracked into the traditional ÖVP narrative when he noted that Austria "had fought longer than any other country against Hitler and National Socialism," without explicitly referencing Dollfuss' "resistance" against the Nazis. Both speakers took a deep bow before founding fathers such as Leopold Figl. Both saw European integration and the European Union's peace project as an antithesis to the nationalisms that fueled World War II.[58]

On 15 May, the old *Proporz*-coalition historical narrative triumphed again (Vice-Chancellor Hubert Gorbach from the coalition partner BZÖ was curiously absent as a speaker). Fischer again stressed that the liberation of Austria and the defeat of Hitlerite Germany in April 1945 was the starting point of Austrian independence and democracy after the war; then 1955 brought "full freedom and independence." He thanked the representatives of the four Allies who were represented at the State Treaty ceremony for the sacrifices of their soldiers in liberating Austria and for their economic support to make Austria viable after the war. He noted the difficult path of negotiating the Austrian State Treaty and the "heavy burden" the Austrian people felt from the ongoing four-power occupation after the war. As is customary in the SPÖ, Fischer praised Austria's peace-oriented neutrality policy after 1955. Schüssel addressed the changing geopolitical context in 1955 and the "great luck" Austria had in seizing the moment to complete the State Treaty. Austria received back "the precious gift of her freedom," which it used to join the United Nations and the European Council. He recounted the success story of Austria's economic miracle after the war—thanking Americans for the Marshall Plan—and its importance as a bridge between East and West in the Cold War. He obliquely paid lip service to the fact that Austria paid restitution and damages, albeit too late, without mentioning the specific victim groups benefiting from these restitutions. He concluded that Austria was a latecomer to nation building, yet recorded with pride that Austrians' enthusiasm for their nation was great.[59] There was a lot of trite commentary in the traditional consensual rhetoric of these speeches, and critics made fun of the "teflon memory" in these empty rhetorical formulas.[60]

At the same time, there was a lot of speechmaking during the opening of the historical exhibits at the Schallaburg in Lower Austria and at the Castle Belvedere in Vienna in mid-April and mid-May. Both these exhibits also displayed the original copy of the Austrian State Treaty on loan from Moscow for a few weeks, a piece of material history that was a great hit with hundreds of thousands of visitors. The Schallaburg show *Österreich ist frei* concentrated on the occupation period and the Austrian success narrative culminating in the signing of the State Treaty in 1955. The Belvedere exhibit *Das Neue Österreich*, which came together very late due to political controversy surrounding it about finances and conceptualization, gave the entire narrative of the two Austrian Republics, starting in 1919 and including the World War II era.[61] These two exhibits tended to support the master narrative of the success story of postwar Austria. This was obviously the principal narrative the Schüssel government was promoting throughout the memory year 2005 with some minor dissonances, complimenting the story of Austrian hardship after the war and triumph after the end of the four-power occupation. Clearly, as one critic noted acerbically, the war years were not counted in the celebration of the postwar success story and "Austria celebrated its non-existence" in those difficult years when it was a victim of the Nazis.[62]

In the contested narratives of Austrian history, the representations in these exhibits staged and reproduced the postwar myths designed to silence the conflicted past (which included Austrofascism, Austrian war criminals, postwar procrastinations in restitution policies, and the like). These exhibits thus were constructed to intensify the uncontroversial master narrative of Austrian history. These exhibits therefore acted as "privileged spaces for the will to dramatize very specific conceptions of identity," averred Heidrun Zettelbauer.[63]

What Schüssel called the "playful" *25 Peaces* was the most curious and controversial production of the Federal Chancellery's *Planungsbüro*. Twenty-five events (as many as there were EU states at the time) were staged as reminders of the hard times during and after the war. The equestrian statues on Vienna's *Heldenplatz* were camouflaged as they had been during the war, when they were protected from Allied bombs; next to them a vegetable garden was planted as had been done in 1945 when the Viennese were starving. The night of 12 March 1945, when the inner city of Vienna was subjected to its most severe Allied air attack, was restaged on 12 March 2005, by way of fearful light and sound installations. In the days prior to the key State Treaty anniversary on 15 May, a herd of cows grazed in the Belvedere gardens, as bovines had done during the occupation period. A copy of the Belvedere balcony was sent with a crane around the country for Austrians to reenact Figl's famous yet spurious "*Österreich ist frei*" balcony scene on 15 May (this was termed "do-it-yourself Figl"). The famous "four in the Jeep" patrolled Vienna again, and the zonal borders were painted on the streets of the capital to remind the Viennese of the four-power partition of their city during the occupation decade. The planners of the *25 Peaces* wanted to encourage Austrians to think creatively about their nation's past through these staged representations in the public space. "History as happening" was designed to appeal to the younger generations of Austrians who usually do not visit museums and exhibits.[64]

Critics savaged the *25 Peaces* and the combative mastermind behind such historical "event culture," Wolfgang Lorenz. The "son-et-lumière spectacle" (Robert Menasse)—the recreation of the "*Bombenstimmung*" after an Allied air-attack—was especially seen as "event history" and a trivialization of the past (Lisa Mayr). Writer Marlene Streeruwitz told Lorenz that to make a complex history appealing to a younger crowd was condescending and mendacious ("*Schwieriges zu entschwierigen ist Lüge*"). In an interview with the Viennese weekly *Der Falter*, the combative Lorenz rejected the notion that his *25 Peaces* were cheap "infotainment" and attacked all consumers of high-brow culture as bores (*fad*), implying that his low-brow historical entertaining reenactments at least sported considerable excitement among participants.[65] The funniest attack on the *25 Peaces* was an alleged "cow-napping" by a group of Internet activists. Newspapers reported an Internet story of the kidnapping of one of the cows, peacefully grazing in the Belvedere gardens, by unknown terrorists who also demanded that Chancellor Schüssel and the CEO of Austrian Television publicly admit that "they had been misleading the Austrian population in 2005 with lies about history and inciting them towards nationalism."[66] There is no question that tens of thousands of people were attracted to the "hands-on" form of "everyday history" (*Alltagsgeschichte*) by participating in the discourses sparked by the *25 Peaces*. Whether it produced the thoughtfulness (*nachdenken*) intended by the event producers and thereby allowed Austrians a more profound understanding of the past by way of immersion in their history is impossible to assess empirically.

Next to this official master narrative celebrated in anniversary speechmaking and the exhibitionism of luscious and uncontroversial historical shows, there was a counter narrative issued at every turn of the anniversary celebrations by critics and intellectuals, some of it shrill and much of it unforgiving, attacking and demeaning the official mindset, often in the best tradition of Karl Kraus.[67] The main points of contention were the "stubborn revival of the victim's myth" and the "celebration of the Austrian perpetrators collective as the Austrian victims collective."[68] The real victims of World War II such as the Jews and the Holocaust were largely marginalized during the memory year. The State Treaty anniversary of 1955 was privileged over the liberation of Austria in 1945 in the Schüssel government's "hegemonic" historic discourses. April

1945 was interpreted as the end of the war rather than the liberation from the Nazis. Some Austrian elites apparently were still having a hard time determining whether the end of the war spelled defeat or liberation.[69] Dwelling on Figl's famous 1955 dictum "Austria is free" as the beginning of Austria's newborn postwar freedom rather than the election of 1945 was appalling. The fact that a majority of Austrians perceived the fall of the Hitler regime as defeat and did not welcome the Allied liberators was strictly ignored.[70] In the age-old Josephinian tradition, the historical master narrative of Austria's postwar "success story" of liberation both from the Nazis and then the Allies and integration into the European Union was ordered from the top down by the "chief administrator" of the state and his comrades "responsible for ideology."[71]

Conclusion: Legacies—*Was bleibt?*

The legacy of Schüssel's *Vergangenheitspolitik* is ambiguous. On the one hand, no postwar Austrian chancellor embarked on more ambitious restitution policies. His prominent ÖVP predecessors on Vienna's Ballhausplatz, Leopold Figl and Julius Raab, had hemmed and hawed and procrastinated, and so did long-serving SPÖ Chancellors Bruno Kreisky and Franz Vranitzky. Kreisky's active role in *Vergangenheitspolitik*, by the way, ever since he served in high office was as determined as Schüssel's in reinforcing Austria's victim's status and celebrating Austrian resistance during the war.[72] Schüssel, determined to impose *his* master narrative on an unsuspecting public, did backtrack on the 1990s paradigm shift in Austrian World War II memory. Next to the restitution payments to slave laborers and Jews, the Schüssel government quietly passed legislation to pay restitution indiscriminately also to Austrian prisoners of war, who had fought on all fronts during the war. To demonstrate politically correct gender consciousness for good measure, the postwar "*Trümmerfrauen*," namely those women who cleaned up the rubble in Austria's cities after the war, received symbolic token restitution payments, too.[73] It did not matter whether the Austrian POWs had been fervid *Wehrmacht* fighters or the *Trümmerfrauen* had been members of the Nazi Party; their suffering needed to be acknowledged sixty years after the war. This tended to reinforce the myth of Austrians (both on the frontlines and the home front) as victims rather than as perpetrators. Even though Schüssel expanded the traditional Austrian World War II collective of victims in his commemorative speechmaking, he stubbornly insisted in early February in a much-quoted interview with the *Neue Zürcher Zeitung* that "Austria was a victim," namely the "first military victim of the Nazis." As early as

July 2000, he had stressed in a parliamentary debate: "Austria was a victim of National Socialism; Austria was wiped off the map, disappeared, was a victim." In November 2004, he reiterated the same notion an interview with the *Jerusalem Post*: "The Nazis took Austria with force. The Austrians were the first victims."[74] He made no mention of his own party's Christian Social predecessors and their pre-Anschluss authoritarian regime that cast a willful death sentence over democratic governance.

Coupled with outrageous statements from the camp of his coalition partner that the Auschwitz gas chambers did not exist and that *Wehrmacht* deserters were "murderers of their comrades" (*Kameradenmörder*)[75]—statements that Schüssel to his credit did publicly disavow[76]—it appeared to many critical observers that the opportunity for a real breakthrough in Austria confronting the crimes of National Socialism and mastering its World War II past was missed once again. Schüssel and his party's *Schlussstrich* mentality lacked contrition for Austrians' complicity in World War II war crimes. They went a step forward on restitutions, but two steps backward on a critical reflection and confrontation of Austria's ambiguous recent past.[77]

Heidemarie Uhl, the most distinguished historian of Austrian World War II memory discourses, concluded with resignation that the State Treaty and the consensual year 1955 replaced the controversial year 1945 as the crucial founding myth. In public opinion polls, 20 percent of Austrians have a fond image of the State Treaty, but only 1 percent hold positive associations with 27 April 1945. She adds that the Schüssel government reactivated the narrative of the Austrian "success story" in the 2005 anniversary year and superimposed it over the post-1986 critical narrative of Austrian responsibility for the crimes of National Socialism. In 2005, Austria missed the opportunity to embrace the European trend of finally abandoning exculpatory postwar mythology and placing the memory of the Holocaust as the principal European site of memory into the center of its cultural memory.[78] In his brazen effort to encourage Austrians to reflect critically about their troubled past during the war and reinforce the positive national identity of the country's success story after the war, Schüssel reinvented the hidebound Austrian tradition of the contested *Opferdoktrin*, which had been eroding since the mid-1980s and was increasingly abandoned. While most Germans have engaged in a culture of contrition, many Austrians seem to wallow still in their "victim culture."[79]

In 2005, Schüssel's ÖVP indulged in a commemorative carnival while the opposition SPÖ seriously engaged in mastering the embarrassing Nazi detritus (*braune Flecken*) in its own past. While the Socialist Party in 2002 began a serious scholarly investigation into former Nazis that served in various postwar party organizations and posts and published the report in 2005, Schüssel's ÖVP refused to launch such a critical self-study. In the national elections of 1945, both parties vied for the votes of former Nazis. Moreover, 10.7 percent of SPÖ and 12.8 percent of ÖVP deputies in Parliament and higher legislative bodies were former Nazis. Both parties failed to thoroughly de-Nazify their membership after the war and maintained these "brown spots" in leadership positions. But unlike the Socialists, Schüssel's People's Party refused to confront this seedy past in its history. American historian Matthew P. Berg, who participated in one of the SPÖ's self-studies, is on the mark in concluding that the SPÖ belatedly held a "genuine claim to moral high ground" by demonstrating "its willingness to acknowledge the active complicity of many of its members in the Third Reich." Moreover, unlike the Christian Socials, the prewar predecessor party of the ÖVP, the SPÖ "never supported any form of dictatorship," a fact that the ÖVP was even less willing to concede.[80] As ÖVP leader, Schüssel failed to press his party to confront *both* dictatorships, the first one many of its members had supported and are still trying to exculpate.

Schüssel's *Geschichtspolitik* in the memory year 2005 made clear that *popular* and *scholarly discourses* probably will always coexist next to each other. Apart from the chattering classes of high-brow print media commentaries and superficial discussions on television, these two communities are separated by deep chasms of professional boundaries and do not communicate with each other much (other than the few scholars privileged to have been invited to the Chancellor's roundtable as consultants). The vast array of historical exhibits staged during the memory year 2005 all over Vienna and across the country and attracting more than a million visitors (310,000 alone in the Belvedere exhibit *Das Neue Österreich*[81]), may be the only medium where more complex scholarly perspectives were presented to a larger public.[82] Yet, as noted, some of these extravaganzas presented uncritical trajectories of consensual success history. It should be added that the scholarly community gathered in numerous symposia and conferences to reflect on the state of postwar history and historiography.[83]

Apart from a few high profile keynote lectures and opening speeches, the historians communicated among themselves and did not interact much with the political leadership. Nor were Schüssel's chief antagonists Menasse, Streeruwitz, and Maimann present at such high-brow scholarly gatherings—acting the part of classical Austrian contrarians and *Raunzer*, writing from the margins, and pursuing their own partisan political agendas. Alexander Pollak is right in observing that "the state of knowledge (*Wissensstand*) of a society rarely corresponds with the insights of its scientific community."[84] While the intellectual perspectives on the memory year were critical and deeply reflective, the public at large seems to have followed the official management of history and welcomed and embraced the events of the 2005 memory year and, thus, Schüssel's consensual *Geschichtspolitik*.

Notes

1. The authors would like to thank Heidemarie Uhl, Matthew Berg, Hans Haider, Nicole L. Immler, and Renate S. Meissner for providing valuable materials for this essay. Matthew Berg was kind enough to comment on an earlier draft of the essay.

2. Tina Rosenberg, *The Haunted Land: Facing Europe's Ghosts after Communism* (New York: Vintage Books, 1995), xiii.

3. Stuart E. Eizenstat, an Undersecretary of the Treasury and President Bill Clinton's, special mediator in negotiations about Holocaust-era assets, attest Schüssel had a deep knowledge of the restitution agenda and an unusual willingness for a government leader to enter substantive negotiations on the matter; see Stuart E. Eizenstat, *Imperfect Justice: Looted Assets, Slave Labor, and the Unfinished Business of World War II* (New York: Public Affairs, 2003), 298. Schüssel gathered historians and philosophers to consult about ideas for the agenda of the memory year 2005; see Stefan Karner, "Replik: Österreich verloren," in *Was bleibt: Schreiben im Gedenkjahr*, ed. Helene Maimann (Vienna: Czernin Verlag, 2005), 47. Graz historian Karner's personal friendship with Schüssel involved him deeply in the Chancellor's politics of history; after being on the team of historians that was supposed to design the main anniversary exhibit in the Belevedere Palace—a team effort that failed but was resurrected by another group of prominent Austrians—Karner received the commission to conceptualize the exhibit *Österreich ist frei* in the Schallaburg and thus contributed to the writing of the master narrative of the memory year 2005. See Ljubomir Bratic, "Die Ausstellung als Ort der Macht," in *Rebranding Images: Ein streitbares Lesebuch zur Geschichtspolitik und Erinnerungskultur in Österreich*, ed. Martin Wassermair and Katharina Wegan (Innsbruck: StudienVerlag, 2006), 31. For another critical view of the discursive construction of Austrian identities in the memory year 2005, see Rudolf de Cillia and Ruth Wodak, eds., *Gedenken im "Gedankenjahr": Zur diskursiven Konstruktion österreichischer Identitäten im Jubiläumsjahr 2005* (Innsbruck: StudienVerlag, 2009).

4. For a first effort to summarize and analyze Schüssel's restitution policies, see Günter Bischof, "'Watschenmann der europäischen Erinnerung?' Internationales Image und Vergangenheitspolitik der Schüssel/Riess-Passer-ÖVP/FPÖ-Koalitionsregierung," in *Austria in the European Union: Assessment of her Membership*, ed. Michael Gehler et al., vol. 7, Schriftenreihe des Herbert-Batliner-Europainstitutes (Vienna: Böhlau, 2003), 445-78.

5. Elazar Barkan, *The Guilt of Nations: Restitution and Negotiating Historical Injustices* (Baltimore: Johns Hopkins UP, 2000).

6. Ibid.

7. Andreas Khol et al., eds., *zukunft denken: Festschrift für Wolfgang Schüssel* (Vienna: Verlag für Geschichte und Politik, 2005).

8. Matthew P. Berg calls it a "paradigm shift" of Austrian cultural memory; see his "Commemoration versus *Vergangenheitsbewältigung*: Contextualizing Austria's *Gedenkjahr* 2005," *German History* 26.1 (2008): 53-55.

9. The literature on Austria's postwar historical memory production is huge. The best guide to the complex trajectory of postwar memory is Heidemarie Uhl; see "The Politics of Memory: Austria's Perception of the Second World War and the National Socialist Period," in *Austrian Historical Memory & National Identity*, ed. Günter Bischof and Anton Pelinka, vol. 5, Contemporary Austrian Studies (New Brunswick, NJ: Transaction, 1997), 64-94. Uhl's documentation and analysis of the 1988 "memory year" discourses is a good starting point; see *Zwischen Versöhnung und Verstörung: Eine Kontroverse um Österreichs historische Identität 50 Jahre nach dem "Anschluß"* (Vienna: Böhlau, 1992). The clarion call for the scholarly paradigm shift of Austrian postwar memory in the 1980s may well have been the essays in Anton Pelinka and Erika Weinzierl, eds., *Das grosse Tabu: Österreichs Umgang mit seiner Vergangenheit* (Vienna: Edition S, 1987); Uhl has penned many essays on postwar memory. For the 2005 discourses in the context of the changes since the mid-1980s, see her "Europäische Tendenzen, regionale Verwerfungen: Österreichs Gedächtnis und das Jubiläumsjahr 2005," in *"Heiss Umfehdet, Wild Umstritten ...": Geschichtsmythen in Rot-Weiss-Rot*, ed. Werner Koroschitz and Lisa Rettl (Klagenfurt: Drava, 2005), 21-26; on the postwar "*Opferdoktrin*" and its erosion, see Thomas Albrich, "'Es gibt keine jüdische Frage': Zur Aufrechterhaltung des österreichischen Opfermythos," in ibid., 51-73; see also Günter Bischof, "Founding Myths and Compartmentalized Past: New Literature on the Construction, Hibernation, and Deconstruction of World War II Memory in Postwar Austria," in *Austrian Historical Memory and National Identity*, ed. Günter Bischof and Anton Pelinka, vol. 5, Contemporary Austrian Studies (New Brunswick, NJ: Transaction, 1997), 302-41; idem, "Victims? Perpetrators? 'Punching Bags' of European Historical Memory? The Austrians and Their World War II Legacies," in *German Studies Review* 27 (February 2004): 17-32; for recent analyses, see David Art's chapter on "victim culture" in *The Politics of the Nazi Past in Germany and Austria* (Cambridge: Cambridge UP, 2006), 101-44; and Alexander Pollak, "Vergangenheit und Reflexion: Konsens- und Streitlinien im Umgang mit der NS-Vergangenheit in Österreich," in *Zeitgeschichte als Streitgeschichte: Grosse Kontroversen seit 1945* (Munich: Verlag C.H. Beck, 2003), 326-46.

10. The fact that Clinton appointed Stuart Eizenstat as a high level Deputy Secretary of the Treasury and Special Representative of the president and Secretary for Holocaust Issues indicated how seriously he took this agenda. See Jan Surman, "'Unfinished Business' und Holocaust-Erinnerung: Die US- Geschichtspolitik der 90er-Jahre zwischen 'Holocaust-era assets' und Menschenrechtsdiskurs," in *Zeitschrift für Geschichtswissenschaft* 53.4 (2005): 345-55; see also Eizenstat, *Imperfect Justice*.

11. Benno Nietzel, "'Business Finished': Transnationale Wiedergutmachung historischen Unrechts in Europa seit 1989," *Zeitschrift für Geschichtswissenschaft* 57.1 (2009): 26-50; Oliver Rathkolb, ed., *Revisiting the National Socialist Legacy: Coming to Terms with Forced Labor, Expropriation, Compensation, and Restitution* (Innsbruck: StudienVerlag, 2002).

12. Barkan, *Guilt of Nations*, xv-xli. For the Austrian context of commissioned history as the basis for restitution, see the essays by Günter Bischof, Brigitte Bailer-Galanda/Eva Blimlinger, Martin Eichtinger, Dieter Stiefel, Oliver Rathkolb, and Margit Reiter in the Forum, "Commissioning History: Austria and World War II Restitution and Reconciliation," in *The Dollfuss/Schuschnigg Era in Austria: A Reassessment*, ed. Günter Bischof et al., vol. 11, Contemporary Austrian Studies (New Brunswick, NJ: Transaction, 2003), 212-66.

13. For the summary report, see Clemens Jabloner et al., *Schlussbericht der Historikerkommission der Republik Österreich: Vermögensentzug während der NS-Zeit sowie Rückstellungen und Entschädigungen seit 1945 in Österreich. Zusammenfassung und Einschätzungen* (Vienna: Oldenbourg, 2003), and the thirty-two volumes of special

reports on specific issues. For a first review summarizing this vast and complex material in English, see Timothy Kirk, *Austrian History Yearbook* [forthcoming 2009]. Kirk concludes that the Austrian Jews were "subjected to one of the most vicious pogroms in modern European history."

14. A balance sheet about Austrians' roles in World War II is attempted in Günter Bischof et al., eds., *New Perspectives on Austrians and World War II*, vol. 17, Contemporary Austrian Studies (New Brunswick, NJ: Transaction, 2009). David Art has shaped a "contrition index," showing that Austrian parties show considerably less contrition about Nazi war crimes than German parties, the ÖVP and FPÖ being the least contrite; see Art, *Politics of the Nazi Past*, 135-39.

15. Make no mistake about it, scholars of comparative European authoritarianism/fascism in the interwar period clearly place the Dollfuss/Schuschnigg dictatorships in the fascist continuum; see Tim Kirk, "Fascism and Austrofascism,' in *The Dollfuss/ Schuschnigg Era in Austria*, 10-31; Robert O. Paxton, *The Anatomy of Fascism* (New York: Knopf, 2004), 97f; see also Mark Mazower, *Dark Continent: Europe's Twentieth Century* (New York: Knopf, 1999)

16. The published critical self-studies are Wolfgang Neugebauer and Peter Schwarz, *Der Wille zum aufrechten Gang: Offenlegung der Rolle des BSA bei der gesellschaftlichen Reintegration ehemaliger Nationalsozialisten* (Vienna: Czernin, 2005); and Maria Mesner et al., eds., *Enteignung und Rückgabe: Das sozialdemokratische Parteivermögen in Österreich 1934 und nach 1945* (Innsbruck: StudienVerlag, 2007); Maria Mesner, ed., *Entnazifizierung zwischen politischem Anspruch, Parteienkonkurrenz und Kaltem Krieg* (Vienna: Oldenbourg, 2005). For Berg's shrewd analysis, see "Commemoration versus *Vergangenheitsbewältigung*," 58-65, especially 64f.

17. Jabloner et. al., *Schlussbericht der Historikerkommission der Republik Österreich*, 451-57. For an overview of the Austrian restitution and compensation programs in the first postwar decades, see Brigitte Bailer-Galanda and Eva Blimlinger, *Vermögensentzug—Rückstellung—Entschädigung: Österreich 1938/1945*-2005 (Innsbruck: Studien Verlag, 2005), 40-69; *idem*, „Restitution and Compensation of Property in Austria, 1945-2007," in *New Perspectives on Austrians and World War II*, ed. Günter Bischof, Fritz Plasser, and Barbara Stelzl-Marx (*CAS* XVII) (New Brunswick, NJ: Transaction, 2009), pp. 306-24; Helmut Wohnout, "Eine 'Geste' gegenüber den Opfern? Der Nationalfonds für Opfer des Nationalsozialismus und der schwierige Umgang Österreichs mit den Überlebenden nationalsozialistischer Verfolgung," in *Geschichte und Recht: Festschrift für Gerald Stourzh zum 70. Geburtstag*, ed. Thomas Angerer et al. (Vienna: Böhlau, 1999), 250-58; Christian Thonke, *Hitlers langer Schatten: Der mühevolle Weg zur Entschädigung der NS-Opfer* (Vienna: Böhlau, 2004), 50-82. For a comparison between Austria and the Federal Republic of Germany on the restitution agenda, see David Forster, *"Wiedergutmachung" in Österreich und der BRD im Vergleich* (Innsbruck: StudienVerlag, 2001).

18. Bundesgesetz über den Nationalfonds der Republik Österreich für Opfer des Nationalsozialismus, BGBl. 432/1995. For the genesis of the National Fund and more information, see Wohnout, "Eine 'Geste' gegenüber den Opfern?", 259-68, or the official homepage, *National Fund of the Republic of Austria for Victims of National Socialism*, http://www.en.nationalfonds.org/, accessed 7 January 2009.

19. Wohnout, "Eine 'Geste' gegenüber den Opfern?", 262.

20. Hannah M. Lessing et al., "'Wir können nur anklopfen, wo die Tür offen ist'—Der lange Weg zu Anerkennung und Entschädigung," in *Ausgeschlossen und entrechtet: Raub und Rückgabe—Österreich von 1938 bis heute*, ed. Verena Pawlowsky and Harald Wendelin (Vienna: Mandelbaum, 2006), 241.

21. The restitution discourses also gave individual victims the opportunity for psychological release by voicing their experiences of suffering under National Socialism, thereby making it part of the collective memory. Restitution thus played an important role as "mediator" between family memory and collective memory, argues Nicole L. Immler; see her "Restitution and the Dynamics of Memory: A Neglected Trans-Generational Perspective," in *Mediation, Remediation and the Dynamics of Cultural Memory*, ed. Astrid Erll and Ann Rigney (Berlin: D Gruyter, 2009).

22. According to the National Fund law, the following persons are eligible to receive symbolic payments: "those who were persecuted by the National Socialist regime on political grounds, grounds of origin, religion, nationality, sexual orientation, on grounds of a physical disability or mental handicap or on the basis of accusations of so-called asociality, or who in other ways fell victim to typically National Socialist injustice or left the country to escape such persecution," found at "Eligibility for Payments and Filing Applications," *National Fund of the Republic of Austria for Victims of National Socialism*, http://www.en.nationalfonds.org/cgi-bin/dynamic?id=200604121510160058&temp=, accessed 7 January 2009; see also "Nationalfonds der Republik Österreich für Opfer des Nationalsozialismus" and "Allgemeiner Entschädigungsfonds für Opfer des Nationalsozialismus," *10 Jahre Nationalfonds: Zahlen. Daten. Fakten*, ed. Renate S. Meissner im Auftrag des Nationalfonds (Vienna: Nationalfonds der Republik Österreich für Opfer des Nationalsozialismus, 2005), 10-16.

23. "Medieninformationen des Nationalfonds der Republik Österreich und des Allgemeinen Entschädigungsfonds für Opfer des Nationalsozialismus (Stand: November 2008)," *National Fund of the Republic of Austria for Victims of National Socialism*, http://www.de.nationalfonds.org/docs/medieninformation_11_2008.pdf, accessed 7 January 2009), 5.

24. For the project database of the National Fund, see "Notes on Projects and Grants," *National Fund of the Republic of Austria for Victims of National Socialism*, http://de.nationalfonds.org/sites/dynamic.pl?action=db3, accessed 7 January 2009.

25. See the summary of the international "Holocaust era assets" debate in Thonke, *Hitlers langer Schatten*, 83-145; the Swiss Nazi gold lawsuit is a main chapter in Barkan, *Guilt of Nations*, 88-111; see also Independent Commission of Experts Switzerland—Second World War, *Switzerland, National Socialism and the Second World War: Final Report* (Zurich: Pendo, 2002).

26. *Der Standard*, 22 September 2006.

27. This can be loosely translated as "I am in favor of prolonging this thing." See the classic documentation by Robert Knight, ed., *"Ich bin dafür, die Sache in die Länge zu ziehen": Die Wortprotokolle der österreichischen Bundesregierung von 1945 bis 1952 über die Entschädigung der Juden* (Frankfurt am Main: Athenäum, 1988).

28. Eizenstat, *Imperfect Justice*, 284f.

29. Bundesgesetz über den Fonds für freiwillige Leistungen der Republik Österreich an ehemalige Sklaven- und Zwangsarbeiter des nationalsozialistischen Regimes (Versöhnungsfonds-Gesetz), BGBl. I 74/2000. The most detailed summary of the negotiations on the forced laborers issue can be found in Hubert Feichtlbauer, *Forced Labor in Austria, 1938-1945: Late Recognition, History, Tragic Fates* (Vienna: Austrian Reconciliation Fund, 2005), 165-94; see also *Fund for Reconciliation, Peace, and Cooperation*, http://www.versoehnungsfonds.at/, accessed 15 January 2009; Maria Schaumayer, "Austria's Contribution to Reconciliation," in *Revisiting the National Socialist Legacy: Coming to Terms with Forced Labor, Expropriation, Compensation, and Restitution*, ed. Oliver Rathkolb, vol. 3., Bruno Kreisky International Studies (Inns-

bruck: StudienVerlag, 2002), 24-29; for the U.S. perspective on the negotiations, see Eizenstat, *Imperfect Justice*, 279-314.

30. Feichtlbauer, *Forced Labor in Austria*, 183, 198ff, 215, 287f, 296f, 310f; see also the *Future Fund of the Republic of Austria*, http://www.zukunftsfonds-austria.at/, accessed 15 January 2009.

31. Ursula Kriebaum and Ernst Sucharipa, "Das Washingtoner Abkommen. Die österreichische Restitutionsvereinbarung vom 17. Jänner 2001," in *Die Republik und das NS-Erbe: Raub und Rückgabe—Österreich von 1938 bis heute*, ed. Verena Pawlowsky and Harald Wendelin (Vienna: Mandelbaum, 2005), 164-69; Ernst Sucharipa, "Revisiting the National Socialist Legacy, Restitution: Why Now? The Austrian Experience," in *Revisiting the National Socialist Legacy*, 30-40; Thonke, *Hitlers langer Schatten*, 147-51; Eizenstat, *Imperfect Justice*, 293-314.

32. Änderung des Bundesgesetzes über den Nationalfonds der Republik Österreich für Opfer des Nationalsozialismus, BGBl. I 11/2001.

33. "Medieninformationen des Nationalfonds und des Entschädigungsfonds," 6.

34. Bundesgesetz über die Einrichtung eines Allgemeinen Entschädigungsfonds für Opfer des Nationalsozialismus und über Restitutionsmaßnahmen (Entschädigungsfondsgesetz) sowie zur Änderung des Allgemeinen Sozialversicherungsgesetzes und des Opferfürsorgegesetzes, BGBl. I 12/2001.

35. Hannah Lessing and Fiorentina Azizi, "Austria Confronts Her Past," in *Holocaust Restitution: Perspectives on the Litigation and Its Legacy*, ed. Michael J. Bazyler and Roger P. Alford (New York: New York UP, 2006), 231-34; Kriebaum and Sucharipa, "Das Washingtoner Abkommen," 169-85; *National Fund of the Republic of Austria for Victims of National Socialism*, http://www.en.nationalfonds.org/, accessed 17 January 2009.

36. Bundesgesetz, mit dem das Entschädigungsfondsgesetz geändert wird, BGBl. I 142/2005.

37. "Statistics on Application Processing," *National Fund of the Republic of Austria for Victims of National Socialism*, http://www.en.nationalfonds.org/cgi-bin/dynamic?id=20061215235128007&temp=, accessed 17 January 2009).

38. Sucharipa, "Revisiting the National Socialist Legacy," 31f.

39. Schüssel told Eizenstat during a private meeting that he did not learn until he was sixteen that his father was a member of the National Socialist German Workers' Party, "a revelation that led to a lifelong estrangement"; see Eizenstat, *Imperfect Justice*, 305.

40. See, for instance, *Der Standard*, 1 February 2002; *Die Presse Online*, 13 November 2002, http://diepresse.com, accessed 29 March 2009.

41. Feichtlbauer, *Forced Labor in Austria*, 193.

42. Sucharipa, "Revisiting the National Socialist Legacy," 37.

43. Bundeskanzleramt Östereich and Teresa Indjein, eds., *Österreich 2005: Das Lesebuch zum Jubiläumsjahr mit Programmübersicht* (Salzburg: Residenz Verlag, 2004).

44. The elaborate homepage documenting all the activities and events is still up; see *Jubilee Year 2005*, http://www.oesterreich2005.at/, accessed 26 December 2008.

45. Bundeskanzleramt and Hans Haider, eds., *2005: Gedanken – Termine – Bücher: 1945 – 1955 – 1995 – 2005* [hereinafter cited as *Gedanken*]; *2005. Ein Gedankenjahr*; DVD I: *Die grossen Jubiläen*; DVD II: *Quer durch Österreich*; DVD *2005: 25 Peaces; Die Zukunft der Vergangenheit* (Vienna, 2006).

46. Maimann, ed., *Was bleibt.*

47. Wassermair and Wegan, *Rebranding Images.*

48. See Katharina Wegan, "Memory Boom: The 'Year of Reflection' 2005," and Günter Bischof, "Austrian Exhibition-ism: The Year 2005 and its Commemorations of the Recent Past in Exhibition Catalogues," in *Sexuality in Austria*, ed. Günter Bischof, Fritz Plasser and Dagmar Herzog (*CAS* XV) (New Brunswick, NJ: Transaction, 2007), 172-224.

49. Berg, "Commemoration versus *Vergangenheitsbewältigung*," 47-71; Art mentions Chancellor Schüssel's early defiant statements about "Austria as victim" in 1938, but does not analyze 2005 as a memory year; see Art, *Politics of the Nazi Past*, 135f.

50. Maimann, ed., *Was bleibt*, 11, 21.

51. The smallest Austrian state, the *Land* Vorarlberg, issued a comprehensive documentation of its commemorative activities; see Ulrich Nachbauer and Christian Niederstätter, eds., *Aufbruch in eine neue Zeit: Vorarlberger Almanach zum Jubiläumsjahr 2005* (Bregenz: Vorarlberger Landesarchiv, 2006).

52. The official website can be accessed at *Jubilee Year 2005*, http://oestereich2005.at. Morak's and Schüssel's speeches are reprinted in *Gedanken*, 9-82; for critical perspectives, see the essays by Anton Pelinka, "Die Gedanken sind frei: Na und?", and Armin Thurnher "Ein Hintergedankenjahr," in *Was bleibt*, 22-38; the "patriotic 'jubilee machine'" is mentioned in Uhl, "Europäische Tendenzen, regionale Verwerfungen," 23.

53. One of the co-authors of this essay, for example, participated in symposia in Minneapolis, New Orleans, and Ottawa, none of them recorded in the extensive, supposedly final list of "*Termine*" in *Gedanken*, 83-115.

54. Schüssel zum Auftakt des Gedenkjahres im Parlament, 14 January 2005, in *Gedanken*, 17; Raab's letter to Nahum Goldman, 12 November 1953, cited in Albrich, "Es gibt keine Jüdische Frage," in *"Heiss Umfehdet, Wild Umstritten . . ., "* 69.

55. Robert Menasse, "Österreich: Wende und Ende," in *Was bleibt*, 77, quote is on 76. Menasse's controversial essay was first published in the high-brow weekend addition *Spektrum* of the Viennese daily *Die Presse* and produced a heated debate among readers. The contentious essayist and gifted polemicist Menasse is probably Schüssel's fiercest antagonist.

56. Schüssel's and Fischer's speeches are reprinted in *Gedanken*, 15-20.

57. The keynotes by EU Commission President José Manuel Barroso and Foreign Minister Ursula Plassnik, 25 February 2005, are both reprinted in *Gedanken*, 29-41.

58. Fischer and Schüssel's April 27 speeches are reprinted in ibid., 45-52.

59. Fischer's and Schüssel's 15 May speeches are reprinted in ibid., 55-63.

60. Georg Spitaler, "Von der Normalitätsdebatte zur 'Normalposition' des Erinnerns?" in *Rebranding Images*, 76.

61. On these exhibits and their catalogues, see Bischof, "Austrian Exhibition-ism." For a critical perspective on the Belevedere exhibit, see Martin Wassermair, "*Privatisiert und eingestampft!,*" *in Rebranding Images*, 37-40.

62. Oliver Marchard, "Die ungezählten Jahre," in *Rebranding Images*, 58.

63. Heidrun Zettelbauer, "Das Identitätsbegehren nach musealer Repräsentation," in *Rebranding Images*, 147-59 (here 148, 152).

64. See brochure and DVD documentation of the *25 Peaces* in the *Planungsbüro*'s three-volume set.

65. Lisa Mayr, "Anders als gedacht: Gegenstrategien zum 'Gedankenjahr'," in *Rebranding Images*, 161-69 (here 168); Marlene Streeruwitz, "Gedenkkultur. Jänner 2006," ibid., 41-50 (here 43); Robert Menasse, "Österreich: Wende und Ende," and Wolfgang Lorenz, ""Die Anderen sind so fad!'," in *Was bleibt*, 76, 137-41 (quote is on 139).

66. Mayr, "Anders als gedacht," in *Rebranding Images*, 161.

67. The most ambitious effort in 2005 to capture the ambiguous narrative of Austrians' conflicted World War II roles and memories is the superior scholarly collection of essays in the exhibit catalogue *'Heiss Umfehdet, Wild Umstritten...'*, ed. Koroschitz and Rettl. These state-of-the-art essays constitute the ambiguous counter-narrative to Schüssel's official success narrative. Strangely, yet appropriately, the exhibit and the catalogue were produced by the city museum of Villach, in the heart of Haider country and defiant Austrian World War II revisionism—yet another example of popular and scholarly narratives at war.

68. Marchard, "Die ungezählten Jahre," in ibid., 55.

69. Art, *Politics of the Nazi Past in Germany and Austria*, 136.

70. Marchard, "Die ungezählten Jahre," 55; Anton Pelinka, "Gedanken sind frei," 22ff.

71. Bratic, "Die Ausstellung als Ort der Macht," 36.

72. Elisabeth Röhrlich, "Kreisky's Aussenpolitik: Zwischen österreichischer Identität und nationalem Programm," Ph.D. diss, University of Tübingen, 2008, 93-96, 177-85.

73. For a thoughtful essay on the "*Trümmerfrauen*," see Irene Bandhauer-Schöffmann and Ela Hornung, "'Trümmerfrauen'—Deutungsmuster für eine Ikone der Nachkriegszeit," in *Rebranding Images*, 79-92.

74. All citations are from Marchard, "Die ungezählten Jahre," 55f. These Schüssel quotes were cited frequently in the attacks on his *Geschichtspolitik* in 2005, suggesting that he refused to abandon the old victim's doctrine.

75. Berg, "Commemoration versus *Vergangenheitsbewältung*," 65-69.

76. In his April 27 speech, he disavowed those "who pooh-poohed the horrors of the [Hitler] regime and qualify the existence of camps and gas chambers"; see *Gedanken*, 50.

77. After the *Jersualem Post* interview, the Greens rightly charged that this was "an unbelievable step backward in Austria's process of confronting history"; quoted in Art, *Politics of the Nazi Past*, 135.

78. Uhl, "Europäische Tendenzen, regionale Verwerfungen," in *"Heiss Umfehdet, Wild Umstritten ...,"* 21-23.

79. Art, *Politics of the Nazi Past*, 202.

80. See note 14.

81. Ever since he invited and engaged Austrian intellectuals and professionals to think about the future of Austria (*Österreich zukunftsreich*), Schüssel had been a chief promoter of the idea of a national Austrian history museum, concentrating on the two Austrian Republics. In his final months as chancellor, he returned to the controversial plans for a museum of contemporary history (*Zeitgeschichtemuseum*,) supporting the suggestion of using the contents of the successful Belvedere exhibit as the core for such a museum. His historian friend Stefan Karner had been his chief consultant in planning such a history museum. The vast majority in the community of professional *Zeitgeschichtler* opposed Schüssel's plan, being suspicious of his identity politics. They

pleaded for a Holocaust Museum/"Museum of Tolerance," or a contemporary history museum with a European focus. For an excellent summary of this long-standing museum controversy with its confrontational politics of history, see Martina Nussbaumer, "'Haus der Geschichte', Version 05-06," *Rebranding Images*, 197-210; see also Heidemarie Uhl, "Haus der Konflikte," *Falter*, 15 November 2008, 18.

82. Next to the 1.1 million visitors, 475 different meetings were staged and 170 books published on the memory year 2005; for these numbers, see Franz Morak, "Editorial," *Gedanken*, 25.

83. Prime examples of outstanding scholarly publications produced as part and parcel of the *Gedankenjahr* are Arnold Suppan et al., eds., *Staatsvertrag 1955: Internationale Strategie, rechtliche Relevanz, nationale Identität/The Austrian State Treaty 1955: International Strategy, Legal Relevance, National Identity* (Vienna: Verlag der Österreichischen Akademie der Wissenschaften, 2005); and Stefan Karner and Barbara Stelzl-Marx, eds., *Die Rote Armee in Österreich: Sowjetische Besatzung 1945-1955*, 2 vols. (Graz: Oldenbourg Verlag, 2005).

84. Pollak, "Vergangenheit und Reflexion," 342.

Economic Policies and Economic Change

Johannes Ditz

Introduction

In the past fifty years, Austria has undergone a transformation; initially a "poorhouse," it has become one of the most prosperous nations in Europe. This change—measured as gross domestic product (GDP) per capita—shows that Austrian economic policy has been able to find, generally speaking, the right answer to its many domestic and international challenges. Without a drastic change of course in its economic policies in the mid-1980s, this positive development in Austria would not have been possible.

After restoration of stability in the mid-1950s, Austrian economic policy took a market-oriented direction and focused on economic and social policies supportive of a social market economy that would also be strongly shaped by the Austrian representation of interests by employers and employees (a social partnership). With an economic policy aimed at the promotion of exports and investments, accompanied by a responsible wage and income policy, Austria was able to achieve above-average growth rates. A cautious expansion of the government spending ratio and the continuous development of the social system made possible the attainment of a higher standard of living for all Austrians. Similar to the "German economic miracle," Austria's economic rise was also a success, and it was able to decrease its unemployment rates year after year.

At the start of the 1970s, full employment was a reality. Thanks to the Social Democratic Party of Austria (*Sozialdemokratische Partei Österreichs*, or SPÖ) leading a one-party government during the 1970s and early 1980s (the Kreisky era), a step-by-step transition to an Austro-Keynesian economic model took place. Based on Scandinavian social structure and following John Kenneth Galbraith's thesis on "public poverty," Austria took advantage of the 1970s boom to heavily increase state operations, to expand the transfer systems, and to develop an Austrian welfare model. Compared to other countries, the recessions of 1974-1975 and 1981-1982 were well managed through Keynesian demand management, employment increases in the public sector, "decreed" employment accommodations at the state's utility companies, and waivers of termination rights at the nationalized primary industries.

The negative consequences and high costs of these policies became evident in the mid-1980s. The federal deficit, which grew from just under 50 billion shillings (Euro 3.63 billion) in 1970 to almost 750 billion shillings (Euro 54.5 billion) in 1988, increasingly constricted the budgetary financial margin. Interest payment expenditures increased from 2.8 billion shillings (Euro 0.2 billion) in 1970 to 50.2 billion shillings (Euro 3.65) in 1988. The total tax rate increased heftily from 34.3 percent (1970) to 41.1 percent (1985).

The limitations of the tax burden began to show. The cash flow development and equity capital formation of Austrian companies was negatively influenced, in an increasing manner, due to tax changes in balance sheet regulations (2nd Tax Amendment Law of 1977).

The motivation and willingness of Austrian employees to take risks were eroded due to rising tax progression and extremely high marginal tax rates. A value-added tax of 30 percent increased the prices of luxury and semi-luxury products (cameras, furs, and so forth). The nationalized industry lost billions as a result of the exertion of political influences, a false diversification strategy, and speculative operations. Looming insolvency had to be averted through widespread assumptions of liability and capital grants by the state (the ÖIAG Law of 1987).[1] As a result of evident structural weaknesses, the national unemployment rate began to increase from 1.9 percent (1980) to 5.6 percent (1987).

The need for a fundamental political change of course—from a state-run demand-based policy to a supply-based policy oriented toward competition, deregulation, and exports—became more and more apparent. This change, of course, was programmatically prepared by the Austrian People's Party (*Österreichische Volkspartei*, or ÖVP) and implemented by the Grand Coalition that was formed after the National Council elections of 1987. Robert Graf (the economic spokesperson), Johannes Ditz (head of the ÖVP's Political-Economic Department), Josef Taus (industry spokesperson), and Wolfgang Schüssel (secretary general of the Austrian Business Federation) were primarily responsible for the ÖVP's economic program.

The changes focused on revisions in the budget structure and expenditure-related budget reorganization measures, the prompt integration of Austria into the European single market, deregulation and privatization measures, and relief-oriented tax reforms.

As a coalition negotiator (1987), minister of economic affairs (1989-1995), and vice-chancellor (1995-2000), Wolfgang Schüssel decisively helped to shape the transition from demand-based to supply-based economic policy in Austria. As Austrian chancellor (2000-2007), he deepened and strengthened the supply-based economic course.

Figure 1
Austrian National Ratios as a Percent of GDP

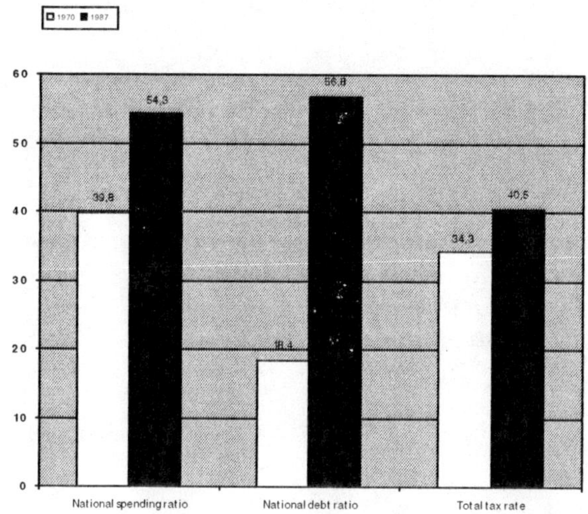

Source: Statistics Austria.

Figure 2
Austrian Unemployment Rate in Percent

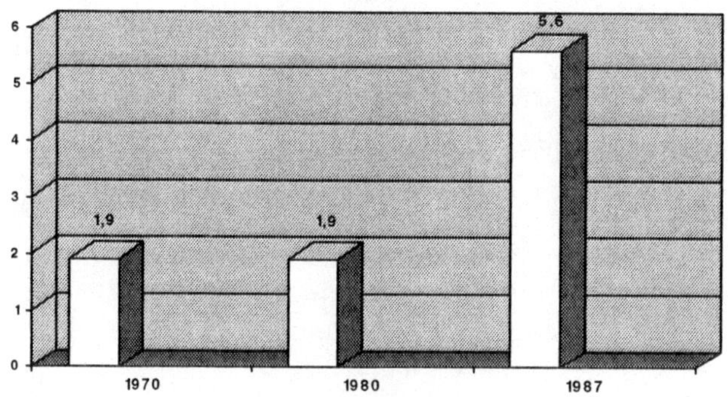

Source: Wirtschaftsforschungsinstitut (WIFO).

Change of Course during the Vranitzky-Mock Government

The change of course in the economic policy of the SPÖ-ÖVP's Grand Coalition concerned, primarily, financial policy. Budget policies attempted to reduce the government spending ratio, to slow down the deficit growth, and to decrease taxes. Additional growth and higher employment rates were to be achieved in the future through a competitive economy, dynamic exports, and increased internationalization.

Budget Policy

In budget policy, a multi-year concept was developed with the goals of reducing the number of government agencies, decreasing the transfer tasks by abolishing services, and limiting subsidies to social insurance agencies to an achievable level. The efficiency of public companies was increased, and less financing was made available to local authorities down the line for residential construction and other public services. The organization of the labor market administration was improved, and unemployment benefits were statutorily re-regulated and limited. Pay raises in the public services sector and the review of pensions were postponed for a half-year (wage freezes).

As a result of these measures, the government spending ratio and federal net deficit were markedly reduced, and deficit growth was slowed. When in the middle of 1994 the SPÖ increasingly challenged the budget restructuring course and, subsequently, the nation's net deficit climbed again to more than 5 percent, the ÖVP realized that growth and stability were at risk, and re-elections took place (Figure 3).

The SPÖ won the election with social-oriented promises, but the ÖVP pushed through the continuation of the budget restructuring course at the following coalition negotiations. Under the direction of Minister Viktor Klima (SPÖ) and Minister Johannes Ditz (ÖVP) and at the request of regional government heads, both parties agreed upon a consolidation package that was comprised of two-thirds savings and approximately one-third earnings increases. Personnel reductions, changes in employment law, and moderate wage increases stabilized personnel expenditures in the public services sector. Within two years, 9,200 service positions were eliminated. The Austrian Post & Telekom was outsourced and converted into a public limited company. Structural reforms in civil service pension law limited early retirement benefits for public servants. The General Social Security Act (ASVG) made the path to early retirement unattractive because it reduced benefit amounts. Additional savings measures involved transfer payments for the nursing/care area, unemployment benefits, and family-related services.

Figure 3
Austrian Net Deficit as a Percent of the GDP

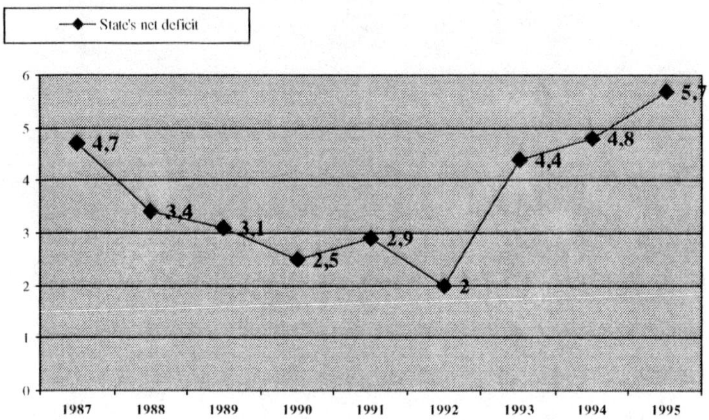

Source: Bundesministerium für Finanzen (BMF).

On the income side, tax loopholes were closed by eliminating exemption clauses and timely tax subventions, and by including gas and electricity in tax assessments.

Thanks to these measures, it was possible to reduce the government spending ratio from its highest point of 56 percent to 51.4 percent in 2000. The net deficit as a percentage of the GDP dropped from 5.7 percent to 1.7 percent, also in 2000.

Overall, the Grand Coalition was able to bring budget development under control with multiple budget restructuring concepts. Budgetary maneuvering room for tax relief measures was achieved; stabilization of the debt ratio, on the other hand, was not. The debt ratio grew significantly more slowly than it had during the Kreisky years, but an increase from 56.8 percent (1987) to 65.6 percent (2000) could not be avoided.

Figure 4
Austrian National Debt Ratio in Percent

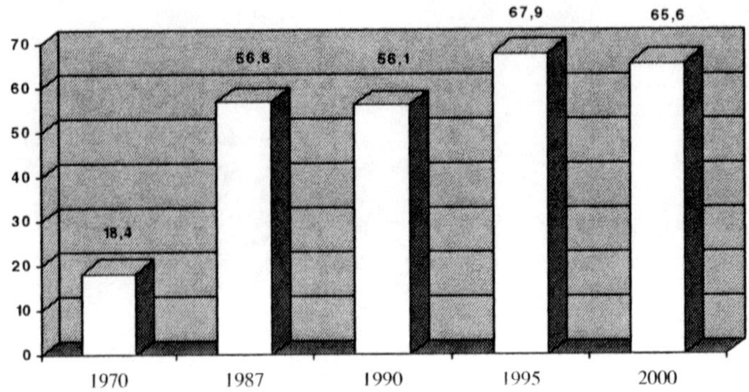

Source: Wirtschaftsforschungsinstitut (WIFO).

Tax Reform Policy

In order to stimulate the economy and growth, the Grand Coalition's main goal was to reduce the tax burden that had grown heavily during the 1980s and to improve the tax framework conditions for industry, commerce, trade, and tourism.

Tax Reforms I (1989) and Tax Reforms II (1994) that were conceived by Finance Minister Ferdinand Lacina (SPÖ) and State Secretary Johannes Ditz (ÖVP) dramatically changed the tax policy landscape in Austria. In addition to fiscal recognition of performance and profit, the executed tax reform measures focused on a strengthening of equity capital formation (corporate income tax reform), an improvement in competitive capabilities, and a fortification of private demand. The 30 percent value-added tax on luxury and semi-luxury products that was introduced under Chancellor Kreisky was repealed. The Austrian tax system was rebuilt with two large reform stages. The first reform stage involved wage and income taxes, and corporate taxes for public and private limited companies. In line with the basic premises of Reagan-era tax reforms, tax rates were reduced for wages and income, but in return, tax exemption provisions and tax loopholes were eliminated. Exemption limits were increased, and the number of tax rate brackets was reduced. The top income tax rate was decreased from 62 percent to 50 percent. Among the middle-income brackets, the three tax brackets of 39 percent, 45 percent, and 51 percent were combined into a single tax bracket of 32 percent. In total, the number of tax brackets was reduced from ten to five:

- The marginal tax rate was reduced from 21 percent to 10 percent.
- Between 50,000 and 150,000 shillings (approx. Euro 3,600 and Euro 11,000), the marginal tax rate became 22 percent instead of the earlier 27 percent and 33 percent, respectively.
- Between 150,000 and 300,000 shillings (approx. Euro 11,000 and Euro 22,000), the marginal tax rate became 32 percent instead of the earlier 39 percent, 45 percent, or 51 percent.
- Between 300,000 and 700,000 shillings (approx. Euro 22,000 and Euro 51,000), the tax rate became 42 percent instead of 55 percent and 58 percent.
- Starting from 700,000 shillings (approx. Euro 51,000), the marginal tax rate became 50 percent, instead of 58 percent, 60 percent, or 62 percent.

The corporate tax, which until 1989 had also been progressively designed and which amounted to 55 percent for the majority of Austrian companies, was reduced to 30 percent. The government also abolished the preferential taxation for distributed profit. Thus, the taxation for company-retained profits was radically reduced, and self-financing was significantly improved.

As part of the second stage of tax reform, the abolition of the trade earnings tax and business capital taxes significantly increased the attractiveness of Austria as a location for industry. Extraneous equity capital formation was fostered and made attractive through the expansion of the Austrian model for capital gains tax on stocks and *GesmbH*[2] shares. In Austria, interest is uniformly taxed at 25 percent at the source. This tax also satisfies the income, capital gains, and inheritance tax burdens.

The tax reforms and tax reduction measures of the Lacina-Ditz tenure led to a turnaround in the tax policies and tax philosophy of the Kreisky era. While high tax rates were combined with comprehensive tax incentives during the 1970s, the objective in the 1980s was to make the achievement and reporting of profits attractive. The government recognized that a structural conversion would be achieved through high-yielding businesses and not through national sponsorship, and a sufficiently high equity stake would mean security in times of crisis for companies. In the mid- 1990s, all economic policy decision makers understood that positive developments in growth and employment in a small country such as Austria would only be achieved through increasing exports, internationalization, and competitive businesses.

EU Entry: Prerequisite for Export Dynamics and Internationalization

The new orientation of Austrian foreign trade policy was, next to budget and taxation policy, the third important change in the reformulation of Austrian economic policy which was no longer based on the state, but on internationalization and competition. Vice-Chancellor and Foreign Affairs Minister Alois Mock must be given historical credit for introducing, in the mid-1980s, a positive shaping of public opinion on the topic of Austria's accession to the European Union and for seizing this initiative. The fall of the Iron Curtain and the incipient opening of the East encouraged the Vranitzky/Mock government to strive for rapid admittance to the European Union and not to accept the integration of European Free Trade Association (EFTA) nations into the European market area, which was initially proposed by the Union, as a long-term solution.

Austria realized that its growth and economic chances as a small country in the heart of a newly-forming Europe would only be protected by a clearly Westernized orientation and barrier-free access to the newly-created EU single market. In order to improve export opportunities for Austrian companies to the former Council for Future Economic Assistance (Comecon) countries, Austria entered into free trade agreements with Poland, Hungary, Bulgaria, Romania, Slovakia, the Czech Republic, and Turkey between 1991 and 1993. In doing so, Austrian foreign trade and economic policy was well aware that the desired bridge-building function and internationalization in the direction of Central Europe could only be successful if Austria became a full-fledged member of the European Union and the European heartland.

Negotiations for EU admission were initiated on 1 February 1993. The federal government was well prepared for them. Financial and support programs were to be developed for those branches that would be particularly affected by the changes. The government presented the Austrian population with the reasons for and the advantages of EU admission, within the scope of a national information and education campaign. This helped to promote speedy negotiations. On 12 June 1994, 66.58 percent of the Austrian population approved EU admission, with 81.27 percent voter participation.

Admission on 1 January 1995 led to comprehensive changes in Austria's economic structure. Due to competitive pressures, old structures were broken, upcoming liberalization and privatization plans were accelerated, and political influences were extensively eliminated. As a result of EU admittance and these developments, Austria's exports increased heavily, and a strong surge in direct financial investments in Austria and by Austria occurred. Strong growth in the area of exports and services led to an above-average growth rate as compared to other countries.

Figure 5
Austrian Exports in Billion Euros

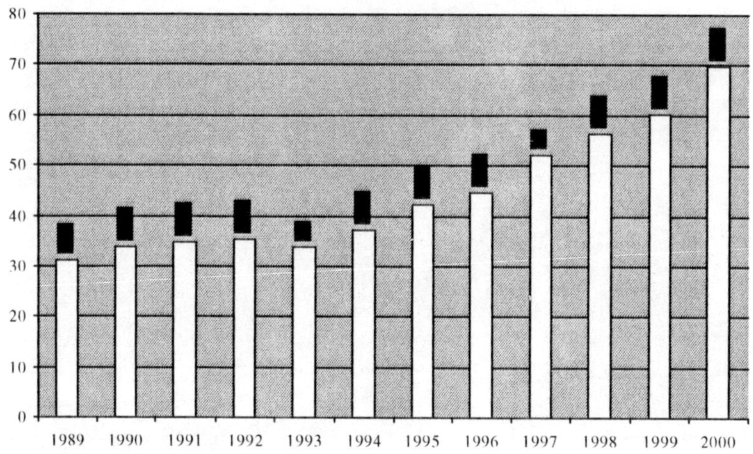

Source: Wirtschaftskammer Österreich (WKO).

Restructuring and Privatization of Nationalized Industry

With the formation of the 1987 Grand Coalition, the government planned the first partial privatizations in the public sector industry. The financing help needed for ÖIAG (Österreichische Industrie Aktiengesellschaft) operations was tied to a comprehensive restructuring and reorganization agreement. Following initial restructuring successes, repeated restructuring setbacks led to a total change of course that affected Austrian private sector industry. The objective pursued until then, to achieve an internationally successful Austrian conglomerate (Austrian Industries), was abandoned with the 1993 ÖIAG Law in favor of a clear privatization strategy.

With the 1993 amendment to the ÖIAG Law,[3] negotiated by Minister Viktor Klima (SPÖ) and State Secretary Johannes Ditz (ÖVP), the ÖIAG obtained a new assignment of duties. The newly-appointed ÖIAG management was statutorily obligated to sell off the majority of directly-owned shares in industrial companies within a specific time period. Privatizing these companies would ensure that Austrian industrial firms and industrial added value would be preserved insofar as economically justifiable.

Based on this law, twenty-seven privatization measures were initiated until 1999. Smaller participations were sold by up to 100 percent to private owners, such as AT&S and Schoeller-Bleckmann Oilfield Equipment AG, for example—both internationally reputable companies and sought-after ATX values nowadays. Initial public offerings (IPOs) and the disposal of majority shares through the stock exchange were planned for the larger holdings VA-Steel, VA-TEC, and Böhler-Uddeholm.

In 1994, the majority privatization of VA-TEC and OMV-AG took place. In 1995, VA-Steel had its IPO, in the course of which 31.7 percent of shares were sold. In March 1996, the majority privatization of Böhler-Uddeholm AG took place. The AMAG, which was reporting losses, was restructured. At the end of 1996, it was fully sold to an Austrian industrial group as part of a management buyout.

Overall, privatization earnings in the amount of 23 billion shillings (Euro 1.7 billion) were achieved between 1994 and 1996. The successful work of the ÖIAG as a privatization agency led to the transfer of additional privatization candidates in their areas of competence. In 1997, the Austria Tabak (Austria Tobacco) IPO took place. A strategic partner was sought for the mobile network operator Mobilkom Austria, which was divested from the Post as part of a controlled auction process. This resulted in strategic partnerships between Telekom Austria and Telecom Italia in the area of mobile units and later also in the fixed-line area. (Figure 6)

With its entry to the European Union, privatization, tax reform policies, and budget consolidation, the Grand Coalition undertook a remarkable and, above all, successful change of course in economic policy in the 1990s, accomplishing its goals without social unrest or strikes, as was the case in other countries.

Critical to this success was not just the ÖVP's espousal of this change of course, but also the acknowledgement and contributions on the part of the SPÖ's leading economic politicians (Franz Vranitzky, Ferdinand Lacina, Rudolf Streicher, and Viktor Klima).

The political success was primarily ascribed, however, to the SPÖ and not to the ÖVP, which was the initiator. At the end of the 1990s, the joint reform process began to lose steam. Daily politics increasingly focused on short-term measures, pending privatization projects were postponed, and the implementation of already agreed-upon savings measures was slowed down and often evaded. Due to these occurrences, the focus of budget restructuring increasingly shifted from the budget's expenditure side to the earnings side. The total tax rate, which had averaged 40.6 percent under Lacina-Ditz between 1987 and 1995, increased in only four years by 3 percentage points, or Euro 9 billion, to an average of 43.6 percent under the Finance Ministers Klima/Edlinger.

Figure 6
ÖIAG Figures in Million Euros

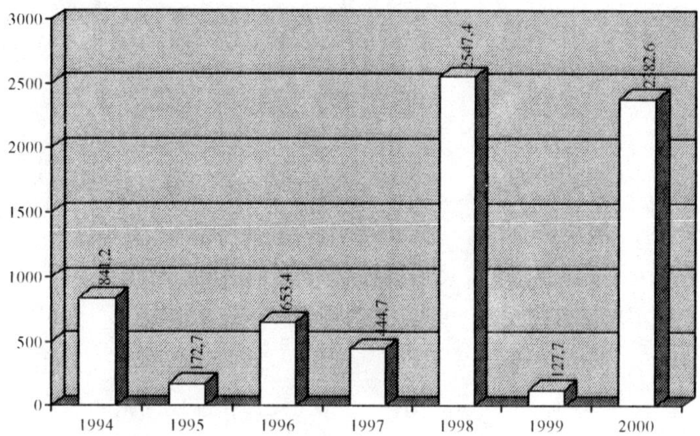

Source: Österreichische Industrie Aktiengesellschaft (ÖIAG).

Economic Policy under Federal Chancellor Wolfgang Schüssel, 2000-2007

The re-formation of a Grand Coalition, which was sought in the year 2000, failed largely due to a debate on whether policy that was oriented towards denationalization, deregulation, and budget consolidation should be intensely pursued (ÖVP), or should be weakened or corrected in order to prevent "social hardships" and to preserve the exertion of state influence in sub-areas (SPÖ). With the newly-formed government of Wolfgang Schüssel (ÖVP) and Susanne Riess-Passer (FPÖ), the answer clearly pointed in the direction of "less state and more private ownership." In preparation for the introduction of the Euro, highest priority was given to reducing the national debt ratio and the deficit. Following the successful IPOs of formerly state-run companies, the Schüssel government planned, for the first time, the total handover of owner functions to the private sector (100 percent privatization). The government fostered the development of a functioning capital market, drastically increased the research ratio, and continuously improved the framework conditions for Austria as a location for industry.

In 2001, the highest priority in budget consolidation was given to the highest total tax rate of the Second Republic, 44.8 percent. The wage and income tax amendment of 2005 limited itself to relief for low-income earners and an increase in exemption limits. Since there was also no permanent revision of tax rates for wages and income under Schüssel/Grasser, the wage and income tax burden for middle-bracket incomes in Austria is almost 50 percent higher at present than at the beginning of the 1990s.

Reduction of Government Spending and Debt Ratios

The primary goal of the Schüssel government was to meet the convergence criteria of the Maastricht Agreement and to pursue consistently a reduction of the debt ratio, a goal that was introduced with the 1995 restructuring package.

Both objectives were met. The debt ratio declined from its highest point of 66.5 percent in 1995 to 61.7 percent in 2006. In 2007, the Maastricht criterion of having a debt level below 60 percent was met by Austria for the first time with 59.1 percent. The objective of achieving a balanced budget (zero deficit), also propagated by the federal government, was achieved for the whole country in 2001 through heavy tax increases and reductions in personnel and social expenditures. (Figure 7)

The resulting economic slowdown of approximately 0.6 percentage points and the elimination of about 6,000 people from the labor force prompted the Austrian federal government to take countermeasures. The recent annulment of measures to stimulate investment activity was rescinded. As a result of this development, Maastricht-conforming national deficits of between -0.5 percent (2002) and -1.4 percent (2006) were reported between those years.

Figure 7
Austrian Public Debts According to National Accounting, as a Percent of the GDP

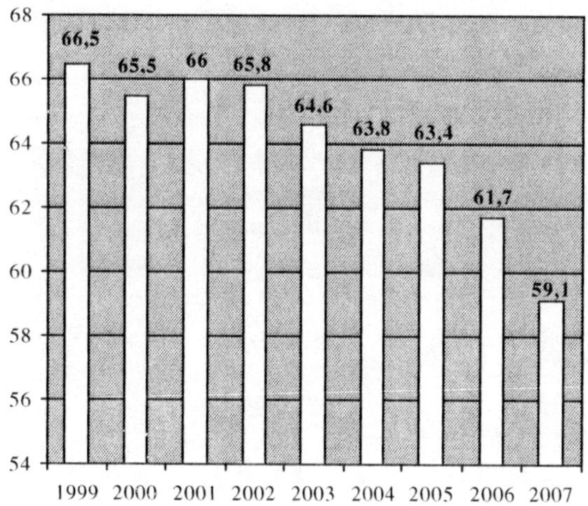

Source: Bundesministerium für Finanzen (BMF).

Figure 8
Total Austrian National Deficit as a Percent of GDP

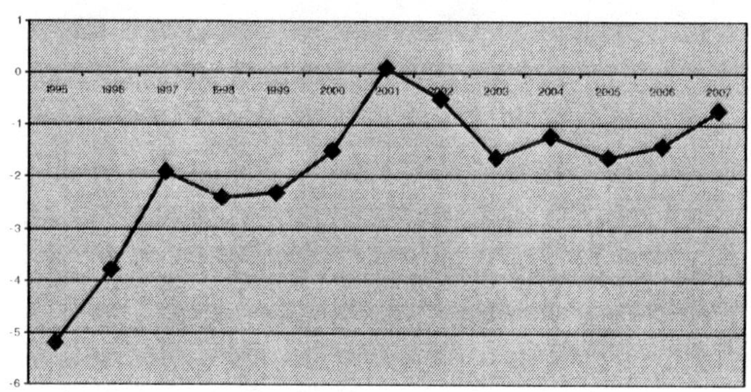

Source: Bundesministerium für Finanzen (BMF).

The government spending ratio, which had clearly risen to more than 50 percent toward the end of the Kreisky era, for the first time sunk below the 50 percent mark during the Schüssel government through savings measures and the divestment of state-run companies to private enterprise administration. An "affordable" level of 48.2 percent was achieved—without permanent tax increases.

The divestments included the Austrian universities, the state's Property Administration, museums, the financial market regulating authorities, and a few more. The 2003 Federal Railway Structure Act fundamentally reformed the Austrian state railways by improving capital backing and limiting subsidies. The Austrian Federal Railway Holding (ÖBB-Holding-AG) established individual public limited companies for passenger transportation, transportation of goods, the infrastructural sector, and services. Personnel savings were achieved primarily in the area of finance and customs administration, as well as through the consolidation of the police and gendarmerie.

Figure 9
Austrian National Spending Ratio as a Percent of GDP

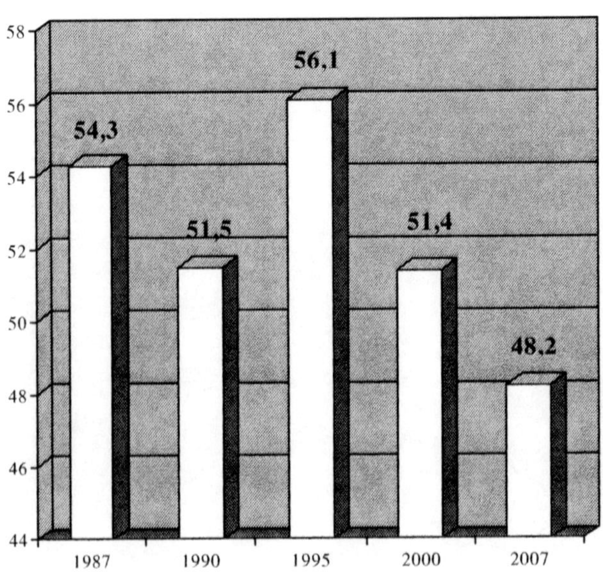

Source: Bundesministerium für Finanzen (BMF).

The core of the reform measures on the expenditures side was, without a doubt, the adaptation of the Austrian pension system to the changed demographic framework conditions and the increased life expectancy for the Austrian population. While the Grand Coalition merely positioned select measures and corrected erroneous developments, the Schüssel government attempted to achieve a uniform pension system for the future using a comprehensive package of measures. The eligibility age for retired persons was increased through cancellation of earlier benefits, thus improving markedly the long-term financial viability of the system. Early retirement pensions based on long insurance terms and unemployment were eliminated. The upvaluation factors for retirement pensions were reduced, and the standard retirement age was set at sixty-five years. A newly-established age range to receive retirement benefits provided some flexibility as to the actual age at which people retire. The retirement age in Austria will range in the future between sixty-two and sixty-eight years. Those retiring before sixty-five years of age will incur pension reductions, and those who retire later will receive increases. The 2005 Pension Harmonization Law modified the system to implement personal retirement accounts for every individual with the goal of achieving, in this manner, more transparency for every benefits recipient based on a modern and fair pension system.

The pension reform showed the ÖVP-FPÖ government's will to achieve reform. The parties were ready to implement unpopular performance standard measures in order to guarantee the necessary safety of pensions in the long term.

Strengthening of Austria as a Location for Industry

With the barrier-free access to the European single market and the almost simultaneous establishment of market-oriented economic structures in the former Comecon nations, the framework conditions for the Austrian economy changed fundamentally during the second half of the 1990s. The strengthened competition and the abolition of trade barriers compelled the Austrian economy, which was structured around medium-sized enterprises, toward change, innovation, and internationalization. Successful innovations and internationalization measures opened up new opportunities in the European markets and worldwide. In particular, the intensely-growing markets of Central and Eastern Europe offered the Austrian economy new investment, participation, and export possibilities. As a result, the level of internationalization of the Austrian economy increased from just under 5 percent of GDP to more than 25 percent within ten years. Investments from foreign countries have almost quadrupled in the last ten years, the greatest investments coming from companies in Germany, Italy, the Netherlands, and Switzerland. Austrian investments abroad concentrated primarily on the new markets in Central and Eastern Europe. Financial direct investments have more than quintupled from Euro 12.9 billion (1997) to Euro 72.2 billion (2007). Today, Austria is the largest investor in Romania, Slovenia, Bulgaria, Croatia, Serbia, and Bosnia-Herzegovina. In the neighboring countries of Slovakia, Hungary, and the Czech Republic, Austria ranks as the third largest investor.

Figure 10

Development of Direct Austrian Investments in Billions of Euros by Year

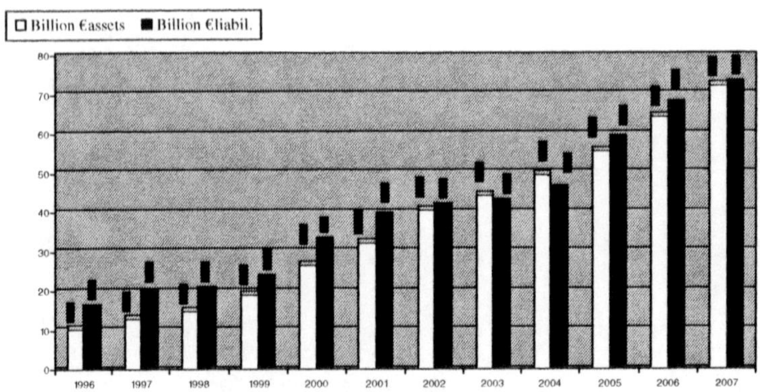

Source: Wirtschaftskammer Österreich (WKO)

The Schüssel government supported this development with an offensive regional economic policy. Through numerous initiatives and reform measures, the attractiveness of this industrial location increased, and continuous strengthening of the Austrian economy's competitiveness occurred. Austrian competition law was reformed. Austrian industrial regulations, which govern professional access for the self-employed, were liberalized and debureaucratized. In general, market access for small and medium-sized enterprises was facilitated and improved. Business hours of operation were formulated more flexibly and liberally. The mobility and flexibility of Austrian labor laws and working-time legislation were markedly increased. Thanks to the procurement of employee provision funds and the conferment of rights to severance pay, employee ties to one particular company were abandoned in favor of added mobility. The government initiated liberalization of the energy markets, and liberalization of the telecommunications market supported market development in the communications area. Austria restructured its procurement law to be EU compliant. Tax measures and the "Go International" initiative supported international integration of the Austrian economy. Research tax sponsoring, institutional reforms, and greater funding of research programs greatly expanded research and development (thus increasing the Austrian research quota). In terms of infrastructure, high priority traffic routes toward Central and Eastern Europe were built and expanded. The state-run labor market administration was reshaped as a modern labor exchange agency, placing great value on quality management. The main focus of the labor market administration's development program was on qualifications and skills.

The Schüssel government also placed a focus on location-relevant measures for tax policies. A reduction in the corporate tax rate from 34 percent to 25 percent and the introduction of modern group taxation for international company groups, which fiscally allows for net loss carry-overs for foreign subsidiaries in Austria, improved the attractiveness of Austria as a location for company headquarters and holding companies. In terms of the taxation of public limited companies, Austria finally went from being a high-tax country at the end of the 1980s to a low-tax country by the middle of 2005.

The tax yield from corporate taxes increased during this period from 0.8 billion Euros to 5.7 billion Euros, despite radical tax rate decreases, because companies' conduct also changed with the reduction in the tax burden. While attempts were made in the 1980s to keep reported profits as low as possible through technical balancing methods, company revenue was considered evidence of success in Austria after the tax reforms of the 1990s. This had as consequence a type of "Laffer effect": the lowering of tax rates led to a heavy increase in the tax yield (see Figure 11).

The regional economic policies described herein turned Austria into a dynamic and attractive industrial location at a time of globalization, integration, and the opening of Eastern markets. The Austrian export economy became the critical growth engine. Between 1996 and 2006, the number of Austrian exporters tripled. The average growth rate of Austrian exports (goods and services) totaled 8.8 percent and was, thus, significantly higher than that of the EU-15 (6.5 percent) and higher than the rate for the rest of the world (7.5 percent). Further, the increase in the export rate from 35.9 percent (1996) to 58.3 percent (2007) (see Figure 12) was a key contributor to Austria's rise as the third wealthiest country of the European Union.

Figure 11
Austrian Government Income from Corporate Taxes in Billion Euros

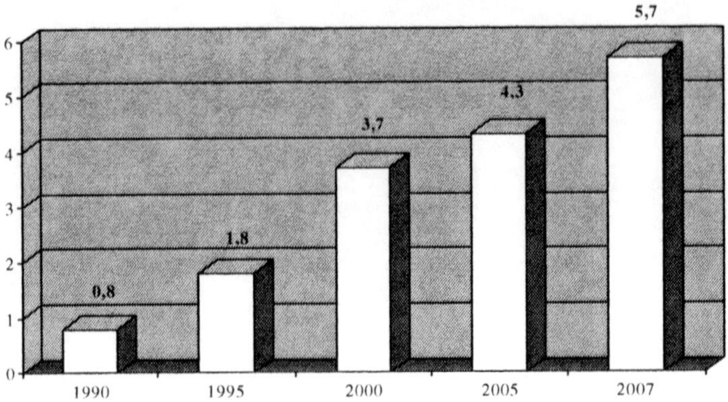

Source: Bundesministerium für Finanzen (BMF).

Figure 12
Number of Austrian Exporters (rounded) Triples following EU Admission

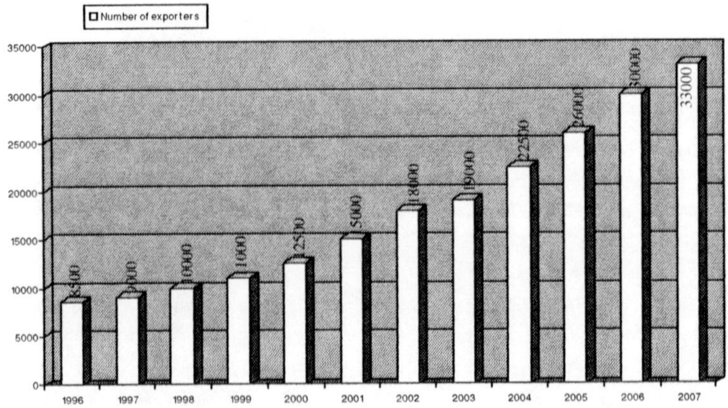

Source: Wirtschaftskammer Österreich (WKO).

Figure 13
Development of the Austrian Export Rate as a Percent of GDP

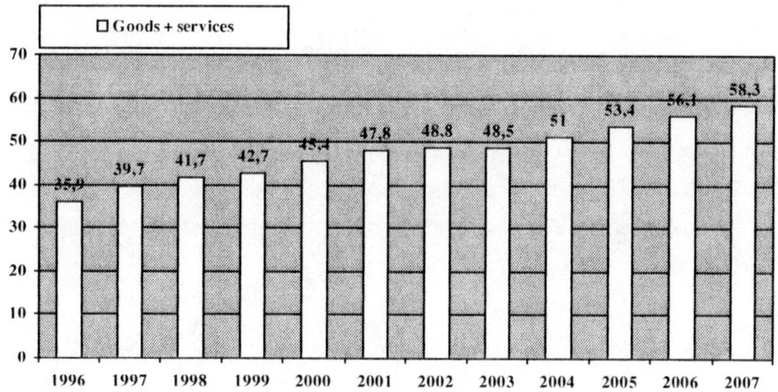

Source: Bundesministerium für Wirtschaft und Arbeit (BMWA).

Development of an Austrian Capital Market

Until the middle of the 1980s, the financing of the Austrian economy occurred almost exclusively through foreign financing (bank loans) and domestic financing (cash flow). Financing through financial markets played no role due to cemented ownership positions and extremely high tax rates. The Vienna Stock Exchange (*Wiener Börse AG*, or WBAG) was overshadowed by these conditions. With the change in corporate tax assessments in the 1990s and the privatization of formerly state-run companies through the Vienna Stock Exchange, the first steps were taken toward the formation of an Austrian capital market. The Schüssel government recognized how important an efficient Austrian capital market would be for growth, innovation, and employment and subsequently promoted the systematic development of the Austrian capital market.

In 2001, the government launched an information and internationalization campaign for an Austrian capital market and appointed a capital market representative. Collaborations with other central European stock exchanges were initiated, and an international ownership structure for the Vienna Stock Exchange was sought and found. The Austrian Corporate Governance Code provided an internationally adequate regulatory framework for good company leadership and control that would be accepted as a guideline by both the stock-listed companies as well as by the investors. With the purchase of premium retirement planning products, which would benefit Austria during tax assessment—40 percent of the capital paid in would be invested in an "underdeveloped" European Equity Fund (EEA) Stock Exchange's shares—the Vienna Stock Exchange was supported and, at the same time, a concrete push was given towards more self-insurance.

A result of this capital market initiative was an increase in the market capitalization at the Vienna Stock Exchange, from 32.2 billion Euros in 2002 to 146.2 billion Euros in 2006.

Figure 14
Market Capitalization of the Vienna Stock Exchange Increases, in Billion Euros

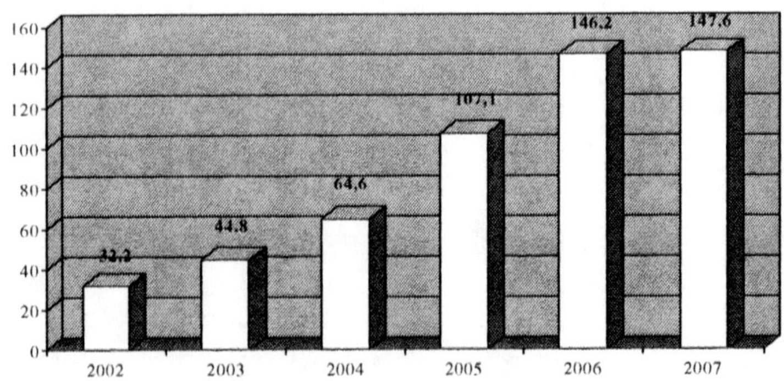

Source: World Federation of Exchanges (WFE); Economica Institut.

The average trade turnover in domestic shares grew from 1 billion Euros in 2002 to 13.7 billion Euros in 2007 (see Figure 15).

The increase in the proportion of international turnover among total turnover of 16.6 percent (2002) to 52.3 percent (2006), together with the simultaneous reduction in the national percentage, reflected the growing internationality of the Austrian exchange (see Figure 16).

The good performance of Austrian companies as market leaders in niche markets with successful Eastern European engagements, attractive price-to-earnings ratios, and solid dividend policies were critical to the successful establishment of the Vienna Stock Exchange in 2002. The ATX index markedly outperformed the established indices between 2002 and 2006, whereby 95 percent of ATX companies operated in Central and Eastern Europe. The goal of becoming the leading stock exchange in Central and Eastern Europe has become more of a reality

Figure 15
Average Monthly Turnover of Domestic Shares in Billion Euros and Including 2007 Avergage Daily Revenue for Profit-Sharing and Participation Certificates*

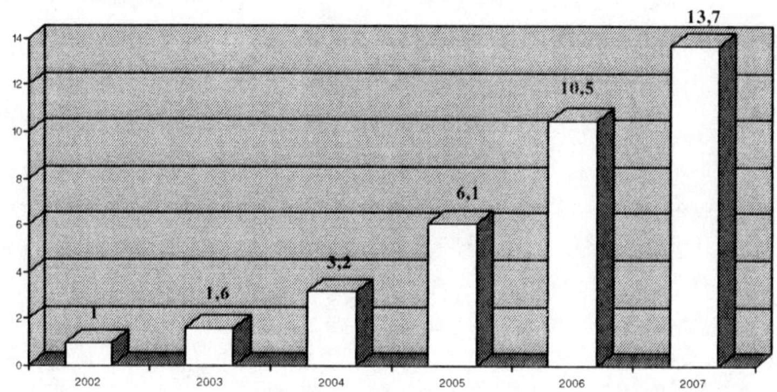

*624 million Euros, an increase of +1224 percent
Source: World Federation of Exchanges (WFE); Economica Institut.

Figure 16
Domestic and International Trade Turnover at the Vienna Stock Exchange, in Percent

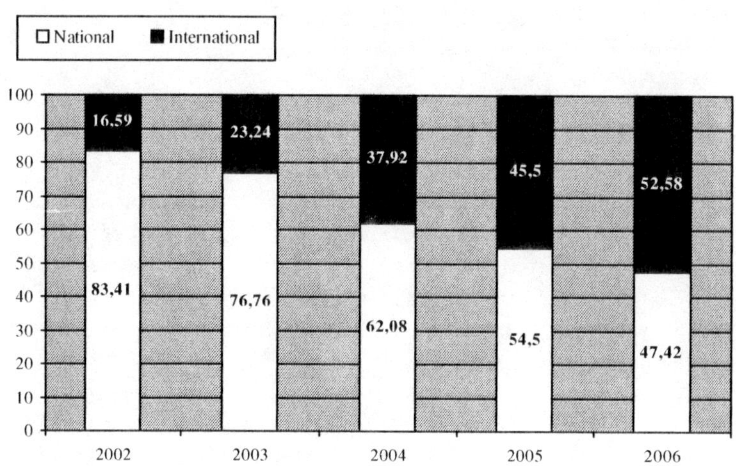

Source: World Federation of Exchanges (WFE); Economica Institut.

for the Vienna Stock Exchange in the last few years. In the opinion of research economists, the Vienna Stock Exchange has clearly functioned in recent years as a catalyst for growth. The Vienna Economic and Social Research Institute calculates a cumulative growth effect of 1.1 billion Euros and a positive employment effect of 5,900 additional jobs for the years 2003 to 2005.

Return to Private Ownership and Reduction of Government-Backed Debts through the ÖIAG

The 2000 amendment to the ÖIAG Law, prepared by the ÖIAG (Hollweger/Streicher/Ditz) for the coalition negotiations between the SPÖ and ÖVP, was adopted by the Schüssel government without any changes to its content. The amendment provided for the fusion of the ÖIAG, PTBG (Postbeteiligungs Gesellschaft) and PTA (Post & Telekom Austria), whereby the ÖIAG's portfolio expanded with inclusion of the Österreichische Post AG, Telekom AG, and PSK (Postsparkasse). At the same time, all of these companies' state-guaranteed debts were transferred to the ÖIAG. The amendments further provided for the annulment of the nation's refund obligations and liabilities and for the repayment of all debts (within one legislative period) through privatization revenue. The law's objective was clear: to bring the old nationalized policies of the Kreisky era to a final and visible end with a comprehensive privatization program and the total abolition of state-backed debts. While the partial privatizations and IPOs of earlier state undertakings were the norm during the Vranitzky government, the Schüssel government aimed for the total withdrawal of the state as proprietor. The national core shareholder, ÖIAG, was to be replaced by private proprietors, while preserving Austrian interests as much as possible. While privatization revenue had only been used until the year 2000 to service interest payments, the Schüssel government began to reduce liabilities on its own. The privatization contract formulated by Schüssel/Grasser provided for the 100 percent privatization of the PSK, Austria Tabak AG, Printmedia Austria AG, Flughafen Wien AG, Österreichischen Staatsdruckerei GesmbH, Österreichischen Dorotheum GesmbH, and Telekom Austria AG.

In 2000, the 100 percent sale of PSK shares to the Bank für Arbeit und Wirtschaft AG (BAWAG) took place within the scope of a controlled auction process. Telekom Austria was made public despite difficult framework conditions. The ÖIAG's approximate 46.4 percent share in Austria Tabak AG was sold to Gallagher AG Europe under specific strategic conditions. The privatization of VA-TEC was configured with difficulty, but following some turbulence, respected buyers were found in Siemens Austria and Andritz. The ÖIAG participation in Böhler-Uddeholm was ceded to a private group and is now part of the portfolio of the also privatized VOEST-Alpine AG. VOEST-Alpine AG—the core of the former nationalized industries of the Kreisky era—has become in the last fifteen years an internationally recognized, expanding group of steel companies with top stock performance, headquartered in Austria. The same applies to the OMV Group and the Böhler-Uddeholm group. These former state-run companies have become stock listed corporations and market leaders in niche markets, whose shares are coveted by international investors due to their good performance and successful internationalization strategies.

Even Telekom Austria has achieved, on its way to the stock exchange, the conversion from bureaucratic public utility to international communications and services provider in a relatively short time. The Austrian Post AG was taken public in 2006. This action was oversubscribed eight-fold; more than half of all Post Group employees in Austria became shareholders of the company in the course of this operation. The goal of the Schüssel government to reduce ÖIAG debts with privatization revenue was achieved. The ÖIAG debts, amounting to Euro 6.3 billion in the year 2000, were completely paid off. At the end of 2006, there was a surplus of liquid assets totalling Euro 252 million (see Figure 17).

Figure 17
Austrian Debt Level in Billions of Euros by Year

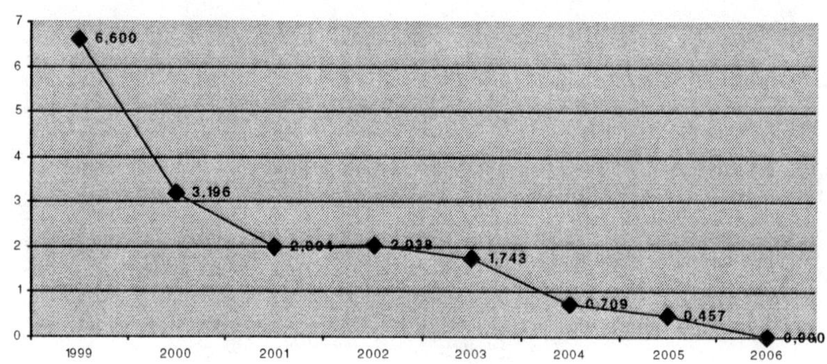

Source: Österreichische Industrie Aktiengesellschaft (ÖIAG).

The result of investment management that focused on value appreciation and shareholder value consciousness was that the portfolios still managed by the ÖIAG increased in value by more than half between 2000 and 2006, from Euro 5.0 billion in 2000 to Euro 8.2 million in 2006, despite comprehensive privatizations. The ÖIAG's portfolio is composed today of only the stock-listed participations in Austrian Airlines AG, OMV AG, Telekom Austria AG, and Österreichische Post AG.

Figure 18
ÖIAG Share Performance, in Million Euros by Year

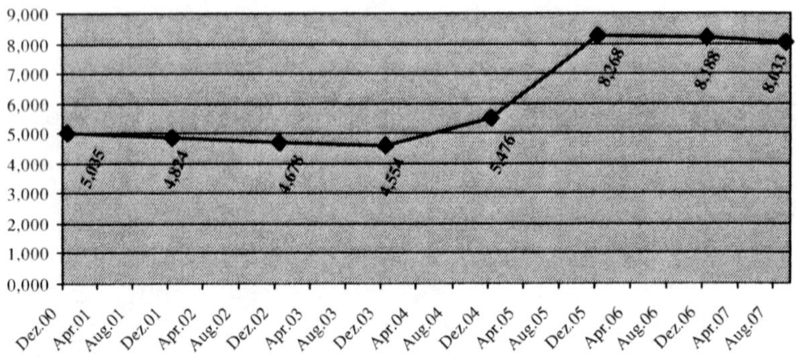

Source: Österreichische Industrie Aktiengesellschaft (ÖIAG).

The difficult nationalized industry, which had burdened the budget and the employment market so massively at the end of the 1980s, was finally closed down twenty years later by the Schüssel government following numerous reforms.

Increase of the Total Tax Rate: A Growing Burden for Mid-Sized Companies

The focus of Schüssel/Grasser's financial policies was oriented toward stabilization and reduction of the budget deficits. In order to achieve these objectives, tax increases and an increase of the total tax rate of almost 2 percentage points, from 42.9 percent to 44.8 percent, were implemented during the first year of the Schüssel government. Following this tax burden increase, relief measures were implemented, and the average total tax rate of 43 percent for the Schüssel period slightly underperformed the average total tax rate (43.6) for which Chancellor Klima and Finance Minister Edlinger (SPÖ) were responsible. It was markedly higher, however, than the average tax rate for the Lacina/Ditz periods which totalled just 40.7 percent, almost 3 percentage points or Euro 9 billion less than during its highest phase.

Figure 19

Average Total Austrian Tax Burden as a Percentage of GDP

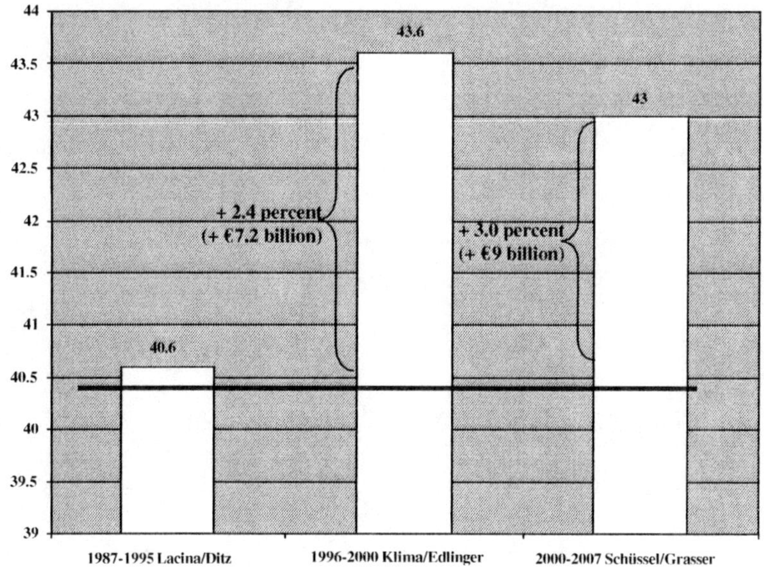

Source: Bundesministerium für Finanzen (BMF).

The tax relief measures that were part of the 2005 tax reforms concentrated mainly on incentives and tax cuts for companies. There was no perceptible relief in mid-level incomes due to a sinking of wage and income tax rates. The "cold progressive scale effect" that commenced with the large income tax rate reform of 1989 was not made retroactive. However, tax exemption limits for lower incomes were noticeably raised. When the threshold was exceeded, however, an income tax rate of 38.3 percent became effective. The tax progression subsequently increased sharply and reached the top tax rate of 50 percent with a taxable annual income of 51,000 Euros. With this progression, the wage and income tax burden for middle-bracket incomes has increased by approximately 50 percent in the last twenty years. The steep progression that is in place for annual incomes of 15,000 to 50,000 Euros is being increasingly seen by Austrian taxpayers as unfair. The growing tax burden is faced, however, with a broadly diversified system of budgetary transfer payments. Since these transfer payments are not allocated in a coordinated and bundled manner, taxpayers increasingly feel like they are "the losers of the system." The total tax rate, which has been reduced from its highest mark of 44.8 percent in 2001 to approximately 42 percent at present, is less the result of systematic relief policies, and more the result of decreasing revenue elasticity in the Austrian tax system.

The portion of quantity-dependent taxes and the value-added tax system in place have led to the tax yield increasing by only 0.95 percent with growth of 1 percent. During boom times, they lead to an automatic sinking of the total tax rate.

Summary and Outlook

In 2005, the reform dynamics of the Schüssel government began to weaken. In the run-up to the 2006 National Council elections, the government limited itself to listing its successes. Reforms that had been discussed in the Austrian education sector were no longer initiated and, in part, no longer deemed as necessary. Organizational and financial problems in social policies were recognized too late, and it was no longer possible to apply any satisfactory solutions. Macroeconomic success data obstructed the government's view of those who lost in the new system, and it was little acknowledged that all those who contributed to the economy to achieve such successes had to work harder and often had to change their personal wants and habits. Tax policy concentrated too strongly on group headquarters and too little on the needs of small- and medium-sized companies and middle-income wage earners. Further, the opposition parties were able to gain points with excessive promises for better education and social fairness. The opposition gave off the (false) impression that globalization effects could be remedied with more government spending.

With Wolfgang Schüssel's surprising election defeat in 2007, the reform policies in Austria also came to a standstill. The SPÖ-led Grand Coalition was unable to finance and honor the social promises it had made prior to the elections. The new government lacked the awareness of issues necessary for the implementation of pending reforms in the health, administration, and education sectors. In both parties, conservative distribution and social politicians increasingly gained the upper hand and wanted to solve the new problems using old recipes from the 1970s. Furthermore, differing approaches to solutions by both governing parties, together with partisan tactical maneuvers, hindered a joint approach. The government broke up after only eighteen months.

The result of the "Schüssel years," which were in place in Austrian economic policy from 1987 to 2007, is that Wolfgang Schüssel decisively helped to shape the change of course from a state-centred economy to an economy oriented towards internationality and exports through his roles as negotiator of the 1987 coalition agreement, and later as minister of economic affairs and vice-chancellor. He collaborated on the 1989 and 1994 tax reforms and was one of the chief negotiators, along with Foreign Affairs Minister Alois Mock, Finance Minister Ferdinand Lacina, and State Secretary Brigitte Ederer, in the EU admission talks that were so important to the export dynamic.

As chancellor, Schüssel promoted internationalization and pushed the state sector back to a financially viable scale. The national debt ratio was stabilized and restored to a Maastricht level of below 60 percent. With a committed privatization concept, the nationalized industry in Austria was successfully ended, and an Austrian capital market was established starting in 2000. Thus, at the end of 2007, Austria's economy was better equipped for the future than it was two years earlier. Thanks to EU accession, the opening of the East, and successful reform measures, Austria has become, in the past twenty years, an international industrial hub in the heart of Europe. From diverse positions, Schüssel the politician left his mark in the course of more than twenty years in public service.

The excessively large public sector of the mid-1980s was thus reduced, but bureaucracy and the tenacious adherence to outdated structures in fulfilling state duties continue to represent a danger to and a drag on growth and employment. It remains to be seen whether the improvements and adaptations achieved in the public sector are sufficient for ensuring Austria's successful path. Austria must undoubtedly find its way back to a long-term policy of reform in order to continue to be successful in the upcoming years.

Notes

1. The ÖIAG (Österreichische Industrie Aktiengesellschaft) is Austria's state privatization agency.

2. The *GesmbH* is a limited partnership in which the general partner is a limited liability company.

3. More specifically, the Federal Law Gazette No. 973 (1993).

Schüssel and the Welfare State

Max Preglau

This essay offers an overview of the Wolfgang Schüssel years and their longer-term effects in the field of social policy. I start by charting the initial conditions of Schüssel's reform project: the state of the Austrian welfare system established to overcome the "social challenge" in the period of "Fordist" capitalism already beyond its peak at the end of the 1990s; the current transformation of economy and society that seriously challenges the Austrian welfare system, the rise of "post-Fordist" network capitalism and the erosion of "normal" labor, "normal" family, and the culturally homogeneous nation; and the new restrictions and options for social policy resulting from this transformation. The second section turns to social policy under Wolfgang Schüssel's chancellorship. The third section evaluates the impact of Schüssel's reform of the welfare state, exploring if and in which sense his successor Alfred Gusenbauer is still following Schüssel's course of social policy.

Initial Conditions

The Austrian Welfare System: The Status Quo before Schüssel

As in other welfare systems in Europe and the rest of the industrialized world, the Austrian welfare state has been introduced as an answer to the "distribution challenge"[1] at the turn from the nineteenth to the twentieth century.[2] The most important stages in this development are listed below.[3]

The first steps towards the welfare state had been taken during the Austro-Hungarian Monarchy—with the gradual introduction of labor protection measures like the limitation of the daily work time (1884/1885), the introduction of an obligatory insurance against accidents (1887) and of a health insurance (1988), and a pension insurance for white collar workers (1906).

The establishment of the welfare system occurred after the foundation of the First Republic in 1918 powered by the political strength of the Social Democrats. Regulations for the installation of work councils and the Chamber of Labor were passed, the eight hour workday as well as insurance against unemployment were introduced (1918-1920), and a decision about the introduction of a pension insurance for workers had been made, but was not yet implemented (1927).

After a rollback caused by the world economic crises, Austrofacism, and National Socialism, the span of years between the foundation of the Second Republic in 1945 and the State Treaty of 1955 had been used for the restitution of the *status quo* before fascism and its codification within the "General Social Insurance Act 1955" (*Allgemeines Sozialversicherungs-Gesetz*, or ASVG) This act became the basis for all further developments of the social security of employees, but also the guideline for the subsequent inclusion of employers and self-employed people in the system starting in 1979 and for the subsequent harmonization of the different regulations for blue collar workers, white collar workers, and civil servants.

Beyond any doubt, the 1960s and the 1970s (and the period of the Social Democratic one-party government of Bruno Kreisky in particular) had been the "golden age of social policy."[4] On the one hand, the coverage of the system had been extended beyond the group of just employees to include employers, the self-employed, and family members. On the other hand, the scope of entitlements and services had been widened to encompass dynamic improvement of pensions, compensation payments for low pensions, improvements of health and unemployment insurance and holiday entitlements, and introduction of paid parental leave, free prenatal medical care for mother and child, a state subsidy for births, a leave for care of relatives, free school books and university studies, and so forth.

In the 1980s, the scene had begun to change. The economic, social, and political conditions had become turbulent and less favorable. The budgetary margin for social expenditure had narrowed, and the welfare system had turned from expansion to stagnation.

To understand these changes over time and their implications for the Schüssel years, one must also understand the basic structure of the Austrian welfare system. It is based on three columns: paid labor, marriage and family, and citizenship.

Regarding paid (wage) labor, the four social insurance systems (accident, health, unemployment, pension) are funded by contributions of employers and employees defined as a percentage of the wage sum (according to the Bismarck principle), and the entitlement to benefits from these systems result from participation in the work force.

Regarding marriage and family, members of the family of an insured person also benefit from the insurance systems, and further subsidies for families are offered by a public fund for family subsidies

(*Familienlastenausgleichsfond*, or FLAF) financed first and foremost by employers' contributions but also by a percentage of a worker's wages.

Regarding citizenship, Austrian citizens who are either not in the labor force and do not directly benefit from the social insurance systems and/or do not benefit from internal or state-controlled family transfer payments are protected by a "second net of social security" (means tested). This system is financed by taxes and organized on the regional level.

To determine the type of the Austrian welfare system, I refer to Gösta Esping-Anderson's typology of welfare regimes,[5] which distinguishes between liberal, conservative, and social democratic regimes. A "liberal" regime type, present in the United States, Canada, and Australia, puts its priority on "market-based welfare"; social services and transfer payments are means tested and on a low level. A "conservative" regime type, established in countries like France, Germany, or Austria, tends towards state paternalistic protection and provision; social rights and benefits are closely linked with class position and occupational status, and its family orientation is very strong. A "social democratic" regime type, as in Sweden, Norway, or Denmark universally includes all members of the society regardless of their social background in a comprehensive system of social rights and services. In terms of this typology, the Austrian system is basically "conservative," but during its golden age, some "social democratic" elements were also introduced.

The performance of the Austrian welfare system is impressive. The risk of poverty rate is significantly reduced through the social transfer—from 25 percent to 13 percent in Austria (resulting in risk of poverty reduction of nearly 50 percent).[6] Its integrative power can be best appreciated by considering the fact that after its introduction the relationship between the industrial classes had changed from "class struggle" to "social partnership," and the political system had transformed from a labile "conflict democracy" into an ultra-stable "concordance democracy."[7]

Transition from Fordism to Post-Fordism as a Challenge of the Welfare State

As in other welfare systems in Europe and the rest of the industrialized world, the Austrian system is, for better or for worse, linked to a particular societal context: Fordism.[8] The Austrian welfare state emerged as a part of this particular stage of development of capitalism. Among other characteristics, Fordism is marked by

- a system of "mass production" based on full employment; on industrial labor standardized through a Taylorist and bureaucratic organization, mechanization, collective bargaining, and labor and social legislation; and on high wages and on mass consumption;

- the generalization of the bourgeois family model, composed of the "male breadwinner" and the female housewife and mother and guaranteeing the exchange of income, goods, and services between the spouses as well as the transfer of public family allowances;
- a Keynesian economic and social policy, supplying economic stability and growth and collective social advancement through the improvement of social security and redistribution; and
- a "national constellation" in which the nation-based economy is maintained and controlled by tariff and currency policy and in which the national community is largely composed of native citizens.

Table 1
Indicators for Social Change in Austria

Indicator	Change, in Percentage
Declining Labor Volume 1960-1997	- 25
Rising GNP (figures for Germany)	+ 180
"Atypical" labor in the work force 2004	33 (all) / 50 (female)
More Women in Academia	35 (1961) -> 57 (2001)
Rising Female Employment	50 (1951) –> 65 (2004)
Divorce Rate	46 (2006) / 20 (1951)
Ratio of "Normal" vs. "Atypical" Couples and Families 2001	3:1 (2001) / 6:1 (1971) / projected 2:1 (2030)
Increase of FDI in Austria	2005: 400 of 1996
Increase of FDI in the European Union	2001: 900 of 1986
Foreign Workforce and Population 2007	Ca. 10 (1950 < 3)
Foreign-born 2007	Ca. 16

Source: Statistics Austria, EUROSTAT.

Since the 1980s, capitalism seems to have entered a new stage—"post-Fordism,"[9] or, in terms of M. Castells' more positive notion, "network capitalism" and "network society."[10] The most relevant properties of this new stage of capitalism in our context are the following (see Table 1):

- A production system of "flexible specialization,"[11] based on scientific knowledge, on flexible network organization, on electronic information and communication technologies (ICT), on pluralization, flexibilization, "disorganization"[12] and deregulation of labor, and on diversification of products and services. Economic prosperity and growth are no longer linked to full employment and growth of labor volume. The highly qualified core parts of the workforce in the advanced network sector of the economy are winning in terms of labor autonomy and income, and the traditionally qualified workforce is progressively marginalized—be it as part-time and temporary project workers, as "new entrepreneurs" in the network sector, or as part of the workforce in declining traditional industries, and people without any qualifications are in danger of complete exclusion.

- The transformation of gender roles in the family occurs as women's participation in education and labor rises, family ties get looser, and new forms of partnership and family—with or without marriage, with or without children, hetero- or homosexual, staying single, and so forth—are developed.[13]
- "Neoliberal" supply-oriented monetarist economic and social policies that distrust state ownership and regulation and trust instead private investments and self-regulated markets, while espousing anti-interventionism develop.[14]
- "Post national constellation"[15] in which national states operate on liberated and deregulated markets; in order to remain attractive as locations for globally operating capital, they have to invest in infrastructure (knowledge and qualification, communication, transport, energy), cut taxes, and reduce labor regulations and "unproductive" expenses. Moreover, they are exposed to competition with other states for investments on liberalized and deregulated markets. At the same time, migration has led to a changed composition of the societal community and challenged its nationalist identity.

Restrictions and Options for Social Policy in the Age of Post-Fordism

This societal development seriously affects the nature of the state in general and of the type of social policy established in the era of Fordism in particular. Unlike in the era of Fordism, the state is not primarily a welfare state any more, but a "national competition state,"[16] engaged in a zero sum competition with other national states. Regarding their competition strategy, the state, in principle, has two choices. First is the offensive strategy which involves investing in knowledge and education in order to attract investors and create new jobs in the new knowledge economy while at the same time investing in social policy in order to enable the population to participate in and maintain their employability in a flexible network economy. This strategy has been successfully practiced in Scandinavian countries like Finland and Sweden and in the Netherlands.[17] Second is the defensive strategy which avoids an outflow of capital and unemployment through cutting taxes, abolishing labor regulations, reducing social expenses, and increasing the pressure on the labor force. Some "liberal" countries like the United States or Great Britain are following that strategy; some "conservative" countries complement this strategy with protectionist measures like incentives for women to stay away from the labor market and barriers for migrant workers. Of course, these two strategies can also be combined.

Furthermore, the paradigm of social policy is shifting from "active full provision" towards "activation."[18] The new paradigm of social policy entails not only a reduction, but also a redirection, of social expenditure as new modes of care and social services provision are introduced (see Table 2).

Table 2
Modes of Care and Social Services Provision

Mode of Provision	Fordist		Post-Fordist
	Informal	Formal	Hybrid
Unpaid	family care	volunteers	paid and unpaid family and institutional service,
Paid	paid domestic service	(private and public) service facilities and institutions	allowances and tax credits for family care and market service, public financial support for paid domestic service

Source: Fine, own adaptations.[19]

The forms established in the Fordist welfare system—paid or unpaid, formal or informal provisions—are complemented and/or substituted by mixed "hybrid forms." At the same time, organization and management of formal care is reorganized to include contracting with private providers, embracing new administrative arrangements (introduction of monitoring surveillance, funder-provider splits, output-based funding, management by objectives, and so forth, known as "new public management"), overcoming the fragmentation of and improving the coordination between services (case management, one-desk principle, networking of services, and so forth), encouraging less intensive and cheaper service through substitution policies, and improving the targeting of services.[20]

Regarding the broader socio-political orientation of social policy, basically two versions of activating social policy may be distinguished. First is the "progressive" version which accepts the reality of post-Fordist network society and aims at the empowerment of people to get along with the new flexible working and living conditions. Second is the "conservative" version which still clings to the Fordist past and tries to keep the people on board the "sinking ships" of a full employment economy, family, and nation.

The Transformation of the Austrian Welfare State in the Schüssel Years, 2000-2006

"Neo-Liberal" Social Policy

The containment of social expenditure in Austria had already started under the Grand Coalition of the Social Democratic Party of Austria (*Sozialdemokratische Partei Österreichs*, or SPÖ) and Austrian People's Party (*Österreichische Volkspartei*, or ÖVP) the in the 1990s for a rather pragmatic reason: the need to adapt to reputedly factual budgetary constraints. Two "austerity packages" passed in 1994 and in 1995 entailed more restrictions, cuts, and/ or deductibles in the areas of health, unemployment, and pensions insurance.[21]

The new center-right coalition between the ÖVP and the Freedom Party of Austria (*Freiheitliche Partei Österreichs*, or FPÖ), in office since February 2000, inspired by the "neo-liberal" trust in markets and "self-responsibility," continued and even intensified this approach to social policy. The coalition's "neo-liberal" agenda of reduction and transformation of the supposedly overdeveloped welfare system followed the principle "less welfare state, more entrepreneurship," according to Minister of Finance Karl-Heinz Grasser.[22]

This neo-liberal agenda of the ÖVP-FPÖ coalition was put into practice via different channels. One channel was the change of formal administrative structures and political decision-making procedures. The competence for labor affairs was transferred from the Ministry for Social Affairs to the Ministry for Economic Affairs.[23] Additionally, in order to increase its influence on social policy, the new government tried to cut the autonomy of the corporatist Economic and Social Partnership (ESP). The first initiative in this direction was undertaken in summer 2001,[24] but was reversed in autumn 2003 by the Constitutional Court[25]; the second initiative in this direction at the end of 2004 was successful.[26] Finally, Schüssel's government also broke with the tradition of the non-autonomous ESP—that is, the inclusion of employer, employee, and farmers' organizations in the process of parliamentary decision making—for instance, on the occasion of the pension reform of 2003.

The other channel for the neo-liberal agenda of Schüssel's government was material decision making. In its first period, several measures were significant. Under the headline "Measures for Budget Consolidation," mass taxes and dues were raised, a fee for outpatients' departments and a tax on accident benefits were introduced,[27] tuition fees as well as restrictions on the pension system (for example, elimination of early retirement) and on unemployment insurance (for example, lower replacement rates, cuts of family surcharges, longer waiting periods for repeated claims, harsher sanctions for abuse) were implemented.[28] In terms of social policy, Schüssel's first cabinet can be credited with the "Billion for Handicapped Persons"[29] which was funded in the budgets for 2001 and 2002.

A far-reaching change of the welfare system was the introduction of two private pillars into the hitherto purely public pension system: a company pensions scheme[30] and a scheme for individual retirement provisions.[31]

In its second term in office, the ÖVP-FPÖ/ BZÖ coalition continued with this agenda:

Labor and Labor Market Policy

Schüssel's cabinet agreed upon a further liberalization of business hours[32] and upon a reduction of part-time work for older employees[33] as well as of unemployment insurance (resulting in stricter definitions of "acceptable" employment and "acceptable" commuting distances).[34] Also part of the agenda of the ÖVP-FPÖ/BZÖ government[35] (ÖVP/ FPÖ 2003), but not realized was the introduction of unemployment insurance for employers and the self-employed.

In the area of labor market policy, Schüssel's cabinet put its focus on "activating" measures to raise "employability" (according to the relevant guidelines and the "Lissabon Agenda" of the European Union), including a new combination wage model.[36] An important step towards labor market liberalization was abolishing the monopoly for placement services of the state-controlled "Labor Market Service" (AMS).[37]

In the year 2005, the so-called "service check" was created. With this innovation, the government tried to make a step towards the legalization of illegal housework and its integration into the social insurance system.[38]

Pension Reform

After the introduction of two private pillars during its first term in office, the government engaged in the reform of the first public pillar of the system. Basically the government aimed at 1) adaptation of the system to the current demographic transition through a reduction of the payout and 2) harmonization of the different pension systems through the introduction of a unitary system for all occupational groups. In spite of strong resistance from the trade unions and the parliamentary opposition, the relevant decisions were made on 11 June 2003[39] and 18 November 2004.[40] The core issues of the new system:

- the regulation will be in force on 1 January 2005 for all people below the age of fifty;
- the rate of contribution is 22 percent for blue and white collar workers, 17.5 percent for the self-employed, and 15 percent for farmers;
- eligibility occurs after only seven instead of fifteen years of employment;
- up to four (instead of two) years of eligibility may be replaced by time spent on child care;
- time spent on child care (or care for the dying) is rated relatively generously with the average income of women (Euro 1.350), whereas the rating of times of unemployment was reduced;
- regular retirement age is sixty-five; earlier retirement leads to marked deductions;
- replacement rate is 80 percent after forty-five (instead of only forty) years of contribution; the basis of the computation is the average income of the whole occupational carrier (instead of the average of the last fifteen years);
- heavy workers will have a chance for early retirement without a reduction of their pensions[41]; the current regulation for early retirement ("*Hackler-Regelung*" giving the right of retirement after forty-five years of contribution to the pension system) will be extended until 2014;
- minor appreciations of years of contribution occurs, reduced increase of pensions;
- in order to secure sustainability, the system will be automatically linked to further demographic development;
- losses through the reform are limited with a maximum of 5 percent for 2004 up to 10 percent from 2024 onward.

Projected in the coalition agreement,[42] but ultimately not realized, was a minimum pension.

Considering the increase of part-time and discontinuous labor and the minor weight of years of contribution to the pension system (-8 percent) on the one hand and the absence of a minimum pension on the other, a growing part of the younger generation (in general) and women (in particular) will have real trouble safeguarding their future based on the revised pension system.

Health Reform

In the first half of 2003, Schüssel's second cabinet pushed through the harmonization of contributions to health insurance (unitary contribution rate: 7.3 percent; +0.4 percent for white collar and -0.3 percent for blue collar workers), the raise of the contributions to the health insurance for retired persons (+1 percent), and the introduction of deductibles for medical consultations and new contributions for leisure time accidents (0.1 percent).[43]

In October 2004, the federal state and the regional states agreed upon a "package for financing the health system"; this package included among others an increase of the tobacco duty, further deductibles and a temporary elevation of contributions to the health insurance.[44]

At the same time, the ruling coalition prepared an organizational reform of the health system: Within a nationwide health organization structure Austria is divided into four "health zones" and thirty-two "health regions." In order to assure a high quality at reasonable costs the medical activities of hospitals and independent physicians, inpatient and outpatient treatment, standard level- and high level-medical service efforts should be optimized and better coordinated.[45]

Taxes and Fees

Fees were further raised, for example, the fee on fuel. On the other hand, as the first step in a two step-tax reform, the level of tax-free income was raised to _14,500 per year, and taxes were reduced.[46] In sum, the relief amounts to the rather modest sum of Euro 169 million.[47]

The second step of the tax reform with a volume of Euro 2.2 billion contains, among other features, a reduction of corporate tax from 34 percent to 25 percent and a modification of the income tax (less tax brackets, raising of the brackets in order to prevent hidden progression) aiming at a simplification of the system and a reduction of the tax burden. Furthermore, a rise of the single earner tax allowance was part of the reform.[48]

Poverty Reduction

Contrary to its announcements, Schüssel's second cabinet took no significant measures against poverty. Neither the minimum pension nor the nationwide unitary guaranteed minimum income which was supposed to replace the old regional system of subsidies that was neither uniform nor able to secure one's livelihood were put into practice.[49]

With this social policy agenda aiming at a better targeting of social services and an individualization and privatization of the social risks,[50] the "social democratic" elements of Austria's welfare regime were reduced, and additional "liberal" elements were introduced. Faced with the realm of a "post-Fordist" network economy, a "defensive" strategy was chosen to avoid the outflow of capital and unemployment through cutting taxes, abolishing labor regulations, reducing social expenses, and increasing the pressure on the labor force. This strategy was supplemented by two other problematic elements: a conservative gender and family policy and a restrictive migration and integration policy.

Conservative Family and Gender Policy

In terms of family and gender policy, Schüssel's cabinets enforced the "conservative" character of the system inspired by traditional models of family and gender relations, trying to reduce women to the function of housewives and mothers and to keep them dependent upon the male breadwinner and the state-controlled family transfer.

In terms of the formal administrative structure, the abolishment of the Ministry for Female Affairs, the integration of its former areas of responsibility into the Ministry for Social, Family, and Generation Affairs, and the launching of a Department for Male Affairs within this Ministry is symptomatic of the new approach to gender and family issues.[51]

In terms of material policy, the paradigmatic model in this respect is the "children's allowance" (*Kindergeld*).[52] It was introduced during the ÖVP-FPÖ coalition's first term of office as a substitute for the previous policy of paid maternal leave for employees. Admittedly, other groups besides housewives and mothers (for example, students and the self-employed) also benefit from this measure, but the allowance is no surrogate for a regular income, and it tempts women to stay away too long from the workplace. In its second term, Schüssel's cabinet continued with this policy. The children's allowance for multiples was raised,[53] and as already mentioned above, the single earner tax allowance was improved.

Ambivalent in its consequences for the gender relations was the consideration of time spent on childcare for the calculation of pensions and the introduction of voluntary pension-splitting during the child's first four years, both introduced with the pension reform 2003/04. On the one hand, women gained an independent legal claim to a pension; on the other hand, the cash equivalent of that claim is low, and the measure sustains the "male breadwinner" model.

Two further family policy measures of Schüssel II are similarly ambivalent in their consequences. The first measure is the leave for end-of-life care and care for the seriously ill (without salary, up to six months), passed in parliament in May 2005.[54] Its scope is limited to the members of "normal" family, and considering the existing gender differences in their labor market participation and income, it sustains the unequal gender order. The second measure is the right of part time work for employees which was introduced in order to reconcile parenthood and labor passed in parliament on 26 May 2003.[55] Only 25 percent of the employees potentially benefit from this measure; it primarily applies to women and, thus, contributes to the reproduction of the established gender order. Furthermore, step-parents are not included in this regulation.[56]

Shocked by negative results of the PISA Study about the quality of education in Europe, the ÖVP-FPÖ/BZÖ coalition loosened its resistance against institutional child care. In July 2005, it paved the way for the provision of additional day care facilities for 10,000 children.[57]

As far as new forms of marriage and family such as patchwork families or homosexual couples are concerned, both of Schüssel's cabinets consistently refused to face reality and ensure equal treatment. Although the Constitutional Court had ruled out the discrimination of homosexual couples[58] and in spite of the Anti-Discrimination Directive of the European Union, the relevant initiatives of Minister of Justice Karin Gastinger finally were not successful.[59]

At the same time, the ruling ÖVP-FPÖ/BZÖ coalition made a decision with disadvantageous consequences for the legal status of patchwork families. The regulation extending insurance coverage to a partner with whom one was cohabitating was changed so that it no longer applied to non-married couples, be they heterosexual or homosexual.[60] Thus a practice of equal treatment of married and unmarried couples introduced twenty-five years ago was revoked.[61]

In May 2004, the coalition agreed upon a revision of the Equal Treatment Act[62] in order to implement an anti-discrimination directive of the European Union. The new regulation was meant to protect all employees from discrimination at their workplace on the basis of sex, race, ethnicity, religion, age, or sexual orientation. However, the EU directive was implemented only minimally.[63]

During Austria's EU presidency, Schüssel's cabinet launched an action plan against "tradition-bound violence" against women such as female genital mutilation, forced marriage, or honor killing. At the end of January 2006, a relevant network was founded and financed by the EU Fund for Human Rights and Democracy.[64] By the end of March 2006, the Austrian parliament passed measures for the protection of victims of "tradition-bound violence" against women.[65] Without downplaying the importance of the fight against this type of crime, it is noteworthy that it xenophobically associates violence against women with the tradition of the migrant population and goes along with an ignorance and neglect of home-grown violence against women.

Restrictive Immigration and Integration Policy

By means of immigration and integration policy, additional nationalistic, protectionist, and xenophobic elements were introduced into social policy. Most instructive about the approach to migration and integration in Austria is the attitude toward these policy issues at the Ministry of Internal Affairs: migration is perceived as a threat and a matter of homeland security, not as an opportunity, and migrants are not welcomed, but received with distrust.

The most prominent example for the restrictive approach to immigration and integration legislation in the first term of office for Schüssel's ÖVP-FPÖ coalition was the newly introduced "Integration Agreement" that has to be signed by immigrants. Unlike its Dutch model, it offered no new opportunities and positive incentives (such as better access to the labor market and public housing, the right to vote on the communal level, an earlier award of citizenship), but imposed more obligations (language and regional studies courses) and hurdles (health test) and threatened immigrants with negative sanctions such as progressive deductibles, fines, and removal.[66]

In its second term in office, Schüssel's cabinet continued with its restrictive agenda, particularly in the arena of asylum legislation. As far as asylum law is concerned, the ÖVP-FPÖ coalition in 2003 passed legislation involving more complicated application and appeal procedures. In addition, revisions of one's justification of one's application offered in hindsight were prohibited.[67] After the abrogation of this law by the Constitutional Court in October 2004,[68] the ruling coalition made another effort to change asylum legislation including, among others, provisions regarding extensive custody pending deportation, forced nutrition of hunger strikers, and fines for people acting as accessories to the abuse of asylum rights and for fictitious marriages. At least the prohibition of a revision of the justification of one's application in hindsight was moderated. The new law was passed as a part of a comprehensive migration legislation package on 7 July 2005; it was supported by large parts of the oppositional SPÖ.[69]

On 24 March 2004, the Agreement between the Federal State and the Regional States Concerning the Support of Refugees implementing a relevant EU directive was passed unanimously in the parliament.[70] With this measure, the subsistence of asylum seekers was guaranteed.

During the same period, legislation for immigration and citizenship was considerably modified as well. The quota for legal immigration was reduced from 8,518 places for 2001 to 7,000 places for 2006, about 50 percent of which were reserved for immigrants admitted in order to reunite families. In addition, more seasonal migrant workers were admitted in order to accommodate the short-term demand on the labor market. Furthermore, higher requirements within the Integration Agreement, higher requirements (knowledge of language and culture, having one's own means of subsistence) and longer waiting time (twelve instead of ten years) for naturalization, additional difficulties for binational couples and for transnational adoptions, and less security for migrants against deportation were features of the legislation. At least further steps towards a harmonization of residence and labor were taken, and more independent rights for people who came to the country via the family reunion policy were granted. The new laws concerning legal residence and settlement were passed with the approval of the oppositional SPÖ on 7 July 2005[71]; the decision upon the new rules for citizenship followed on 1 March 2006.[72]

A few measures of the ÖVP-FPÖ/BZÖ government sought to reduce discrimination and encourage the integration of migrants. These included the extension of children's and family allowance to migrant women who do not share a household with an Austrian citizen,[73] and the introduction of measures for the promotion of speech development of migrant preschool children and school students.[74]

Reviewing gender, family, migration, and integration policies of the Schüssel era reveals that the administration chose the "conservative" agenda, still clinging to the "sinking ships" of the traditional gender order, "normal" family, and maintaining a nation of aboriginal citizens. With regard to gender and family, it supported the traditional male breadwinner model of family, it discouraged full-value female employment, and it continued with discrimination of deviant couples and patchwork families. As far as migration is concerned, the policies of the ÖVP-FPÖ/BZÖ coalition inhibited immigration and impeded social integration.

Final Evaluation of the Social Policy of the Schüssel Years

A comprehensive retrospect on the "Schüssel Years" shows a clear tendency toward a neoliberal transformation of the welfare state into a national competition state, toward the consolidation of traditional gender order and family, and toward a nationalist exclusion of migrants.

Neoliberal transformation of social policy does not necessarily mean reduction of social expenses. The rate of social expenditure has been stable or has even increased since the 1990s,[75] but focusing on the different sorts of expenses reveals a more mixed and non-uniform picture. Some social contributions have decreased—be it because of reduction (of, for example, unemployment payment, pensions), because of the introduction of deductibles (in, for example, health insurance), or because of their substitution by private arrangements (such as, for example, pensions). Yet expenses for monetary children's and family allowances have increased, whereas the expenditure for institutional child care has stagnated. Compared to other European countries, Austria has developed into a country with a relatively high standard of monetary allowances and a relatively low standard of institutional services.[76]

Except for the introduction of the support of refugees required by a relevant EU directive, the investments in measures for the integration of migrants have been rather moderate. Thus it's no wonder that, according to the Migration and Integration Policy Index, Austria ranks as the second to the last of all EU countries in this policy area.[77]

In its turn to embrace the national competition state model, Schüssel's two cabinets chose the "defensive strategy" of reducing the tax burden and wage subsidies to create more capital and "activating" labor by means of negative incentives. The socio-political orientation in the Schüssel era was "conservative," enforcing promotion of the traditional gender order and "normal" marriage and family and engaging in the continuous discrimination of unmarried couples and patchwork families. Simultaneously, the discrimination of the migrant population continued and was even intensified. Thus the ÖVP-FPÖ/BZÖ coalitions did not account for the emerging "network society" and (mis-)invested in the sinking ships of normal labor and full employment, the male breadwinner family model, and the nation of aboriginal citizens.

The effects of this backward policy orientation are numerous. The inequality of incomes increased,[78] and poverty continues in Austria. Five percent are acutely poor, a further 7 percent are at risk of poverty, and a further 20 percent are affected by restrictions of their standard of living. The primary risk groups are female widows and (predominantly female) single parents and migrants.[79] The number of people living on public social support has increased more than threefold since 1999.[80]

The system of public social transfer reproduces and even amplifies these inequalities.[81]

The gender gap of professional status and income continues[82]; women have been driven "back to the kitchen," (re-)entry into the labor market after parental leave ends has become more difficult,[83] and the restrictive migration and integration policy has led to labor market problems (shortage of qualified labor and/ or care takers) as well as to structural social exclusion and cultural isolation of the migrant population.[84]

The coalition agreement of the subsequent SPÖ-ÖVP-coalition[85] contained some projects in the area of social, gender and family, migration, and integration policy issues promising a reorientation of policy along the lines of EU trends. Initiatives like the guaranteed minimum income; the inclusion of employers, the self-employed, and freelancers in unemployment insurance; the improvement of professional training and occupational retraining; and the introduction of the comprehensive school indicate a shift from a "defensive" to an "offensive" competitive strategy prepared to invest in human capital and in social security as a precondition of flexible labor.

Initiatives like the flexible nature of the children's allowance, the expansion of institutional child care, or the abolishment of discrimination against homosexuals, non-married couples, and patchwork families indicate a shift from a "conservative" to a "progressive" socio-political orientation and to the acknowledgement of the new model of network society which includes flexibility in work and life and pluralism of ways and styles of living.

Because the ÖVP was neither prepared to give up basic principles and core results of the Schüssel era, nor to concede major political successes to its ally, in the political practice of the coalition many of those projects were either diluted (as in the comprehensive school) or retarded (as in the introduction of the guaranteed minimum income) and/or finally completely prevented (as in the equal treatment of homosexuals, non-married couples, and patchwork families).

Furthermore, there was also much continuity provided for in the coalition agreement. The competitive strategy still included "defensive" elements such as the further liberalization of opening hours and working hours for shops or further restrictions on unemployment insurance. Unimpressed by the criticism expressed by human rights organizations and the supreme jurisdiction of the European Union, the SPÖ-ÖVP coalition consensually continued with the restrictive agenda of migration and integration policy, thus staying on the "conservative" socio-political course of its predecessor.

Thus state and social policy in Austria currently are in a state of uncertainty—undecided and torn apart between an "offensive" and a "defensive" competitive strategy and between a "conservative" and a "progressive" socio-political orientation. Schüssel's ÖVP was not prepared to make a fundamental turn, whereas Gusenbauer's SPÖ was not strong enough to push the turn through by force; it was also unwilling to change the conservative course in the area of migration and integration policy. Thus even Gusenbauer's policies remained dependent on the path taken by Schüssel, and social policy was shaped by Schüssel beyond the years of his chancellorship.

Notes

1. Stein Rokkan, *Staat, Nation und Demokratie in Europa: Die Theorie Stein Rokkans aus seinen gesammelten Werken rekonstruiert und übersetzt von Peter Flora* (Frankfurt: Suhrkamp, 2000).

2. Jens Alber, *Vom Armenhaus zum Wohlfahrtsstaat: Analysen zur Entwicklung der Sozialversicherung in Westeuropa* (Frankfurt/Main: Campus, 1982), Tables A2-A6, 232-39.

3. See Gerda Bohmann, "Kapitalistische Wirtschaft und Wohlfahrtsstaat," in *Ökonomie und Gesellschaft: Eine Sammlung von Studientexten*, ed. Johann August Schülein and Gerda Bohmann (Vienna: Springer, 1994), 214-29; Emmerich Talós, "Krise des Sozialstaates," in *Solidarität: Option für die Modernisierungsverlierer*, ed. Paul Zulehner et al. (Innsbruck: Tyrolia, 1996), 36-50; and Emmerich Talós, "Sozialstaatsbilanz," *Diskurs Sozial* 1 (1996): 5-20.

4. Talós, "Sozialstaatsbilanz."

5. Gösta Esping-Andersen, *The Three Worlds of Welfare Capitalism* (Cambridge: Polity, 1990).

6. Within the European Union, Austria forms a middle group together with most of the other "conservative" systems. The Scandinavian countries and the Czech Republic do better (above a 60 percent risk of poverty reduction, while most of the countries of the southern and eastern parts of Europe do worse (below a 30 percent risk of poverty reduction). These figures are for 2004; see the Statistical Office of the European Communities (EUROSTAT), http://epp.eurostat.ec.europa.eu/portal/page?_pageid=1090, 30070682,1090_33076576&_dad=portal&_schema=PORTAL, accessed 30 November 2008.

7. See Rainer Nick and Anton Pelinka, *Bürgerkrieg - Sozialpartnerschaft: das politische System Österreichs. 1. und 2. Republik, ein Vergleich* (Vienna: Jugend und Volk, 1984).

8. Joachim Hirsch and Roland Roth, *Das neue Gesicht des Kapitalismus: vom Fordismus zum Post-Fordismus* (Hamburg: VSA-Verlag, 1986).

9. Ibid.

10. Manuel Castells, *The Information Age: Economy, Society, and Culture*, 3 vols. (Cambridge, MA: Blackwell, 1996, 1997, and 1998).

11. Michael J. Piore and Charles F. Sabel, *The Second Industrial Divide: Possibilities for Prosperity* (New York: Basic Books, 1984).

12. Scott Lash and John Urry, *The End of Organized Capitalism* (Cambridge: Polity, 1996).

13. See Ulrich Beck, *Risikogesellschaft. Auf dem Weg in eine andere Moderne* (Frankfurt: Suhrkamp, 1986) and Ulrich Beck and Elisabeth Beck-Gernsheim, *The Normal Chaos of Love* (Cambridge: Polity, 1995).

14. For a critical review, see Tim Engartner, "Privatisierung und Liberalisierung—Strategien zur Selbstentmachtung des öffentlichen Sektors," in *Kritik des Neoliberalismus*, ed. Christoph Butterwege et al. (Wiesbaden: VS Verlag für Sozialwissenschaften, 2007), 87-133.

15. Jürgen Habermas, "Die postnationale Konstellation und die Zukunft der Demokratie," in *Die postnationale Konstellation: Politische Essays* (Frankfurt: Suhrkamp, 1998), 91-169.

16. Joachim Hirsch, *Vom Sicherheits- zum nationalen Wettbewerbsstaat* (Berlin: ID-Verlag, 1998).

17. See Felix Stalder, *Manuel Castells: The Theory of the Network Society* (Cambridge: Polity, 2006), 120.

18. See Bernhard Blanke and Stefan Plaß, "Vom schlanken Staat zum aktivierenden Staat. Leitbilder der Staats- und Verwaltungsmodernisierung," in *Ausblicke auf den aktivierenden Staat: Von der Idee zur Strategie*, ed. Fritz Behrens et al. (Berlin: Edition Sigma, 2005), 27-42.

19. Micheal D. Fine, *A Caring Society? Care and Dilemmas of Human Service in the Twenty-First Century* (New York: Palgrave Macmilian, 2007).

20. See ibid., 200-02.

21. See Talós, "Sozialstaatsbilanz," 13-18.

22. See *Der Standard Online*, Newsroom, 5 Feb. 2002, http://www.derStandard.at, accessed 30 Nov. 2008.

23. See ÖVP/FPÖ, "Österreich neu regieren: Regierungsprogramm der österreichischen Bundesregierung für die XXI. Gesetzgebungsperiode," (Vienna 2000), 18 Feb. 2002, Bundeskanzleramt Österreich, http://www.austria.gv.at/, accessed 30 Nov. 2008.

24. Amendment to ASVG and parallel regulations, see "Presseaussendungen der Parlamentskorrespondenz," Republik Österreich Parlament, 6 July 2001, http://www.parlament.gv.at/portal/page?_pageid=908,132238&_dad=portal&_schema=PORTAL, accessed 30 Nov. 2008.

25. "Ausgewählte Entscheidungen und Prüfungsbeschlüsse," Verfassungsgerichtshof Österreich (VfGH), 10 Oct. 2003, http://www.vfgh.gv.at/presse.html, accessed 1 Dec. 2008.

26. Parliamentary decision about the third Revision of the Social Insurance Act 2004 (3. *Sozialversicherungs-Änderungsgesetz* 2004), see "Presseaussendungen der Parlamentskorrespondenz," Republik Österreich Parlament, 10 Dec. 2004, http://www.parlament.gv.at/portal/page?_pageid=908,132238&_dad=portal&_schema=PORTAL, accessed 1 Dec. 2008.

27. These measures had to be rolled back after several months because of administrative and legal problems.

28. Revision of Social Legislation (*Sozialrechts-Änderungsgesetz*) 2000, Pensions Reform Act (*Pensionsreformgesetz*) 2000 from 7 May 2000, see "Presseaussendungen der Parlamentskorrespondenz," Republik Österreich Parlament, 5 July 2000, 6 July 2001, and Budget Accessory Act (*Budgetbegleitgesetz*) 2001 from 11 Nov. 2000, 23 Nov. 2000, http://www.parlament.gv.at/portal/page?_pageid=908,132238&_dad=portal&_schema=PORTAL, accessed 30 Nov. 2008.

29. Ibid., 20 Feb. 2002.

30. Company Pension Act (*betriebliches Mitarbeitervorsorgegesetz*) from 12 June 2002, see ibid., 12 June 2002.

31. Individual Provision Act (*Gesetz über die Zukunftsvorsorge*) from 19 Sept. 2002, see ibid., 19 Sept. 2002.

32. Business Hours Act 2003 from 8 July 2003, see ibid., 8 July 2003.

33. Budget Accessory Act passed on 11 June 2003, see ibid., 11 June 2003.

34. Labor Market Reform Act 2004, passed on 16 June 2004, see ibid., 16 June 2004.

35. ÖVP/FPÖ, "Regierungsprogramm der XXII. Gesetzgebungsperiode," 28 Feb. 2003. Bundeskanzleramt Österreich, http://www.austria.gv.at/, accessed 30 Nov. 2008.

36. Employment Promotion Act (*Beschäftigungsförderungsgesetz*) passed on 28 September 2005, see "Presseaussendungen der Parlamentskorrespondenz," Republik Österreich Parlament, 28 Sept. 2005, http://www.parlament.gv.at/portal/page?_pageid=908,132238&_dad=portal&_schema=PORTAL, accessed 1 Dec. 2008.

37. See Herbert Obinger and Emmerich Tálos, *Sozialstaat Österreich zwischen Kontinuität und Umbau* (Wiesbaden: VS Verlag für Sozialwissenschaften, 2006), 144.

38. Parliamentary decision of 12 May 2005, see "Presseaussendungen der Parlamentskorrespondenz," Republik Österreich Parlament, 12 May 2005, http://www.parlament.gv.at/portal/page?_pageid=908,132238&_dad=portal&_schema=PORTAL, accessed 1 Dec. 2008.

39. As a part of the Budget Accessory Act 2003, see ibid., 11 June 2003.

40. Harmonization of Pensions Act (*Pensionsharmonisierungsgesetz*), see ibid., 18 Nov. 2004.

41. In spring 2006, the regulation for the heavy workers was specified. Persons who have worked for forty-five years, are older than sixty, and have done at least ten years of heavy labor within the last twenty years may retire early under advantageous conditions. Revision of Social Legislation (*Sozialrechtsänderungsgesetz*) 2004 from 12 July 2006, see ibid., 12 July 2006. The downside of this regulation is that women and people who have done heavy labor more than twenty years ago don't benefit from it; see "Newsroom," *Der Standard Online*, 16 Feb. 2006.

42. ÖVP/FPÖ, "Regierungsprogramm der österreichischen Bundesregierung für die XXII Gesetzgebungsperiode," Vienna 2003, 28 Feb. 2003, Bundeskanzleramt Österreich, http://www.austria.gv.at/, accessed 30 Nov. 2008.

43. Budget Accessory Act 2003 from 11 June 2003, see "Presseaussendungen der Parlamentskorrespondenz," Republik Österreich Parlament, 11 June 2003, http://www.parlament.gv.at/portal/page?_pageid=908,132238&_dad=portal&_schema=PORTAL, accessed 1 Dec. 2008.

44. Parliamentary decision of 9 Dec. 2004, see ibid., 9 Dec. 2004.

45. Health Reform Act (*Gesundheitsreformgesetz*) 2005, passed unanimously in parliament on 10 Dec. 2004, see ibid., 10 Dec. 2004.

46. Federal Budget Acts (*Bundesfinanzgesetze*) 2003 and 2004 of 18 June 2003, see ibid., 18 June 2004.

47. See "Newsroom," *Der Standard Online*, 19 June 2003 and 13 August 2003, http://derstandard.at/.

48. Tax Reform Act (*Steuerreformgesetz*) 2005 from 6 May 2004, see "Presseaussendungen der Parlamentskorrespondenz," Republik Österreich Parlament, 6 May 2004, http://www.parlament.gv.at/portal/page?_pageid=908,132238&_dad=portal&_schema=PORTAL, accessed 1 Dec. 2008.

49. See Obinger and Tálos, *Sozialstaat Österreich*, 191-200.

50. For more details, see Obinger and Tálos, *Sozialstaat Österreich*.

51. See ÖVP/FPÖ, "Österreich neu regieren: Regierungsprogramm der XXI. Gesetzgebungsperiode."

52. Children's Allowance Act (*Kinderbetreuungsgeldgesetz*) of 4 July 2002, "Presseaussendungen der Parlamentskorrespondenz," Republik Österreich Parlament, 4 July 2002, http://www.parlament.gv.at/portal/page?_pageid=908,132238&_dad=portal&_schema=PORTAL, accessed 1 Dec. 2008.

53. Revision of the Children's Allowance Act of 10 July 2003, see ibid., 10 July 2003, and Revision of the Children's Allowance Act of 24 May 2006, see ibid., 24 May 2006.

54. Family Hospice Leave (*Familienhospizkarenz*), see ibid., 25 May 2005.

55. See ibid., 26 May 2004.

56. See "Newsroom," *Der Standard Online*, 7 and 10 October 2003, http://derstandard.at/.

57. School Law Package (*Schulrechtspaket*) 2005 of 8 July 2005, see "Presseaussendungen der Parlamentskorrespondenz," Republik Österreich Parlament, 8 July 2005, http://www.parlament.gv.at/portal/page?_pageid=908,132238&_dad=portal&_schema=PORTAL, accessed 1 Dec. 2008.

58. Decision of 10 Nov. 2005, see "Ausgewählte Entscheidungen und Prüfungsbeschlüsse," Verfassungsgerichtshof Österreich (VfGH), 10 Nov. 2005, http://www.vfgh.gv.at/presse.html, accessed 1 Dec. 2008.

59. See "News," 9 July 2006, http://www.orf.at/, and "Newsroom," *Der Standard Online*, 13 July 2006.

60. Passed as a part of the Revision of Social Legislation Act (*Sozialrechtsänderungsgesetz*) 2006 on 12 July 2006, see "Presseaussendungen der Parlamentskorrespondenz," Republik Österreich Parlament, 12 July 2006, http://www.parlament.gv.at/portal/page?_pageid=908,132238&_dad=portal&_schema=PORTAL, accessed 1 Dec. 2008.

61. See "Newsroom," *Der Standard Online*, 24 May and 2 June 2006, http://derstandard.at/.

62. Revision of the Equal Treatment Act (*Gleichbehandlungsgesetz*) of 26 May 2004, see "Presseaussendungen der Parlamentskorrespondenz," Republik Österreich Parlament, 26 May 2004, http://www.parlament.gv.at/portal/page?_pageid=908,132238&_dad=portal&_schema=PORTAL, accessed 1 Dec. 2008.

63. See "Newsroom," *Der Standard Online*, 5 Nov. 2005, http://derstandard.at/.

64. Ibid., 5 Sept. 2005 and 26 Jan. 2006.

65. Parliamentary decision of 29 March 2006, see "Presseaussendungen der Parlamentskorrespondenz," Republik Österreich Parlament, 29 March 2006, http://www.parlament.gv.at/portal/page?_pageid=908,132238&_dad=portal&_schema=PORTAL, accessed 1 Dec. 2008.

66. Revision of the Settlement and Residence Act (*Niederlassungs- und Aufenthaltsgesetz*) 2002 of 9 July 2002, see ibid., 9 July 2002.

67. Revision of the Asylum Law (*Asylgesetz-Novelle*) 2003 of 23 Oct. 2003, ibid. 23 Oct. 2003.

68. "Ausgewählte Entscheidungen und Prüfungsbeschlüsse," Verfassungsgerichtshof Österreich (VfGH), 3 Oct. 2003, http://www.vfgh.gv.at/presse.html, accessed 1 Dec. 2008.

69. Migration Law Package (*Fremdenrechtspaket*) 2005, see "Presseaussendungen der Parlamentskorrespondenz," Republik Österreich Parlament, 7 July 2005, http://www.parlament.gv.at/portal/page?_pageid=908,132238&_dad=portal&_schema=PORTAL, accessed 1 Dec. 2008.

70. See ibid., 24 March 2004.

71. As a part of the "Migration Law Package (*Fremdenrechtspaket*) 2005," see ibid. 7 July 2005.

72. Revision of the Citizenship Law (*Staatsbürgerschaftsrechts-Novelle*) 2005, see ibid., 1 March 2006.

73. See "Newsroom," *Der Standard Online*, 24 Nov. 2005, http://derstandard.at/.

74. As a part of the School Law Package (*Schulrechtspaket*) 2005, see "Presseaussendungen der Parlamentskorrespondenz," Republik Österreich Parlament, 7 Dec. 2005, http://www.parlament.gv.at/portal/page?_pageid=908,132238&_dad=portal&_schema=PORTAL, accessed 1 Dec. 2008.

75. See EUROSTAT, Yearbook 2003, and "Statistics," 2005, Statistics Austria, http://www.volkszaehlung.at/web_en/statistics/index.html, accessed 1 Dec. 2008.

76. See "OECD Family Database," Organization for Economic Co-operation and Development, http://www.oecd.org/document/4/0,3343,en_2649_34819_37836996_1_1_1_1,00.html, accessed 11 Aug. 2008.

77. "Key Findings," 2007, Migrant Integration Policy Index (MIPEX), British Council/Migration Policy Group, http://www.integrationindex.eu/findings/, accessed 11 Aug. 2008.

78. See *Bericht über die soziale Lage 2003-2004* (Vienna: Bundesministrium für Soziale Sicherheit, Generationen und Konsumentenschutz, 2005).

79. See Statistics Austria, ed., *Einkommen, Armut und Lebensbedingungen: Ergebnisse aus EU-SILC 2006*, 11 Aug. 2008 http://www.statistik.at/dynamic/wcmsprod/idcplg?IdcService=GET_NATIVE_FILE&dID=64402&dDocName=030260, accessed 1 Dec. 2008.

80. "Statistics," 2001-2007, Statistics Austria, http://www.statistik.at/.

81. See Statistics Austria, ed., *Einkommen, Armut und Lebensbedingungen 2006*.

82. "Statistics," 2001-2007, Statistics Austria, http://www.statistik.at/.

83. Christiane Rille-Pfeiffer and Olaf Kapella, eds., *Kinderbetreuungsgeld: Evaluierung einer familienpolitischen Maßnahme* (Innsbruck: Studienverlag, 2007).

84. Heinz Fassmann, *2. Österreichischer Migrations und Integrationsbericht 2001-2006* (Klagenfurt: Drava Verlag, 2007).

85. SPÖ/ÖVP, "Regierungsprogramm der österreichischen Bundesregierung für die XXIII. Gesetzgebungsperiode," 2007, Bundeskanzleramt Österreich, 11 Aug. 2008, http://www.austria.gv.at/DocView.axd?CobId=19542, accessed 1 Dec. 2008.

The Demise of "Minoritenplatz-Schleicherei": Eighty-Four Month of *Wende* Higher Education Policy in Austria

Josef Leidenfrost[1]

Introduction

It is remarkable that the policy field of "higher education" is included in this volume on the Schüssel years in Austria 2000-2007. Higher education is regularly ignored when taking stock of historical developments in any given era.[1] In the basic handbook *Politik in Österreich* edited by several Austrian political scientists,[2] thirteen different key policy areas were covered; "higher education" was not among them. Oswald Panagl's and Peter Gerlich's *Wörterbuch der politischen Sprache in Österreich*[3] has entries on fraternities and student politics (*Studentenverbindungen* and *studentische Politik*), but none on higher education policies (*Hochschul-/Universitätspolitik*), let alone higher education reforms (*Hochschul-/Universitätsreform*), even though Austrian higher education marched at least through five major reforms since 1945. Only Nikolaus Dimmel and Josef Schmee's *Politische Kultur in Österreich 2000-2005* contains a contribution by Claudia von Werlhof that carries at least "*Hochschul*" in its title.[4] Occasionally, celebratory *Festschriften* for declared experts in the field of higher education politics (such as Manfried Welan, Christian Brünner, and Wolfgang Mantl[5]) may cover some specific aspects of higher education

---

1. The author would like to thank the following people for sharing first hand information and helping to find books, articles, and web entries: Ursula Brustmann, Renate Eisenbock, Wolfgang Fingernagel and his team, Martin Haidinger, Anni Horak, Heinz Kasparovsky, Gudrun Luger, Norbert Neumann, Ramona Reschenhofer, Christian Ruhs, Alois Söhn, Kurt Sohm and Fritz Wendl and his team. He would also like to thank Elisabeth Fiorioli, Heinz Kasparovsky, Helmut Konrad, and Barbara Weitgruber for their critical comments on the draft mansucript, and Günter Bischof for a thorough editing of the text and translations of quotations into English. Leopold Lippert and Terrence McElhaney helped the author to get the manuscript ready for press. Responsibility for the contents exclusively rests upon the author.

policy in general, while they shy away from the partisan political discourses of higher education policies in Austria.

Higher education reform, however, was high on the agenda during the years 2000 to 2007 of the coalition governments of Wolfgang Schüssel with the FPÖ/BZÖ of Susanne Riess-Passer, Herbert Haupt, and Hubert Gorbach. Higher education as a policy field went through changing paradigms, some as a result of careful planning in the domestic arena, others unfolding almost by coincidence or as a result of outside pressure.[6] Granting Austrian universities autonomous rules and charging modest tuition fees to Austrian students for the first time in a generation represented dramatic changes. New access regulations for foreign students and selection procedures for Austrian students in certain academic disciplines at public universities as a result of a European Court decision in 2005 represent yet two other major changes. So do the new laws affecting higher education governance as a result of long planned reforms as well as of short-term decisions coming along with the implementation of the "Bologna goals" after 1999. Extensive media coverage of higher education issues made these paradigmatic changes part of a wider Austrian conversation. The policy decisions unleashing some of the most important changes are the subject of this essay.

Elisabeth Gehrer and the Resetting of the Higher Education Policy Agenda

After several weeks of negotiations for a new coalition government between the Social Democratic Party of Austria (*Sozialdemokratische Partei Österreichs*, or SPÖ), the conservative Austrian People's Party (*Österreichische Volkspartei*, or ÖVP), and the right-wing Freedom Party of Austria (*Freiheitliche Partei Österreichs*, or FPÖ) in which all possible variations and combinations of parties had been discussed[7], the new coalition was presented to the media and to the public on 4 February 2000. The result, namely a small coalition between Wolfgang Schüssel's ÖVP and Jörg Haider's FPÖ, was a big surprise to all observers. For the first time, the populist right-wing Haider party was included in a governing coalition in Austrian politics.

Whereas some of the nine FPÖ ministers and secretaries of state in the Schüssel/Riess-Passer team were mostly unknowns, the name of the new higher education minister Elisabeth Gehrer was familiar to the majority of the Austrians. In 1980, Gehrer, a former primary school teacher, had become a member of the city council of Bregenz, Austria's westernmost provincial capital. Ten years later, she joined the Vorarlberg provincial government, in charge of the education portfolio. In both positions, she had been strongly involved in setting the agenda and making decisions in education policy on the provincial level. Gehrer entered Vienna politics with a reputation of toughness. When she was first appointed federal minister for Education and Culture in 1995, the press dubbed her the Alpine "power lady" and "miracle lady" (*Powerfrau aus den Alpen, Frau Wunderwuzzi, Mutter Courage vom Bodensee*).[8]

Her new office as minister was located in the Palais Starhemberg in Vienna's first district on the Minoritenplatz, ever since the late nineteenth century the "powerhouse" of education politics in Austria.[9] In the new Schüssel/Riess-Passer coalition government, Gehrer's new portfolio was widely expanded on 1 April 2000. The Education Ministry was merged with the former Ministry of Science and Transport and became the new super Ministry of Education, Science, and Culture. Such a merger of the several educational competences had already been discussed publicly during the late 1990s in the discussion forum of experts *Österreich Zukunftsreich* (originally launched by then Vice-Chancellor Wolfgang Schüssel), and during the election campaign of 1999, Gehrer herself raised the issue of such a merger.[10] At the time of the late 1999/early 2000 coalition negotiations between the SPÖ and ÖVP, even the chief negotiators Chancellor Viktor Klima and Wolfgang Schüssel had talked about it.[11]

This accumulation of tasks and duties turned Gehrer's ministry into one of the new key ministries (*Schlüsselressorts*) in the new ÖVP/FPÖ coalition government and gave Gehrer added cache to Schüssel's cabinet. With the merger it became "the highest administrative and planning institution of the Republic of Austria for schools, higher education (in particular universities and *Fachhochschulen*), adult education, scientific research and international affairs in the field of science, the federal museums, and for the protection of historical monuments."[12]

Gehrer as the new conservative ÖVP minister for education, science, and research tried to turn the traditionally "red" ministry "black." Yet even with the new "black" boss, the institution was —for the time being— largely Social Democratic "red" since many of the key positions within the higher education administration had been held by Social Democrats, who had been appointed by the previous SPÖ ministers Hertha Firnberg, Heinz Fischer, Hilde Havlicek, Rudolf Scholten, and Caspar Einem (between 1970 and 2000). Only during the years of ÖVP Minister Erhard Busek (1989-1995) had some changes been made with the appointments of a few conservatives in leading positions within the ministerial hierarchy.[13] Gehrer's taking office and sweeping changing of colors in the ministry (*Farbwechsel im Ministerium*) were naturally welcomed by ÖVP officials as well as some university people.[14]

After February 2000, then, education policy in Austria was dominated by Minister Gehrer and her advisers, who had served in previous administrations or were new appointments. Some operated discreetly in the background like Gehrer's *chef de cabinet* since 1995 Peter Mahringer who was the *eminence grise* in the powerful ministerial bureaucracy. "P.M." (his initials) had already served Erhard Busek as close adviser during the latter's term as Vice Mayor of Vienna.[15] Another force to be reckoned with was Sigurd Höllinger, the "red" director general of the ministry and mastermind behind many of the reforms in higher education during the 1990s.[16] He had been hired by Hertha Firnberg in 1976, and Minister Heinz Fischer promoted him to director general for higher education in 1986.[17] Some observers even characterized him as the quasi-minister (*eigentlicher Wissenschaftsminister*).[18]

Gehrer handpicked her own team of experts. Among the seven new directors general in the ministry appointed during her tenure from 2000 to 2007, she chose three women, namely Brigitte Böck, Heidrun Strohmeyer, and Barbara Weitgruber, a renowned expert on the internationalization of higher education,.[19] Outside the ministry, Gehrer regularly consulted experts of her personal choice.[20] The most political body was Chancellor Schüssel's personal kitchen cabinet starting off the week every Monday morning at ÖVP party headquarters. Andreas Khol (third president of the National Assembly), Wilhelm Molterer (ÖVP party whip at the parliament), and Minister Gehrer faithfully attended these sessions that were chaired by the Chancellor and reviewed old policies and set strategies for the new policy initiatives.[21] The agenda with which Gehrer had to contend as minister was mostly determined by preset conditions; the inheritance she accepted was burdensome.

The 1990s: The Maastricht Criteria Confront the Mass Universities

The first center-right government of the Second Austrian Republic began its work in difficult times. On the one hand, the new political actors in Vienna were confronting a deep aversion to tackling the backlog of reforms (*Reformstau*) left by the increasingly paralyzed grand SPÖ/ÖVP coalition government of Viktor Klima and Wolfgang Schüssel. On the other hand, many of the new "incoming" decision makers and their new (and not so new) advisers were obsessed with the desire to change things now that they were in the position to bring about fundamental turnabout—the *Wende*. [22]

In the field of higher education, the legacies of the past were distinct and multi-faceted. They had been shaped by strong and weak ministers and their administrations, some cooperative, others oppositional. Four higher education ministers had been from the Socialist Party, namely Hertha Firnberg (1970-1983), Heinz Fischer (1983-1987), Rudolf Scholten (1995-1997), and Caspar Einem (1997-2000); two had been from the conservative ÖVP, namely Hans Tuppy (1987-1989) and Erhard Busek (1989-1995).

When Chancellor Bruno Kreisky established his Socialist government in 1970, he appointed Hertha Firnberg as the first Minister for Science (in fact, Higher Education!) and Research in postwar Austria.[23] The trained social scientist Firnberg emerged as the "*grande dame*" of higher education during her thirteen years in power.[24] Her most far reaching reform was the *Universitätsorganisationsgesetz* (UOG) 1975, which "democratized" the Austrian universities and did away with many of the hierarchical structures. It probably was a delayed outgrowth of the 1968 student movement in Austria.[25]

Heinz Fischer's term as science minister in the SPÖ/FPÖ coalition governments led by Fred Sinowatz and then Franz Vranitzky (1983-1987) was unspectacular, continuing the policies set into place by Firnberg. In the first SPÖ/ÖVP coalition government under Chancellor Vranitzky and Vice Chancellor Alois Mock, the pendulum started to swing in the other direction. In early 1987, the respected university professor Hans Tuppy was appointed Minister for Science and Research. He had been a candidate for a ministerial post ever since the late 1960s. A favorite for the position of the minister of education under ÖVP Chancellor Josef Klaus, party strategists favored a younger candidate, so Klaus appointed the upstart Alois Mock instead.[26] After seventeen years of "red" control over higher education policies, Tuppy in 1987 was the first "black" science minister. As a university professor for biochemistry and a former rector of the University of Vienna as well as a former president of the Austrian Academy of Sciences, he was met with high hopes. During his term as minister, the introduction of the bachelor degree in Austrian higher education was widely discussed for the first time. It was rejected at that time but was implemented ultimately more than ten years later when Austria *had to adopt* the bachelor/master system through the "Bologna process" with its new system of higher education degrees.[27] Also during the Tuppy years, Austria entered the dynamic processes of the European student mobility programs even before the country joined the European Union in 1995 in the fourth enlargement round. Austria organized its own "pre-ERASMUS" student mobility program, a privately funded scholarship to support the mobility of university students within Europe.[28]

In the spring of 1989, Erhard Busek succeeded Tuppy on the Minoritenplatz. He brought strong credentials to the job of Minister of Science and Research, having served as the People's Party speaker for higher education issues in the Austrian Parliament during the late 1970s. The fall of the Iron Curtain and the opening of the "new democracies" along Austria's eastern border (*Ostöffnung*) unleashed a profound boom in European integration. Busek was an intellectual in his own right and had been a key participant in the "*Mitteleuropa*" debates of the 1980s. He initiated innovation and major changes in higher education, including the new regulations in study law as a first step towards the *Europeanization* of curricula in Austria.[29] Busek also created the *Fachhochschulen*, a new tier of applied sciences in the Austrian higher education system.[30] In 1993, he also pushed through parliament a new organizational law for university reform (*Universitätsorganisationsgesetz*, or UOG 1993).

Rudolf Scholten, a former banker, succeeded Busek in 1995 as science minister in a new SPÖ/ÖVP coalition government again led by Franz Vranitzky and now Wolfgang Schüssel (in direct succession of Erhard Busek). He had already served as Minister of Education and Culture since 1990, being noticeably more interested in culture and the arts than in general education policies.[31] When Scholten began negotiations for the first annual budget under the new Social Democratic–Conservative coalition in early 1996, it soon became apparent that higher education would also be affected by the budget cuts necessary in all branches of the federal government. These were driven by the so-called "Maastricht criteria." European Union member states who wanted to join the European Economic and Monetary Union (EMU) and adopt the Euro as their currency were forced to lower their budgetary deficits under a certain percentage determined by Article 121(1) of the Treaty of Maastricht (European Community Treaty).[32]

These necessary budget cuts, which soon became known as the government's savings plan (*Sparpaket*),[33] were also severe in higher education. The cuts included the reduction of student social support funds from the public coffers (now awarded by the students' academic achievements rather than mere social need), as well as the reduction of extra teaching assignments (*Lehraufträge*) for teachers, which amounted to a sizable pay cut for non-tenured lecturers. Moreover, free public transportation for students, one of the major achievements of the Kreisky years, was canceled.[34]

A wave of resistance swept onto Austria's streets to fight these cuts in higher education. Tens of thousands of university students marched in the streets;[35] some rectors (that is, university chancellors) gave aggressive press conferences (one of them even wearing the costume of the Grim Reaper);[36] other rectors published open letters in newspapers, alerting the public to the severe consequences of a declining higher education system which would result from the planned budget cuts.[37] The protests culminated on 12 March 1996, when the members of the new Vranitzky/Schüssel government walked across the *Ballhausplatz*—above ground—from the Federal Chancellery to the Federal President's offices. There they were greeted with previously unheard of catcalls and jeers.[38] This moment was more than symbolic, signaling the beginning of the end of twenty-five years of Social Democratic higher education policies.

Rudolf Scholten's tenure as science minister was short-lived, lasting for a mere 122 days since Chancellor Vranitzky himself resigned in mid-January 1997 and handed the reigns to his successor Viktor Klima. In the following reshuffle of cabinet positions, Caspar Einem was appointed as the new Minister for Science and Transport [sic!] in the new Klima/Schüssel SPÖ/ÖVP coalition government. Einem had started out as Secretary of State in the Federal Chancellery before he became Interior Minister in spring 1995.[39] Contrary to his predecessor Scholten, Einem actually showed initiative in his job as Science Minister. He acted as an honest agent of societal change, including higher education issues.[40] He tackled several topics and ignited some spectacular initiatives such as the plan to send management consultants to observe professors' academic performance in the classroom.[41]

On the occasion of Austria's first presidency of the European Union in 1998, Einem published and presented to the public an ambitious "White Paper on Higher Education in Austria."[42] There he drew up a road map for changes, but could not implement it because he lost his job after the snap national elections in the fall 1999. Still Einem left a lasting legacy to higher education in Austria. During his tenure, he signed the "Bologna Declaration" for Austria in June 1999, which introduced the three-tiered degree system (bachelor/master/doctorate) into Austrian higher education.[43]

While Einem served as minister, the implementation of the UOG 1993, initiated by Busek, entered into its final phase. This thorough organizational reform agenda initiated new tasks, organizational structures, and rights and duties for the principal university governing bodies (senates, rectors, vice rectors, faculty bodies, deans, and joint curricular committees). It also allowed for expanded latitude for decision making in the individual universities.[44] Initially, the UOG 1993 legislation had been praised. Yet later on critics denounced it for coming into effect over such an extended period of time, its costliness, and the morale problems it created among many university employees.[45] At a time when the ongoing reforms had not yet been fully implemented, an even more radical reform agenda was already pushed, namely the full legal autonomy of universities (*Vollrechtsfähigkeit der Universitäten*).[46]

From Kowtowing to Autonomy: The University Act of 2002 and the Demise of the *"Minoritenplatz-Schleicherei"*

The new coalition government sworn in on 4 February 2000 was determined to redevelop the university organization reforms beyond the UOG 1993 and its half-realized reform that had been stopped in its tracks by the 1999 elections. The agreement adopted by the ÖVP and FPÖ coalition partners included the commitment to embark on a reform process resulting in the full autonomy of Austrian universities.[47] Only a few weeks into her new office, Minister Gehrer announced that high on her priority list was making autonomous universities full legal entities.[48] Experts from Austrian universities had compiled and debated a comprehensive position paper about the restructuring of Austrian universities in a global competitive environment in the late 1990s.[49] This was a groundbreaking step towards the positioning of universities independent from the daily petty interferences of the political system and the heavy-handed ministerial bureaucracy.[50]

Minister of Education, Science and Culture Elisabeth Gehrer and the mastermind of university reforms in Austria, Director General Sigurd Höllinger

picture credits:
Toms Grinbergs, University of Latvia, Riga

Stefan Titscher who had acted as the coordinating editor of this study was a recognized expert in organizational development and change management. As the former head of the Senate of the Vienna University of Economics and Business Administration, he had gained a lot of experience in changing university governance.[51] Late in the year 2000, Gehrer hired him to help conceptualize and write the law and prepare the implementation of the new system. Titscher and Sigurd Höllinger, the still powerful Director General, monitored the details in the reform steps together. The new law's cornerstones were the full legal capacity of universities, multi-year performance contracts with the Ministry, global budgets covering several years, new regulations for teaching staff, promotion of talent within the universities, simplified administrative processes, the shortening of the duration of studies for all majors, and compulsory evaluation systems with appropriate follow-up measures.[52]

In August 2001, in the midst of the summer holidays when most Austrians are vacationing, a draft proposal (*Gestaltungsentwurf*) was presented to public. According to the critics, this tactic was both prudent and sly. Subsequently the draft law (*Gesetzesentwurf*) was made public in early March 2002. The deadline for comments and further feedback was again set very tightly for 19 April 2002.[53] During this short ten-week consultation period, predominately negative and critical statements from stakeholders, lobbying groups, and individual citizens surfaced.[54] As is usual with such bold reforms, narrow-minded insistence on tradition and resistance to change in the universities were profoundly challenged. It was hotly discussed in the communities affected by it and had both defenders and critics.[55]

For the first time in modern higher education politics, the discussion was also carried on electronically via the worldwide web, which was deliberately utilized during the gestation phase of the new law. The Ministry even set up a special "*Weltklasse*" (world class) homepage to engage in a discourse about the coming systemic changes.[56] Critics in the Viennese weekly magazine *Falter* made fun of the notion of Austrian "world-class" universities, arguing that,

> "*Weltklasse*" is a slogan used in the lingo of educational reforms on the university level. According to the present federal government and the responsible Minister Gehrer, the Austrian universities are destined to be "tops in Europe in education and research." The way stations on the road to *W.* [world-class] are the new university teacher contractual employment law, the development of profiles, and the university law 2002. Critics think that the boasting inherent in the term *W[eltklasse]* is laughable.[57]

Indeed, the rhetoric "*Weltklasse*" was used extensively as a marketing tool by the Ministry via the "*Weltklasse*" homepage. At the same time, it was savaged by the critics and antagonists in and outside of the university.[58]

The university communities were given the chance to make their voices heard too and present their views to a wider public. Erwin Niederwieser, the long-time Social Democratic member of parliament and education party spokesman from the Tyrol, launched yet another web page.[59] In addition, the universities of Innsbruck and Vienna[60] operated their own sub-web pages dedicated exclusively to the discussion of the new law. This parallel public sphere ran counter to the government's campaign (*Gegenöffentlichkeit*). Rarely has Austrian civil society engaged public higher education issues with such intensity.

The opponents of the *Universitätsgesetz* 2002—some of them plainly partisan—engaged in several other forms of public discourse, countermanding the government rhetoric in promoting the new law. The Austrian Green Party organized a day-long parliamentary symposium with leading educational experts on the pointed question "University Law 2002: World-Class or Cul-De-Sac?" ("*Universitätsgesetz 2002: Weltklasse oder Sackgasse*?"). The Social Democrats filed an official complaint with the Austrian Constitutional Court against some specific clauses of the law.[61] This court confirmed the basic constitutionality of the law—with only three clauses on the performance agreements being revoked in the end.[62] The plenary session of the Austrian Parliament at last took up the law, debated it, and passed it on a partisan majority vote by the ÖVP and FPÖ representatives on 11 July 2002.[63]

As the new law was being implemented, it broke with many traditions dear to the stakeholders in the Ministry and the universities. Traditional paradigms were shifted as better measurable performance and productivity were being expected. The new multi-year contracts—the performance agreements (*Leistungsvereinbarungen*) between the universities and the Ministry—signaled the end of hidebound traditions such as the old-fashioned negotiation of resources between ministers and their favorite professors (*Minoritenplatz-Schleicherei*).

Minoritenplatz-Schleicherei served as an accurate yet disrespectful description of the sneaky deal-making in the Ministry's corridors. The groveling and kowtowing of university staff to the top ministerial decision-makers (the director general, the Minister's *chef de cabinet*, or even the minister him/herself) in their pompous first- and second-floor offices in the Ministry located on the Minoritenplatz was legendary. It took non-Austrians to publicly denounce these special habits. Academic immigrants from Germany, namely Stefan Laske, professor of business administration and chairman of the academic senate at the University of Innsbruck, and Wolf Dietrich Freiherr von Fircks-Burgstaller, rector of the Vienna University for Veterinary Medicine,[64] were among the first to use this specialist term to castigate the brazen favoritism. *Minoritenplatz-Schleicherei*, as a time-worn technique well established in the former imperial capital, was aptly characterized by seasoned observers from the provinces such as Helmut Konrad, rector of the University of Graz from 1993 to 1997, nevertheless an intimate connoisseur of the Vienna power games himself:

> [...] the Ministry always doled out the budget appropriations to the individual institutions using less than transparent criteria [...] The Minoritenplatz in Vienna, seat of the [Science] Ministry, was the rarefied center of power. This favored the Vienna universities, who knew how to play the channels of intervention more directly. To express it more pointedly: the number of flower bouquets often served the crucial advancement of one's causes.[65]

A similar view of the system is held by Kurt Grünewald, a professor at Innsbruck University (and member of the Green party). He saw the Austrian universities' desire for autonomy as directly related to the frustrations and disappointments with lengthy and complicated bureaucratic ways of decision-making in the Ministry. But he also criticized the universities for having played their share in the opaque inflexibilities of the old system:

> The struggle for personnel, supplies, new instruments, necessary renovations, and new buildings, as well as the regular experiences with questionable new [professorial] appointments [...] were the main factors [in the call for more autonomy]. To be fair, the universities and their governing bodies contributed their share to the ongoing mismanagement. Both the Ministry and the universities were characterized by inside favoritism, deceptions, vanity, and snobbery to the point of arrogant condescension and lusting for power. Yet the opposite was the case too.[66]

Sigurd Höllinger, the long-serving high Ministry official and himself one of the key actors on the Minoritenplatz has his own opinion on the pre-2002 kowtowing university crowd. Soon after his retirement in the fall 2005, he was first asked in an interview: "You once observed that your daily fare consisted of griping assistant professors, intriguing department chairs, and incompetent student representatives."[67] His answer was stunning:

> Much has changed, yet this still goes on. Once something does not work out well in the new system, then the search begins for support from the Minoritenplatz. [...] It will take time before one knows where the political critique is going [...] It also happens that errant scholars end up in the Ministry, demanding that the decision of a chancellor be reversed.[68]

The agenda and duties of the Ministry have changed as a result of the paradigmatic role reversal in the new UG 2002 era, the power shifts from the center to the periphery of the universities in the provinces, and the pending necessity for reorganization. When Minister Gehrer was grilled in Parliament about the consequences of the university reform in her Ministry, she put it bluntly: "Of course, the [University Law of 2002] had repercussions inside the Ministry. The Ministry will be leaner, fewer people will work in it, they will engage in and are already being trained for new tasks."[69] When Gehrer left office in January 2007, the Ministry's staff indeed had been cut by some 300 positions.[70] Time will tell whether those staying are properly trained for their multiple new duties.

The new university law came into full force on 1 January 2004, after a transitional period that followed its passing by Parliament in the summer of 2002. The implementation, at times, was rather turbulent. An incident at the University of Vienna in early 2004 illustrates the turmoil. It happened when emotions had been stirred up during the decision-making process of the controversial new organizational plan for the university. Students had already disturbed a meeting of the university's Senate and occupied a meeting room a week before a panel discussion was scheduled for the eve of 20 January 2004. The partisan think-tank *SPÖ Zukunfts- und Kulturwerkstätte* organized a forum on universities between decline and world-class status.

The invited panel featured some illustrious speakers, namely Georg Winckler, the rector of the University of Vienna; Höllinger, the general secretary of the Science Ministry; Josef Broukal, a former TV anchor and Socialist higher education spokesman and member of parliament; and Patrice Fuchs, chairwoman of the Austrian National Union of Students. Fuchs opened the discussion with her statement. When it was Höllinger's turn, the audience started applauding and booing, and continued to do so for several minutes. Banners were unfurled with slogans such as "Stop Studying—Begin Comprehending," "Smash the Org[anization] Plan," and "Winckler is ruining the University."[71]

Then a person jumped onto the podium and threw a cake at Winckler—it was a cream cheese cake. A few moments later another cake—this time a chocolate cake—flew in Höllinger's direction.[72] The scene quickly turned into pandemonium, and the forum was suspended. Chancellor Schüssel denounced the students' actions as a poor showing (*Armutszeugnis*); Minister Gehrer criticized it as an "incredible escalation" (*unglaubliche Eskalation*).[73] Whereas the chairpersons of the Austrian Student Association Patrice Fuchs and Ralph Schallmainer refused to take responsibility for the sticky sweet protests, other student representatives called the pie-tossing "a creative political means of protest" (*kreatives, politisches Mittel des Protests*).[74]

The *Universitätsgesetz* 2002 has been called the "law of the century," a *Jahrhundert-Gesetz*, yet it has already been amended three times since its first promulgation. This seems to indicate that not all of its regulations were written for the long-term. Another revision and fine-tuning is pending at the time of writing this article.

The Minister Leaving Through The Back Door: The Difficult (Re)Introduction of Tuition Fees

During the 1990s, the numbers of students at Austrian universities made serving them less manageable. Any Austrian high school graduate with a "*Matura*" diploma was entitled to attend any Austrian university free of charge.[75] Yet at the same time that student numbers increased dramatically, public expenditures for higher education were cut. This produced major bottlenecks in higher education financing and challenges for university governance and in over-filled lecture halls that no politician really wanted to explicitly address.[76] The progressive education reforms of the Kreisky years provided the children of the baby-boom generation unrivaled access to higher education in Austria. During the late 1990s, the political class was challenged to address the transfusion of these high school graduates into the higher education arena.

The budgetary cuts (*Sparpaket*) of 1996 induced by the "Maastricht criteria" mentioned above intensified debates about the financing of higher education. The students vigorously protested the cutting of social entitlements. The public discussion began to drift to topics such as alternative ways of financing higher education. It also began to address the alleged privileges of universities, including financial ones. Soon, the discourse arrived at the introduction of tuition fees. Newspapers commented critically on the student protest movement against budget cuts and even only discussing about tuition fees.[77]

Some politicians and parts of the university community began to favor the introduction of tuition fees. Even Social Democrats such as Helmut Konrad, the rector of the University of Graz, publicly made the case *for* tuition fees. He averred that tuition fees would be fairer than a *numerus clausus* and also more efficient than budget cuts (namely additional *Sparpakete*).[78] Elisabeth Gehrer, at that time Minister for Education and Culture but not responsible for higher education, started talking in public about the introduction of tuition fees at Austrian universities. She noted, "I have problems regarding the issue of charging tuition fees in universities since it might result in a war over basic beliefs [*Glaubenskrieg*]." She also stated that for the SPÖ coalition partner any public debate was *verboten*, which did not help matters.[79] Expert studies by economists Richard Sturn and Gerhard Wohlfahrt on tuition-free access to universities looked into alternative models of financing higher education.[80]

In the end, though, it was left to the *Wende* government to initiate change. The ÖVP/FPÖ coalition agreement of February 2000, entitled quite tellingly *Österreich neu regieren,* did not contain a policy goal on tuition fees. Yet the section on budget policies included a clause on "reviewing the targeting and equitable distribution of public spending" (*Überprüfung von öffentlichen Ausgaben auf Treffsicherheit und Verteilungsgerechtigkeit*), which called for a closer look into the adequacy of existing social support schemes.[81] Wolfgang Mazal, a University of Vienna professor of labor and social law, was asked to compile such a study during the summer of 2000. Like the coalition agreement, Mazal's report also did not contain recommendations on the introduction of tuition fees.[82]

However, during a mid-fall cabinet strategy session at the Federal Chancellery four days before a decisive Cabinet meeting, the die was cast in favor of tuition fees. On the evening of Friday, 15 September 2000, Chancellor Schüssel, Minister of Finance Karl-Heinz Grasser (at the time still a Ph.D. student in business administration at the University of Klagenfurt),[83] and Martin Bartenstein, the Minister of Economics and Labor, confronted Elisabeth Gehrer with the concrete plan to introduce tuition fees for *all* university students by 2001. The youthful Grasser played hardball with Gehrer and threatened to reduce Gehrer's budget by 2 billion Austrian Schillings unless she agreed on charging tuition fees. A reluctant Gehrer relented.[84] She felt manhandled, though, and was considering resigning from her post right after that meeting. Her chief of staff Mahringer talked her out of taking such a step.[85]

On 19 September 2000, the *Ministerrat* took the final decision to introduce tuition fees in all Austrian public universities.[86] This put an end to one of the most prominent achievements of the early years of Social Democratic education policy: in 1972 the Kreisky government had abolished all tuition fees.

The new regulations were presented to the press by Chancellor Schüssel and Vice Chancellor Riess-Passer who briefed the press in the *Pressefoyer* after the cabinet session. Minister Gehrer was not present during this press conference.[87] She had left the Chancellery by way of the backstairs.[88] The same evening, Gehrer went public during the primetime news program on Austrian Public Television, *Zeit im Bild*. She put a brave face on the introduction of tuition fees in explaining the new policy to the public:

> Even when I was minister of state [in Vorarlberg], I was favoring tuition fees in *Fachhochschulen*. I also support the partial introduction of fees for golden agers, long-time students, and those who work on second and third doctorates. 5,000 [Austrian] Schillings in tuition fees per semester is a very moderate amount; the socially weak will be safeguarded by stipends that will be available.[89]

In a newspaper interview published the next day, Gehrer characterized the sudden introduction of tuition fees as the result of a weekend brainstorming session! The partial introduction of fees for only certain students was not feasible. After all, the principal reason for tuition fees was to increase the quality of studies.[90]

The public outrage was immediate. Both students and university administrators reacted with prompt rejection of the announced tuition fees.[91] The Green and SPÖ opposition parties filed urgent motions in Parliament (*Dringliche Anfragen*). The ÖVP and FPÖ coalition partners, in turn, passed a special decision in Parliament (*Entschließungsantrag*) defending fees. They promised to increase scholarships and improve services offered by the universities. They also decided to install a student ombudsman with a new agenda of fighting deficiencies, maladministration, and poor services at universities.[92]

Students organized a broad range of nationwide protest activities.[93] Demonstrations were held in several cities. Sometimes these protests were actively supported by university chancellors such as Rector Winckler of the University of Vienna.[94] Similar to the public debate about the University Law 2002, the affected community communicated extensively via the worldwide web on the issue of tuition fees.[95] On the Minoritenplatz in Vienna, a quite spectacular sit-in action took place in the Ministry offices. In early October 2000, some students occupied the office of Director General Höllinger on the second floor of the Palais Starhemberg for two and one-half hours.[96] The government did not bow to the street protests. Based on the Cabinet's decision, the *Hochschultaxengesetz* was amended in early 2001 which finally made university tuition fees public law.

The (re)introduction of tuition fees in Austria produced some immediate results. For one, the number of enrolled students decreased from 227,948 (2000/01) to 182,805 (2001/02). Media commentaries had a heyday with this decline.[97] Probably it was the exclusion of the "*Karteileichen*" from the official statistics, namely those students who maintained their enrollment but did not take classes for multiple reasons, that explained the significant reduction in enrollment.[98] This improved the recording of active students, hence allowing administrators to plan more efficiently and improve teacher-student ratios. By 2004, enrollment figures were on the rise again. In the long run, it seems, the tuition fees did not lead to a permanent reduction of student numbers.[99]

Did the (re)introduction of tuition fees, along with a whole range of quality and efficiency measures for institutions of higher learning, enhance the efficiency in public universities? Economists Gudrun Biffl and Joe Isaac argued affirmatively in a position paper on the impact of tuition fees. They averred that it would produce more effective teaching methods and restructure the system towards faster graduation rates.[100] The fees, in the most rose-colored assessment, were supposed to improve overall study conditions in the universities—which only happened to some extent. Awareness among faculties and students has grown, however, about their respective responsibilities in the more effective use of public funds.[101]

Hans Robert Hansen, the former rector of the Vienna University of Business Administration, dismissed the introduction of tuition fees as the "triumph of fiscal over education policies."[102] In addition, educational scientist Hans Pechar stated that tuition fees represented yet another (involuntarily) contribution by students to consolidate the country's budget like already in the mid 1990s. The universities, though, would continue to survive. There would not be a state of emergency, but distrust and cynicism would increase, which were poisoning the climate in higher education politics already for years, "*'Regieren neu' eben*."[103]

A European Court of Justice Decision and Its Consequences for Austrian Higher Education

The Republic of Austria has a population of some eight million inhabitants and accommodates approximately 250,000 students within its higher education system. Germany, Europe's most populous nation, has some 83 million inhabitants, among them approximately 1.9 million students. In the late 1980s, the Austrian Science Ministry began to initiate new efforts to increase the international mobility of Austrian university students.[104] Yet at the same time, the regulations were tightened for incoming students wanting to study in Austria.[105] This regulation pursued a hidden agenda, namely the augmentation of student mobility for linguistic reasons. The goal was to increase student mobility between countries with different languages, not among countries with the same language (such as Germany and Austria or France and French-speaking southern Belgium).

The issue of trans-border access to higher education institutions had not been raised during the negotiations for Austria's accession with the European Commission. A problem began to emerge only when European integration, including free movement of people and students, was rapidly progressing. The issue of foreign students' admission entered the political agenda in the late 1990s, ironically as the result of a case involving an Austrian citizen who had passed her general qualification exams in Germany, but was not admitted to a German university because the major she wanted to pursue was subject to the *numerus clausus*. The student could not secure admission to an Austrian university either (her second choice). She filed a complaint with the Austrian Constitutional Court, charging that admission regulations to Austrian universities were unconstitutional; moreover, that it was a breach of European Community law. The High Court rejected the motion. It determined that it was the legislation's objective to prohibit a massive inflow of foreign students (especially German medical students barred from German medical schools), who wanted to circumvent the admission restrictions in their home countries. Austrian regulations on university admission thus passed the domestic constitutional test. The Constitutional Court, however, did not rule out that European Community law may have been violated.[106]

In the following months, politicians simply ignored the problem while university representatives repeatedly warned about a potentially serious problem on the horizon. In November 1999, while the negotiations to construct a governing coalition were carried out after the important October elections, the European Commission sent a letter to the Austrian government. It was the first formal notification about major shortfalls in Austrian admission standards violating Articles 12, 149, and 150 of the Treaty of Amsterdam.[107]

When Elisabeth Gehrer became the new science minister in February 2000, she entered a contentious arena *vis-à-vis* European Union demands of opening admission to Austrian universities to foreigners. The admission issue had been passed back and forth like a hot potato between Vienna, Brussels (the seat of the European Commission), and Luxembourg (the headquarters of the European Court of Justice). At the time, the implementation of the University Act of 2002 was on a tight schedule and represented the highest priority in higher education innovations. The foreign student access and admission issue obviously was not. The Science Ministry did not pursue a clear and proactive strategy, nor did it prepare a "Plan B" for the worst-case scenario of the European Court forcing the issue of admission of foreign students.

On 20 January 2005, Judge Francis G. Jacobs, the Court's Advocate General, went public with his opinion (*Schlussantrag*). Jacobs recommended a selective admission standard, including the introduction of entry exams and admission procedures based on a system similar to a *numerus clausus*.[108] This decision of the European Court of Justice fanned the public debate in Austria to a flame. A radio report analyzed the coming dilemma well. Its title said it all: "The European Court of Justice's Decision May Be the End of Open Access to Universities" ("*EuGH-Urteil könnte offenen Hochschulzugang kippen*").[109] Georg Winckler, the chancellor of the University of Vienna and chairman of the national Austrian Rectors' Conference at the time, recommended a *Studieneingangsphase,* a kind of trial period for university freshmen during their first two semesters. Newspapers injected some scaremongering headlines into the debate. The Vienna daily *Der Standard* wrote, "The European Court of Justice Wants to Open the Lecture Halls" ("*EuGH-Anwalt will Hörsäle öffnen*"). The daily *Salzburger Nachrichten* entitled its story "Access to University is Endangered, Students Will Face High Hurdles" ("*Uni-Zugang in Gefahr. Studenten drohen hohe Hürden*").[110] Meanwhile, some rectors were beginning to adopt Judge Jacobs' argument that free access to Austrian universities would have to end.[111]

German students who had been denied access to their own universities had the biggest stake in the European Court's ruling. The German media therefore homed in on the story, too. The German weekly news magazine *Der Spiegel*, always good for caustic headlines, entitled its story "Alarm over the *Piefkes* in Vienna: The Germans *Ante Portas*" ("*Piefke-Alarm: Die Deutschen vor Wien*").[112] While the *Spiegel* article praised the dismantling of access limitations for international students at Austrian universities, the advantages of the same language for German students, and the low tuition fees, Rector Winckler raised the specter of an influx of as many as 23,000 German "*numerus clausus* refugees." This was the number of rejected applicants to German medical schools in 2004/05. He warned that other disciplines regulated by the *numerus clausus* at German universities might also be forced to open admission for international (particularly German) students in Austria.[113]

While this crisis was brewing, officials in Vienna responsible for dealing with this impending problem of a run on Austrian universities by German students, still simply watched. Insiders in Austria agreed that the pending court decision in Luxembourg would produce major problems, yet nobody seemed to be working on preparing for this scenario of open access for foreign students. The Vienna conservative daily *Die Presse* ridiculed the laggard ministry officials with their appeasing tactics:

> Those responsible in the Education Ministry are playing the waiting game and are —credibly—claiming that they have not been working on strategies. They first want to read the fine print in the decision of the European Court. They are passing the buck to the universities, along the lines of the motto—once the European Court gives the green light to foreign students in April or May then it's time for the universities to find ways to master the onslaught of students. It will come in July when the enrollment period begins for the upcoming semester.[114]

In mid-April 2005, Director-General Höllinger at last began to ponder alternative scenarios in case the European Court followed the Advocate General's opinion. He suggested a simple amendment to the

University Act of 2002 that would enable universities to introduce special access standards for specified majors during a period of two years. This amendment would become law before the registration period began at universities.[115] In essence, this signaled the end of free access for Austrian students to their native universities—yet another dramatic change in Austrian higher education politics.

The enrollment period for the 2005/06 fall semester began by sheer coincidence in early July during the week prior to the announcement of the European Court's decision. Consequently, last-minute admission regulations were established in great haste. The Medical University of Vienna introduced a "first come-first served" principle, assigning study slots according to the original application date.[116] Prospective medical students spent an entire night camping out in a park next to the Vienna Medical University to be first in line for registration when it opened up the next morning.[117] Four-hundred and seventy applicants registered successfully during the next (that is, the first) day of the official admission period.[118]

At last, on 7 July 2005, the European Court of Justice in Luxembourg issued its verdict in the case C-147/3. It followed much of the wording of the Advocate General Jacobs' opinion issued in January: the Republic of Austria had failed to comply with the obligations of the respective articles in the Treaty of Amsterdam. In the afternoon of the same day, Minister Gehrer announced the amendment to the University Act of 2002 that Höllinger had been talking about in April. The amendment covered special admission regulations in the fields of medicine, veterinary medicine, dentistry, biology, psychology, pharmacy, and business administration. This list corresponded to the list of *numerus clausus* restricted majors at the German universities.[119] Less than forty-eight hours after the European Court decision, the ÖVP and their new coalition partner, the BZÖ, passed this amendment regulating access to Austrian universities.[120]

For the first time since the early 1970s, Austrian universities introduced selective admissions standards, partly disguised as changes of curricula. This triggered more critical media coverage and added further confusion to the situation. Worried students-to-be and their parents launched protests about the untenable situation. Aggressive German students—who were applying to the medical universities in Vienna, Graz, and Innsbruck—along with their lawyers threatened to sue these universities. They both argued that these measures introduced rank inequality and injustice into the system.[121]

Student representatives were stunned. "This is another sad day on the path to eliminate open and free access to universities," complained the Austrian Student Union (*Österreichische Hochschülerinnen und -*

hochschülerschaft, or ÖH).[122] The media perceived these changes differently:

> The ÖH's protests [...] seem odd. Their "life's dream" allegedly was destroyed by ending open access. It seems that the Student Union is grieving over the demise of nocturnal waiting lines and public auctions for seminar slots. Select admission will allow all those who are serious about studying to do this all the same under fair and fine conditions. The introduction of gateways for improving quality should be a rational mandate—before the German asylum seekers arrived and now even more so.[123]

Reviewing these changes in Austrian higher education in the summer of 2005 almost four years later, it must be said that the ratio of Austrian to international students enrolled in the popular majors that supposedly came under siege by the influx of German students did not change too much. However, a significant increase occurred in the field of medical studies. One year after the European Court's dramatic decision, Austrian medical universities were forced to introduce a quota system for Austrian students as a result of the enormous interest of German students in Austrian medical universities.[124] In 2005/06, the Vienna Medical University had 1,500 Austrians and the same number of German applicants competing for only 1,560 study slots. The Innsbruck Medical University had 500 slots to fill from 447 Austrian applicants and 2,147 German applicants. For the 300 open slots at the Graz Medical University, 917 Austrians and 1,964 Germans competed.[125]

It is a fact that some universities had waited for the day when they would be able to launch selection procedures by introducing entrance standards and entrance exams. The *Salzburger Nachrichten* offered a shrewd obituary in the summer of 2005:

> Behind the scenes, official sources will admit that the European Court decision did not strike Austria with the force of lightening. The chance to put up access hurdles by way of speedy procedural changes through the welcomed back door from Europe was gratefully accepted. What had hitherto been a clandestine good-bye to free access, now enjoys the force of law [...] Rectors have long tried to unleash a debate about access to universities. Now the European Court decision allegedly forced both ministers and rectors to introduce access restrictions at once and without much debate. Free access to universities became history from one day to the next by way of sheer fly-by-night activism. This hectic activity was homemade. The government and the rectors had years to plan for such a European

Court decision which would be handed down sooner rather than later.[126]

The Brave New World of "Bologna": Systemic Challenges and Changes Far Beyond 2010

In June 1999, the northern Italian city of Bologna became the center of higher education in Europe. Delegates from twenty-nine countries gathered in Bologna in June 1999 and signed the Joint Declaration of the European Ministers of Education.[127] Its main goal was the development of the European Higher Education Area (EHEA) by the year 2010. The Declaration's six initial focus areas have concentrated on the adaptation of a system of easily readable and comparable degrees, the adoption of a common European high education degree structure based on undergraduate and graduate (BA/MA) degrees, the establishment of the European Credit Transfer System; the further promotion of student mobility, European cooperation in quality assurance, and the European dimension in higher education.[128] Austrian Science Minister Caspar Einem signed the declaration, committing the country to take part in the implementation of the above-mentioned goals.[129]

The "*Bologna goals*," as it turned out over the years, have become yet another catalyst in the planning and execution of ongoing university reforms in Austria. "Bologna's" importance as a means to pursue important goals in higher education policies became clear soon after Minister Gehrer took office in 2000. During the first "Austrian Bologna Day" in June 2000 held in Vienna all the Bologna goals were part of the agenda, among them quality assurance and accreditation, both relatively new to the Austrian higher education system.[130] Barbara Weitgruber, the high official at the Science Ministry in charge of international relations of Austrian higher education institutions, emphasized the motivation needed in universities to implement the necessary reforms of the "Bologna process."[131] Director General Höllinger was pushing universities into high drive in pursuit of the reform agenda, noting, "To put it mildly, the approach to the new possibilities is very cautious. Unless we have quick success in this transformation process, we will fall back in our competitiveness."[132]

Ever since the year 2000 and Gehrer's arrival in the Ministry, several changes in higher education in Austria have been designed as a reaction to some of the Bologna goals, such as the reform of doctoral programs and the introduction of Anglo-American degree titles. But also "homemade" topics like the multi-year allocation of budgetary funds to universities based on performance agreements with individual universities and the granting of full institutional autonomy in curricular and organizational matters have been dealt with.[133]

The systemic changes unleashed by the Bologna goals in the higher education arena have been massive in most countries. Needless to say, the Bologna goals also garnered considerable criticism and opposition. One of the most prominent Bologna critics in Austria is the Viennese philosopher Konrad Paul Liessmann. He has criticized vociferously the ideas behind these reforms and the way they have been carried out.[134] Student representatives have also castigated the Bologna goals as well as their hasty implementation, as is documented in the *Black Book of the Bologna Process* published by the European Student Union.[135]

In the field of quality assurance—one of the chief elements of the Bologna process—two sectors of higher education in Austria are ahead of public universities, the *Fachhochschulen* and the private universities.[136] Private universities are a new phenomenon in Austria's higher education system. They had to run through accreditation from the very beginning. Moreover, unlike public universities, they are evaluated and re-accredited by the Austrian Accreditation Council on a regular basis. For the periodic evaluation and accreditation of *Fachhochschulen*, the *Fachhochschulrat* was established as early as 1993. Unlike public universities, both these institutions choose their students via selection procedures, entrance exams, and personal interviews. Unlike public universities, they limit their openings every academic year and also issue individual student contracts.

The education ministers have gathered biannually for Bologna follow-up meetings since 1999. One outcome of the meeting in London in 2007 was that evaluation and accreditation mechanisms should be introduced for all sectors of higher education, also in Austria, and hence also for public universities. Yet Austria seems to be taking its time in this area.[137] Indeed, immediately before the completion of the European Higher Education Area by 2010, future challenges in Austrian higher education remain in terms of the full implementation of these mechanisms, especially in the field of Standards and Guidelines for Quality Assurance.[138]

Within the higher education community in Austria today, public universities are still the most important providers of post-secondary education. They are now full legal entities in their own right with the highest degree of independence possible. Public universities now have complete responsibility and liability for implementing the Bologna goals.[139] Still, the Science Ministry has the right and obligation to supervise the universities under the Universities Act 2002, including the monitoring of full compliance with Austrian law.[140] The basis for cooperation between the government and the public universities is new mechanisms of "performance agreements," which also represent the universities' medium-range strategic plans. The first set of these performance agreements for the years 2007 to 2009 were signed in early 2007 and have been published via the worldwide web.[141] The next set is concluded in late 2009 for the years 2010 to 2012. Critics have strongly denounced this new tool as a "sham" and a "*carte blanche*" for business as usual.[142]

A reality check on the new autonomy of universities after almost three years of practice reveals some deficiencies. An illustrative example of a prevailing mentality of "as-you-like-it" remains the issue of waiting lists. Although access regulations have been set up, more students still populate some disciplines than stated openings would accommodate. Students are carried along in this system because they fulfill all the requirements for continuing their studies but are unable to do so due to the lack of university resources.

Cases from two medical universities were first brought to the attention of the Student Ombudsman and the National Ombudsman in 2005/06. The government authorities were then forced to deal with such problems of available slots in required classes repeatedly prior to the introduction of performance agreements in 2007 as well as after such agreements had been signed.[143] Public critiques were issued and recommendations made.[144] The University Act 2002 clearly mandates that public universities prevent the unnecessary prolongation of studies as a result of limited course openings. Public universities are mandated to offer extra courses to accommodate all students admitted, if necessary even during semester breaks.[145] The universities ignored the Ombudsman's reprimands and got away with it. In the fall 2008 semester, there were still cases of inadequate student access to required classes.[146]

During 2008, the Auditor General (*Rechnungshof*) investigated the Science Ministry's required monitoring of the performance of Austrian universities. It strongly urged the establishment of an overall national strategy for public universities. At the same time, the Auditors General demanded student numbers to be included in the "performance agreements" as planning indicators for future projections of the instructors needed and courses to be offered.[147] This, in turn, will lead to yet a final paradigm shift in Austria's higher education arena, namely access limitations and standards for *all* majors offered in public universities.[148]

Conclusion

The comparative analysis *Two Decades of Reform in Higher Education* published in 1990 defined the main reform agenda in Europe for the last decade of the second millennium: management, finance and control, financial aid to students, curriculum and teaching, access and internationalization.[149] When reviewing the seven years of Schüssel/Gehrer *Wende* policies in Austria's higher education system, several of these priorities were addressed proactively, others still are in need of being addressed, and some remain out of reach. The coincidental (re)introduction of tuition fees was one of the agenda items tackled and so was the granting of full autonomy to universities—a long-term goal that had already been initiated in the early 1990s. The prying open of access and admission to Austrian universities for international students was bound to happen anyway. It came as a result of massive outside pressure from the European institutions. The nagging issue of overcrowded lecture halls and restricted access to seminars in some disciplines at public universities did not go away.

Analyzing the details of higher education policies raises bigger issues about Austria's politics that cannot be answered here. What is the importance of higher education policy in a society's social progress? Do politicians and political parties muster sufficient depth and profile to shape policies in such crucial areas of public life that define a nation's mental maps and core values? Are they capable of and do they have the courage to recruit the right people at the right time for the right leadership positions? How big is the room to maneuver anyway for a politician such as Elisabeth Gehrer—blessed with the expertise of many advisers—over a period of (only?) some seven years?

Higher education policies, as in any policy field, are subject not only to the political marketplace but also to populist temptations. The shelf-life of political decisions, laws, and administrative measures can be very short, though. Tuition fees, one of the cornerstones of the *Wende* higher education policy, were mandated in 2001, but abolished only seven years later. A spur of the moment "coalition" of Social Democratic, Green, and FPÖ members of parliament voted for the abolition of tuition fees three days before the general elections scheduled for the fall of 2008. The conservative ÖVP, along with their erstwhile coalition partner the BZÖ voted against it. On 24 September 2008, the plenary assembly of the Austrian Parliament thus became the stage ultimately for a rebellion against the legacies of the ÖVP/FPÖ-BZÖ era (2000-2007). Since the Gusenbauer/Molterer grand coalition in early 2007 had only partially revoked tuition fees, the (now campaigning) SPÖ in a *pro tempore* coalition with the Greens and FPÖ thus took revenge on its own —outgoing—leaders.

Have the *Wende* reforms really been carried out under the mere pretext of neoliberalism?[150] Have all the described reforms increased the *Studierfähigkeit* ("studyability," a term created in the course of the Bologna process) for students at higher education institutions and furthered the *Beschäftigungsfähigkeit* (or "employability," a term first used in this context during the British EU Presidency in 1998) of graduates? If nothing else, these reforms at least have given us these impressive "new speak" expressions. What can we expect next in the higher education arena in the next decade? Answers to these questions can only be offered by the individuals studying and working at the institutions themselves and by society at large.

Notes

1. Still the most comprehensive and general view of the development of higher education in Austria during the Second Republic up to the early 1970s is Bernd Schilcher, "Hochschulen," in *Österreich: Die Zweite Republik*, vol. 2, ed. Erika Weinzierl and Kurt Skalnik (Graz: Styria, 1972), 347-67; this basic survey has never been amended, updated, or continued since then. For an elaborated survey on research policy and research funding in postwar Austria up to 2005, see Rupert Pichler et al., eds., *Forschung, Geld und Politik: Die staatliche Forschungsförderung in Österreich 1945-2005* (Innsbruck: StudienVerlag, 2007).

2. Herbert Dachs et al., eds., *Politik in Österreich: Das Handbuch* (Vienna: Manzsche Verlags- und Universitätsbuchhandlung, 2006).

3. Oswald Panagl and Peter Gerlich, eds., *Wörterbuch der politischen Sprache in Österreich* (Vienna: öbvhpt VerlagsgesellschaftmbH & Co. KG, 2007).

4. Nikolaus Dimmel and Josef Schmee, eds., *Politische Kultur in Österreich 2000-2005* (Vienna: Promedia Druck- und VerlagsgesmbH, 2005).

5. Christian Brünner, ed., *Kultur der Demokratie: Festschrift für Manfried Welan zum 65. Geburtstag* (in Studien zu Politik und Verwaltung) (Vienna: Böhlau, 2002); Gerhard Schnedl and Silvia Ulrich, eds., *Hochschulrecht—Hochschulmanagement—Hochschulpolitik: Symposion aus Anlass des 60. Geburtstages von Christian Brünner* (Vienna: Böhlau, 2003); Hedwig Kopetz et al., eds., *Soziokultureller Wandel im Verfassungsstaat. Phänomene politischer Transformation: Festschrift für Wolfgang Mantl zum 65. Geburtstag* (Vienna: Böhlau, 2004).

6. Günther Sandner, "Paradigmenwechsel? Hochschulpolitik seit dem Jahr 2000," in *Schwarz-Blau: Eine Bilanz des Neu-Regierens*, Emmerich Talos (Vienna: LIT Verlags GesmbH, 2006), 279.

7. For the critical period from election day, 3 October 1999, to the inauguration of the new government on 4 February 2000, see Günther R. Burkert-Dottolo and Bernhard Moser eds., *Die Regierungsbildung in Österreich 1999/2000* (Vienna: Eigenverlag der Politischen Akademie der ÖVP, 2000). Insightful eyewitness reports by the political actors are recorded by Heinz Fischer, *Wende-Zeiten: Ein österreichischer Zwischenbefund* (Vienna: Kremayr & Scheriau, 2003), and Andreas Khol, *Die Wende ist geglückt: Der schwarz-blaue Marsch durch die Wüste Gobi* (Vienna: Molden, 2001); on critical reports by journalists, see Gerfried Sperl, *Der Machtwechsel: Österreichs politische Krise zu Beginn des 3. Jahrtausends* (Vienna: Molden, 2000), and Michael Fleischhacker, *Wien 4. Februar 2000 oder Die Wende zur Hysterie* (Vienna: Czernin Verlag, 2001).

8. Hans Haider, *Elisabeth Gehrer: Reportage eines politischen Lebens* (Vienna: Edition Steinbauer, 2008), 42. Some of her accomplishments in provincial *Land Vorarlberg* politics are listed in ibid., 30f.

9. Wolfgang Fingernagel, ed., *Das Haus am Minoritenplatz, Bundesministerium für Unterricht, Kunst und Kultur / Bundesministerium für Wissenschaft und Forschung*, 2nd ed. (Vienna: Bundesministerium für Unterricht, Kunst und Kultur / Bundesministerium für Wissenschaft und Forschung, 2008), 37ff.

10. Gerald Schöpfer, "Bildung als eine neue Utopie im Zentrum der Gesellschaft," in *Österreich Zukunftsreich. Denkpfeiler ins 21. Jahrhundert. Eine Initiative von Vizekanzler Wolfgang Schüssel*, ed. Stefan Karner (Graz: Promedia Verlag, 1999), 245-60. Haider, *Elisabeth Gehrer Reportage*, 90.

11. Sperl, *Machtwechsel*, 157.

12. Academic Portal Austria, http://www.portal.ac.at/owa/portal.ogn_alph_en?otp_id_in=3, accessed 14 November 2008. A useful overview on the institutional development of the "science ministry" and its structural transformations and name changes is given in Elmar Schübl's chapter "Das Wissenschaftsressort," in idem, *Der Universitätsbau in der Zweiten Republik: Ein Beitrag zur Entwicklung der universitären Landschaft in Österreich* (Horn: Berger, 2005), 50-55.

13. Thomas Götz, "Der Chef," in *Erhard Busek: Ein Porträt*, ed. Elisabeth Welzig (Vienna: Böhlau, 1992), 232ff.

14. Haider, *Elisabeth Gehrer Reportage*, 97.

15. On Gehrer's unique relationship with her chief of staff Dr. Peter Mahringer and the changes in the ministry's operational style after Mahringer's premature death in the summer of 2003, see Haider, *Elisabeth Gehrer Reportage*, 76f.

16. For an early appraisal of changes needed in higher education policy in Austria in the 1990s, see Sigurd Höllinger, "Eine wirkliche Hochschulreform, 27 Anstöße zur Diskussion," *Zukunft* 7 (1990); idem, *Universität ohne Heiligenschein: Aus dem 19. ins 21. Jahrhundert* (Vienna: Passagen Verlag, 1992). The journalist and Gehrer biographer Hans Haider characterizes Höllinger as an "experienced and reform friendly top official, who has been moving towards autonomous universities and tuition fees for a long a time"; see *Elisabeth Gehrer Reportage*, 98.

17. Haider, *Elisabeth Gehrer Reportage*, 98.

18. Sperl, *Machtwechsel*, 157.

19. On Weitgruber's appointment, see "Gesetze, Personalbesetzungen, Auslandstermine," *Die Presse*, 27 November 2002, 8. For profiles of Weitgruber, see "Vielsprachiges Energiebündel für Forschung," *Der Standard*, 13 December 2002, 2k, and "Unsere Frauen 2003," *Women* 1, 3 January 2003, 29f.; for a first interview with Weitgruber about her plans, see "Ich hoffe auf die erste Rektorin," *Die Furche*, 9 January 2003, 11.

20. Haider, *Elisabeth Gehrer Reportage*, 98.

21. Ibid., 96.

22. Markus Haider defines "*Wende*" in Panagl's and Gerlich's Wörterbuch der politischen Sprache as "incisive change, changing direction of events and developments" ("*einschneidende Veränderung, Wandel in der Richtung eines Geschehens oder einer Entwicklung*"); Haider likens the "*Wende*" in Austria in February 2000 and the following months and years to the events in the German Democratic Republic in the fall of 1989. See also the comprehensive Ewald Ehtreiber's entry "*Schwarz-blaue Wende*" in the same dictionary, with an extensive list of publications, 376-78. For deeper analyses of the "*Wende*" from various perspectives, see Andreas Khol et al., eds., *Österreichisches Jahrbuch für Politik 2000* (Vienna: Wissenschaftsverlag, 2001).

23. For Kreisky's motivations in setting up the new and independent Ministry of Science and Research in 1970, see his memoirs, *Erinnerungen: Das Vermächtnis des Jahrhundertpolitikers*, ed. Oliver Rathkolb (Vienna: Kremayr & Scheriau, 2007), 124f. For an early appraisal of Firnberg's ministry, see Wolf Frühauf, ed., *Wissenschaft und Weltbild: Festschrift für Hertha Firnberg* (Vienna: Europa-Verlag, 1975).

24. On Firnberg's achievements as minister, see Hans Joachim Bodenhöfer, "Bildungspolitik," 657, in *Politik in Österreich: Das Handbuch*, ed. Herbert Dachs et al. (Vienna: Manzsche Verlags- und Universitätsbuchhandlung, 2006), 657; her personality is profiled in *Profil*, 10 April 2000, 170.

25. Sandner, "Paradigmenwechsel," 279. For the effects of the global crisis year 1968 on Austrian universities, see Paulus Ebner and Karl Vocelka, *Die Zahme Revolution: '68 und was davon blieb* (Vienna: Ueberreuter, 1998), 160-95, and 204-07. The 1975 and 1993 reforms are reflectively compared in a collection of oral histories with key actors in Henrik Kreutz and Heinz Rögl, *Die umfunktionierte Universitätsreform: Von der Steigerung der Produktivität zur staatlichen Förderung sozialen Aufstiegs politischer Kernschichten* (Vienna: WUV Wiener Universitätsverlag, 1994).

26. Martin Eichtinger and Helmut Wohnout, *Alois Mock: Ein Politiker schreibt Geschichte* (Graz: Styria, 2008), 35.

27. Hans-Joachim Bodenhöfer, "Die Einführung des Bakkalaureats in Österreich—Ausgangslage und Erwartungen," http://www.oefg.at/text/workshop/beitrag_2.html, accessed 4 May 2009.

28. On the early years of internationalizing Austria's higher education system, see Josef Leidenfrost et al., "Austria," in *National Policies for the Internationalisation of Higher Education in Europe*, ed. Torsten Kälvemark and Marijk van der Wende (Stockholm: Högskoleverket, 1997), 42-59. On the early years of ERASMUS in Austria, see Josef Leidenfrost, "Austria," in *Education in a Single Europe*, ed. Colin Brook and Witold Tulasiewicz (London: Routledge, 2000), 45-47.

29. On the early Europeanization of Austrian higher education in a comparative view, see ibid., 49-69. A more recent publication on the same issue focused on Austria alone, see Manfred Prisching et al., eds., *Bildung in Europa: Entwicklungen und Perspektiven* (Vienna: Verlag Österreich, 2005).

30. On the creation of the new *Fachhochschule* sector in Austria, see the programmatic publication, containing the basic message in the book title, Sigurd Höllinger et al., eds., *Fachhochschulen—unbürokratisch, brauchbar und kurz* (Vienna: Passagen Verlag, 1994).

31. For a biographical entry, see "Dr. Rudolf Scholten" on the webpage of the Austrian Parliament, http://www.parlament.gv.at/WW/DE/PAD_02789/pad_02789.shtml, accessed 4 May 2009.

32. "Eckpfeiler eines 'nachhaltigen' Budgets für Wien: Deutliche Rückführung der öffentlichen Haushaltsdefizite," *Neue Zürcher Zeitung*, 16 March 1996, 11.

33. "*Sparpake*t" is a composite term with considerable rhetorical utility; it was deliberately used to make budget cuts more appealing to the citizens (*bürgerfreundlicher*); see Panagl and Gerlich, eds., *Wörterbuch der politischen Sprache*, 398f. The term itself entered the *Österreichisches Wörterbuch* for the first time in the 1997 edition.

34. Anna Magdalena Hollwöger wrote an incisive op-ed piece on the impact of the budget cuts from the point of view of an assistant professor, see "Ein vielseitiges Paket: Es geht nicht nur um's Geld," *Kleine Zeitung*, 13 March 1996, 30.

35. *ÖH 60 Jahre* (Vienna: Österreichische Hochschülerinnen- und Hochschülerschaft, 2006), 70.

36. "Requiem der Rektoren: 'Man kann auch zu Tode sparen'," *Kurier*, 6 March 1996, 2.

37. See the open letters to the minister "Offener Brief an Herrn Minister Scholten!" by the Verband der Professoren der Karl-Franzens-Universität Graz, *Kleine Zeitung*, 16 March 1996, 19, and "Offener Brief von Rektor Heinrich Otruba, Wirtschaftsuniversität Wien," *Salzburger Nachrichten*, 16 March 1996, 17.

38. "Buhrufe und Pfiffe am Weg zur Angelobung," *Neue Zeit*, 13 March 1996, 5; "Studenten spotteten Klima aus," *Täglich Alles*, 13 March 1996, 3.

39. For Einem's vita and his reasons for entering politics, see Caspar Einem, "Der Fußweg war doch etwas länger," in *Wie ich Politiker wurde*, ed. Hubertus Czernin (Vienna: Czernin, 2004), 45-53.

40. On Einem's emancipatory agenda, see Caspar Einem, *Ein neuer Staat befreiter Bürger* (Vienna: Molden, 1999).

41. "Proteststurm gegen 'Stasi-Methoden' Caspar Einems," *Die Presse*, 3 February 1998, 7, and "Jetzt suchen wir Unis, die bereit sind," *Die* Presse, 4 February 1998, 7.

42. Caspar Einem, Federal Minister of Science and Transport, *White Paper on Higher Education in Austria* (Vienna: Federal Ministry for Science and Transport, 1998). A previous official government document on Austrian politics with similar ambitions dated back to 1995, *Weissbuch der österreichischen Bundesregierung: Österreich in der Europäischen Union* (Vienna: Bundeskanzleramt, 1995); it contained only a small section on universities and *Fachhochschulen*, 136-38.

43. For a brief summary of Einem's achievements as minister, see Haider, *Elisabeth Gehrer Reportage*, 104f.

44. For a comprehensive overview of the main issues of the UOG 1993, see Frank Landler, *The Austrian University System* (Vienna: Federal Ministry for Science and Transport, 1998), 13-26.

45. Different approaches on the UOG 1993 implementation are described in Anneliese Legat, ed., *Wege in das UOG 1993. Materialien zum Reformpropzess an den österreichischen Universitäten* (Graz: Leykam, 2000)

46. Sandner, "Paradigmenwechsel," 280. An exemplary report on the many setbacks caused by the ongoing reform as seen from the perspective of the dean of the Medical Faculty of the University of Graz is Thomas Kenner, *Sechs Jahre Amtszeit als Dekan*, http://www.meduin-graz.at/physiologie/mitarbeiter/kenner/rektorat, accessed 4 May 2009. The estimated costs of the UOG 1993 and its implementation at major universities amounted to approximately 80 million Austrian Schillings, the restructuring of the ministry cost another 3.7 million Schillings; for the details, see the Parlamentarische Anfrage Grünewald und Freundinnen und Freunde, "Kosten der Implementierung des UOG 93 an den Universitäten," 659/J XXI. Gesetzgebungsperiode and Gehrer's reply 674/AB XXI. Gesetzgebungsperiode.

47. See the Coalition Agreement *Österreich neu regieren*, 57.

48. "Gehrer nun auch für Universitäten zuständig," *Wiener Zeitung*, 11 February 2000, 3.

49. Stefan Titscher et al., eds., *Universitäten im Wettbewerb: Zur Neustrukturierung österreichischer Universitäten* (Munich: Rainer Hampp Verlag, 2000).

50. Ibid., 12.

51. Stefan Titscher's publications on organizational innovation include *Studiendauer, Studienerfolg und ihre Faktoren* (Vienna: Bundesministerium für Unterricht, 1966) published in 1966 (!), and *Struktur eines Ministeriums: Eine verwaltungssoziologische Studie zur Ministerialbürokratie* (Vienna: Österreichischer Bundesverlag, 1975); on Titscher, see also "Univ.Prof.Dr. Stefan Titscher," Institüt fur Soziologie und Empirische Sozialforschung, Wirtschafts Universität Wien, http://www.wu-wien.ac.at/sozio/institut/person_detail/titscher, accessed 16 November 2008.

52. For a detailed overview of the principal elements, see Stefan Titscher, "Die Weiterentwicklung des Universitätsbereichs," in *Österreichisches Jahrbuch für Politik 2001*, 559-84.

53. Entwurf: Bundesgesetz über die Organisation der Universitäten und ihre Studien (Universitätsgesetz 2002), BMBWK GZ 34.190/2-VV/B/4/2002.

54. *ÖH 60 Jahre*, 45. Of the almost 400 comments on the draft law during the parliamentary discussion process more than 90 percent were negative. Kurt Grünewald and Johannes Gadner, *Universitätsgesetz 2002—Weltklasse oder Sackgasse? Eine kritische Auseinandersetzung* (Vienna: Verlag Österreich, 2003), 11.

55. For commentaries in favor of the reforms, see Stefan Titscher,"Theoretische Grundlagen, Interpretationsvarianten und mögliche Auswirkungen des Universitätsgesetzes," and Sigurd Höllinger, "Die Entwicklung von der staatlich gelenkten zur autonomen und europäischen Universität," in *Die österreichische Universitätsreform: Zur Implementierung des Universitätsgesetzes 2002*, ed. Sigurd Höllinger and Stefan Titscher (Vienna: WUV Wiener Universitätsverlag, 2004), 51-59, 73-123. For commentaries arguing against the reforms, see Franz Ofner, "Die unsichtbare Hand greift nach den Universitäten," in *Österreichische Zeitschrift für Soziologie* 26.1 (2001): 68-87; Othmar Pruckner, "Schluß mit Gaudeamus," *Trend*, 1 May 2001, 52; Christian Fleck, "Die Stronach-Uni," *Falter*, 3 April 2002, 16; Sigrun Nickel, "Die Reform des Grauens," *Die Zeit*, 19/2002, 2 May 2002, 35; for a comparison of the Austrian and German situations, see Sigrun Nickel, "Erduldete Transformation. Hochschulreform als Spielball der Politik," in *die hochschule* 1 (2002): 101-12.

56. The website, once located at http://www.weltklasse-uni.at/, is now defunct.

57. "*'Weltklasse' ist das bildungspolitisches Schlagwort für die Ziele der Universitätsreformen. Die österreichischen Hochschulen sollen nach Ansage der derzeitigen Bundesregierung und der zuständigen Ministerin Gehrer in fünf Jahren ‚Europaspitze in Bildung und Wissenschaft' sein. Etappen auf dem Weg – Richtung W. sind das neue Hochschullehrerdienstrecht, die Profilentwicklung und das Universitätsgesetz 2002. Kritiker empfinden den Begriff W. wegen seines inhärenten Selbstlobes als lächerlich.*" See the Uni-Lexikon entry "Weltklasse," HEUREKA. Das Wissenschaftsmagazin im FALTER 2 / 2004, http://www.falter.at/web/heureka/archiv/02_4/a.php, accessed 21 November 2008. For a profound international critique of the term "world-class university," see Jan Sadlak and Liu Nian Cai, eds., *The World-Class University and Ranking: Aiming beyond Status* (Bucharest: UNESCO/CEPES, 2007), 17-23.

58. Barbara Sporn accentuated the political aims; see "World-Class Reform of Universities in Austria," International Higher Education, Fall 2002, http://www.bc.edu/bc_org/avp/soe/cihe/newsletter/News29/text011.htm, accessed 19 November 2008. Birgit Wagner takes the philosophizing approach; see "Weltklasse: Eine Internet-Erzählung," http://www.dieuniversitaet-online.at/beitraege/news/welklasse-eine-internet-erzahlung, accessed 19 November 2008.

59. The web site is Forum Wissenschaft, http://www.forum-wissenschaft.at/, accessed 19 November 2008, and was still online in early 2009; on Niederwieser's vita, see Bio-

grafie von DDr. Erwin Niederwieser, Republik Österreisch Parlament, http://www.parlament.gv.at/WW/DE/PAD_01052/pad_01052.shtml, accessed 19 November 2008.

60. For the University of Innsbruck, see http://www.uibk.ac.at/public-relations/aktuelles/unireform with individual statements by university members and discussion threads; for the University of Vienna, see http://ug02.wordpress.com/ug-2002-entwurfe, which leads to the amendments planned in 2008, offering blogs on special aspects.

61. "Universitätsgesetz vor Verfassungsgerichtshof angefochten," http://www.vsstoe.at/default.asp?Hauptmenue=2&Untermenue=1&ID=901&Tabelle=, accessed 21 November 2008.

62. Sandner, "Paradigmenwechsel," 286.

63. "Uni Neu: Die größte Veränderung seit 153 Jahren," *Die Presse,* 11 July 2002, 7.

64. The expression "*Minoritenplatzschleicherei*" has been widely used in the Austrian press, see "Überrascht von der Minoritenschleicherei" [sic], *Die Presse*, 29 January 2002, 2, and "Fakultätenstreit," *Die Presse*, 13 March 2004, 6. It was also mentioned in one of the official statements on the draft university law in 2002, written by Ekkehard Kappler et al., "Auf Umwegen in die Autonomie?—Der Entwurf zur Vollrechtsfähigkeit der österreichischen Universitäten," http://www.uibk.ac.at/iol/forschung/autonomie.pdf, accessed 16 November 2008. Laske had described this phenomenon earlier, using the more polite terms "*Antichambrieren*" and "relationship management"; see Stefan Laske and Alfred Zauner, "Architektur und Design universitärer Verhandlungssysteme: Zur Konzeption und Praxis mehrfach geschichteter Rahmensteuerung," in *Universität im 21. Jahrhundert: Zur Interdependenz von Begriff und Organisation der Wissenschaft*, ed. Stefan Laske et al. (Munich: Rainer Hampp Verlag, 2000), 445-87 (quotes 466).

65. *[E]s war immer das Ministerium, das die Geldmittel auf die einzelnen Institutionen nach wenig transparenten Gesichtspunkten verteilte [...] Der Wiener Minoritenplatz, Sitz des Ministeriums, war die ausschließliche Machtzentrale. Dies begünstigte naturgemäß die Wiener Universitäten, da deren Interventionskanäle direkter zu bespielen waren. Zugespitzt könnte man es so formulieren: Oftmals war die Anzahl der Blumensträuße für die Durchsetzung von Anliegen ausschlaggebend.*
See Helmut Konrad and Elisabeth Fiorioli, "Die Struktur der österreichischen Qualitätssicherung," in *Handbuch Qualität in Studium und Lehre*, ed. Winfried Benz et al. (Bonn: Raabe Verlag, 2007), 2f.

66. "*Der Kampf um Personal, Sachausstattung, Geräteeinsatz, notwendige Sanierungen und Neubauten sowie laufende Erfahrungen mit fragwürdigern Berufungsentscheidungen waren...treibende Kräfte [für den Wunsch nach mehr Autonomie]. Fairerweise sollte hier aber hinzugefügt werden, dass nicht nur das Ministerium, sondern auch die Universitäten und ihre Gremien selbst ihren Teil an den immer wieder kolportierten Missständen beitrugen. Unrühmliche Seilschaften, Täuschungen, Eitelkeiten, Standesdünkel bis zur Hochstapelei und Machtverliebtheit gab es da wie dort, aber auch das Gegenteil.*"
See Kurt Grünewald, "Universitätsgesetz 2002—die umstrittene Reform," in *Österreichisches Jahrbuch für Politik 2003* (Vienna: Verlag für Geschichte und Politik, 2004), 153-77 (quotation p. 157).

67. "Sie vermerkten einmal, Ihr Arbeitstag bestehe in der Abwehr raunzender Assistenten, intrigierender Institutsvorstände und inkompetenter Studentenvertreter." See "Einflüsterer für fünf Minister," *Vorarlberger Tageszeitung*, 2 October 2005, 2.

68. "*Da hat sich viel geändert, aber das gibt es auch jetzt noch. Wenn im neuen System etwas nicht klappt, dann gibt es die Suche nach Halt am Minoritenplatz [...] Es wird noch dauern, bis man versteht, wohin die politische Kritik gehen soll [...] Gelegentlich*

kommen auch noch Wissenschaftler als Irrläufer zum Ministerium, die verlangen, dass man eine Entscheidung eines Rektors aufhebt." Ibid.

69. "*Natürlich hat es [das UG 2002] Auswirkungen auf das Ministerium. Das Ministerium wird schlanker, es wird weniger Leute dort geben, sie werden neue Aufgaben haben, und die Leute werden darauf eingeschult.*" See Stenografisches Protokoll der 101. Sitzung des Nationalrates, XXI. GP, 11 July 2002, 116.

70. Haider, *Elisabeth Gehrer Reportage*, 97.

71. Indymedia Printausgabe: Studierendenproteste an der Universität Wien, 22 January 2004, http://docs.indymedia.org/pub/Local/Austria, accessed 16 November 2008.

72. The event was filmed and publicized by the university channel Universitätsfernsehen Wien (UTV); it was originally online at http://www.utv.at/direct.php?id=161, but is no longer available there. See Youtube, http://de.youtube.com/watch?v=YZR8rsLLP18, accessed 15 November 2008, "Magnifizenz georg winkler [sic!] kriegt eine torte in die fresse :--)." The event was also covered extensively by the press; see "Rektor nach Tortenwurf: 'Ich mag Topfentorten'," *Krone Online*, 22 January 2004, http://www.krone.at/S25/object_id_14417/hxcms_popup/index.html, accessed 15 November 2008; "Uni Wien: Rektor Winckler getortet," *Der Standard*, 22 January 2004, 4; Martin Haidinger, "'Uni-Krieg': Keine Einigung in Sicht," 21 January 2004, http://science.orf.at/science/news/102117, accessed 15 November 2008.

73. "Aufregung nach Tortenwurf," *Salzburger Nachrichten*, 22 January 2004, 2.

74. "Studentenprotest: Torten als kreative Form des Protests," *Die Presse*, 23 January 2004, 7; interview with Vera Schwarz, Referat für Öffentlichkeitsarbeit der ÖH Uni Wien by *TATblatt*, http://www.tatblatt.net/207/207uniorg.html, accessed on 15 November 2008. It states that Winckler and Höllinger's piece had not been anticipated; hence no statements had been prepared by the ÖH. According to Martin Haidinger, ORF radio journalist and the moderator of the planned discussion, Josef Broukal had told rector Winckler the evening before that he should wear old clothes the next day because something might happen (personal information provided by Martin Haidinger). In the commemorative publication *ÖH 60 Jahre* (Vienna: Hochschülerinnen- und Hochschülerschaft, 2006), 68, a picture of Winckler taken right after the moment the pie hit him, was subtitled with little sensitivity: "The protest for university democracy turns sweet" ("*Der Protest für universitäre Demokratie nimmt süsse Formen an*").

75. In 1990/91, 193,479 students studied at Austrian universities; 227,948 attended in 1999/2000. *Statistisches Taschenbuch 2001* (Vienna: Bundesministerium für Bildung, Wissenschaft und Kultur, 2001), 37.

76. This development during the early and mid-1990s has been analysed by Hans Pechar, "Funding Higher Education in Austria: Present Mechanisms and Future Trends," in *European Journal of Education* Vol.33, No. 1 (1998): 41- 54.

77. See the commentaries by Samo Kobenter, "Protest ohne reale Chancen. Die Universitäten werden das Sparpaket wohl oder übel annehmen müssen," *Der Standard*, 6 March 1996, 32; Alfred Payrleitner, "Uni-Krise: Die auffallende Abwesenheit von Sympathie," *Kurier*, 11 March 1996, 2; Kurt Horwitz, "Studieren oder Protestieren?," *Neues Volksblatt*, 13 March 1996, 2; Dieter Lenhardt, "Sorgenkinder der Gesellschaft," *Die Presse*, 13 March 1996, 2; Peter Rabl, "Auch Universitäten können gekränkt sein," *Kurier*, 17 March 1996, 2. The tenor of these articles is generally unfavorable to the student demands.

78. See Helmut Konrad's commentary "Bildungsoffensive ist nur einnahmenseitig zu lösen," *Kleine Zeitung*, 12 March 1996, 35.

79. "Gehrer will Kampf gegen Mentalität des Nulltarifs," *Die Presse*, 25 June 1996, 8.

80. Richard Sturn and Gerhard Wohlfahrt, *Der gebührenfreie Hochschulzugang und seine Alternativen* (Vienna: Verlag Österreich, 1999). See also Christian Keber and Hans Pechar, eds., *Abschied vom Nulltarif: Argumente für sozialverträgliche Studiengebühren* (Vienna: Passagen Verlag, 1996).

81. *Österreich neu regieren: Regierungsprogramm 2000-2003*, 103-04, http://www.bka.gv.at/2004/4/7/Regprogr.pdf, accessed 4 may 2009.

82. See Erich Witzmann's commentary "Höhenflug und Absturz: Fünf Jahre E. Gehrer," *Die Presse*, 22 September 2000, 3. See Wofgang Mazal, "Erhöhung der Treffsicherheit des Sozialsystems," in *Österreichisches Jahrbuch für Politik 2000* (Vienna: Verlag für Geschichte und Politik, 2001), 161-78. Mazal in this essay states how he was surprised about the government's intention to introduce tuition fees for university students (p. 170), yet in the same essay he welcomes the idea of tuition fees as a means to improving conditions at universities both for students and their professors (p. 171).

83. See the entry "Karl Heinz Grasser," http://www.nationmaster.com/encyclopedia/Karl_Heinz-Grasser, accessed 24 November 2008; and "Doktoratsstudent Grasser erschien nicht zur Wahl," http://doktorat.at/Presseschau/Dokoratsstudent_Grassser_erschien-nicht-zur-Wahl.html, accessed 24 November 2008.

84. Gehrer's low point is mentioned in news articles in the week after the meeting, see "Heisser Herbst: Schüssel gegen Studenten, Arbeitslose und Frauen," *News*, 21 September 2000, 14; "Gehrer, ein Wendeopfer?," *Format*, 25 September 2000, 27; and "Das Studentenleben wird härter: Studiengebühren in Österreich," *Der Spiegel Online*, 12 October 2001, http://www.spiegel.de/unispiegel/studium/0,1518,druck-161938,00.html, accessed 24 November 2008. *Format* mentions the Grasser ultimatum. On the evening before the meeting of the Council of Ministers on 19 September 2000, the VP and FP members of Parliament in charge of higher education policy were informed about the decision the evening before the Council's Meeting, see *Protokoll der 72: Sitzung der XXIII. Gesetzgebungsperiode*, 24 September 2008, 4. Gehrer used Grasser's arguments for the first time in public during the "press hour" on Austrian Public Television on 24 September 2000; see also "Gehrer: 'Gratis ist nichts'," *Salzburger Nachrichten*, 25 September 2000, 2.

85. Haider, *Elisabeth Gehrer Reportage*, 100f.

86. Vortrag an den Ministerrat 29/19, BMWA GZ 434.001/134-SVI/00; BMSG GZ 10.302/9-MinBüro/2000; BMF GZ 04701/120-Präs.4/00; BMBWK GZ 10.720/43-I/2000.

87. "Studiengebühren kommen überraschend," *Wiener Zeitung*, 20 September 2000, 1.

88. "Wenn eine Ministerin über die Hintertreppe flüchtet," *Kurier*, 20 September 2000, 2. She later stated on this reproach that she was in a hurry to arrive on time to the closed government meeting scheduled to begin on the evening of the same day in Burgenland.

89. *"Ich war schon als Landesrätin für Studienbeiträge an den Fachhochschulen. Ich habe mich auch klar dafür ausgesprochen, dass man für Senioren, für Längerstudierende, für solche, die ein zweites, drittes Doktorat machen, einfach Beiträge einhebt. Dieser Studienbeitrag von 5000 Schilling pro Semester ist sehr moderat, er wird abgesichert durch erweiterte soziale Stipendienmöglichkeiten."*
See ORF-Zeit im Bild 1 transcription, 19 September 2000, Dokumentation ÖVP-Parlamentsklub. Gehrer and Sigurd Höllinger had first expressed their positive views on introducing tuition fees for *Fachhochschule* students during a symposium in Bregenz in 1994. There the two met for the first time; see Haider, *Elisabeth Gehrer Reportage*, 30.

90. "Streitthema Studiengebühr: Studentenchef Martin Faißt fühlt sich von Bildungsministerin Gehrer 'voll belogen': Sie kontert," *Kleine Zeitung*, 21 September 2000, 6.

91. "Aktionismus an den Universitäten: Studenten erhalten bei ihren Protesten Schützenhilfe von den Rektoren," *Der Standard*, 22 September 2000, 10.

92. *Stenographische Protokolle, 39. Sitzung des Nationalrates der Republik Österreich, XXI. Gesetzgebungsperiode*, 12 October 2000, 57-59. The Styrian governor Waltraud Klasnic first introduced the idea of a student ombudsman during the regional election campaign in Styria in the fall of 2000. See "Steiermark-Wahl: Klasnic kündigt 'Studentenanwalt' an," Austrian Press Agency APA0280, 9 October 2000. Minister Gehrer adopted this proposal; see "Studiengebühren: 'Studentenanwalt' soll im November Arbeit aufnehmen, Gehrer greift Vorschlag Klasnics auf," APA0322, 10 October 2000. The SPÖ criticized Gehrer's announcement since a student ombudsman had first been installed by Minister Scholten as early as 1996; see "Einfallslose ÖVP-Ministerin Gehrer nimmt Anleihen bei SPÖ-Vorgängern," APA OTS0239, 11 October 2000. For a background article on the new ombudsman based on an interview with the new team leader Josef Leidenfrost, see "Ich werde mich für die Studenten zerreißen," *Die Presse*, 7 March 2001, 9. For articles on the work of the new ombudsman, see "Ombudsmann für Studenten," *Wiener Journal*, September/October 2002, 24-25; "The Studierendenanwaltschaft at the Austrian Ministry for Education," *Austrian Education News* 34 (March 2003): 1-2, and "The Austrian Ombudsman for Higher Education: A Regulator with Teeth?," in *Student-Institutional Relationships in Times of New University Management: Ombudsmen in Higher Education*, ed. Kristl Holtrop et al. (ENOHE Occasional Paper Number 1, Vienna 2006), 61-64.

93. *ÖH 60 Jahre*, 44.

94. *Handelsblatt*, 12 October 2000, 6.

95. Strike Action, http://strike.action.at/conz.htm, accessed 16 November 2008.

96. Ibid. As a result of this "break-in" incident, the main entrance to the minister's office on the first floor of Palais Starhemberg was equipped with a touchdown telephone access control system. Before the incident, it was only equipped with a closed-circuit television system, which had been installed first right after a series of letter bombs ("Briefbombenserie") had been sent to several government officials through the mail in 1993/94.

97. Statistics provided courtesy of Anni Horak, Federal Ministry of Science and Research. For media coverage of reduced student numbers, see the commentary by Martin Haidinger, "Studiengebühren: 70,000 Studenten weniger," 13 November 2001, http://science.orf.at/science/news/18884, accessed 27 November 2008.

98. These students also stayed enrolled so they would not be transferred into new curricula; due to other obligations in life such as jobs and family, they were unable to take the exams. See the critical article by Robert Czepel, "Leichen im Karteikeller," *Heureka*, January 2003, http://www.falter.at/web/heureka/archiv/01_3/11.php, accessed 28 November 2009.

99. Hans Pechar and Angela Wroblewski, "Weniger Scheinimmatrikulationen, gleichbleibende Studienaktivität—Über die Auswirkungen der Studiengebühren auf die Zahl der Studentinnen und Studenten an österreichischen Universitäten," *Beiträge zur Hochschulforschung* 2 (2001): 219-41.

100. Gudrun Biffl and Joseph E. Issac, "Should Higher Education Students Pay Tuition Fees?," *WIFO Working Papers* 172 (Vienna: WIFO, 2001), 1.

101. "Fünf Jahre Studiengebühren—eine Bilanz," Radiokulturhaus, 21 June 2006 (a recording of this Austrian radio discussion is in the author's personal archives); see also the article Hans Pechar on ORF Science Online, http://science.orf.at/science/news/144842, accessed 28 November 2008.

102. "Fiskalpolitik vor Bildungspolitik?," *Wiener Zeitung*, 21 September 2000, 6.

103. See Hans Pechar's commentary "Gebührenpeitsche," *Falter*, 29 September 2000, 5.

104. See Friedrich Faulhammer, "Maßnahmen zur Umsetzung des EU-Rechts in das österreichische Hochschulrecht," and Heinz Kasparovsky, "Rechtliche Grundlagen der EU-Bildungspolitik im Hochschulbereich," in Leidenfrost, ed., *Österreichs Hochschulausbildung*, 17-23, 55-57.

105. Tim Birtwistle and Josef Leidenfrost, "Policy and Law – The Context for Mobility in Europe and the Austrian Case Study," in "Legal Aspects of Higher Education in an International Context: Disputes, Resolutions, Methods and Safeguards," *EAIE Occasional Paper* 21, ed. Tim Birtwistle (Amsterdam: EAIE, 2008), 23.

106. Roland Winkler, "Development of Education Law in Austria," Part II: Higher Education, *European Journal for Education Law and Policy* 2 (1998): 63-64.

107. Birtwistle and Leidenfrost, "Policy and Law," 23.

108. *Numerus clausus* is a preferred method for universities to select among competing applicants in popular fields in order to limit the pool of qualified applicants. The selection can be handled differently such as making it dependent on high school grade point averages or entrance exams or both. For the most popular subjects the *numerus clausus* was implemented nationwide. For details on current regulations for medicine in Austria, see http://www.eignungstest.ch/nc_oesterreich_medizinstudium.php#Austria, accessed 17 November 2008.

109. ORF Science Online, 19 January 2005, http://science.orf.at/science/news/132019, accessed 16 November 2008.

110. Both headlines appeared on 21 January 2005.

111. *Kurier*, 31 January 2005, 2.

112. "Die Deutschen vor Wien," *Spiegel Online*, 3 February 2005, http://www.spiegel.de/unispiegel/studium/0,1518,druck-339872,00html, accessed 16 November 2008.

113. Ibid. Other estimates predicted up to 80,000 German students seeking admission to *numerus clausus* subjects at Austrian universities; see *Der Standard*, 12 April 2005, 7.

114. *"Die Verantwortlichen im zuständigen Bildungsministerium warten ab und versichern—glaubhaft!—, dass sie sich noch keine Strategien überlegt haben. Man wolle erst das Kleingedruckte im EuGH-Urteil lesen. Somit wird den Universitäten der Schwarze Peter zugespielt, etwa nach der Devise: Kommt im April oder Mai vom EuGH das grüne Licht für ausländische Studierwillige, dann sollen halt die Universitäten selbst Konzepte finden wie sie dem Ansturm Herr werden. Und dieser könnte Anfang Juli einsetzen, wenn die Inskriptionszeit für das kommende Studienjahr beginnt."*
See "Die Ausländer kommen! Brüssel und die Unis," *Die Presse*, 23 March 2005, 31.

115. "Diskussion zum Hochschulzugang," APA, 19 April 2005.

116. "Medizin: First Come—First Serve—Prinzip," *Der Standard Online*, 29 June 2005, http://derstandard.at/druck/?id=2094975, accessed 30 June 2005; "Wer schnell inskribiert, hat den Platz so gut wie sicher," *Der Standard Online*, 29 June 2005, http://derstandard.at/druck/=?id=2095190, accessed 30 June 2005].

117. "Österreich fürchtet deutschen Studentenansturm," *ARD-Tagesschau,* 7 July 2005, http://www.tagesschau.de/ausland/meldung 174842, accessed 16 November 2008.

118. "Inskription ab heute möglich," *ORF Online*, 4 July 2005, http://wien.orf.at/stories/43326, accessed 15 November 2005.

119. "Gehrer erlaubt Unis Beschränkungen," APA press communique, 7 July 2005, http://www.forumromanum.de/member/forum/forum.php?action=ubb-show&entryid, accessed 16 November 2005.

120. For a detailed description of the legal process, see Eva Schulev-Steindl, "Hochschulzugang in Österreich: Die Rechtslage nach dem Urteil des EuGH in der Sache C-147/03," *Juristische Blätter* 1 (January 2006): 2-17.

121. Birtwistle and Leidenfrost, "Policy and Law," 24. "Unis droht nun Flut von Klagen," *Heute*, 11 July 2005, 7.

122. This information was once available online at http://www.beschraenkt.at/eugh-urteil-oesterreich, accessed 16 November 2008; it is no longer available online.

123. On 9 July 2005, the *Kleine Zeitung* reported:

> *"Seltsam [...] der Protest der ÖH. Ein 'Lebenstraum' sei mit dem Ende des offenen Zugangs geplatzt. Offenbar trauert die Hochschülerschaft den nächtlichen Warteschlangen und Seminarversteigerungen nach. Beschränkun-gen ermöglichen, dass all jene, die ein Studium ernsthaft betreiben möchten, dies zu gleich fairen und guten Bedingungen auch tun können. Was ist daran studentenfeindlich? Die Einführung qualitativer Schleusen ist ein Gebot der Vernunft. Sie war es schon ohne deutsche Asylwerber und jetzt erst recht."*

See "Warum dem freien Uni-Zugang niemand nachtrauern muss: Ein Dogma aus den Siebzigern wurde bestattet—viel zu spät," *Kleine Zeitung*, 9 July 2005, 12.

124. Sandner, "Paradigmenwechsel," 288. The quotas established were 75 percent for Austrians, 20 percent for EU citizens (including Germans), and 5 percent for non-EU citizens.

125. "German-speakers Rush to Austria," *cafebabel – The European Magazine*, 10 October 2005, http://www.cafebabel.com/eng/article/14957/german-speakers-rush-to-austria.html, accessed 14 November 2008.

126. *"Dass das EuGH-Urteil Österreich nicht wie ein Blitz aus heiterem Himmel getroffen hat, wird hinter vorgehaltener Hand auch von offizieller Seite zugegeben. Doch die Chance, Zugangshürden im Hauruckverfahren quasi durch die europäische Hintertür einzuführen, wurde dankbar angenommen. Der bisher schleichende Abschied vom freien Zugang steht nun im Gesetz [...] Die Rektoren wollen seit langem eine Debatte über den Uni-Zugang lostreten. Mit dem Pseudo-Sachzwang des EuGH-Urteils im Rücken konnten Ministerin und Rektoren die Beschränkungen gleich—und ohne jede Diskussion— einführen. Der freie Uni-Zugang war in einer hektischen Husch-Pfusch-Aktion von einem Tag auf den anderen Geschichte. Die Hektik war hausgemacht. Regierung und Rektoren hatten Jahre Zeit gehabt, sich auf das absehbare Urteil vorzubereiten."*

See "Gekommen, um zu bleiben," *Salzburger Nachrichten*, 30 September 2005, 7.

127. Europaeum, http://www.europaeum.org/index2php?option=com_content&task=view&id=58, accessed 4 May 2005.

128. Gottfried Bacher, "Higher Education in Austria and the Bologna Process: How It All Began," 1, 5 October 2004, http://ostina.org/html/bridges/article.htm?article=1177, accessed 5 May 2009.

129. Since then, follow-up conferences have been conducted biannually to monitor the progress of the implementation of the Bologna goals. In addition, biannual national reports have been published by the Science Ministry on the implementation of the Bologna goals in Austria. The Minstry published the first report in 2001. See *Erster Bericht über den Stand der Umsetzung der Bologna-Erklärung in Österreich 2001* (Vienna: Bundesministerium für Bildung, Wissenschaft, und Kultur, 2001); the most recent report was published in April 2008; see http://www.bmwf.gv.at/fileadmin/user_upload/europa/bologna/Austrian_Country_Report_2007-2009.pdf, accessed 4 May 2009.

130. "Reformtag an der Wiener Universität," *Die Presse*, 19 June 2000, 7.

131. "Erster Bologna-Tag: Unis werden europäischer," *Der Standard*, 21 June 2000, 47.

132. "*Der Umgang mit neuen Möglichkeiten ist, freundlich gesagt, sehr behutsam. Wenn wir die Umstellung nicht rasch schaffen, wird die Konkurrenzfähigkeit sinken.*" See his op-ed "Weckruf an die Unis: Effizienz, Mobilität steigern," *Die Presse*, 23 June 2000, 6.

133. Bologna Process Template for National Reports, 9 May 2006, http://www.bmwf.gv.at/fileadmin/user_upload/europa/bologna/National_Reports-Austria_2006.pdf, accessed 4 may 2009; see also *Im Blickpunkt: Strukturen des Hochschulbereichs in Europa 2006/07—Nationale Entwicklungen im Rahmen des Bologna-Prozesses* (Brussels: European Commission, 2007), 76-81.

134. Konrad Paul Liessmann, "Bologna: Die Leere des europäischen Hochschulraumes," in idem, *Theorie der Unbildung: Die Irrtümer der Wissensgesellschaft* (Vienna: Zsolnay, 2006), 104-23.

135. National Unions of Students in Europe, ed., *The Black Book of the Bologna Process* (Bergen: ESIB, 2005); Manja Klemencic, "European Students in the Bologna Process," *International Higher Education* 50 (Winter 2008), http://www.bc.edu/bc_org/avp/soe/cihe/newsletter/Number50/p23_Klemencic.htm, accessed 4 May 2009.

136. *Higher Education in Austria: Reforms 2001* (Vienna: Federal Ministry for Education, Science, and Culture, 2001), 17.

137. Konrad and Fiorioli, "Struktur der österreichischen Qualitätssicherung," 7. On the issue of European evaluation models and their potential implications for Austrian higher education, see Helmut Konrad, "Europäische Evaluierungsmodelle und deren Anwendbarkeit für Österreich," in *Untersuchungen zum Organisations- und Studienrecht*, ed. Rudolf Strasser (Vienna: Manzsche Verlags- und Universitätsbuchhandlung, 1999), 27-36.

138. *Bologna Process Stocktaking London 2007*, ed. U.K. Department for Education and Skills (London: NP, 2007), 63.

139. For two comprehensive recent publications on this issue, see Werner Hauser, "Responsibility and Liability in Education: Austria," in *European Journal for Education Law and Policy* 6 (2002): 59-67, and Manfred Prisching et al., eds., *Die (Rechts-)Stellung von StudentInnen in Österreich* (Vienna: Verlag Österreich, 2007).

140. Universities Act 2002, as of April 2008, Chapter 4, §45, (1), http://www.bmwf.gv.at/fileadmin/user_upload/wissenschaft/recht/englisch/E_UG.pdf, accessed 4 May 2009.

141. Uni-data, Datawarehouse Hochschulbereich, http://eportal.bmbwk.gv.at/portal/page?_pageid=93,1172892&_dad=portal&_schema=PORTAL, accessed 4 May 2009.

142. See, for example, Christian Fleck, "Die Stronach-Uni," *Falter*, 3 April 2002, 16.

143. "Auch gute Studenten müssen ewig warten," *Kurier*, 29 September 2007, 1; *ATV Nachrichten*, 22 August 2008.

144. "Verzögerungen im Zuge des Studiums der Humanmedizin und Zahnmedizin," in *Bericht der Volksanwaltschaft an den Nationalrat und den Bundesrat 2006* (Vienna: Volksanwaltschaft, 2007), 1-14; and "Studienverzögerungen an den Medizinischen Universitäten," in *Bericht der Volksanwaltschaft an den Nationalrat und den Bundesrat 2007* (Vienna: Volksanwaltschaft, 2008), 1-5.

145. This regulation is set up in the University Act 2002, § 54 (8). The problem with long waiting lists at medical universities was covered by the special TV program V*olksanwalt—Gleiches Recht für alle*, in April and October 2006, and in the magazine *ORF Nachlese*, October 2006, 45.

146. *ATV Abendnachrichten*, 17 September 2008 (A recording of this TV program is in the author's personal archives.)

147. "Rechnungshof kritisiert Uni-Politik massiv—Gesamtstrategie fehlt," APA 0136, 19 January 2009.

148. This topic has been discussed on many occasions, but most prominently in connection with the decision of the European Court of Justice; for a survey of historical developments and the changes needed, see Christoph Badelt et al., eds., *Hochschulzugang in Österreich* (Graz: Leykam, 2007).

149. *Two Decades of Reform in Higher Education in Europe: 1989 Onwards* (Brussels: European Commission, 2000), 4.

150. Hannes S. Auer, *Neoliberalismus in Österreich? Hochschulpolitik, Gesundheitspolitik und Wirtschaftspolitik der ÖVP-FPÖ/BZÖ-Koalition auf dem Prüfstand* (Munich: Grin Verlag, 2008).

Legacies of the Schüssel Years

Anton Pelinka

Introduction

Wolfgang Schüssel has been a visible actor in Austrian politics for decades. In the following analysis, the term "Schüssel years" will be used for the years 2000 to 2006 only—a period that can be rightfully called the "Schüssel era."

Schüssel had been no newcomer to the Austrian government when he was appointed federal chancellor in February 2000, and he did not leave politics after the appointment of his successor, Alfred Gusenbauer, in January 2007. Schüssel had started his career as secretary of the Austrian People's Party (*Österreichische Volkspartei*, or ÖVP) caucus in parliament and secretary general of the ÖVP's Business League (*Österreichischer Wirtschaftsbund*). A member of parliament, beginning in 1979, he became minister of economic affairs in the coalition of the ÖVP and the Social Democratic Party of Austria (*Sozialdemokratische Partei Österreichs*, or SPÖ), shaped by Franz Vranitzky and Alois Mock, and then—beginning in 1995—ÖVP chairman, vice-chancellor, and minister of foreign affairs. In the period between January 2007 and September 2008, when the ÖVP was the junior partner in the coalition cabinet led by the SPÖ, Schüssel was—as a member of parliament—the ÖVP's floor leader in the National Council. But the years during which his name and his personality made such a decisive impact on Austrian politics were his years as chancellor in the ÖVP-FPÖ (and, from 2005 to 2006, Alliance for the Future of Austria—*Bündnis Zukunft Österreich*, or BZÖ) coalition government. This is the period which—for good reasons—can be called the Schüssel Era.

The summary of the almost six years during which Schüssel was the head of the government can be divided into two arenas: politics and policies. The basic argument of this article is that the era's significant impact has been in politics.

Regarding policies, the overall conclusion is that the Schüssel era was characterized by "more of the same." The general trend towards "Westernization," which has dominated Austrian politics at least from the 1980s onward, was also followed between 2000 and 2006. It can be argued that the Schüssel government functioned as a catalyst—implementing certain policies within the logic of "Westernization" faster than it would have happened otherwise, but it cannot be argued that the Schüssel years reversed the general trend Austria had been following for decades. The Schüssel era did not contradict the years when Vranitzky—in cooperation with ÖVP ministers like Alois Mock, Erhard Busek, and Wolfgang Schüssel himself—stood for a clear Austrian response to the end of the East-West conflict. If there is no (ideological, military, economic) East, if there is no bloc confrontation any more, Austria's position cannot be defined by a "third" way like permanent neutrality or "mixed economy." Austria's position is defined by the general trends (Western) European societies follow.

Regarding politics, the Schüssel years were characterized by dramatic upheavals. The rise of the FPÖ to a coalition partner of equal footing in 2000, the FPÖ's deep fall in 2002, and the party's split in 2005 are one aspect of a fast process of electoral de- and realignment. The victory the ÖVP enjoyed in 2002 was followed by a rather deep decline in 2006. The SPÖ's ability to conquer the ÖVP's traditional strongholds in some of the Austrian states (*Länder*), followed by reconquering the (electoral) number one position and the office of the chancellor in the reestablished Grand Coalition dominated the years 2004 to 2006. The overall decline of political participation (expressed by electoral turnout and party membership) and party concentration (defined by the long-term electoral weakening of both major parties) has to be included in any kind of summary. The deep crisis organized labor experienced in 2006 when the Austrian Trade Union Federation (ÖGB) almost went bankrupt due to business practices of the ÖGB owned bank are the main indicators of an extremely volatile situation.

The overall trend that the Schüssel years did not start, but on some levels accelerated or slowed down, can be best described by the term "Westernization." Beginning with the end of the 1970s, but especially in the early 1980s, Austrian policies and politics became increasingly similar to those in other Western European political systems. Austria began to lose—for better or worse—some of its special characteristics.

The "Westernization" or "de-Austrification" of Austrian politics started earlier than the "Westernization" of Austrian policies. The end of the first Grand Coalition was followed by the period of one-party governments—four years of the ÖVP and thirteen years of the SPÖ. This in itself could be seen as a decline of the political culture so typical of post-1945 Austria when inter-party arrangements between the ÖVP and SPÖ as well as intra-party arrangements in both major parties reduced the impact of political competition and when the corporatist network between business, labor, and agriculture—known as Social Partnership—limited the consequences of economic competition.[1] But the one party governments under Josef Klaus (ÖVP) and Bruno Kreisky (SPÖ) were built on an extremely solid basis characterized by

- a highly concentrated party system in which more than 90 percent of the voters preferred either the ÖVP or the SPÖ, a concentration almost unheard of in a multi-party system with proportional representation;
- a very high electoral turnout, such that more than 90 percent of Austrian voters went regularly to the polls, a turnout being one of the highest marks among pluralistic democracies; and
- an extremely high organizational density of the party system, evidenced by the fact that both major parties had about 25 to 30 percent of their voters organized as party members.

All these indicators started to decline in the 1980s. At the end of the Schüssel years, this process seemed to be accelerating even faster than before.

Regarding policies, this acceleration is exemplified in Austria's typical pattern of corporatist intervention in the economy, in combination with partial state ownership in major industries and in major banks—a rather unique for a system which principally has been based on a market economy. It is further exemplified in Austria's declaration of permanent neutrality in 1955, followed by a rather specific policy of neutrality, and by Austria's tradition of an extremely high degree of "statism," of direct government control in higher education.

The most important consequences of Austria's neutrality had been Austria's abstention from joining the European Communities (based on the Rome Treaties 1957) and the North Atlantic Treaty Organization (NATO). The first aspect has been already revised in the 1980s, when Austria—represented by a Grand Coalition—applied for European Union (EU) membership in 1989. But even the economic and social policies had been changed during the 1980s: It had been under the Grand Coalition led by an SPÖ chancellor and an SPÖ minister of finance when Austria started to privatize almost all its nationalized industries and all its nationalized banks. Moreover, Austria's tightly governmentally controlled universities had already been given significantly more autonomy in the 1990s.

When the Schüssel era began, Austria's policies as well as politics were not in a paralyzed state. Of course, it can be argued that "Westernization," especially of Austrian policies, slowed down after EU membership had been achieved. It can be argued that the Grand Coalition had accomplished its mission when Austria had joined the European Union in 1995, the (partly) supranational "club" of almost all Western (and very soon of almost all Eastern) European states. By fulfilling this mission, the Grand Coalition had lost its major function. The beginning of the Schüssel years can be seen as the attempt to Westernize Austria even more and even more quickly due to the now Westminster-style situation of a major party in the role of parliamentary opposition.

Westernization in Policies

The Westernization process occurring in the field of policies can be demonstrated in three major areas: economic policy, foreign policy, and policy of higher education. In the field of the economy, "Westernization" implied a tendency to strengthen market orientation and to play down state intervention and corporatism—the two major characteristics of "Austro-Keynesianism" so typical of Austria until the 1980s. In the field of foreign policy, "Westernization" meant stressing the need to act within the framework of the European Union. In education, "Westernization" meant a retreat from direct governmental influence. In all these areas, the Schüssel government did not reinvent an orientation, but continued policies defined especially during the first years of the Grand Coalition governments, beginning with 1987.

This aspect has been overshadowed by two phenomena: the conflicts between the government and the opposition and the crisis between Austria and its EU partners in 2000. The latter phenomenon contradicted the "Westernization" agenda that at least Schüssel's ÖVP had been following for a long time.

The economic and social policies the Schüssel government implemented had been the reason for the opposition from the left—especially from the SPÖ and the ÖGB—to accuse the government of "social coldness," an argument which would have had less weight if social democratic politicians would have still been responsible for this overall trend as had been the case prior to 2000. The same must be said about the tendency to strengthen "law and order"—a tendency criticized by human rights activists—and about the government's intention to make it more difficult for refugees and migrants to get legal status or citizenship. These tendencies had emerged before 2000—and some of the decisions had been backed by the Social Democratic opposition after 2000. Most importantly, all these tendencies had been part of a broader, ongoing European trend.[2] To criticize the Schüssel government for being responsible for increasing inequality and for emphasizing "law and order" is one thing, for during the years the ÖVP-FPÖ coalition was in power, the gap between the rich and the poor became deeper and "security" became a dominant issue. But one cannot overlook the fact that these tendencies began years earlier, in some cases at the beginning of the 1980s, at the end of the Kreisky era.

It can be said that the Schüssel government did not succeed in reversing a trend which had started before—and which has been (and still is) a trend with which practically all highly industrialized democracies in Europe and North America have to contend. It would be difficult or even impossible to single out the Schüssel years for being particularly hard-hearted regarding and especially responsible for the deepening social gap and closing Austria's borders to more and more refugees and migrants.

Perhaps the most significant change in government policies could be seen in the Schüssel government's agenda regarding gender relations. The FPÖ particularly emphasized the role of mothers in society, discussing this issue more than had been the case in terms of government policy on this issue. The government's decision to pay "*Kindergeld*" (children money)—a very popular slogan in the FPÖ electoral campaign 1999—had to be seen as a change of focus: gender equality became less important, incentives for motherhood more.[3]

About the increase in social (especially income) inequality, it is at least dubious to see the government's intentions as being responsible for this situation. But regarding the trend to privatize what had been left of the state-run economy, the Schüssel government clearly had the intention to go ahead and—embracing "Westernization" once more—reduce the state influence by reducing state property rights. This policy orientation may be criticized for being too fast for giving away the republic's "family silver" for too cheap a price. Because the trend to privatize state industries and state banks had been started more than a decade earlier, the Schüssel years can be seen a period in which a policy of the previous years' administrations had been accelerated.

When Schüssel became chancellor, the debate about the meaning of Austria's neutrality within the European Union had been going on for years. It was Schüssel's party which, within the Grand Coalition, had openly discussed the possibility for officially ending Austria's neutral status by joining NATO. In 2001, the Schüssel government—without changing the Neutrality Act of 1995—declared Austria non-aligned (*bündnisfrei*), a status less formal than neutrality.[4] But despite this rhetoric, the ÖVP-FPÖ government never tried to make the next step—opting for NATO membership and, by doing so, abandoning neutrality legally. When Schüssel left office, the rather ambivalent status of a neutral country participating in the EU's "Common Foreign and Security Policy" had not changed.

The European and foreign policy of the Schüssel years was overshadowed by the bilateral diplomatic boycott the governments of the fourteen other EU member states (EU14) declared in February 2000 and lifted in September of that year. For that very reason, Schüssel's overall Western orientation became blurred and almost invisible for the domestic as well as Western (especially European and American) audience. The reasons for the EU14 to declare such a boycott had been the character or the "nature" of Schüssel's ally, the FPÖ. The EU14 wanted to send a strong signal that in the European Union not everyone is welcome as partner.[5]

This may be a rather paradoxical, even tragic aspect for any kind of summary regarding the Schüssel years: a government whose main foreign policy actors (chancellor and foreign minister) had designed a European policy to become more and more "streamlined" within the European Union became the symbol of violating "European values." A government most eager—concerning its ÖVP leadership which was responsible for foreign and European policy—to demonstrate the self-evidence of Austria's status as an average Western European country actively participating in the EU's deepening and widening, became seen as the stumbling stone of the EU's ambitious program. The Schüssel years, which—according to Schüssel himself and his foreign ministers Benita Ferrero-Waldner and Ursula Plassnik as well as to the government's program and the ÖVP's party platform—should have become a period of embedding Austria more decisively into the European Union, made Austria a suspicious case within Europe.

Of course, this effect has been neither Schüssel's nor his party's intention, nor did it happen without the co-responsibility of other actors, like the SPÖ-opposition and organized labor. When in 2004 Austria had to decide whether and to what extent it should use the transition period to bloc the opening of the Austrian labor market for citizens of the newly accepted EU member states, Austria opted for the least possible opening—for a seven year period. Moreover, the pressure of the ÖVP's coalition partner as well as the short-term interest of organized labor (ÖGB and Chamber of Labor) made the Austrian labor market less open than the ÖVP, Schüssel himself, and Austrian business interests would have liked.

There had even been a debate about whether Austria should veto the EU enlargement of 2004, especially regarding the Czech Republic's access to the Union. This debate was the result of pressure by the FPÖ and by some environmentalist groups. Thanks to Schüssel's ÖVP, this debate did not have any other result but the loss of Austria's image as the frontrunner in all matters regarding EU enlargement. The consequence: Austria is considered a "hesitating candidate for [a] leadership role in Central Europe."[6] Despite the strong performance of the Austrian economy in the new EU member states, Austria is seen underperforming politically.

The result of all these mixed messages Austria sent to its European partners is that Austria was on the brink of losing its position as one of the most reliable members in the European Union. When at the end of the Gusenbauer-Molterer coalition in June 2008 the SPÖ left the consensus the two major parties had demonstrated in all EU matters even during the Schüssel years, the message became even more damaging: Austria can no longer be considered the vanguard of European integration. Austria has lost this particular position, and when it comes—as a result of the non-ratification of the Constitutional Treaty and potentially of the Reform Treaty—to the development of a "core Europe" consisting of members states interested in going ahead with the deepening of the integration, there is not much left of the possibility that Austria would be part of that core group.

In the field of educational policies, an argument could be made that the Schüssel government by deciding to introduce tuition for Austrian students at Austrian universities had changed direction. This policy was met with strong opposition from the SPÖ and the Greens as well from the students' representatives. The promise to reverse this decision had been a key plank of the SPÖ's electoral campaign in 2006—a promise the SPÖ was unable to fulfill due to the coalition with the ÖVP that was agreed upon in 2007. But what could be seen as a rather significant step away from a policy designed to guarantee social openness for all Austrians is of lesser significance when two factors are taken into account. First, in the 1990s the Grand Coalition led by Vranitzky and Busek introduced the system of polytechnics (*Fachhochschulen*) intended to offer a new option for post-secondary education. The polytechnics, competing with the universities for the same clientele, were asking for tuition from the very beginning. The start of a tuition-based, public post-secondary education system was not the result of the Schüssel years, but of the Grand Coalition of the 1990s. Second, the basic argument against the university tuition has been social openness. The argument that tuition would make it more difficult for students coming from low income families to enter universities is basically true. But as any study about the social stratification of Austrian academics and students demonstrates, the Austrian educational system is socially unjust: the percentage of students from low income families is very low, and the percentage of students coming from families with an academic background very high. The Schüssel years did not improve this situation—but the addition of university tuition did not deteriorate this situation either.

Because tuition-based public university systems have been the rule in Western democracies for a long time, the introduction of university tuitions can be called part of the Westernization process, but once more, this particular step has been started already before Schüssel became chancellor. The Schüssel policies—legitimized by the governing majority of the ÖVP and FPÖ, implemented by ÖVP Minister Elisabeth Gehrer—has accelerated a process which has started much earlier.

This trend toward Westernization in education can also be seen in the University Act (UG), passed in 2002 and implemented in 2004. The public universities, traditionally seen—following their history as institutions controlled for centuries by the Emperor and the Catholic Church—as state institutions, were transformed in highly autonomous institutions of post-secondary learning. Now, the government provides the universities with general rules and a budget which is the result of formal agreements between each university and the government. Any other strategic and operative decision (for example, which studies will be offered where and who will be appointed to which position) is within the autonomy of the university, especially of the rector.[7] This development gives the Austrian public universities a status very much like the status of U.S. public universities, with one significant exception: the Austrian universities still have to live with an open access to principally all the studies—meaning that the universities have no control over the number of their students. Nevertheless, the University Act of 2002 can be seen as an important step in the direction of Westernization.

But again, this policy change did not start with the Schüssel era in 2000. In the 1990s, the Grand Coalition had begun to move the Austrian universities towards more autonomy—through steps like the University Organization Act (UOG) of 1993. The Grand Coalition of the 1990s also emphasized the concept of inter-university competition by permitting the establishment of private universities. These trends—more autonomy, more competition—can be rightfully put into the category "Westernization." But this process is not the special effect of the Schüssel years. The Schüssel government proceeded down the same path its predecessor had followed—perhaps a little bit more decisively and faster, but not differently at all.

What the Schüssel years are responsible for is coming to terms with some aspects of the Nazi past. To demonstrate that the inclusion of the FPÖ in the government did not mean any special favor for the heirs of Austrian Nazism, the Schüssel government tried to finish deals with representatives of Nazi victims. The two major topics were returning looted Jewish property and paying for slave labor.[8]

Two aspects help to evaluate this policy of belated justice: Schüssel's and his government's interest in softening Western criticism concerning the FPÖ's access to the government and—once more—the fact that this kind of policy had already started more than one decade earlier, when the Austrian government began to re-define the Austrian position regarding the Nazi past from "being Hitler's first victim" to Austria's "co-responsibility" for Nazism. It has been the last Grand Coalition before 2000—Viktor Klima for the SPÖ and Wolfgang Schüssel for the ÖVP—which established the historical commission responsible for the ground work leading to the consensus with the victims after 2000.[9]

Westernization in Politics

The Schüssel years had a significant impact on Austrian politics. The most visible aspect is that the FPÖ, for the first time since Jörg Haider became party chairman in 1986, succeeded in breaking out of its isolation on the federal level. Of course, it can be argued that it had been the SPÖ which—by accepting the pre-Haider FPÖ as a coalition partner in 1983—had started this process of upgrading the FPÖ to a fully accepted partner for both major parties. The FPÖ of 1983 could be seen as even more forbidding than the FPÖ of 2000 because the influence of the old Nazi leaders—like Friedrich Peter, an officer in the SS—had been much more visible in 1983 than seventeen years later. But Peter and his group tried to mainstream the FPÖ, making it a centrist party, accepted as liberal by major European liberals like the German Free Democratic Party (*Freie Demokratische Partei*, or FDP), the Dutch People's Party for Freedom and Democracy (*Volkspartij voor Vrijheid en Democratie*, or VVD), or the British Liberals. Haider reversed that strategy of mainstreaming. He had played the right-wing populist card successfully, making an old right-wing middle class party a catch-all party with increasing proletarian profile, by using anti-European and xenophobic rhetoric. When Haider became chairman, the SPÖ immediately cancelled its coalition with the FPÖ and tried to isolate the old-new FPÖ in a kind of "cordon sanitaire."

Schüssel broke with this policy of isolating the FPÖ after this party had risen to the size of 27 percent of the votes in 1999. In that respect, Schüssel had crushed the SPÖ's (and especially Vranitzky's) attempt to define the FPÖ as a party with which no other party dares to be associated. It remains to be seen whether the post-Haider FPÖ under Hans Christian Strache who is trying to repeat Haider's recipe of the 1980s and 1990s can be kept isolated as was the case after the 2006 elections—or whether Schüssel's breaking of the taboo will find imitators, either in the SPÖ or in the ÖVP.

The question of whether a party like the FPÖ should be accepted as a legitimate coalition partner has a European dimension. Because the FPÖ is linked to extreme right-wing parties, all of which are mavericks within the European party system, any kind of integration of the FPÖ in the inner circle of potential governing parties would contradict the Westernization paradigm. Almost all the European parties view a coalition with the FPÖ similarly negatively. Only the case of Slovakia provides a certain parallel, when—after the elections of 2005—the (socialist) SMER ("Direction") established a coalition with two right-wing parties with a nationalistic and xenophobic outlook, making these two as isolated on the European level as the FPÖ. In Western Europe, no other right-wing party has been able to gain acceptance as a coalition partner—neither the French Front National nor the Belgian *Vlaams Belang*, two parties with which the FPÖ tries to cooperate on the European level. The Danish People's Party—a right-wing populist party, but without the FPÖ's Nazi background—backs a conservative minority cabinet without joining the government directly. Other parties, sometimes seen in a connection with the FPÖ like Italy's Forza Italia, had been accepted and integrated into the system of European party families which is expressed by the party groups in the European Parliament: the Forza Italia is a member of the European People's Party.[10]

The ability of the FPÖ to mobilize more than a quarter of the electorate by using a xenophobic, anti-European message had not changed during the Schüssel years. Because the FPÖ seems to have learned a lesson from its deep fall in 2002, the party will probably not easily fall into the trap of becoming junior partner of a coalition in which the necessary pragmatism will destroy its populist appeal. The FPÖ is the most important factor in Austrian politics contradicting the overall trend towards Westernization.[11]

One lesson from the Schüssel years is the reduced role of the federal president when it comes to forming a cabinet after the election of the National Council. In 1999/2000, Thomas Klestil had made it clear that he would very much prefer the revival of the Grand Coalition. He tried to prevent the ÖVP-FPÖ coalition. It had been the first time that the president asked the leader of the strongest party in parliament—Viktor Klima from the SPÖ—to form a government, but had to give in finally and appoint a chancellor (Schüssel) who never had a presidential mandate.

After the parliamentary election of 2002, Klestil again openly preferred a Grand Coalition, but in the end he accepted the prolongation of the ÖVP-FPÖ alliance, this time even with the presidential mandate for Schüssel. Heinz Fischer, elected in 2004, tried to be as careful as possible when it came to forming a government after the 2006 election of the National Council. Before the Schüssel years, all the federal presidents had followed an unwritten script of charging the leader of the strongest party in parliament with forming a government and accepting any cabinet proposal the newly-appointed chancellor put forward. Klestil, in 1999/2000, had tried to rewrite this script by claiming a much more active role for the presidency. He could do it with reference to the constitution. But he failed in his attempt because—due to the necessity that the cabinet has to have at least the toleration by the National Council's majority—Klestil finally had to accept that the will of a parliamentary majority is stronger than the will of the president. The lesson has been that the Austrian political system is a parliamentary one. Its presidential elements are of only secondary importance.[12]

The Schüssel years changed the implications of Austrian federalism. For decades, the ÖVP had been seen as the party defending state rights—and the SPÖ had been the party tempted to reduce the states' power in favor of more power at the federal level. When Schüssel took office in 2000, six out of nine states (*Länder*) had ÖVP governors (*Landeshauptleute*). All these six states had been under the control of an ÖVP governor in the decades since 1945. When Schüssel left office at the beginning of 2009, the ÖVP had lost control of two of these states. As a result of decisive ÖVP losses in regional elections, Salzburg and Styria—always governed by ÖVP (previously Christian Social) governors—had SPÖ governors. In 2008, the SPÖ controlled Vienna, Burgenland, Salzburg, and Styria, and the ÖVP had kept control in Lower Austria, Upper Austria, Tyrol, and Vorarlberg. Carinthia has stayed in the realm of the BZÖ (formerly the FPÖ).[13]

Federalism has become a mixed argument with mixed consequences. An old pattern had seen ÖVP governors openly opposing their central party leadership. As a result of changes in the Schüssel years, SPÖ governors started to oppose the SPÖ leadership and the SPÖ chancellor. Strengthening a party's state level does not necessarily strengthen the party as a whole. The SPÖ governors—like their ÖVP counterparts who are first and foremost interested in winning their state elections—are tempted to distance themselves from "Vienna," meaning not the state and the city, but the federal government and their own central party leadership. What had been almost exclusively an ÖVP problem has become a significant SPÖ problem also.

At the end of the Schüssel years, Austrian politics had become significantly different. It was defined by an extremely volatile party system with an extremely unpredictable voting behavior and by a dramatic retreat of the voters from organized loyalties like party membership. Had the 2002 election seemed to reverse this trend by strengthening the two major parties at the cost of the FPÖ, the 2006 as well as the 2008 elections made clear that 2002 was just an exception in an ongoing trend of decline that both the SPÖ and ÖVP have to face. This has been accompanied by a significant decline in electoral turnout.

Table 1
Voting Behavior from 1975 Onward, in Percentage[14]

National Council Elections

Year	Votes for Parties					Electoral Turnout
	SPÖ	ÖVP	FPÖ	Greens	Others	
1975	50.4	43.0	5.4	-	1.2	92.9
1979	51.0	41.9	6.1	-	1.1	92.2
1983	47.7	43.2	5.0	3.3*	0.9	92.6
1986	43.1	41.3	9.7	4.8	0.8	90.5
1990	42.8	32.1	16.6	4.8	3.3	86.1
1994	34.9	27.7	22.5	7.3	7.9**	81.9
1995	38.1	28.3	21.9	4.8	6.9**	86.0
1999	33.2	26.9	26.9	7.4	5.7****	80.4
2002	36.5	42.3	10.0	9.5	1.8	84.3
2006	35.3	34.3	11.0	11.1	8.2*****	78.5
2008	**29.3**	**26.0**	**17.5**	**10.4**	**16.8********	**78.8**

*In 1983, two different green parties had presented candidates; **Liberal Forum (LIF) 6.0; ***LIF 5.5; ****LIF 3.7; *****BZÖ 4.1; ******BZÖ 10.7
Source: Official data from the Austrian Federal Ministry of the Interior.

Comparatively speaking, the concentration of the party system, reflecting the dominance the SPÖ and ÖVP enjoyed until the beginning of the 1990s, had been extraordinary. Considering the effects of proportional representation, an electoral system usually responsible for deconcentration by indirectly favoring smaller parties, the indicators of the Austrian party system until the 1980s can be called unique. The decline of the two major parties must be seen as an Austrian adaptation to average (Western) European standards, another proof of the ongoing "Westernization" and "de-Austrification" of the Alpine nation.

This can be underscored by an evaluation of party density. Austrian voters, who until the 1980s had been highly (even extremely) willing to be organized by the major parties in the form of ("card carrying") membership, started to leave the parties. SPÖ and ÖVP membership declined sharply. This could be explained as a parallel phenomenon of the two parties' declining capacity to mobilize voters. But because the winners of the de-concentration process—the FPÖ and the Greens—

never reached any kind of organizational density comparable to that of the SPÖ and the ÖVP, it must be argued that the losers of the overall trend are all parties as such—and not just the SPÖ and ÖVP.

In 1979, the SPÖ claimed to have 720,000 members. In 2005, this number had fallen by more than 50 percent to 350,000. The ÖVP membership cannot be easily compared, for the ÖVP does not have a uniform concept of direct party membership. Instead, it counts membership by the different sub-parties (*Teilorganisationen oder Bünde*) separately. But it can be assumed that the decline of the ÖVP's organizational strength is not so different from the SPÖ's. Significantly, the FPÖ in its years of dramatic electoral victories has never risen beyond 50,000 members—and the Greens, claiming to have a principally different understanding of organizing grassroots support, are claiming less than 5,000 members.[15]

The Second Republic, defined by a political culture of a highly concentrated party system and the dominance of densely organized political parties, has lost its major characteristics. But this has not been the specific result of the Schüssel years. Despite some moments of a short-term reversal of the general trend—like the outcome of the 2002 general elections, the Schüssel years cannot be seen as having an ongoing impact on the Austrian party system.

One process the Schüssel government started could be addressed by the post-Schüssel government. The process started by the Schüssel government was that of constitutional reform. After the 2002 election, the Schüssel government—as well as the opposition plus the nine states, the social partners, representatives of religious denominations, and other groups—had been assembled as a "Constitutional Convention" (*Verfassungskonvent*) to discuss and promote a new federal constitution for Austria. Following the examples of Switzerland and the European Union, the plan was to redefine the relationship between the union (*Bund*) and the nine states (*Länder*), to re-edit (and reform) basic rights and to make the constitution more coherent and understandable by reducing the numerous special constitutional norms. The Constitutional Convention did not succeed because too many veto players guaranteed this non-result. This is a process which could be restarted rather easily in a new administration.[16]

A post-Schüssel government could also focus on the issues of proportional representation in a constitutional revision process. After the 2006 elections, a debate started about the possibility of changing the special constitutional provision guaranteeing the rules of proportional representation for the National Council as well as for the State Diets (*Landtage*) and local parliaments (*Gemeinderäte*). The rationale behind this discourse is to improve the chances of clear majorities in parliament and to escape the need to form coalitions between unwilling partners. If such a proposal—which could be discussed more fully after the 2008 elections—were to be implemented, this would strongly favor the SPÖ and ÖVP and strongly disfavor all the other parties, especially the FPÖ and the Greens. Just as at the end of the Schüssel years, the difficulty of finding clear as well as stable majorities in the National Council has not been reduced compared with 1999, and this topic will not disappear fro Austria's political agenda.[17]

Remaining Austrian Peculiarities

Had Schüssel left Austrian politics after his electoral success in 2002, perhaps the most significant of his legacies would have been the downfall of Jörg Haider and the FPÖ. Schüssel could have claimed that—intentionally or not—the power-sharing arrangement with Haider had been the reason for the FPÖ's demise. Schüssel, the St. George of Austrian politics, could have been seen as the knight successfully killing the dragon. The FPÖ, for many reasons a burden for Austria's international reputation and credibility within Europe, had been crushed, evidenced by its decline from 27 percent of the votes in 1999 to 10 percent in 2002. There is no disputing that the main reason for the FPÖ's fall had been the impossibility of reconciling the right-wing extremist opposition rhetoric with the necessities of government pragmatism. More than 60 percent of the FPÖ electorate left the party disillusioned with the FPÖ's performance.

But the picture became rather different in 2006. Beginning in 2005, the split between the BZÖ, backed by Haider and most of the FPÖ's elite in parliament and government, and the FPÖ—now under Hans-Christian Strache—enabled the FPÖ to repeat its success as a party outside and against the Austrian mainstream. All the anti-European, anti-migration, xenophobic, and (regarding the Nazi past) revisionist rhetoric again had credibility because it was not tarnished with a government policy that could never deliver. At the end of the Schüssel years, the dragon was back.

Schüssel's legacy cannot be seen as responsible for the strength of a party which—in the European context—is seen as an ally of the French Front National, the Belgian *Vlaams Belang*, and the Bulgarian *Ataka*. The potential strength of the FPÖ—a party within the tradition of the Pan-German ideological camp, a tradition which includes the heritage of the Austrian National Socialist German Workers' Party (NSDAP or Nazi Party)—is the biggest of any extreme rightist party within the European Union. The FPÖ in the late 1980s and 1990s, starting from about 5 percent (1983), demonstrated with its 27 percent success in 1999 the size of this segment of angry modernization losers, who are in their great majority neither "Nazis" nor simple "fascists," but who don't care about the European consensus as articulated by the European Union and the Austrian political mainstream. The potential FPÖ electorate is "anti-system," and by being so, it accepts at least a rhetorical alliance with hardcore, right-wing extremism.

In Austria, the concept of a French style *cordon sanitaire*[18] never had been implemented, despite attempts by Vranitzky's SPÖ and Busek's ÖVP to do so. In this context, *cordon sanitaire* means accepting extremist parties in parliament, but never accepting them in any kind of cooperation, especially not as a coalition partner on any level. The *cordon sanitaire* did not work on the regional level in Carinthia, when a non-FPÖ majority in the Carinthian diet was unwilling to prevent Haider's governorship—with the exception of 1991, when the SPÖ and ÖVP united using their majority to vote Haider out of office. His return to the governorship in 1999 was *de facto* accepted by the majority still controlled by the SPÖ and ÖVP.

But the major break of any attempt to keep the FPÖ out of government came after the 1999 elections when Schüssel opted to become chancellor by forming an alliance with Haider. Schüssel got the position of head of government—and the FPÖ received proof of being respected. That this proof was not transformed in European respectability was demonstrated by the diplomatic boycott between February and September 2000,

Paradoxically, Schüssel's rather significant personal impact on the perception of Austria's chancellorship must lead to the recognition of the structural weakness of the chancellor's position. The Austrian federal chancellor is—by constitutional design—nothing more than the *primus inter pares* in the cabinet.[19] The executive power is not concentrated in the chancellor's position, neither is it concentrated in the position of the federal president. The executive power is with the single federal ministers. The sectoral power of such a minister is limited by law, not by the president or the chancellor. Because the Austrian Federal Cabinet consists of federal ministers of equal standing—among them the federal chancellor and the vice-chancellor—and because all the ministers enjoy a high degree of autonomy, the executive power in Austria neither rests with the head of state (the federal president) nor with the head of government (the federal chancellor). The Austrian government is not presidential—but it is neither parliamentarian in the sense of a prime minister-oriented Westminster democracy. Austria is governed by individual ministers; it is a republic of ministers.

Extra-constitutional factors may strengthen the chancellor's role. The most decisive factor among those is the aspect of the chancellor's role within his or her party. The intra-party authority of a chancellor may give him or her special authority over the cabinet members coming from his or her own party. As a party leader whose role is seen as decisive for the party's electoral success, the chancellor will have power not only based on the constitution, but also on his or her intra-party standing. But this does not lead to a special authority regarding cabinet members nominated by and belonging to a coalition partner.

As soon as the federal government is based on coalition agreements between two or more parties, the chancellor has no extra-constitutional authority whatsoever regarding policies designed and implemented by the second (or third) party in government. On the contrary, any coalition—and especially the coalition between parties of more or less equal strength—makes the vice-chancellor, usually the leader of the second governing party, a kind of second chancellor. It is the vice-chancellor who could be able to use his (her) intra-party standing for influencing policies of ministers of his (her) party in addition to the constitutional rules. According to these rules, the chancellor (as well as the vice-chancellor as his or her deputy) is just an ordinary member of the federal government without any special authority above the authority of every (other) single federal minister.

The question remains why the Schüssel years have been especially identified with the chancellor. There are two aspects to be considered as responsible for Schüssel's personal importance. First is Schüssel's special role in shaping the alliance of February 2000 against the declared intention of the federal president, Thomas Klestil, and against the unwritten rule that the leader of the strongest party in the National Council is entitled to the chancellorship. After his party's rather dramatic defeat of October 1999, Schüssel, the leader of the third-strongest party and—on the surface—extremely weakened by his responsibility for the ÖVP's worst electoral performance ever, "conquered" the chancellorship by making the deal with Haider and the FPÖ. In that respect, due to the breaking of unwritten rules, intentions, and expectations, the ÖVP-FPÖ coalition has been identified as "Schüssel's government." Second is the structural weakness of Schüssel's coalition partner. The FPÖ, rising fast as a radical, right-wing populist opposition party, was not prepared to govern. Soon it became obvious that the FPÖ's electorate could not be satisfied by the government's performance generally and by the FPÖ's performance in particular. The deep fall of the FPÖ became the reason why Schüssel—considered responsible for the ÖVP's big electoral success in 2002—had been seen as more powerful than any other chancellor with the exception of the one-party-government chancellors Josef Klaus and Bruno Kreisky. As the initially balanced ÖVP-FPÖ coalition became more and more unbalanced, the government became identified with Schüssel as the leader of the dominant party.

The legacy of the Schüssel years has become the burden of Schüssel's successors in government and in Schüssel's party. Because the consequence of the October 2006 elections has been the coalition between two partners of practically identical strength in parliament, the expectations—raised by the SPÖ in the almost seven years of opposition—could never have been fulfilled by Alfred Gusenbauer, chancellor of the SPÖ-ÖVP coalition. Moreover, because the ÖVP, used to being seen as the dominant Austrian party for almost seven years, had to learn to be satisfied with a much lower share of government power, the authority of Wilhelm Molterer, Schüssel's successor in the ÖVP, has been challenged from the very beginning of the Gusenbauer-Molterer coalition. Gusenbauer had to prove his authority—but this would have been possible only at the cost of Molterer's authority, and Molterer had to face the same situation on his side.

The Schüssel years had been responsible for unrealistic expectations—first and foremost regarding the power of an Austrian chancellor, limited not only by the constitution and by the absence of any kind of formal ranking within the cabinet, but also by the power sharing arrangements with an equally strong coalition partner.

Conclusion

The Schüssel years should not be overestimated—either in a negative or a positive way. The Schüssel government did not start a policy of pushing back the economic role the government had in Austria since 1945. The Schüssel government did not begin to reduce the government control over universities. The Schüssel government has not been the main reason why the social partners lost some of their traditional influence. In addition, the Schüssel government cannot be blamed for the decline of the Austrian party state—of the quantitative and qualitative dominance of two major parties not over politics, but over society.

But the Schüssel government will be rightfully linked to two major experiences. First, Schüssel's pact with Haider at the beginning of 2000 created a major European and international crisis, reminding Austria and the Austrians that the country is perceived, especially by the West, as the nation which had tried to make the world forget the participation of so many Austrians in the crimes of the Nazi regime. Second, despite the hardening of the confrontation between a government seen as being very much on the far right and a rather embittered leftist opposition, the rules of the democratic game never seemed to be in danger. The Schüssel years have to be considered an important proof of Austria's democratic stability.

Is Austria—the Austrian society, the Austrian political system—a different one because of the Schüssel years? The Austria of 2008 is different from the Austria of the post-1945 years. Political stability as guaranteed by consensus democracy and social partnership is not what it used to be. But this trend did not start in the year 2000. Like Austrian corporatism, the very much discussed "social partnership," the meaning of stability has been redefined as stability within the European Union.[20]

Austria can't go it alone. Austria is not an island of the blessed. Austria needs ever-deepening integration into the European Union. But this is not the result of the Schüssel years. The Schüssel era has been one period in an ongoing development.

Notes

1. Günter Bischof and Anton Pelinka, eds., *Austro-Corporatism: Past, Present, Future*, vol. 4, Contemporary Austrian Studies (New Brundwick, NJ: Transaction, 1996), 5-146; see all the topical essays in this volume by Andrei S. Markovits, Emmerich Tálos and Bernhard Kittel, Randall W. Kindley, Hans Seidel, and Ferdinand Karlhofer.

2. Emmerich Tálos, *Vom Siegeszug zum Rückzug: Sozialstaat Österreich, 1845-2005* (Innsbruck: StudienVerlag, 2005), 72-76; Alfred J. Noll, "Vor dem Sicherheitsstaat?," *Österreichische Zeitschrift für Politikwissenschaft* 1 (2004): 33-48, especially 39-47; Rainer Bauböck, "Migration und innere Sicherheit: Komplexe Zusammenhänge, paradoxe Effekte und politische Simplifizierungen," *Österreichische Zeitschrift für Politikwissenschaft* 1 (2004): 49-66, especially 63-66.

3. Rosenberger, "Die rechte und die linke Hand der Wendepolitik: Am Beispiel der Geschlechterordnung," *Anlassfall Österreich: Die Europäische Union auf dem Weg zu einer Wertegemeinschaft*, ed. Ferdinand Karlhofer et al. (Baden-Baden: Nomos, 2001), 47-60, here 55.

4. Gunther Hauser, *Österreich—dauernd neutral?* (Vienna: Braumüller, 2002), 110-24.

5. Sonja Puntscher Riekmann, "Österreich und die Europäische Union: Ein Blick zurück auf die Maßnahmen der Vierzehn," in Karlhofer et al., eds., *Anlassfall Österreich*, 131-40, here 137f.; Jacques Le Rider, "The Austrian Crisis as Seen by a French Scholar of Germanic Culture," in *Austria in the European Union*, vol. 10, Contemporary Austrian Studies, ed. Günter Bischof et al. (New Brunswick, NJ: Transaction, 2002), 56-66, here 59f.; Waldemar Hummer and Anton Pelinka, *Österreich unter "EU-Quarantäne": Die "Maßnahmen der 14" gegen die österreichische Bundesregierung aus politikwissenschaftlicher und juristischer Sicht: Chronologie, Kommentar, Dokumentation* (Vienna: Linde, 2002), 32-38; Rebecka Ulfgard, *Norm Consolidation in the European Union: The EU14-Austria Crisis in 2000* (Växjö: Växjö UP, 2005), 53-77.

6. Bretislav Dancák and Vit Hlousek, "The Concept of Leadership in Central Europe: Discussing the Austrian and Polish Cases," *Österreichische Zeitschrift für Politikwissenschaft* 2 (2006): 127-40, here 129.

7. See the articles by Elisabeth Gehrer, Georg Winckler, Wolf Rauch, and Kurt Grünewald in *Österreichisches Jahrbuch für Politik 2003*, ed. Andreas Kohl et al. (Vienna: Verlag für Geschichte und Politik / Oldenburg, 2004), 117-78.

8. Stuart E. Eizentstat, *Imperfect Justice: Looted Assets, Slave Labor, and the Unfinished Business of World War II* (New York: Public Affairs, 2003), 279-314.

9. Clemens Jabloner et al., *Schlussbericht der Historikerkommission der Republik Österreich: Vermögensentzug während der NS-Zeit sowie Rückstellungen und Entschädigungen seit 1945 in Österreich* (Vienna: Oldenburg, 2003), 17-79.

10. Cas Mudde, *The Ideology of the Extreme Right* (Manchester: Manchester UP, 2000), 9; Cas Mudde, *Populist Radical Right Parties in Europe* (Cambridge, UK: Cambridge UP, 2007), 172, 178f., 288-90.

11. Ruth Wodak and Anton Pelinka, eds., *The Haider Phenomenon in Austria* (New Brunswick, NJ: Transaction, 2002).

12. Anton Pelinka and Sieglinde Rosenberger, *Österreichische Politik: Grundlagen, Strukturen, Trends*, 3rd.ed. (Vienna: facultas.wuv, 2007), 136-40; Iris Ullmann, "Causa Austria: Österreichs Weg vom Sonderfall zu demokratischer Normalität unter besonderer Berücksichtigung des Faktors Leadership," PhD. diss., University of Innsbruck, 2008, 216-19; David Wineroither, "Struktur, Mechanismen und Dynamik von Regierungsmacht: Die Kanzlerschaft Wolfgang Schüssels," PhD. diss., University of Innsbruck, 2008, 156-76.

13. Michael Steger, ed., *Baustelle Bundesstaat: Perspektiven und Weiterentwicklung des politischen Systems Österreich* (Vienna: Braumüller, 2007), especially 57-64, 119-53.

14. Fritz Plasser and Peter A. Ulram, eds., *Wechselwahlen: Analysen zur Nationalratswahl 2006* (Vienna: facultas.wuv, 2007), 289.

15. Anton Pelinka, *Vom Glanz und Elend der Parteien: Struktur- und Funktionswandel des österreichischen Parteiensystems* (Innsbruck: Studien Verlag, 2005), 63.

16. Johannes Pollak and Peter Slominski, "'Konstitutioneller Moment' und Verfassungsreform: Eine Einschätzung des Österreich-Konvents," *Österreichische Zeitschrift für Politikwissenschaft* 4 (2005): 337-48, here 342-46.

17. Michael Fleischhacker, "Wir brauchen Euch nicht mehr. Oder: Das Ende der Zweiten Republik ist überfällig," in *Österreichisches Jahrbuch für Politik 2007*, ed. Andreas Khol et al. (Vienna: Böhlau, 2008), 645-50, especially 648f.

18. Mudde, *Populist Radical Right Parties*, 288-90.

19. Manfried Welan and Heinrich Neisser, *Der Bundeskanzler im österreichischen Verfassungsgefüge* (Vienna: Verlag Brüder Hollinkek, 1971), 93-106; Pelinka and Rosenberger, *Österreichische Politik*, 140-45; Wineroither, "Struktur, Mechanismen und Dynamik von Regierungsmacht," 306-16.

20. Emmerich Tálos, "Vom Vorzeige- zum Auslaufmodell? Österreichs Sozialpartnerschaft 1945-2005," in *Sozialpartnerschaft: Österreichische und Europäische Perspektiven*, ed. Ferdinand Karlhofer and Emmerich Tálos (Vienna: LIT, 2005), 185-216, here 208f.

FORUM

"Disturbing Creativity?"[1]: Austrian Literature, Studies, and Cultural Politics

Maria-Regina Kecht

Between 2005 and 2008, I had the honor and pleasure of serving as the editor of the international journal *Modern Austrian Literature* (*MAL*). For readers not familiar with the publication, I should provide a few pieces of contextual information. The beginnings of *MAL* date back to the early 1960s when the Arthur Schnitzler Society (founded in the United States) wanted to create its own research venue. In 1968, however, the publication initially dedicated exclusively to scholarship on Schnitzler was renamed *Modern Austrian Literature* clearly expanding its focus and, thus, also its readership. For several decades, *MAL* was inextricably associated with Professor Donald Daviau (University of California, Riverside) and Professor Jorun Johns (California State University, San Bernardino), who devoted their energy to the development and internationalization of the journal.

In the course of time, the Arthur Schnitzler Society decided to be officially in synch with the contents of its scholarly publication and, accordingly, chose to transform itself into the Modern Austrian Literature and Culture Association (MALCA). The Association and its journal adopted a series of new standards and practices for the organization of its annual symposium and the editorial work related to its quarterly, *MAL*. So, for example, the position of editor is filled on the basis of a national announcement, and the editor serves for a three-year term. The journal has an international advisory board consisting of scholars in

1. The term refers to the question (and title) of the roundtable discussion at the 2008 conference of the German Studies Association, which is the basis for this "Forum."

Austrian Studies working at U.S. institutions or overseas. The board members are instrumental in the blind peer review of submitted manuscripts as well as in the selection and nomination of the best *MAL* essay for the annual Max Kade Prize. Each *MAL* issue contains four or five articles and approximately twenty book reviews. The acceptance rate of submitted manuscripts is less than 25 percent. The print version of the journal is widely available in U.S. and overseas research libraries, and all archived issues (from the journal's inception to today) are also accessible electronically via EBSCO. This has greatly contributed to the growing distribution of *MAL*.

Since *MAL* is the journal of MALCA, it goes without saying that the publication reflects the philosophy and research direction of the organization. Several years ago, the executive council of MALCA and the organization's members agreed to emphasize the "C" (cultural) component of Austrian Studies in its annual conference and in the journal so as to respond successfully to the currents of the discipline as well as to accommodate our readers' scholarly interests. Particularly among the junior colleagues in our profession, the research identification with cultural studies is more prevalent than with literary studies.

A glance at any of the *MAL* issues of the last several years demonstrates that the scholarly spectrum in Austrian Studies—as presented by MALCA—has not only grown far beyond the original focus on Arthur Schnitzler, but also beyond strictly literary topics. The conventions and criteria scholars use in their selection of research issues have changed; methods and approaches have undergone various kinds of shifts; a plurality of critical readings can co-exist without any professional indictment; and interdisciplinarity brings together various perspectives that allow *MAL* readers to recontextualize familiar texts and/or authors. Quite clearly, the notions of what is canonical and what might be peripheral or marginal have changed, which, in turn, has brought about a very productive decentralization in Austrian Studies and placed Austrian literature and culture in a much wider, Central European framework that comprises the cultural production of the regions/countries that were part of the Habsburg Empire.

Quite generally one can observe a trend towards a "wider angle" and broader views that offer more complex connections and establish reference points that link diverse fields of inquiry and different systems of thought. Literary analysis may be placed in various kinds of contexts, which may emerge from intellectual history, social history, psychology, philosophy, media theory, technology, and so forth. Neither in principle nor in terms of disciplinary conventions are there any limits to this sort of "mix and match." This kind of freedom may be conducive to intellectual creativity, but may also undermine analytical stringency and methodological coherence.

When leafing through the *MAL* issues that have appeared over the last several years, we can discern the following trends and thematic clusters: transnational or transhistorical analyses, comparative papers, interdisciplinary approaches, gendered perspectives on female and male authors, canonical works in new contexts, popular culture as an object of inquiry, and inter-media studies (linking texts with film or photography). It seems as if the pursuit of theory for theory's sake is a thing of the past, and there is no competition for any particular theory's superiority. Innovation and originality emerge from the specific contexts scholars succeed in establishing.

When we take a look at the abstracts that summarize the published articles in *MAL*, we notice a wealth of inter- or trans-disciplinary research areas into which the articles can be subsumed: cultural transfer, literary history and literary politics, social history of cultural contributors (such as writers), intertextuality, performativity, translation, systems theory, media history and media theory, cultural theories. Only rarely do we find a strictly philological paper or an essay that could be categorized as a "close reading" in the original sense of the term.

Quite logically, the Kade prize-winning essays of *MAL* reflect the direction noted above. Here are some examples. In 2005, the award was given to an essay on the relatively little-known author Caroline Pichler (1769-1843) whose work in two of her historical plays "traces Pichler's journey from advocating for a German-speaking nation under Habsburg rule to realizing the inherent instability of the Habsburg hold on power in the emerging nationalist discourse" (quote from abstract). Board members considered the article as "exemplary scholarship in its combination of aesthetic and historical analyses, and its strict attention to the micro-politics of the Habsburg nineteenth century." In 2006, the winning essay on the Nobel prizewinner Elfriede Jelinek and her *Prinzessinnendramen* was praised for its "fascinating and well-argued case of literary 'sampling' or intertextuality, well-tracked in terms of its cultural reference and the meanings thereof." Reviewers were impressed with the compelling analysis of the question of literary inscription in Jelinek's textual and political solidarity with (and tribute to) Ingeborg Bachmann, Marlen Haushofer, and Sylvia Plath. A year later, another well researched and highly perceptive article was singled out for the Kade prize. This time, the editorial board chose a piece on the Viennese satirist Karl Kraus and his writings on etiquette. "With nuance and detail," the commentary reads, "[the author] situates Kraus's critique within turn-of-the-century Vienna as well as within the larger functions and systems of language." The essay was a superb example of well-done work in *Kulturwissenschaft*.

The national identity—Swiss, Austrian, and Swedish—and professional status of the Kade prize winners—college professor, independent scholar, and doctoral candidate—indicates diversity at a different level. It is actually quite noteworthy that over the past years, many of the contributors to *MAL* have not been American and do not necessarily teach German Studies at U.S. institutions. A good number of scholars submitting their manuscripts to *MAL* work in Europe—not necessarily at universities and not necessarily at departments of *Germanistik*. A growing number of submissions, which is not the same as saying the number of printed articles, have come from scholars in Eastern Europe—from the Czech Republic, Poland, Slovenia, Croatia, or Hungary. Many of them have had access to *MAL* thanks to the newly founded *Österreich Bibliotheken* and are eager to connect and exchange ideas internationally with colleagues in Austrian Studies. These efforts in international cooperation are also reflected in the collaborative research projects that individual *MAL* issues have been presenting.

So, given our discussion, we need to ask whether in the pages of *MAL* we can find innovation, originality, ingenuity, or "disturbing creativity"? Ultimately, of course, the readers of the journal have to come to their own conclusions and pass a verdict. The process of anonymous, blind peer review guarantees that the best of the submitted manuscripts are accepted for publication and that the printed essays offer provocative insights, stimulate scholarly discussion, and inspire further research. The noteworthy bricolage of theoretical concepts and frames of reference, which characterizes a good number of articles, can be fascinating, interesting, and also impressive, but it can also be considered "disturbing" when the reader discerns a certain, perhaps quite intentional, arbitrariness that instrumentalizes the selected text for a performance—an intellectual show—on the part of the scholar/author. Objectively, there is no way we can come up with a clear-cut definition of what might be "disturbing" about the scholarly creativity in the pages of *MAL*—whether this is in the positive sense of the term, implying thought-provoking, out-of-the-box cogitation, or in the negative sense of the term suggesting irritation, frustration, or confusion. Most likely only hindsight will allow us to ascertain whether examples of "disturbing creativity" are more than manifestations of critical fads shared by the contemporary scholarly community.

It seems to me that the development of *MAL* over the past several years indicates a vibrant, healthy, and exciting international research climate that benefits tremendously from the commitment and contributions of young scholars both inside and outside the United States. We can observe plenty of creativity, which may be related to the disappearance of boundaries at various levels, for example, great interdisciplinarity, broad and multiple modes of contextualization, intermedia perspectives, and a wide spectrum of literary and literary historical connections that locate authors and texts in innovative and unexpected ways.

I can only wish that this trend will continue and that many readers of *Contemporary Austrian Studies* will want to make their own contribution to *MAL's* "disturbing creativity."

Austrian and German History and Literature

David S. Luft

Austrian literature in relation to the broader context of German and Austrian history and literature is a topic I discussed in the early 1980s with Wendelin Schmidt-Dengler, as well as Hilde Spiel and Kurt Fischer, and I have returned to these concerns in various ways since then. As a historian, these questions are particularly interesting to me. In particular, I have always wondered what the relationship of literature is to the broader context of intellectual life—including philosophy, politics, and the social and natural sciences. In my current research, I am exploring these questions in two related projects. *The Austrian Tradition in German Culture* is an intellectual history of German-speaking Austria that emphasizes Cisleithanian Austria in the geographical sense (that is the Austrian and Bohemian hereditary lands of the Habsburgs) from the eighteenth century to 1918—and the Austrian Republic thereafter. My second project, *Hugo von Hofmannsthal and the Austrian Idea*, is a translation edition of Hofmannsthal's essays on culture and politics, which explores his understanding of Austrian intellectual life in relation to a broader German culture. My general concern is the importance of specifying the historical, linguistic, geographical, and social context of discussions of Austrian literature.

For the purposes of this discussion, I want to recall the reservoir of meanings and relationships that we draw on when we speak of Austrian literature. One clear approach to this subject is to emphasize the period since 1945 or since the collapse of the monarchy in 1918. In either case, we have at least a relatively clear region that includes primarily German-speakers. But even in such approaches, questions always arise: What is the relationship of this Austria to the larger Austria in its various forms from the tenth century to the early twentieth? What is the relationship of this little Austria to German language and culture, or even to other languages and cultures? Does Austria have its own literature? What would it mean to say that it does?

Austrian national identity came to consciousness and clarity largely after the fact—in the 1970s and 1980s—and then began to disappear into the European Union. In the immediate postwar era, this conception of Austrian national identity grew out of efforts to reestablish a connection to the imperial past. In my project on the Austrian tradition in German culture, I am interested in clarifying what we mean by the Austrian intellectual tradition since the eighteenth century. I have found it important to underscore the connection to Bohemia, and I have learned a great deal in this regard and in related matters from Hofmannsthal. Indeed, at the heart of any discussion of Austrian culture are the mature essays of Hofmannsthal, yet historians are often unaware of the extent of his influence on discussions of this theme. Hofmannsthal had very clear ideas on this subject, although he examined the question in a variety of different ways, and his ideas have not always been accurately recalled. In addition, Hofmannsthal's conception of the Austrian idea also blurs into his idea of Europe and into his understanding of what is German, and he repeatedly insisted that these meanings are not static, but change over time.

Hofmannsthal's most striking definition of the Austrian idea appears in his essay by that title in 1917: "This primary and fateful gift for compromise with the East; let us say it precisely: toward compromise between the old European, Latin-German and the new European Slavic world, this only task and *raison d'être* of Austria [...]."[1] This definition touches on many dimensions of Austrian intellectual history from Bernard Bolzano and Adalbert Stifter to Peter Handke and Ingeborg Bachmann, but what was central for Hofmannsthal was the special relationship between the Alpine lands and Bohemia until 1918. He makes very clear that, when he says "Austria," he is thinking of Cisleithanian Austria and not about the Habsburg Monarchy as a whole. Like Franz Grillparzer, Hofmannsthal thought of Bohemians and Moravians as he did about Styrians and Tyroleans, as part of the long-standing core of the monarchy. Grillparzer did not count Hungary as part of Austria any more than he did Spain, indeed less so. One might say that all the clichés about Austria are true, especially the ones that derive from Hofmannsthal—but they refer not to the Habsburg Monarchy and not to Vienna or to the present-day Austrian Republic, but to Austria and Bohemia, especially during the four centuries before the First World War.

Hofmannsthal often thought about "Austrian" and "German" in ways that blur into each other—usually in the sense of Austria as an expression of Germanness (*deutsches Wesen*). His decisive examples precede 1871 and often connect in some way to the early modern period or even to the Middle Ages. In "Austria in the Mirror of Its Literature" (1916) he even offers an unfamiliar description of the Germans who conquered the world: "That German essence, which once conquered the world, which penetrated both East and West, which sent its architects, its businessmen, its scholars, its generations of peasants across the Lower Rhine, across the Oder and down the Danube, who pursued and developed trade, enlightened and enriched, colonized without conquering, led without ruling [...]."[2]

German historians have often seen the Holy Roman Empire as a frustratingly decentralized precursor of the real Germany, whereas Hofmannsthal saw it as the mainstream of what he took to be German. Hofmannthal's vision of the development of German culture since the Middle Ages is not without its problems to be sure, resonating in some respects with the experience of Europeans in the American West. But, instead of limiting himself to Austria as a region or a state, he discusses German culture in a much larger sense that evokes a dualism between Austria and a sense of "Germany" that goes beyond temporary forms of Prussian Germany or the possibilities of the 1860s. This is, in many respects, truer than the conventional accounts of German nationalism, and it accounts for much of the ambiguity in the way Hofmannsthal writes about Germans and Austrians, here and elsewhere. He frequently contrasts Austria not to the German state, but to cosmopolitan German culture. This way of thinking is hardly even accessible today, perhaps even to German historians. But Austrian historians, of course, have a substantial stake in this cosmopolitan notion of Germanness, which includes Otto von Bismarck and Gottfried Wilhelm Leibniz, as well as Prince Eugene and Franz Joseph. Hofmannsthal has a number of ways of seeing the Austrian idea, but he consistently keeps alive a broader sense of Germanness that is richer and more cosmopolitan than the nationalisms of 1871, 1938, or 1989—or even 1914.

Indeed, if Hofmannsthal were alive today he might be in a position to argue that Germany represents Austrian or European ideas more than Austria does.

> If we see Austria as the one part of the old German empire in which the energies of German history are living and working, the implication for the German is: Austria is not merely something that still exists but an unfinished task. Much that could not find resolution in the new empire that was founded in 1870, and yet was a German mission, inner German life, something that has impact and is willed by fate, should and will be solved here.[3]

But German culture in this cosmopolitan sense (Michael Steinberg has used the term "cosmopolitan nationalism"[4]) was also not a specifically Austrian idea—nor did Hofmannsthal think it was—but, rather, the linguistic and spiritual sources of the whole people in the sense that William Shakespeare could be said to symbolize for the English-speaking world—and this is roughly what Johann Wolfgang von Goethe was for Hofmannsthal. This view leads Hofmannsthal to a third definition, which links the first two: "Austria is the special task that is posed to the German spirit in Europe. It is the field, directed by destiny, of a purely intellectual and spiritual imperialism. For it does not require the intervention of German political force, but to be sure the constant influence by the German spirit."[5] On the other hand, even in 1915, he was alert to the dangers of this dependence on Germany: "If Germany gives us something less than its highest and purest, it will become for us a poison."[6]

Notes

1. Hugo von Hofmannsthal, "Die österreichische Idee," *Reden und Aufsätze II, Gesammelte Werke*, ed. Bernd Schoeller and Rudolf Hirsch, vol. 9 (Frankfurt am Main: Fischer Taschenbuch, 1979), 456-57.

2. Hugo von Hofmannsthal, "Austria in the Mirror of Its Literature," *Reden und Aufsätze II*, 22-23.

3. Hugo von Hofmannsthal, "Wir Österreicher und Deutschland," *Reden und Aufsätze II*, 393.

4. Michael P. Steinberg, *The Meaning of the Salzburg Festival: Austria as Theater and Ideology, 1890-1938* (Ithaca, NY: Cornell UP, 1990).

5. Hofmannsthal, "Wir Österreicher und Deutschland," *Reden und Aufsätze II*,. 393-94.

6. Ibid., 394.

Austrian-Jewish Studies?

Leslie Morris

In thinking about the future or the viability of Austrian Studies, I would like to pose a question about the place of Jewish Studies within Austrian Studies. German-Jewish Studies has become a recognized subfield within both German Studies and Jewish Studies, with Austria and the legacy of the Habsburg Monarchy folded into it. Yet in probing the contours of the future of Austrian Studies, I propose to sidestep the now rather tired debates about the viability of national literatures as an area of study; in fact, in many respects Austria, as a former empire and ongoing borderland region, presents a way out of the usual conundrum of thinking about literary studies and national spaces. Scholars in Austrian Studies have long pleaded for the cultural and historical specificity of an inquiry into Austria that is not subsumed by German culture; indeed, let me suggest that *if* it is perhaps time to craft a more conscious field of Jewish Studies within the context of Austrian Studies, we need to enable Austrian-Jewish Studies to evolve and flourish in a different interpretive space than German-Jewish Studies.

Significant scholarly work on the multiple intersections of Jewishness and other national cultures in the former Habsburg lands exists; much of this recent work has been indelibly shaped by Gilles Deleuze and Felix Guattari's conception of Franz Kafka's work as exemplary of a "minor" literature.[1] Significantly, the explorations of Jewishness and "the minor" have complicated the notion of Vienna as the center of Austrian-Jewish culture. Let me single out the case of Czernowitz—either celebrated or critiqued as the famed "topos" of a literary world—as the test case for mapping out the relationship between real and imaginary literary and geographical spaces and between text and memory.[2] If the task of a new Austrian-Jewish Studies is to re-read the textual spaces of Jewish memory, then Czernowitz is the place/text par excellence, for it reveals the fault lines between literary text, cultural and historical memory, and geographical and textual sites of memory. An Austrian-Jewish Studies might be one way to articulate the ongoing complex and often violent enmeshment of Austrianness and Jewishness.

So what would an Austrian-Jewish Studies look like? First, it would have to do more than merely point a finger at the deliberate silences and erasures of Jewish history and Jewish experience enacted in the Second Republic and the failure to create any sort of Jewish visibility or legibility as the nation-state was emerging. Second, I would make a plea not simply to put at the center of inquiry the Jewish figures who made significant contributions to Austrian culture— in other words, not to create a Jewish Studies that relies largely on biographical and historical "Jews" as an antidote to their later expulsion and exclusion. Rather, perhaps the case of Austria, where debates about Jews both present and absent have come much later to the surface, gives a chance for literary and cultural studies scholars to approach the question of the links between Jewishness and textuality, that is, of the viability of an Austrian-Jewish Studies that might be understood as a complex relationship of textual correspondences. To do this, we would need not to position Jewishness and Austrianness as diametrically opposed categories, but rather, as Matti Bunzl has suggested,[3] as "symptoms of modernity"—to reimagine Jewishness as an integral part of Austrianness and to reimagine Austrianness as the partial product and reflection of specifically Jewish contributions.

Let me illustrate this more concretely. While Elfriede Jelinek has attracted widespread and deserved attention in cultural circles for her work in postdramatic theater and her innovative prose works, there has also been an attempt to categorize her as "Jewish" author, drawing on her (however tenuous) Jewish family history. Yet Jelinek places herself not so much for reasons of family history (she is not halachically Jewish) within a trajectory of Austrian-Jewish writing from Karl Krauss[4] to the present. In this way, the taxonomy of Jewish writing can be expanded beyond the biographical to include textual relationships. Thus Dagmar Lorenz's volume on Austria in the University of Nebraska Press's series on contemporary Jewish writing includes Jelinek alongside more canonically "Jewish" authors such as Erich Fried, Elias Canetti, Paul Celan, Ruth Klüger, and Robert Schindel.[5] If an Austrian-Jewish Studies is to forge these textual definitions of Jewishness, we need to expand beyond the parameters of what can be anthologized as "Jewish" writing in Austria. To this end, I want to cite the approach found in Regina Kecht's recent work exploring Jelinek's novel *Die Kinder der Toten* as part of a corpus of Jewish text.[6] Kecht gives a reading of the frontispiece of the novel, suggesting its function as a metaphorical mezuzah that draws the reader into textually Jewish space. It is precisely this sort of reading that gives the possibility of merging work in Jewish literary studies, Jewish textuality, with Austrian Studies. Leaving aside the problematic question of whether or not Jelinek is

Jewish, or Jewish enough, Kecht turns instead to the complex interplay between Jelinek's work and a Jewish textual tradition.

If we are to move into an Austrian-Jewish Studies that has the capacity to navigate the foundational links between text, memory, history, Austrianness, Jewishness, and beyond, then we must do precisely this kind of work: unveiling and excavating the complex enmeshments of Jewish culture and Austrian culture that might enable us, for instance, to see not only the contribution of Jewish artists and thinkers to the project of modernity, but even more significantly, modernism and the avant-garde as a movement that enabled a new approach to and interpretation of Judaism. It is thus the interplay between the hermeneutic meanings of Judaism as cultural discourse—Jewishness as the trope of the avant garde—in particular as this discourse evolved in Vienna at the turn of the century, that might be a good place for an Austrian-Jewish Studies to lay its anchor. In other words, an Austrian-Jewish Studies would not just turn its attention to the Jewish contributions to Austrian culture, but instead would open up new discussions of the complex interactions and interplay between Austrian and Jewish culture, and the formative way in which Jewishness as trope of the modern has to be part of any approach to Austrian Studies.

Notes

1. See Gilles Deleuze and Felix Guattari, *Kafka: Toward a Minor Literature*, trans. Dana Polan (Minneapolis: U of Minnesota P, 1986).

2. See Andrei Corbea-Hoisie, *Czernowitzer Geschichten: Über eine städtische Kultur in Mittelosteuropa* (Vienna: Böhlau, 2003); Winfried Menninghaus, "Czernowitz/ Bukowina als Topos deutsch-jüdischer Geschichte," *Merkur* 3/4 (1999): 345-57; Leslie Morris, "Translating Czernowitz: The Non-Place of East Central Europe," *Studies in 20th and 21st Century Literature* 31.1 (2007): 187-205.

3. Matti Bunzl, *Symptoms of Modernity: Jews and Queers in Late Twentieth-Century Vienna* (Berkeley, CA: U of California P, 2004).

4. See Paul Reitter, *The Anti-Journalist: Karl Kraus and Jewish Self-Fashioning in Fin-de-Siecle Europe* (Chicago: U of Chicago P, 2008).

5. See Dagmar C.G. Lorenz, ed. *Contemporary Jewish Writing in Austria* (Lincoln, NE: Nebraska UP, 1999).

6. Kecht, Regina, "The Polyphony of Remembrance: Reading *Die Kinder der Toten*," in *Elfriede Jelinek: Writing Woman, Nation, and Identity*, ed. Matthias Konzett and M. Lamb-Faffelberger (Madison, NJ: Fairleigh Dickinson UP, 2007), 189-217.

Disturbing Creativity: Phantom Pains, Arts, and Cultural Policies in Postwar Austria

Andreas Stadler

Austria is known worldwide as a much sought after tourism destination, with its capitals of high culture, such as Vienna and Salzburg, as well as its alpine ski resorts. However, this positive and inviting image has been marred in recent years by crime scandals such as the Josef Fritzl (2008) and the Natascha Kampusch (2006) cases. More or less implicitly, these human tragedies were attributed to a specifically Austrian characteristic: the failure to come to terms with Autria's Nazi past.[1] Even if this oftentimes claimed connection is not empirically verifiable, the discourse shows that a diffuse, sometimes even manifest, suspicion does, in fact, exist.

This stereotype of an "unsettled past" began to emerge in the 1980s during the course of the Waldheim Affair, and resurfaced in the year 2000 when the Wolfgang Schüssel (ÖVP) and Jörg Haider (FPÖ) government made international headlines and triggered political sanctions by fourteen member states of the European Union. The most recent elections in September 2008, where Austria's right-wing populist Freedom Party of Austria (*Freiheitliche Partei Österreichs*, or FPÖ) won 17.5 percent and its younger brother, the Alliance for the Future of Austria (*Bündnis Zukunft Österreich*, or BZÖ) won 10.7 percent of the vote, have once again focused the world's attention on Austria. However, open criticism was mostly missing from the international media.

The lack of criticism can probably be attributed to three factors. First, even Austria's harshest critics may have realized that the 2000 vote did not really represent a danger to democracy. This was surely aided by a strong showing of the civil society, supported and even headed by the cultural sector and artistic community. Second, Austrian President Heinz Fischer, head of state since 2004, is an internationally respected personality who stands for democracy and stability. Third, and finally, it was apparent very early on that once again the government would consist of a coalition between the Social Democratic Party (*So-*

zialdemokratische Partei Österreichs, or SPÖ), which had won 29 percent of the vote, and the Austrian People's Party (*Österreichische Volkspartei*, or ÖVP), which had won 26 percent of the vote. In any case, the U.S. media showed no sign of serious concern in their appraisals of the Austrian elections.

Today, Austria represents a contemporary cultural nation with a distinct civil society. Besides its so-called "high culture" at the Staatsoper and the Salzburger Festspiele, artistic traditions such as the unsettling "Viennese Actionism" are also associated with Austria. Especially within the visual arts, Actionism is considered Austria's decisive contribution to post- World War II art.

Names such as Günter Brus, Hermann Nitsch, Otto Muehl, and Rudolf Schwarzkogler are included in most standard volumes on art history. Their works, as well as those by their younger colleagues, like Valie Export (b. 1940), fetch record prices and are included in many important international art collections.

But from where does this inclination of Austrian artists toward scandal and irritation, this disturbing creativity, come?

Austrian artistic expression most certainly correlates with the enormous upheavals of the twentieth century and constitutes a tradition that dates back at least to the masters of classical modernism like Gustav Klimt (1862 to 1918) and Egon Schiele (1890 to 1918), who were repeatedly labeled as troublemakers and often suffered tremendous public rejection. Another well-known representative of this era, Oskar Kokoschka (1886 to 1980), was added to the Nazis' list of "degenerate artists" and banned, as were too many others.

The next generation of artists, those who followed World War II, fought against cultural conservatism up to the point of self-destruction. After all, the prevailing cultural policies after 1945 were meant to safeguard the Austrian state ideologically and reinvent the "Austrian nation." In order to achieve this, a rural and/or alpine aesthetic was embraced, which was fused with the country's baroque and monarchistic legacy. Peter Rossegger and Heinrich Waggerl were the "poet laureates" that dominated school curricula well into the 1970s. National feats of strength were performed in the years of liberation/occupation from 1945 to 1955 to reconstruct the destroyed State Opera House and the Burgtheater.

Operettas as counterparts to musicals became important hallmarks of musical theater. A decisive influence was Robert Stolz, for example, who fled to the United States to escape the Nazis and returned to Austria in 1946. The 1954 film *Echo der Berge: der Förster vom Silberwald* provides an exemplary perspective of the new elite's self-perception.[2]

However, this cultural avoidance strategy was not able to cope with the loss of a multi-ethnic empire and the monarchy, nor with the painful legacy of National Socialism. Thus, in the beginning of the 1960s, representatives of the younger generation protested against cultural conservatism as well as against the still evident remnants of Nazi ideology. In the years from 1962 to 1965, a prominent public debate exploded about the case of university professor Taras Borodajkewycz, who glorified National Socialism in his lectures at the Vienna University of Economics. Heinz Fischer, a student at the time, accused Borodajkewycz publicly on the basis of notes taken by Ferdinand Lacina, and was convicted and fined for defamation of character.

But artists also revolted against this prevailing culturally conservative mood. Of course, the scandalous aesthetics of Actionism have their roots and role models in the American Happenings and were inspired by the Fluxus movement. However, the actionists' special inclination toward aggression and—even more importantly—auto-aggression (Rudolf Schwarzkogler, Günter Brus) was a unique Austrian contribution. This radical stance should be interpreted, in my opinion, as an expression of the phenomenon of phantom pain which was exceedingly felt after the collapse of the multiethnic empire, but mainly after the annihilation and expulsion of the Jewish elements of Austrian society and culture. The severing of this Jewish and multiethnic, Slavic cultural heritage effectively led to self-criticism and castigation, which the sensitive artists of this generation—often subconsciously— undertook and articulated for the rest of society.

A key example is the Action from 1968 entitled *Kunst und Revolution* (Art and Revolution), which became a huge scandal. Otto Mühl (b. 1925), Peter Weibel (b. 1944), Oswald Wiener (b. 1935), and Günter Brus (b. 1938) simultaneously performed so-called actions. In his "Action 33," his body analysis action, Brus undressed, cut his chest and thighs with a razor, urinated into a glass and drank it. He defecated and then smeared his body with excrement. Finally, he lay on a table and proceeded to masturbate while singing the national anthem. Günter Brus was sentenced to six months in prison for vilification of Austrian symbols and creating a public nuisance through amoral behavior. Following this, he went to Germany, but continued to work as an artist. In 1996 he was awarded the Grand Austrian State Prize for art by then Minister of Education and Culture Rudolf Scholten. Today, that action has become an icon of Actionism, Austrian art history, and postwar historiography.

In his experiments on himself and his bondage actions, the artist Rudolf Schwarzkogler (1940 to 1969) also came very close to this disturbing and self-destructive phantom-pain reaction.

The liberal international mood of the 1960s and 1970s helped to expand areas of freedom. In Austria, troublemaker artists were also given platforms by politicians and, thus, by society. In his 1970 government policy declaration, the newly incumbent Federal Chancellor Bruno Kreisky (1911 to 1990) expressed his hopes for a youth that would challenge the existing system and establishment with full disrespect. In 1977, Kreisky went so far as to demand a "socio-critical cultural radicalism."[3]

The disturbing creativity of artists was once again evident in the 1980s, especially in the form of reactions to the Waldheim Affair of 1986. Alfred Hrdlicka, for example, used a giant wooden horse for a large-scale demonstration against President Kurt Waldheim as a form of ironic protest. Thomas Bernhard, a poetic surgeon of the abysses of the Austrian soul, started a national debate with his play *Heldenplatz* (1988). In his own way, even the chairman of the Freedom Party at the time, Jörg Haider, contributed by railing against Elfriede Jelinek, Peter Turrini, and Rudolf Scholten during the election campaign.

The literary oeuvre and the assertive and critical stance of Jelinek, who was awarded the Nobel Prize for Literature in 2004, is a further example of the unsettling creative force evident in the Austrian cultural scene.

In the aforementioned year 2000, Christoph Schlingensief created the Container Action *Please Love Austria* (*Bitte liebt Österreich*). Containers with signs reading "Foreigners Out" (*Ausländer Raus*), a Freedom Party campaign slogan, were set up in front of the Vienna State Opera. Various performers and supporters were locked up in them in the style of the TV series *Big Brother*. This Container Action dominated the Austrian political, public, and media landscape for weeks. With the theme "The Other Austria" (*das andere Österreich*), many artists campaigned for months against the so-called "Blue-Black" government,[4] some of them engaging in political opposition, some of them even abandoning Austria altogether, such as the composers Olga Neuwirth and Georg Friedrich Haas, curator Robert Fleck, and architect Raimund Abraham.

Even if tensions have calmed down in the meantime and artists have made peace with their country, the example of Dirk Stermann and Christoph Grissemann's work in 2008 shows that the troublemaking power of Austrian creativity is alive and well. When the duo satirized the public outpourings of sadness on Austrian television following Jörg Haider's death, they received death threats from people in Carinthia and were forced to cancel appearances there. This shows that art—no matter what kind—is still capable of triggering heated emotions, asking disturbing questions, and testing boundaries.

Notes

1. See, for example, John Wray, "Dungeons and Austrian," *New York Times*, 2 May 2008: A21.

2. See, for example, Oliver Rathkolb, *Die Paradoxe Republik*, 2005, English ed. (Oxford: Berghahn Books, forthcoming 2009).

3. See, for example, Marion Knapp *Österreichische Kulturpolitik und das Bild der Kulturnation* (Frankfurt am Main: Peter Lang, 2005).

4. Blue is the FPÖ's color, while black is the ÖVP's color.

BOOK REVIEWS

Anton Pelinka, Hubert Sickinger, Karin Stögner, *Kreisky, Haider: Bruchlinien österreichischer Identitäten* (Vienna: Braumüller, 2008)

Steven Beller

Bruno Kreisky and Jörg Haider would seem at first sight to be an odd pair to bracket in a book about Austrian identities. That is no doubt why the authors thought it necessary for the two essays in this volume—one by Karin Stögner on Kreisky, the other by Hubert Stickinger on Haider—to be connected by an introduction by Anton Pelinka. This introduction is, notably, not on Austrian identities but, rather, on "Austrian and Jewish identity." As someone who has made the case that there is actually a very close, symbiotic relationship between these two identities (and I should declare here that Pelinka ends his introduction with an analysis of my views on this symbiosis), I find much that is praiseworthy in this book and think that the juxtaposition of Kreisky and Haider does open up interesting avenues for understanding postwar Austrian identity and politics. I also think, however, there are points where the book suffers from the flaws in Austrian identity formation that it purports to delineate.

The least problematic part of the book is that on Haider, a fairly straightforward analysis of his political career and the ideological background that went with it. Sickinger makes a very good case that Haider's background, as the son of National Socialists, had a decisive effect on his views during his rise to power, before his wish for power forced him into an embrace of a (still nativist and xenophobic) Austrian national identity. Sickinger also makes a good point that much of the strength of Haider's appeal lay in his demand that postwar Austria's establishment own up to its Nazi past, while at the same time minimizing the evils that were perpetrated by Austrians in Nazism's name. This was, to some extent, a reversal and challenge to the establishment's "life lie" that attempted to deny any substantial Austrian connection to German National Socialism, presenting Austrians as mere victims of Germans. Yet, as Stögner and Sickinger point out, Haider's approach, by transferring responsibility from actual perpetrators and party members to the collective of all Austrians and by then denying "collective guilt," still had the same effect of "making harmless" the Austrian role in the war and in the Holocaust. The last part of the Haider section, chronicling the demise of Haider's movement, makes for ironic reading considering the resurgence of the far right in Austrian politics in the 2008 election and after Haider's death, but overall this is an interesting sketch of the cultural-political history of the (formerly German) nationalist right in postwar Austria.

Stögner's section on Kreisky is also discourse on a high level, and her central contention that Kreisky was the poster child of that attempt by the postwar establishment to move on from the horror of the past by, in effect, denying it (as Germany's fault), is fairly incontestable. Nevertheless, in the details of her argument Stögner is so relentless that she goes too far in raking Kreisky through the mud of Austrian anti-Semitism and willful political amnesia. There is little mention of the fact that Kreisky's enlightened policies and pronouncements did make Austrians, despite their problematic relationship with their past, a much more liberal and progressive, outward-looking and inclusive nation. Whatever Kreisky's function as an alibi for Austrian anti-Semites, Austria's populace in general became far more accepting of others and far less hidebound under Kreisky's rule. One gets virtually nothing of this from Stögner's description.

This is, I suspect, because Stögner sees Kreisky from the perspective of a critical Austrian academic, which is not the same as someone looking at Austrian history from outside. It might not be *sub specie aeternitatis*, but from the external view, Kreisky's rule was one which liberalized Austria and, hence, Austrian identity; from Stögner's position, no doubt, Kreisky looks like someone who aided and abetted the denial of Austria's anti-Semitic past and present, exploiting his own Jewish heritage to boot. As she demonstrates, this was also true, but I suspect Kreisky's riposte would be that he was trying to bring the sort of enlightenment to Austria that is needed before delving into the ethical morass of the past. I am not sure that the positive results of the Waldheim Affair (a sustained discussion of which is strangely absent from this volume) would have been possible without Kreisky's reformation of Austrian society, the media, and the educational system.

Stögner gives us a very learned discourse on various facets of anti-Semitism and its Austrian variant, using them to explicate Kreisky's attitudes, experiences, and image among Austrians when it came to

Jewish matters, especially his (and Austria's) relationship to Israel. The discourse is so learned, however, that it loses touch with reality at times and also loses sight of its own contradictions (ironic given that much of Stögner's argument is based on the theories of the Frankfurt School). It becomes so abstract that Stögner gives the appearance (as does Pelinka) of making a reified anti-Semitism itself the creator of not only Jews as a "community of fate" but also of Zionism (created in response to anti-Semitism, apparently). Stögner is giving anti-Semitism too much credit here: Jews as both a religious and an ethnic group, self-defined by descent, existed before racial anti-Semitism; moreover, Zionism, which in Theodor Herzl's case was prompted by anti-Semitism, was elsewhere much more an emulative response to nationalism, not merely a reaction to anti-Semitic hostility.

Zionism from early on was, in large part, Jewish nationalism, and its leaders acted and thought accordingly, especially once the nation-state of Israel had been founded. Kreisky was against ethnically based nationalism. He fought hard to realize a civic Austrian identity in which ethnic descent would be irrelevant; as Stögner points out, much of his animus in Jewish matters was due to a frustration that such "irrational" questions were still asked. No wonder he was an anti-Zionist. For all of Stögner's complex psychologizing of Kreisky, I am not sure much, if any of it, undermines the rationality of Kreisky's stance on the Middle East, which has proven, after all, prescient. There is another irony about Stögner's critique of Kreisky's anti-Zionism: a central point of this book, with which I wholeheartedly agree, asserts that the "either/or" logic of both anti-Semitism and nationalism is pernicious in human affairs and should be replaced when possible with more of a "both/and," inclusive approach. Hence the best model of Austrian identity is one in which one can be both Austrian and Jewish, having to deny neither, and in which ethnicity and religion are not excluding or decisive factors. Yet Israel as the Jewish state is precisely the contradiction of this inclusive model of the polity. Perhaps the contexts of modern-day Austria and modern-day Israel explain this contradiction, but it is a contradiction that the authors of this book need to recognize more fully when criticizing the admittedly complex, but nevertheless progressive, figure of "King Bruno."

Gerhard Botz, *Nationalsozialismus in Wien: Machtübernahme, Herrschaftssicherung, Radikalisierung 1938/39* (Vienna: Mandelbaum Verlag, 2008)

Hans Petschar, *Anschluss. "Ich hole Euch heim": Der "Anschluss" Österreichs an das Deutsche Reich. Fotografie und Wochenschau im Dienst der NS-Propganda, Eine Bildchronologie* (Vienna: Christian Brandstätter Verlag, 2008)

Evan Burr Bukey

In March 2008, Austrian scholars and journalists devoted relatively little attention to the seventieth anniversary of the Anschluß. Following decades of acrimonious debate and intensive research, they appeared to have reached consensus on the Nazi takeover or politely agreed to a standoff on the divisive issues. Thanks in no small measure to the resurgence of the radical right, they had become engaged in scrutinizing virtually every aspect of life in Adolf Hitler's homeland between 1938 and 1945, most notably popular attitudes toward the regime, the experience of women, the impact of wartime industrialization, and, above all, Austrian complicity in the crimes of the Third Reich. Indeed, those members of the *Historiker Kommission* employed to investigate the wholesale theft of Jewish assets in Vienna now stood in the forefront of those researching the complex process of "Aryanization," not only in incorporated Austria, but also in Greater Germany itself. In addition, other colleagues were publishing highly original, meticulous studies of Austrian involvement in forced labor and the Nazi legal system as well as preliminary studies of those who wore Hitler's uniform, both in the *Wehrmacht* and the SS. To what extent Austrians played a disproportionate role in the Holocaust had also become a topic of multi-archival scrutiny and intense debate, though one that remains unresolved to this day.

With historical scholarship focused primarily on the searing experience of the Second World War, the most significant book to appear on the Anschluß during the commemorative year was Gerhard Botz's *Nationalsozialismus in Wien*, a thoroughly revised, updated version of his pioneering study *Wien vom Anschluß zum Krieg* first published in 1978[1]. While most new editions normally consist of a fresh introduction and an occasional emendation, Botz's work has been sufficiently reworked to stand on its own as a variation of the original text. In it, the author seeks to incorporate three decades of subsequent scholarship and, above all, to demonstrate that what transpired in Vienna in the eighteen months before the outbreak of the Second World War both presaged and contributed to the radicalization of the Nazi regime throughout Greater Germany, notably the despoliation and deportation of the Jews. While Saul Fiedländer has discounted this notion of a *Modell Wien* for the Final Solution,[2] Botz stands by his guns in marshaling new evidence to reveal the significance of murderous local initiatives in the development of Hitler's anti-Semitic measures.

Before turning to his revised study, readers may wish to consider a brief summary of Botz's original work. The book's major thesis is that the Anschluß constituted a pseudo-revolutionary uprising from below, a semi-legal transfer of power from above, and a powerful military intervention from without. Given the interplay of these forces, Nazi rule in Vienna became so pluralistic and complex that it could be understood only within the larger framework of a polycratic model. The study thus comprises five brilliantly organized chapters that analyze in detail 1) the "seizure of power" by the Viennese NSDAP followed by Hitler's triumphal homecoming; 2) the success of the "April Plebiscite" in winning over both the Roman Catholic hierarchy and most of the industrial working class; 3) the incessant duels between Josef Bürckel, Arthur Seyss-Inquart, and the indigenous NSDAP over the disposition of power and booty within the newly transformed *Reichsgau*, especially those involving the status of the municipal bureaucracy, the fate of the Jewish population, and a host of economic problems focused on the elimination of unemployment and a chronic housing shortage; 4) social, economic, and political developments in 1938-1939 that include discussion of the impact Hitler's anti-clerical measures, the horrors of *Reichskristallnacht*, and the difficulties of implementing the Ostmark Act dividing Vienna into state and municipal administrations subordinate to the *Reichstatthalter*; and 5) those features of polycratic rule distinctive to Vienna as adjudicated by Hitler, concluding with examples of popular disillusionment and discontent that on the eve of war constituted the "emergence of political resistance."

In revising and rewriting his classic study, Botz retains his "social historical" conceptual framework to strengthen and underline his account. While one reviewer regrets that this once innovative approach marginalizes significant cultural changes after 1938,[3] Botz has nevertheless modified a number of his conclusions and suggested new ways of considering "the relatively most successful and the least inhumane" period of Nazi rule (p. 9). He begins, for example, by providing an entirely new introductory chapter that summarizes the historiography of National Socialism since 1978. For obvious reasons, he stresses the end of the Cold War as providing a cornucopia of new source materials from Soviet archives, discrediting fashionable Marxist views, and placing the Holocaust at the center of historical research, especially in Austria. More significantly, he suggests that the competitive coexistence of prerogative and legal structures in Hitler's Vienna should best be viewed through the lens of Ernst Fraenkel's *The Dual State*, first published in 1941.[4] Botz does not discount the multidimensional aspects of the Nazi system, but his approach makes sense for the period under consideration. Between the Anschluß and the invasion of Poland, Hitler made significant inroads in establishing Party supremacy, for example, by liquidating Austrian ministries, by throttling the power of the Roman Church, and by subordinating the Viennese bureaucracy to the Brown House in Munich. But in the accelerated run-up to war, the Nazis upheld non-Jewish property rights, refrained from an all-out purge of the judiciary, and left the General Civil Code of 1811 in place. This meant that both the Reich Ministries of Justice and Interior maintained a certain degree of autonomy based on a measure of the rule of law, particularly in civil and domestic legal disputes. While readers may wish that Botz had followed through more fully with his "dual state" interpretation, the insight nonetheless both enriches and enhances his overall narrative.

Botz claims to have rewritten substantial portions of his original chapters on the Nazi takeover and consolidation of power, but for the most part, the account remains unaltered. While he does incorporate new material from recent publications as well as revealing passages from the Josef Goebbels' diaries, his major change is to place greater emphasis on the widespread spontaneity of anti-Semitic savagery of the March days. The account is also enhanced through the inclusion and analysis of the near complete text of Karl Renner's formal endorsement of the Anschluß. Further, the book reveals how Bürckel's efforts to transform the Ostmark into a laboratory for the eventual establishment of a full party state were greatly facilitated by the appointment of Albert Hoffmann as *Stillhaltekommissar*, a shadowy figure who by 30 November 1938 managed to seize the assets of 70,000 associations, charitable organizations, and foundations; helped discipline the Viennese NSDAP; and provided a model for Adolf Eichmann's Central Office for Jewish Emigration.

Throughout his revised work, Botz devotes more attention to Nazi anti-Semitic policies than in previous editions. Drawing on his own extensive research as well as that of others, he argues forcefully that the expropriation of Jewish property constituted a form of "negative social policy" designed to fulfill ambitious social welfare and suburbanization schemes that could not otherwise be financed by the Anschluß regime. Botz does not discount the virulence of popular Judeophobia, most notably in his expanded chapter on *Reichskristallnacht,* which he interprets as the first step in a concerted drive by the municipal administration to deport the remaining Jews to work camps in Gänserndorf. Nevertheless, he uncovers new documentary evidence revealing that the local authorities also drew up detailed plans to expel the entire Czech population long before Hitler ordered Gauleiter Baldur von Schirach to "remove the Czechs and other foreigners" in November 1941 (p. 580-81). Overall, some 400,000 aliens appear to have been slated for deportation from the Danubian metropolis.

Botz in his final chapters attempts to assess the fluctuations of popular sentiment within the parameters of what he calls "regime acceptance and distance" (p. 599). In the first edition, this approach provided fascinating insights, but by ignoring the findings of others, this unaltered chapter seems outmoded and misleading. This is because those who subsequently uncovered and examined new evidence concur that most Germans and Austrians took a split-minded view of Hitler's regime, endorsing certain aspects of National Socialism while rejecting others.[5] On the other hand, Botz concedes that he was mistaken to interpret well-documented incidents of industrial and religious protests as politically charged or motivated. He also admits that it was primarily the disenchantment of the Viennese Nazis that contributed to a general sense of malaise prevailing in the Danubian city on the eve of war. Overall, Botz ends on a somber note by admitting that, while Vienna constituted a special case, Hitler succeeded in winning the allegiance of the municipal population to support what Götz Aly has called a "dictatorship of consent."[6]

For all its stunning qualities, *Nationalsozialismus in Wien* suffers from one minor but irritable shortcoming, namely a lack of comparative perspective. Although Botz is well versed in the diverse and variegated development of National Socialism in other cities throughout Greater Germany, he pays insufficient attention to regional differences distinguishing them from Nazi institutions in Vienna, a task that could have been achieved in a few pages. In a similar way, Botz also provides revealing insights about Hitler's ambivalent, occasionally positive, attitudes toward Vienna that could have been more fully developed. The overall worth of Botz's achievement, however, is immense. While scholars may differ and quarrel over specific aspects of his study, few will deny that it should stand for decades to come both as an authoritative study of the Anschluß and as an indispensable contribution to the history of the Third Reich itself.

As a complement to Botz's volume, Hans Petschar's *Anschluss: "Ich hole Euch heim,"* provides an astonishing collection of photographs, snap-shots, and movie stills taken in the dramatic weeks between the run-up to the Anschluß and the April plebiscite. Without exception, the images in this book portray the unchained, orgiastic enthusiasm with which vast crowds of ordinary people as well as individuals welcomed the birth of the Greater German Reich. Readers familiar with those halcyon days will no doubt recognize pictures published by Weltbild or the Associated Press, but most of the photographs appear in these pages for the first time, many of them taken by ordinary citizens who later stored them in dresser drawers, attics, or basements where they gathered dust. Among the most striking images are snapshots retrieved from two undeveloped rolls of 9.5 mm film purchased in a flea market in the 1980s. These consist of twelve sequential close-ups of a crouched Jew scrubbing the pavement with his bare hands, followed by four shots of giggling young women gathered to enjoy what they and other onlookers considered a raucous street party.

Aside from these and a handful of other revealing images, however, nearly all of the visual material in Petschar's volume consists of pictures taken by two professionals, Alfred Hilscher, an Austrian employed at one time by the Schuschnigg regime, and Lothar Rübelt, a Reich German vacationing in St. Anton am Alberg at the time of the Anschluß. Unlike Goebbels's camera crews, both men had cut their teeth as sports photographers, enabling them to frame events and press the shutter release at exactly the right moment. Petschar admits that their pictures scarcely differ from those produced by cameramen from Berlin, but he is quite right in emphasizing that they capture the spontaneity and depth of popular enthusiasm more effectively than those taken by official photographers. Among the most dramatic images are those of German cyclists motoring through cheering crowds in Innsbruck, Viennese youngsters clamoring aboard a tank, and Lilienfeld residents clad in native garb preparing to vote in the April plebiscite. There are also photos of Hitler chatting with school girls and waving jauntily to ebullient onlookers.

In sifting through thousands of forgotten pictures, Petschar has uncovered photographs of Jews being harried by uniformed storm troopers and vigilantes. There are also shots of Jews lining up for visas at police headquarters in the Wehrgasse as well as a fair number of frames of "Aryanized" shops and cinemas. Petschar argues that these forgotten photographs reveal images that did not conform to Nazi propaganda, an assessment that some may dispute. Contemporary observers and historians have noted, for example, that newspapers, periodicals, and weekly newsreels often featured pictures of SA men harassing Jews or daubing six-pointed stars on Jewish store fronts. There were also frames of gloating storm troopers pillorying individuals accused of "racial defilement."[7] Photos of Jewish round-ups such as those that appear in this volume would hardly have shocked the Austrian public in 1938. Even so, one wonders what criteria or guidelines were followed in deciding what pictorial images to publish and what to leave in the photo shop.

Seventy years after the Anschluß, the Austrian embrace of National Socialism still remains a matter of dispute and debate. For those seeking to explore and resolve the many issues at stake, many fine works of historical scholarship now exist to help them in their quest. Among the very best are the two volumes discussed in this review.

Notes

1. Gerhard Botz, *Wien vom "Anschluß" zum Krieg: Nationasozilistische Machtübernahme und politisch-soziale Umgestaltung am Beipspiel der Stadt Wien* (Vienna: Jugend und Volk, 1978).

2. Saul Friedländer, *Nazi Germany and the Jews: The Years of Persecution, 1933-1939* (New York: HarperCollins, 1997), 247-48.

3. Werner Suppanz, "Review of Botz, Gerhard, Nationalsozialismus in Wien: Machtübernahme, Herrschaftssicherung, Radikalisierung 1938/39," H-Soz-u-Kult, H-Net Reviews, September 2008, http://www.h-net.org/reviews/showrev.php?id=22752, accessed 22 April 2009.

4. Ernst Fraenkel, *The Dual State: A Contribution to the Theory of Dictatorship* (New York: Octagon Books, 1969).

5. Ian Kershaw, *Popular Opinion and Political Dissent in the Third Reich: Bavaria, 1933-1945* (Oxford: Oxford UP, 1983); Evan Burr Bukey, *Hitler's Austria: Popular Sentiment in the Nazi Era, 1938-1945* (Chapel Hill, NC: U of North Carolina P, 2000).

6. Götz Aly, *Hitler's Beneficiaries*, Trans. Jefferson Chase (New York: MacMillan, 2007), 299.

7. See, for example, the photographs in *Das III Reich: Ein Volk, Ein Reich, Ein Führer: Eine historische Collage über den erregensten Abschnitt deutscher Geschichte in Wort, Bild und Ton 1933-1939*, Bd. I (Hamburg: John Jahr Verlag, 1975), 312-23. On Nazi deployment of anti-Semitic visual imagery, see Jeffery Herf, *The Jewish Enemy: Nazi Propaganda During World War II and the Holocaust* (Cambridge, MA: Harvard UP, 2006).

Gerald Steinacher, *Nazis auf der Flucht: Wie Kriegsverbrecher über Italien nach Übersee entkamen* (Innsbruck: Studien Verlag, 2008)

Michael Phayer

This book fills an important gap in ratline literature. We knew that the war criminals fled to Italy after the war and subsequently to oversees destinations. What we did not know is how they got to Italy. Gerald Steinacher ably supplies abundant data tracing the steps of major and minor fugitives from justice from Germany and Austria through the Tyrol and on to Rome, a route Nazis knew as "the Roman Way."

War criminals, the very worst among them, beat a well trodden path to South Tyrol where they gathered at three major locations: Meran, Bolzano, and Bressanone. Jews, survivors of the Holocaust, often took the identical route, for they, too, were headed for Rome. Steinacher tells of one Tyrolean inn (*Gasthof*) that gave overnight lodging to Jews on the second floor and to Nazi criminals on the third.

That brings us to the key question of who exactly it was on the scene in Tyrol that abetted the escape of the fugitives. Steinacher identifies three types: smugglers who had been at it for generations and did not care who was paying for their services, Nazis themselves, and good Samaritans who did not know they were providing assistance for murderers. Three Nazis in particular organized the South Tyrolean ratline: Robert Verleben, Hermann Milleder, and Walter Rauff, creator of the gas van.

Of course, once fugitives got to the Tyrol they needed to know what they had to do when they got to Rome in order to escape from Europe and from the war crimes trials. Two organizations, the International Red Cross and the Catholic Church (and to a much lesser extent the Protestant Church) supplied the necessary information and documentation. Steinacher devotes two chapters to these two organizations, but both of them crop up repeatedly throughout the book, making it clear that absent their help the fugitives would never have escaped or would not have done so in such massive numbers.

The Red Cross, after doing next to nothing to assist Jews during the Holocaust, readily and routinely helped the war criminals. Even before the war ended, SS members got in touch with Paul Ruegger in Switzerland, president of the European Red Cross, so as to get new identities through his organization. In the postwar years, thousands more did the same. In Rome, the Red Cross also passed out "letters of protection," IDs which then served as travel passports. Both in Switzerland and in Italy, Red Cross personnel knew well enough that they were giving assistance to war criminals on the lam.

Just as ready as the Red Cross to lend war criminals a hand was the Vatican. Pope Pius XII set up the Pontifical Commission of Assistance, a strangely ambiguous name for what was, in fact, an emigration bureau, which had national departments that answered ultimately to Giovanni Montini, the pope's close associate. Bishop Hudal, heading the German division, specialized in SS war criminals, Father Gallow in the Hungarian office catered to Arrow Cross fugitives, and Father Draganovic in the Croatian branch led the Ustasha murderers to freedom. Steinacher is in agreement with what was already known about the Red Cross-Vatican operation. A war criminal went first to one of national units of the Vatican emigration bureau and received there a new identity and letter of good standing which he then took to the Red Cross office where he was given the his official ID and travel papers. Some German fugitives already knew before departing Germany that they had to find Hudal when they got to Rome. Otherwise, they learned he was "the man" when they got to the Tyrol where Hudal had set up many contacts, including many in cloisters. On the way to Rome, many SS criminals took what they sarcastically called the "monastery tour" (*Klostertour*). Not infrequently, the fugitives originated the process of shedding their old names by getting "re-baptized" in the Catholic Church (even though this was a violation of Church law if they were Protestants or Catholics as most surely were). Most of these fugitives did not come from affluent homes and, therefore, had to be supplied with money for passage on a ship. New York's Cardinal Spellman supplied Hudal with $1,500 a month, a princely sum in those days, so the Austrian bishop was able to help out the emigrants financially.

Did Pope Pius know that his Vatican emigration bureau was abetting the escape of war criminals? The question would be somewhat analogous to the question of whether Adolf Hitler knew about the Holocaust, but for the fact that the Argentine author of *The Real Odyssa* (see the second edition) Uki Goñi found evidence in the records of the British Foreign Office directly linking the Pope to known Ustasha war criminals. Since Gallow, Hudal, and Draganovic reported to Montini and since the Jesuit Leiber worked closely with Hudal, it is difficult to imagine that Pius did not know. Montini and Leiber were his closest advisers. Steinacher writes that it is "very unlikely" (p. 136) that Montini did not know what Hudal and the others were doing on behalf of fugitives. Again, he writes that it is "hardly imaginable" (p. 148) that top Vatican personnel, including the Pope, did not know that war criminals were hiding out in Rome. Had the Vatican's ratline business become known it would, Steinacher believes, have been faced "with a storm of indignation" (p. 219) because the pictures of dead Jews in concentration camps were still a fresh memory in many people's minds.

In spite of the fact that *Nazis auf der Flucht* provides an abundance of new information, there are some notable gaps. Not a word can be found about the Spanish ratline. This is inexplicable because, although the author probably could not have read my book, *Pius XII, The Holocaust, and the Cold War,* published earlier the same year as Steinacher's, he definitely did read *The Real Odyssa.* This valuable study reveals the work of one of the central figures in the Spanish ratline to Argentina, the head the chief of German foreign intelligence, Walter Schellenberg, whose name nowhere appears in *Nazis auf der Flucht.* For whatever reason, Steinacher chose to ignore the existence of a second major ratline.

There is also a flaw in Steinacher's analysis. He is only vaguely aware that 1947 was the year when U.S. policy opened the country to former Nazis. But Steinacher cannot pin down exactly when this occurred. This is because the author, again for inexplicable reasons, ignored the pursuit by U.S. intelligence agents of Ante Pavelic, the murderous head of the Ustasha. American spies, such as William Gowen, doggedly but unsuccessfully pursued Pavelic in Rome. Just when they found him and were ready to seize him, the hunt was called off in the summer of 1947. The U.S. National Archives at College Park, Maryland, holds all of the files that tell the story about Pavelic. Steinacher made good use of the archives, but ignored the Pavelic material, most of the references to which may be found in *The Real Odyssa.* Had he not ignored the Pavelic files and had Steinacher been more familiar with the Cold War literature of American historians, he would have been much more precise in his narrative.

Steinacher found a treasure trove of information in the Vincent La Vista files, also in the U.S. National Archives. It was because of La Vista's work that the U.S. State Department became aware, finally, of how extensive the ratline operation was. But U.S. intelligence had long been aware of the operation. La Vista worked for state, not intelligence. By the time he filed his report to state, sounding an alarm, U.S. policy was just at that point of opening its doors to all anti-Communists which included Nazi war criminals. In other words, the La Vista report, a boon to historians, had no impact on history. Because Steinacher cannot pin down the turning point (*Wendepunkt*) of U.S. policy, his narrative suffers from being one-sided. It only embraces U.S. efforts to abet the escape of Nazis while ignoring the efforts of American spies to capture them. The 1943 Moscow Declaration on war criminals required the Allies to return putative war criminals to the countries where they perpetrated their crimes in order to stand trial there. Nowhere does Steinacher mention the Moscow Declaration.

Still, Steinacher succeeds admirably in providing the answer as to how the first part of the ratline—the "Roman Way"—functioned through key stops in the Tyrol. Even though we knew much of the rest of the story, the Italian part, Steinacher gives us additional information, thus filling out this part of the picture. Thus the book will be a necessary read for specialists.

ANNUAL REVIEW

Austria 2008

Elections in Tyrol, June 2008
Parliamentary Elections, September 2008
Jörg Haider, 26 January 1950-11 October 2009
Elections in Carinthia and Styria, March 2009
Economic and Statistical Data

Reinhold Gärtner

Elections in Tyrol, 8 June 2008

Since 1945, the Austrian People's Party (*Österreichische Volkspartei*, or ÖVP) had been the strongest political party in Tyrol, with solid majorities of sometimes more than 60 percent (in 1984, 64.6 percent). This changed dramatically in 1989 (48.7 percent), but until 2008, the ÖVP was able to maintain this lead.

In 2008, a new political party ran for election: the Citizens' Forum Austria (*Liste Fritz Dinkhauser—Bürgerforum Tirol*, or Liste Fritz). Fritz Dinkhauser, chairman of this party, was previously a member of the ÖVP and president of the Chamber of Labor (*Arbeiterkammer*) from 1991 until 2008 and had enjoyed reasonable success in the Tyrol. But he decided to form a new political party and run for election.

In this, he was successful. He gained 18.4 percent and seven (of thirty-six) seats in the Tyrolean parliament. The ÖVP lost dramatically (49.9 percent in 2003; 40.4 percent in 2008) and so did the Social Democratic Party of Austria (*Sozialdemokratische Partei Österreichs*, or SPÖ), and the Greens (Grüne). The Freedom Party of Austria (*Freiheitliche Partei Österreichs*, or FPÖ) again led a xenophobic cam-paign and got 12.4 percent of the vote.

Table 1
Election Results in the Tyrol by Percentage/Seats

	ÖVP	SPÖ	Grüne	FPÖ	Liste Fritz
2008	40.5 / 20	15.5 / 9	10.7 / 4	12.4 / 4	18.4 / 7
2003	49.9 / 16	25.9 / 5	15.6 / 5	8.0 / 2	Not Applicable
1999	47.2 / 18	21.8 / 8	8.0 / 3	19.6 / 7	Not Applicable
1994	47.3 / 19	19.8 / 7	10.7 / 4	16.1 / 6	Not Applicable

* The Liste Fritz was founded in 2008, so data from previous elections do not exist.
Source: Ministry of the Interior.

Liste Fritz got a seat in the Federal Council (*Bundesrat*), too. The *Bundesrat* is the second chamber of the Austrian Parliament; Austria has a very unbalanced Parliament with the National Council (*Nationalrat*) as the really important first chamber and *Bundesrat* as the not very important second chamber. Every *Bundesland* has, according to its population, a certain number of seats in the *Bundesrat*. The members of the *Bundesrat* of each single state (*Länder*) are delegated according to the election results. There are five Tyrolean members of the sixty-two total seats in the *Bundesrat*.

In the nine Austrian federal states are two main types of government. In Vorarlberg, Salzburg, and the Tyrol, the majority principle is used, and it is used on the national level as well. This means that a party with the absolute majority of seats can form the government (or make a coalition with another political party). In the other states (Carinthia, Upper and Lower Austria, Styria, and Burgenland), the proportional principle is used; this means that every political party which has a certain number of seats gets a seat in the federal government, as well. Vienna has a slightly different system.

After the election negotiations began and—finally—Tyrol got an ÖVP-SPÖ coalition with new personnel, Governor van Staa resigned, and Günther Platter, the former minister of the interior, was elected as the new governor.

Parliamentary Elections, 28 September 2008

"*Es reicht*" ("That's enough"), said an enervated Vice-Chancellor Wilhelm Molterer in July 2008 after he was informed that Chancellor Alfred Gusenbauer and Minister Werner Faymann (the new strongman in the SPÖ) had written a letter to the editor of the *Kronen Zeitung*, the Austrian daily with the widest circulation. In this letter, they announced that in the future referenda should be held on important EU questions.

The background to this decision was the *Kronen Zeitung*'s campaign against the ratification of the Lisbon reform treaty.[1] This deeply populist act of the Gusenbauer/Faymann coalition was the straw that broke the camel's back and made Molterer quit the coalition. What followed was an election campaign with manifold right-wing populist arguments, especially from the FPÖ and the Alliance for the Future of Austria (*Bündnis Zukunft Österreich*, or BZÖ). Both parties used a lot of xenophobic slogans.

The election was held on 28 September, and the result was, to a certain extent, surprising. First, both the SPÖ and the ÖVP got the worst results in their respective party's history. Second, the ÖVP could not secure first place. Third, the FPÖ was one of the big winners, and the BZÖ was the other one. Fourth, the Greens lost and fell back to fifth place.

Table 2
Parliamentary Election Results by Percentage/Seats

	ÖVP	SPÖ	Grüne	FPÖ	BZÖ*
2008	26.0 / 51	29.3 / 57	10.4 / 20	17.5 / 34	10.7 / 21
2006	34.3 / 66	35.3 / 68	11.05 / 21	11.04 / 21	4.1 / 7
2002	42.3 / 79	36.5 / 69	9.5 / 17	10.0 / 18	Not Applicable
1999	26.9 / 52	33.1 / 65	7.4 / 14	26.9 / 52	Not Applicable

* The BZÖ was founded in 2005; its *de facto* predecessor was the FPÖ.
Source: Ministry of the Interior.

An astonishing element was the BZÖ's performance. It was more or less a one-man show by Jörg Haider. Haider was present throughout the country, and he performed like a moderate statesman, in contrast to the loudmouth Heinz-Christian Strache. Haider's strategy was clear: there were elections scheduled in Carinthia for March 2009, and a loss in the parliamentary elections would have swept the BZÖ out of the *Nationalrat*. Ultimately, Haider's campaign was very successful; in the elections in Lower Austria in March 2008, the BZÖ only got 0.72 percent of votes cast (7,250 votes). In the parliamentary elections six months later, it got 65,851 votes, which was 6.35 percent of the vote—nine times as many as in March. Another example of the effects of this strategy can be seen in the Tyrol; in the state elections in June 2008, the BZÖ did not even run for election, but it got 9.7 percent (or 35,473 votes) in the parliamentary elections in September.

What followed was the formation of a new government. After the FPÖ, BZÖ, and Greens said that none of them would go into a coalition with anyone from the other two parties, the only realistic alternative was an SPÖ-ÖVP coalition. Because the old coalition of the two parties had collapsed due to continuous controversies, the new one had to make sure that its members were willing to cooperate. The government was sworn in on 2 December 2008.

One remarkable aspect of change deserves to be stressed. In Austria are six autochthonous minorities (Slovenes, Slovaks, Croatians, Hungarians, Czechs, and Roma). Nikolaus Berlakovich and Norbert Darabos are both Burgenland Croatians; it can be seen as a very positive development that at least one minority is prominently represented in the new government.

Table 3
Distribution of Cabinet Posts in the SPÖ-ÖVP Coalition Government

Position	Politician	Party
Federal Chancellor	Werner Faymann	SPÖ
Federal Minister of Finance Vice Chancellor	Josef Pröll	ÖVP
Federal Minister of the Interior	Maria Fekter	ÖVP
Federal Minister of European and International Affairs	Michael Spindelegger	ÖVP
Federal Minister of the Economy, Family, and Youth	Reinhold Mitterlehner	ÖVP
Federal Minister of Justice	Claudia Bandion-Ortner	Ind. (ÖVP)
Federal Minister of Agriculture, Forestry, Environment, and Water Management	Nikolaus Berlakovich	ÖVP
Federal Minister of Defense and Sports	Norbert Darabos	SPÖ
Federal Minister of Transport, Innovation, and Technology	Doris Bures	SPÖ
Federal Minister of Science and Research	Johannes Hahn	ÖVP
Federal Minister of Education, Arts and Culture	Claudia Schmied	SPÖ
Federal Minister of Social Affairs and Consumer Protection	Rudolf Hundstorfer	SPÖ
Federal Minister of Women and Administration	Gabriele Heinsich-Hosek	SPÖ
Federal Minister of Health	Andreas Stöger	SPÖ
State Secretary in the Federal Chancellery	Josef Ostemayer	SPÖ
State Secretary in the Federal Ministry of Finance	Reinhold Lopatka	ÖVP
State Secretary in the Federal Ministry of Finance	Andreas Schieder	SPÖ
State Secretary in the Federal Ministry of Economy, Family, and Youth	Christine Marek	ÖVP

Source: Bundeskanzleramt Österreich <http://www.austria.gv.at>.

Jörg Haider, 26 January 1950-11 October 2009

Jörg Haider, governor of Carinthia, died in the morning hours of 11 October 2009 in a car accident. According to the official investigation report, Haider was driving too fast and was under the influence of alcohol. The day before, 10 October, is celebrated in Carinthia in remembrance of the referendum of 1920, when a majority of German and Slovene-speaking Carinthians voted to the stay with Austria.[2] Haider was governor of Carinthia from 1989 to 1991. In 1991, he had to resign because he had praised National Socialist economy policy. In 1999, though, he was re-elected governor and remained in office until his death.

A well-known Austrian politician, Haider also was the FPÖ party chairman from 1986 until 2000, and he certainly was a polarizing person. He emotionalized the so-called foreigners' issue, used xenophobia and right-wing populist rhetoric, and didn't distance himself much from National Socialism. He led the FPÖ to a remarkable electoral success (26.91 percent in 1999), but he also brought the FPÖ back to results of only 10 percent in the 2002 elections. In 2005, he founded the BZÖ and garnered 4.1 percent of the vote in 2006 and as much as 10.7 percent in 2008.

Despite Haider's polarizing right-wing policy, he was praised beyond all measure (especially in Carinthia).

Elections in Carinthia and Styria, 1 March 2009

In Salzburg, the SPÖ achieved first place in the 2004 elections and thus—for the first time since 1945—could nominate the governor and chose Gabi Burgstaller. So one interesting aspect of the 2009 elections was whether or not the party could achieve first place again. Though the SPÖ lost some 6 percent of voters, it managed to keep first place. The FPÖ gained a moderate percentage, and the Greens suffered minimal losses. (Table 4)

In Carinthia, the situation was different. As pointed out, Haider died in October; his successor was Gerhard Dörfler. During the election campaign, Dörfler tried to attract attention with racist jokes and very vulgar appearances during the Carinthian carnival. Despite this performance (or, perhaps, because of it), the BZÖ rather than the FPÖ was very successful. Because the BZÖ was founded in 2005, one must use the FPÖ's election results of 2004 to compare with the BZÖ's results in 2009. The BZÖ won 2.5 percent more than the FPÖ did in 2004. As a result, Dörfler remained governor of Carinthia.

Table 4
Election Results in Salzburg by Percentage/Seats

	ÖVP	SPÖ	Grüne	FPÖ	BZÖ*
2009	36.5 / 14	39.4 / 15	7.4 / 2	13.0 / 5	3.7 / 0
2004	37.9 / 14	45.4 / 17	8.0 / 2	8.7 / 3	Not Applicable
1999	38.8 / 15	32.3 / 12	5.4 / 2	19.6 / 7	Not Applicable
1994	38.6 / 14	27.0 / 11	7.3 / 3	19.5 / 8	Not Applicable

* The BZÖ was founded in 2005; its *de facto* predecessor was the FPÖ.
Source: Ministry of the Interior.

Table 5
Election Results in Carinthia by Percentage/Seats

	ÖVP	SPÖ	Grüne	FPÖ	BZÖ*
2009	16.8 / 6	28.7 / 11	5.1 / 2	3.8 / 0	44.9 / 17
2004	11.6 / 4	38.4 / 14	6.7 / 2	42.4 / 16	Not Applicable
1999	20.8 / 8	32.9 / 12	3.9 / 0	42.1 / 16	Not Applicable
1994	23.8 / 9	37.4 / 14	1.6 / 0	33.3 / 13	Not Applicable

* The BZÖ was founded in 2005; its *de facto* predecessor was the FPÖ.
Source: Ministry of the Interior.

Economic and Statistical Data

Inflation was at 3.2 percent in 2008 (compared to 2.2 percent in 2007), and Harmonized Index of Consumer Prices (HVPI) was at 3.2 percent (compared to 2.2 percent in 2007). The public deficit amounted 0.4 percent in 2008 (0.5 percent in 2007), and public debts amounted to 62.5 percent in 2008 (59.1 percent in 2007).

In 2008, GNP was at Euro 32.570 per capita (compared to Euro 31.070 in 2007).

In 2007, imports amounted Euro 114.254 million (Euro 85.269 from the EU-27), and exports amounted Euro 114.690 million (Euro 83.108 to the European Union). Imports from NAFTA were Euro 4.394 million; exports to NAFTA were Euro 7.043 million.

In the fourth quarter of 2008, 4,097,900 people in Austria were employed (according to the Labor Force Concept; on average 4,027,900 were employed in 2007). Among them were 428,200 foreigners (419,600 in the fourth quarter of 2007); 178,600 of them were EU-27 citizens. The rate of unemployment was at 4.0 percent in the fourth quarter of 2008 (on average 4.4 percent in 2007).

At the beginning of 2008, 8,331,930 people were living in Austria; among them were 854,752 foreigners (and of them, 301,692 were from the EU-27). In 2007, 76,250 children were born alive in Austria, and 74,625 people died. Life expectancy is at 77.3 years (men) and 82.8 (women).

Notes

1. For particulars, see articles in Günter Bischof et al., eds., *New Perspectives on Austrians and World War II*, vol. 17, Contemporary Austrian Studies (New Brunswick, NJ: Transaction, 2008).

2. For more specifics, see articles in Günter Bischof and Fritz Plasser, eds., *The Changing Austrian Voter*, vol. 16, Contemporary Austrian Studies (New Brunswick, NJ: Transaction, 2008).

List of Authors

Steven Beller is an independent scholar living in Washington DC.

Günter Bischof is Marshall Plan Professor of History and the director of CenterAustria, University of New Orleans.

Evan B. Bukey is Professor Emeritus of History at the University of Arkansas.

Johannes Ditz is President of the Julius Raab Stiftung, member of chairmanship from the Austrian SME (= Small and Medium Enterprises) Union.

Reinhold Gärtner is a professor of political science, University of Innsbruck, Austria.

Peter Gerlich is professor emeritus of government at the University of Vienna, Austria.

Reinhard Heinisch is Chair of Austrian Politics at the University of Salzburg, Austria (Lehrstuhl für Österreichische Politik im Europäischen und Internationalen Vergleich, Universität Salzburg).

Otmar Höll is director of the Austrian Institute for International Affairs-oiip and Professor of Political Science at the University of Vienna, Austria.

Ferdinand Karlhofer is associate professor of political science at the University of Innsbruck, Austria.

Maria-Regina Kecht is a faculty member in German Studies at Rice University, Houston, Texas.

Josef Leidenfrost is the student ombudsmann in the Austrian Ministry of Science and Research, Vienna, Austria.

Günther Lengauer is senior researcher of the Austrian National Election Study (AUTNES) at the Department of Political Science, University of Innsbruck, Austria.

David S. Luft is Horning Endowed Chair in Humanities and Professor of History at Oregon State University.

Kurt Richard Luther is Senior Lecturer in Politics at Keele University in the United Kingdom and Convenor of the Keele European Parties Research Unit (KEPRU).

Michael S. Maier is the 2008/09 Ministry of Science Fellow at CenterAustria, University of New Orleans, and doctoral candidate at the Department of Economic and Social History, University of Vienna.

Leslie Morris is Associate Professor of German at the University of Minnesota, where she also serves as Director of the Center for Jewish Studies.

Heinrich Neisser is Professor Emeritus, Department of Political Science, University of Innsbruck, Austria, and former Jean Monnet Professor.

Anton Pelinka is professor of political science emeritus, University of Innsbruck, Austria, and professor of political science at the Central European University of Budapest, Hungary.

Michael Phayer is Professor of History, Emeritus, Marquette University and the Ida E. King Distinguished Holocaust Lecturer, Emeritus, The Richard Stockton College of New Jersey.

Fritz Plasser is professor of political science und dean of the faculty of political science and sociology, University of Innsbruck, Austria.

Max Preglau is professor of sociology at the Department of Sociology at the School of Political Science and Sociology of the University of Innsbruck, Austria.

Andreas Stadler is a political scientist and the director of the Austrian Cultural Forum in New York.

Peter A. Ulram is research manager at GfK-Austria (Institute for Market and Opinion Research) and professor of political science, University of Vienna, Austria.

David Wineroither is a lecturer in comparative political systems in the Department of Political Science at the University of Innsbruck, Austria.

Contemporary Austrian Studies

Günter Bischof and Fritz Plasser, Editors

Transaction Publishers, New Brunswick (N.J.) and London (U.K)

Volume 1 (1993)
Austria in the New Europe

Volume 2 (1994)
The Kreisky Era in Austria
Oliver Rathkolb, Guest Editor

Volume 3 (1995)
Austria in the Nineteen Fifties
Rolf Steininger, Guest Editor

Volume 4 (1996)
Austro-Corporatism: Past – Present – Future

Volume 5 (1997)
Austrian Historical Memory & National Identity

Volume 6 (1998)
Women in Austria
Erika Thurner, Guest Editor

Volume 7 (1999)
The Vranitzky Era in Austria
Ferdinand Karlhofer, Guest Editor

Volume 8 (2000)
The Marshall Plan in Austria
Dieter Stiefel, Guest Editor

Volume 9 (2001)
Neutrality in Austria
Ruth Wodak, Guest Editor

Volume 10 (2002)
Austria and the EU
Michael Gehler, Guest Editor

Volume 11 (2003)
The Dollfuss/Schuschnigg Era in Austria. A Reassessment
Alexander Lassner, Guest Editor

Volume 12 (2004)
The Americanization/ Westernization of Austria

Volume 13 (2005)
Religion in Austria
Hermann Denz, Guest Editor

Volume 14 (2006)
Austrian Foreign Policy in Historical Perspective
Michael Gehler, Guest Editor

Volume 15 (2007)
Sexuality in Austria
Dagmar Herzog, Guest Editor

Volume 16 (2008)
The Changing Austrian Voter

Volume 17 (2009)
New Perspectives on Austrians and World War II
Barbara Stelzl-Marx, Guest Editor